Kırmızı Kedi Yayınevi: 1095

KIRMIZIKEDİ

Kırmızı Kedi Yayınevi: 1095
Actuality: 50

Mustafa Kemal
Yılmaz Özdil

Translation: Peter Klempner

Editorial Director: Enis Batur

Editor: Çağlayan Çevik
Proofreader: Sevda Akyüz
Cover Design: Cüneyt Çomoğlu
Graphic Design: Taylan Polat

First Edition: April 2019, Istanbul
ISBN: 978-605-298-480-2
Kırmızı Kedi Certificate No: 40620

Printing: Pasifik Ofset
Cihangir Quarter, Güvercin Ave., No: 3/1, Baha Business Center, Block A, 2nd floor, 34310 Haramidere/ISTANBUL
Tel: 0090 212 412 17 77 Certificate No: 12027

Kırmızı Kedi Yayınevi
kirmizikedi@kirmizikedi.com / www.kirmizikedi.com
facebook.com: kirmizikediyayinevi / twitter.com: krmzkedikitap
instagram: kirmizikediyayinevi
Ömer Avni Quarter, Emektar St., No: 18, Gümüşsuyu 34427 ISTANBUL
T: 0090 212 244 89 82 F: 0090 212 244 09 48

Yılmaz Özdil

Mustafa Kemal

KIRMIZIKEDI

To Pelin

To see my face
does not mean to see me.
If you understand
my ideas, my thoughts,
that is enough.

He was born in Salonika, now known as Thessaloniki. It was a pink house. He was born in a room with a heating stove on the second floor.

Zübeyde only remembered the season. "I gave birth still in the cold of *Arba'een*," she had said.

It stayed in her mind as the 23rd of *Kânûn-ı Evvel*.

The 23rd of *Kânûn-ı Evvel* is January 4 in today's calendar.

So, it was January 4, in the year 1881.

The year written on his first birth certificate was 1296. This was the Rumi calendar. It encompassed March 13, 1880 to March 12, 1881.

It stayed as 1880 until the time of the Surname Law. He was issued a new birth certificate with the enactment of the Surname Law and it was corrected as 1881.

His father named him Mustafa. It was his grandfather's name.

This was a requirement of Turkish tradition. Ali Rıza had named his first son, Ahmet, after his father, and his third, Mustafa, after his grandfather. The family's second son, Ömer carried the name of Zübeyde's grandfather.

The name of both his maternal and paternal grandmother was Ayşe.

Ali Rıza.

Ali Rıza had a sword from the Russo-Turkish War—what was known as *93 Harbi*. He had served in a battalion of volunteers in Salonika.

The only known photograph of him was taken while he was in this battalion.

He hung the sword over the head of the cradle. Mustafa grew up learning the honor of that sword.

He was a calm baby in his swaddle.

Zübeyde produced little milk, and so a wet nurse was found by the name of Ümmügül. A black woman named Üftade was also hired. She helped with the housework after the birth.

The pink house had three floors and four rooms. There was a landing, basement, kitchen and bathroom. The windows were latticed and in total, it was 3,670 square feet.

Ali Rıza and Zübeyde had been living there as tenants, but bought the house in 1877. Both their names were on the deed. Ali Rıza paid 9,600 *kuruş* and Zübeyde paid 3,900 *kuruş*.

The National Bank of Greece sold the house, officially registered as the Pink House, as an abandoned property to the Seraphimidou family in 1928 for 197,000 drachmas.

The municipality of Thessaloniki expropriated it in 1933 for 650,000 drachmas and presented it to Atatürk.

It was not easy, however, to empty this gift of a house. The family that owned it had rented out each room. Seven separate families lived there as tenants at the time of its expropriation.

It took two years to be emptied and handed over. The house keys were given to Turkey in 1937.

Atatürk did not accept it free of charge. On principle, he never received goods or services throughout his life that he didn't pay for, and he wanted to pay, even if it was symbolic.

Greece produced a symbolic bill of sale. The state of the Republic of Turkey gave the municipality of Thessaloniki 10,000 drachmas for the Pink House.

Ali Rıza and Zübeyde had another house built at the end of the dead-end street where the Pink House was located. It had three floors and five rooms. Again, both their names were on the deed.

They rented it out and didn't have any economic problems.

Then, Ali Rıza passed away at the age of 47.

According to his estate, he had property worth 35,000 *kuruş*, a jacket worth 45 *kuruş*, trousers worth 20 *kuruş*, an overcoat worth 40 *kuruş*, a chest worth 20 *kuruş* and two books worth 15 *kuruş*.

(One of the books was Ahmet Vefik Pasha's *Lehce-i Osmânî—The Ottoman Language*. The other was *Miftah*'ül-Kulûb—*Key to the Hearts*—by Muhammed Nuri Şemseddin.)

(His father's gold-chained watch was left to Mustafa. He used this watch until he was at the Monastir Military High School. He had an intermittent fever with hot and cold fits one night and fainted. The gold-chained watch disappeared that night and he was never able to find who had stolen it.

This is how his only remaining keepsake from his father slipped away.)

After Ali Rıza left the customs office, he traded lumber and salt to provide for his family. He eventually succumbed to tuberculosis of the bowel.

He was buried in the cemetery of the Hortacı Mosque in Salonika.

Having lost the family breadwinner when he was only 6 years old, Mustafa was also in danger of losing his house during this trauma.

This is because Nuri Efendi, a merchant from Salonika's Stamboul market, appealed to the court six months after Ali Rıza's death. He claimed Ali Rıza owed him 28,800 *kuruş* and that he had pledged the Pink House to cover the debt. He said they should either give him the house or sell it and pay the debt.

Zübeyde said there was no such debt left and that the creditor had long ago been paid. The court asked for a witness.

Two Muslim lumber traders from the Stamboul market were brought in. They took the vow to tell the truth and explained that the debt had been paid. They even said they had witnessed the repayment of the debt along with the neighborhood imam and headman.

The court case lasted four months.

At the end, it was ruled that the debt had been paid and the Pink House was saved.

There was now only Mustafa, Makbule and Naciye left.

Zübeyde moved to the small house they had built, now a widow with three children, the oldest 6 years old.

She rented out the Pink House for 11,500 *kuruş* per year.

Tenants moved in but didn't pay the rent. They went to court. Zübeyde eventually won the case and received the rent payment in full, but by then she had fallen on harder times. She sold the small house to make ends meet and moved in with her older brother who oversaw a farm in the village of Rapla in Langadas.

That is where Mustafa was circumcised.

His uncle acted as both father and *kirve*—the one who takes care of the child during the process. Their relatives from Salonika were invited. Rams were slaughtered and a celebratory dinner was prepared. Mustafa was circumcised together with 16 poor children. Afterward, he slept for seven days holding his robe with one hand.

He stayed in Langadas for six months. He left Zübeyde so he could continue his schooling, and to do so, moved to his aunt's house in Salonika.

Zübeyde couldn't stand being away from her son after a year and so moved in with her son in Salonika. They finally got rid of the tenants and moved back into the Pink House.

Zübeyde then remarried a man named Ragıp Abbas. Like her, he was a widower and had four children.

Mustafa was 15 years old.

It wasn't at all easy for him to accept his stepfather.

His uncle had long hinted at the subject, mentioning how Zübeyde was left alone at a very young age—emotionally preparing his nephew with these types of heart to heart talks.

He came home with his uncle after one such conversation.

Zübeyde greeted them with a smile and wearing a new dress. There was a man Mustafa didn't know sitting inside and Zübeyde didn't wear her headscarf araound this stranger. He understood the situation and fell to pieces.

Years later, he described his state of mind at that moment: "I looked over and there was my father's sword hanging on the wall. Instinctively, I wanted to wrap my hand around that sword. And I wanted to attack this gentleman who was at no fault."

He didn't surrender to his emotions. He turned around and left the house without saying a word and ran.

He went to his aunt and didn't go home for months.

And then?

He explained many years later: "I hadn't seen my mother in months. In the end, though, I became close friends with my stepfather—this very noble man, Ragıp Bey. He was kind and polite. He was a very good teacher to me. I also appreciated at a young age that my mother had made such a family bond. My childish feelings were a rebellion against the loss of my father."

His stepbrother, Süreyya, was a lieutenant. Mustafa loved him like a true brother. He gave Mustafa a switchblade that he always carried. "If you need to, protect yourself with this," he had told young Mustafa.

This switchblade was both the first gift Mustafa received and his first weapon.

He was a serious, sombre child.

He didn't join his neighborhood friends in games of leapfrog, slingshots or wrestling, and preferred to watch with his hands in his pockets. He couldn't stand getting his head dirty even when he was 6 or 7 years old. His demeanor was that of an adult.

According to Zübeyde's account, "He had a peculiar personality. Everyone noticed it."

He had older brothers, Ahmet and Ömer. They died in the smallpox outbreak that ravaged Rumelia. Mustafa was 2 years old at the time and never remembered his older brothers.

He had an older sister, as well, Fatima. Mustafa hadn't been born yet when she was lost to tuberculosis.

Naciye was the youngest. Mustafa was 16 when she died.

"She was my favorite among my siblings," he said. "She was soulful beyond her young age. She was keen to learn. She asked for my books when I went to the Military Academy. I had asked my mother to get her an education. She was blonde, blue-eyed and had clear, white skin like my mother. She wasn't at all like Makbule—she was a typical *yörük* girl."

In 1908, he returned to Salonika from his first tour of duty in Damascus. He didn't want to stay with his mother and so bought a house with the savings from his salary.

It was on the dead-end street over from the Pink House. It had two floors, three rooms and was 1,055 square feet.

It was the first and only house he ever bought throughout his life.

Greece expropriated it years later.

The dead-end street where the house stood was connected to the street behind it in 1935. Mustafa Kemal's house was demolished along with the other houses on the dead-end street. Some of the land went to the road and a part was incorporated into the Turkish consulate being built there.

He was in Egypt, returning to Tripolitania when Salonika, his hometown where he was born and raised, was handed to Greece without a single bullet fired.

He later described what he felt at the time:

"I heard my homeland of Salonika, my mother, brother, and all of my relatives and kin had been granted to the enemy. I heard a bell had been placed in the minaret of the Hortacı Mosque and that the dirty feet of Greek soldiers had trodden over my father's bones lying there."

Thessaloniki had been named after Alexander the Great's sister, Thessalonike.

The city was like an ethnographic museum when Mustafa Kemal was born. The population was 130,000, with 60,000 Turks and Muslims and the rest Jewish, Greek, Bulgarian and Levantine.

An unstoppable fire broke out in 1917 that reduced the city center to ashes.

It erased its historic fabric.

Seventy-two thousand people lost their homes.

Salonika rose anew from the ashes of the tragic fire.

İzmir was also born again out of the ashes of a tragic fire.

The shared fate of these two very important cities that were turning points in Mustafa Kemal's life was a turn of history.

∞

Zübeyde Hanım.

Zübeyde had blonde hair and blue eyes.

She was literate, as she had learned from her family, and she spoke with a Rumelian accent.

She was a devout woman and wanted her son to be a cleric.

Mustafa Kemal always opted to buy items such as prayer rugs, headscarves and prayer beads when he got his mother gifts.

When he was in Damascus, for instance, he bought a silver brocade headscarf with his first pay and sent it to her.

She was 30 when her husband Ali Rıza died. She had three children. She only received two *mecidiye* as her widow's pension and had no income other than the 3 *kuruş* rent. She didn't want to be a burden on her brothers and couldn't find an option other than remarrying.

She married Ragıp Abbas. He was the general-director of customs and was well off. He had a house, but Zübeyde didn't want it, so he moved into the Pink House.

She suffered the gravest sorrows a woman can experience. She lost four children and also buried her husband.

She doted on her son.

Mustafa Kemal came to the Pink House one night with his friends. The constitutional monarchy still hadn't been announced. They held a secret meeting.

Zübeyde was curious and listened at the door. She was very worried, couldn't bear it and walked in. "My son, do you all rebel against the sultan and have the strength of seven saints?" she chided.

Mustafa was stubborn and answered the question with a question: "The man you presume to have the strength of a saint has no power, mother. This work is in full swing and I have to be a part of it as an honorable man. Would you bar me from this?"

Despite her motherly love, the sails had already been set.

"You're my son and I wouldn't want you in ruin," she said. "Mainly, I would be sad if I didn't see you with honorable and esteemed men." She left the room and shut the door.

She set off on the road with her neighbors migrating to Istanbul in a convoy of grief when Salonika was lost. It was misery.

Ragıp Bey stayed in Salonika. They didn't get a divorce, but they got separated.

After a long and distressed search, Mustafa Kemal found his mother wrapped in a blanket, sleeping on the ground among migrants in the courtyard of a mosque. He set her up in a house in Akaretler, Beşiktaş, and from there they moved to Şişli.

Seven years passed.

It was dark and nearly bedtime on May 15, 1919. Mustafa Kemal arrived home. His sister Makbule opened the door. He gave her a troubled look and tenderly stroked her cheek. "Set up a table in front of the bedstead in mother's room," he said. "I want to share with you a little of tonight's trouble."

They prepared a low dinner table in Zübeyde's room and put down cushions and pillows. They made roast with mashed potatoes and spinach with eggs. Mustafa Kemal came into the room a little later. He was wearing his uniform. He hadn't changed his hat. He kissed Zübeyde's hand and sat down cross-legged.

He suddenly said he was going.

It was as if a bomb had hit the room.

"It is possible that what came to Salonika could come here, as well. I won't worry myself as I leave. I wouldn't want to be burdened by sorrow while working for the country on your behalf," he said.

Zübeyde fell on her back with a thud. She'd fainted.

They called Doctor Rasim Ferid.
Zübeyde had come to in the meantime.

With the excitement, tension, sorrow and grief, her tired spirit couldn't bear the ceaseless separation. She couldn't sleep until morning and so read the Quran.

They came to the door with the first light of day to say their farewells. Mustafa Kemal was holding a Quran. The mujahed Sheikh Ahmed Sharif as-Senussi had given it to him as a gift during the Tripolitanian War. He had brought it with him wherever he went for eight years. It was always at his side in Sofia, Gallipoli, Damascus, Aleppo and Palestine. He left it with his mother.

Makbule was crying. Zübeyde scolded her with an authoritarian tone: "You're the sister of a soldier—for shame. Do they cry?"

It was as if she wasn't the same person who had fainted from grief the night before. She was trying to stand straight as a statue. She was actually suppressing her own emotions as she consoled her daughter.

"There is no weeping for a man who goes out to battle for his country and dies. Go and prepare some sherbet for the guests!" she snapped.

She'd always had a few gold bracelets. They were all she had brought from Salonika. She gave them to her son. She told him to hold on to them "just in case".

Come 1920, and he really needed them. They were pressed for money in Ankara. They couldn't even buy bread.

Mustafa Kemal called for his aides. "There are some of my mother's jewelry ents in my suitcase. Take them to the Ottoman Bank and exchange them for money," he said.

Ali Çavuş went to the bedroom. He opened the suitcase that was under the bed and found the bracelets wrapped in a handkerchief. He ran to the bank and put them on the table without a word. They counted out 200 liras and held it out for him.

Now they could breathe a little.

With this, Zübeyde's dowry bracelet had its place in the National Campaign.

Her sorrow turned to partial paralysis when a death warrant was issued for her son, and she couldn't move her legs.

She was under constant pressure. The occupation forces often showed up unexpectedly at the house. They searched for Mustafa Kemal as if he were hidden there even though they knew he wasn't. There was a reputed informant called Sarı Ali. He kept watch on Zübeyde's house 24 hours a day and provided a list to the British of who came and went.

Zübeyde didn't shy away despite all of it. She always had her son's back.

In May 1921, patriotic women in Istanbul organized a fair for the benefit of an orphanage. The message given to the sultan with this occasion was quite clear: *We are doing something about the heroic fathers and sons who have fallen in the National Campaign.*

Zübeyde dragged herself to the fair with her paralyzed legs. She sat at the head of a table filled with colored kerchiefs and personally made sales herself.

This was Mustafa Kemal's mother. She showed herself to be the mother to all children of the fallen. She reunited with her son whom she had longed for her entire life after the Victory of Sakarya. He had her brought to Ankara.

The photograph of her in white muslin and glasses that has been burned in all Turks' memory was taken at the Çankaya Mansion.

The famous round glasses were Sabiha Gökçen's. They were brought for safekeeping to the Yapı Kredi Bank archive.

She was a beautiful woman and she aged gracefully.

Halide Edip Adıvar had the following impression the first time she met her in Çankaya: "The elderly woman's face, active body and fiery expression are the same as Mustafa Kemal Pasha's. There wasn't a single wrinkle in the 70-year-old woman's milky white and pink skin. Her dark blue eyes and mouth made one feel compassion despite her short temper. Her white dress, ironed handkerchiefs and white hands reminded me of my grandmother. She was a Macedonian woman through and through. She always scolded Mustafa whenever she wanted when he was in elementary school. She slept on a bed on the floor. She was seriously ill and it was a miracle she was alive. She kissed the cheeks and held the hands of Doctor Adnan, who examined her, and spoke of her birthplace of Salonika. She yearned for Salonika. Her son Mustafa said she had vowed not to make herself a new dress if Salonika wasn't taken back.

She didn't go out much while she was in Çankaya. She passed the days reading the Quran. She also took it upon herself to represent her son if there was a wedding or other ceremony.

She was very fond of Salih Bozok, who was Mustafa Kemal's neighborhood friend and the son of their neighbor. She attended his son's circumcision with the pride of a grandparent and gave him an expensive Longines wristwatch.

Mustafa Kemal entrusted his mother to Salih Bozok every time he went to Tripoli or Sofia. Zübeyde spent more time with him than with her son and he'd become the family's second son.

Salih Bozok also felt the same. "Zübeyde can be considered as my own mother," he said of it. "I truly don't know who I love more, my own mother or Zübeyde."

Mustafa Kemal preoccupied his mother's mind her entire life.

In a letter he wrote to Salih Bozok while in Istanbul, he asked, "If possible, console my mother. There's still my last month's salary. Show her how to access it."

In a letter he sent to Fuat Bey from Tripolitania, he said, "Don't let my mother know where I am and show her my letters from Istanbul from time to time. I've left 40 liras with Kerim Bey to be given to my mother. It strengthens my heart that Salih Bozok is in Salonika with my mother and it doubles my resilience."

He cautioned in a letter sent from Alexandria: "Salih Bozok, my brother, I went to the hospital for a month-long treatment and regained my health. My kind regards. Don't tell my mother of my illness."

There was an enviable bond of respect between mother and son. They wouldn't meet without first making preparations. Even though they lived in rooms only a few feet from each other in the same mansion, Mustafa Kemal would send word and say when he would visit. Zübeyde would prepare as if it were a veritable holiday, wearing her best clothes instead of her everyday clothing, combing her hair and waiting for her son.

He never entered his mother's room without permission and would kiss her hand every time he did.

Zübeyde made her last will a year before she died.

"After I die, I want the whole of the Quran to be read for my soul every year. I want to leave some money for this. Where should I give it?" she had asked.

They suggested the Darüşşafaka—the Home of Compassion—a school for orphans.

She left 20,000 *kuruş* to it.

She stipulated that every year on *Laylat al-Qadr*, one student at the Darüşşafaka would recite the whole of the Quran, and that this good deed be done in dedication to the Prophet Muhammad and his family first of all, as well as the other prophets and saints and the souls of her entire family, past and present.

She didn't forget those who worked beside her. When she died, she left 1,000 *kuruş* to Hayriye Hanım, 1,000 *kuruş* to her stepdaughter Ayşe for her dowry, 2,000 *kuruş* for the education of Mustafa Kemal's adopted son Abdürrahim and 2,000 *kuruş* to Vasfiye Hanım.

Mustafa Kemal learned of the will and had the entire Quran read for his mother every year. He would give an envelope of money to the hafiz who would recite the Quran.

It was January 14, 1923, just before dawn. Mustafa Kemal called for his aide, Ali Çavuş. "Is there news?" he asked.

Ali Çavuş couldn't say that unfortunately there was. "A code came but it couldn't be solved," he mumbled.

A cloud passed over Mustafa Kemal's deep blue gaze. "I had a dream. I was wandering through a green field with my mother when all of a sudden, a storm came and took my mother from me. I know my mother has died," he said.

He couldn't attend her funeral. He sent a telegraph to Salih Bozok who, as usual, was with Zübeyde. He asked him to bury his mother for him: "Perform a burial in a way proper for the deceased. May God give our people life and salvation."

He wanted a modest ceremony to be held, a modest gravesite and modest tombstone. He certainly didn't give permission to French architect Maurice Gauthier, whom the İzmir municipality had brought over for the construction of the 1934 Fair, to have drawings made for her tomb.

"These are ornate, luxurious and costly. Don't do it. Bring a rock, put it at her head and on it have written, *Here lies Atatürk's mother Zübeyde*. Make the area around it a children's park. She loved children so much," he said.

Latife was with Zübeyde until the final moment.

Mustafa Kemal's wife had entertained and maintained her mother-in-law at her mansion in Karşıkaya. She first informed the governor of İzmir upon her death, then she called for the city's 33 best-known hafizes and had them recite the Quran until morning.

She put on a black overcoat and black veil. She wanted to attend the funeral. Everyone objected at first, her family most of all. They said women could not attend funerals.

In response, she got into a closed carriage and followed the funeral procession a pace from the very back. She distributed hundreds of silver *mecidiye* coins to the poor at the site of the tomb as charity. She held a memorial service on the fortieth day and made *ashura* (Noah's pudding) on the fifty-second day.

Mustafa Kemal was able to come 13 days later. He went to his mother's grave. He made what was maybe the most emotional speech of his life.

He spoke of his mother: "My poor mother has been laid in the sacred soil of İzmir, which is ideal for the whole nation.

"Friends, death is the most natural law of creation. Sometimes, however, it's a saddening spectacle. My mother who lies here was a victim of an arbitrary regime that brought the entire nation to the precipice of disaster through strain and torment. To explain this, if you will permit, let me present a few specific examples from her life of sorrow.

"It was during the reign of Abdülhamid. I had just come from school as a staff captain. I was taking my first steps into life. This step wasn't out into life, though, as it ended in prison. They took me and put me in a dungeon of despotism. I stayed there for months. My mother was only able to know of this after I was released from prison. She ran to see me right away. She came to Istanbul. I was able to see her for a few days because the spies and executioners of this despotism surrounded our residence and they took me away. My mother followed after me in tears. My mother was prevented from seeing me as I was boarding the ferry to my exile, she was in tears and left in pain and heartbreak on the Sirkeci pier.

"The dangers I experienced in exile were cause for the pain and tears she suffered.

"There's another point. I had to leave my mother in grief when I left for Anatolia during the armistice. One of my men was with her. When she saw this man whom I had sent to Istanbul from Erzurum, she thought the caliph and sultan's death warrant for me had been fulfilled, and this presumption crippled her.

"She spent years of struggle in sadness. She was under constant pressure and torture from the sultan, his government and the enemies. They raided her residence with a thousand pretexts and bewildered her.

"My mother spent three and a half years in tears day and night. These tears made her lose her eyes.

"I was finally able to save her from Istanbul, and when I was able to be with her, she was already dead physically and was only alive spiritually.

"I am, without doubt, very saddened by the loss of my mother. There is a matter that removes this sorrow and consoles me, though, and that is to see that the government that brought our motherland to annihilation is buried never to return.

"My mother is interred in this soil, but may the national sovereignty be everlasting. This is the only force that comforts me. National sovereignty will continue for evermore.

"Let me repeat the vow of conscience I swore on my mother's soul and those of all my ancestors. I swear at my mother's grave and in the presence of God—I will never be irresolute in protection and defense of the sovereignty that has been gained and that the nation has won through the spilling of much blood, and I will join my mother if necessary.

"May giving my life for national sovereignty be a debt of conscience and honor for me."

His childhood flashed before him like a film strip while he stood at his mother's grave and gave this emotional and historic speech.

Zübeyde wanted Mustafa to get a religious education. Ali Rıza was in favor of new methods of education.

They found a middle path. Mustafa would go to the Fatma Molla Kadın neighborhood school, which would satisfy Zübeyde in her view of the neighbors, and then he would later transfer to Şemsi Efendi's school.

Children at that time started school with a showy ceremony called the amen procession. The students would hang their Quran bags around their necks, be mounted on colorfully decorated horses and handed out candies and *simit* around the neighborhood, and were brought to school to the singing of hymns. The more means and time a family had, the more festive the ceremony was.

Zübeyde wanted to experience this parental joy.

The amen procession came to the Pink House.

They had dressed Mustafa in some new, white clothes. A turban-like hat was placed on his head. He kissed the hands of his mother, father and teacher. Prayers were said. He joined the procession and went to the school next to the mosque as the neighborhood applauded.

Şemsi Efendi.

He transferred to Şemsi Efendi's school after two months.

Şemsi Efendi had been born to a poor family in Salonika. He worked and studied, learned Arabic, Persian and French, and became a teacher.

He started his career as a Turkish teacher at a foreign private school. He decided to open a private primary school. He repaired a ruined, single-story masjid with a courtyard and turned it into a classroom.

He pushed aside the primitive education method of rote learning.

He started to teach classes the other neighborhoods didn't have at the time, such as history, geography and mathematics.

While the spelling method was used at length in the teaching of reading and writing, in its place, he used the method used today based on the sound of the letters and reading words directly.

The classroom was open to girls. It was a revolution. One of the first girls to be a student there was his own daughter.

The classes each lasted an hour and, in between, the students would do gymnastics in the courtyard.

He used things such as desks for students, a teacher's desk, maps, a blackboard, chalk and an eraser.

He would deputize one of the older, hardworking students as a tutor for new students, similar to today's mentoring system.

He attended the freedom meetings organized in support of constitutionalism together with his students. He became a target for bigotry because of his modern and liberal methods. His school was often attacked with slander that he was teaching the children to be infidels and nonreligious. These people would barge into the classroom and smash the desks, table and blackboard.

He temporarily halted classes at the school when he was exposed to bigoted attacks and instead went to each of the students' houses and continued the classes that way.

He started cultural trips. He organized overnight trips to Istanbul after Mustafa's time at the school.

The families trusted him so much that even the girls joined the overnight trips.

He didn't only train the children, but also the community. He distributed books to the neighboring shopkeepers around the school. He bought them out of his own pocket to get the community used to reading and gave the books away for free.

It was this visionary teacher who gave Mustafa Kemal his educational foundation.

When his father Ali Rıza died, they moved to the farm where his uncle worked as a steward.

He had to take a six-month break from school. Then he went by himself to his aunt in Salonika. Şemsi Efendi was there for the rest of his primary school education.

Unfortunately, Mustafa no longer had his father to guide him to modern education. He attended the Salonika civil junior high school at his mother's insistence.

After Şemsi Efendi, it was insufferable.

He was very angry that he was forced to wear traditional shalvar instead of trousers and that he had to wear a wrapped waistband. He especially didn't like having to sit on his knees in writing class. He would often stand up saying his knees hurt and then glower when the teacher told him to sit.

He had an Arabic teacher known as Kaymak Hafiz.

Mustafa was picked on. Kaymak Hafız was always on the lookout for the opportunity to hurt him.

They were memorizing a text and he asked Mustafa to repeat a sentence. He kept quiet. Kaymak Hafız repeated himself, and again Mustafa remained silent.

He started pulling on his ear, enough to draw blood.

It would've been futile even if it tore off. Mustafa had no intention of bending. He wouldn't say it.

He came home and shut himself in his room.

According to the recollection of his sister Makbule, he didn't say a word for four days and his mouth was sealed shut.

Twelve-year-old Mustafa was on the verge of changing the line of fate for both himself and the Turkish people.

He left the house on the fifth day. He found one of his neighbors from the street, Major Kadri Bey, whom he asked for help to go to the military school.

Kadri Bey had him registered for the test.

After that, Mustafa attended the Salonika Military High School.

Zübeyde's authority had come to an end. He had announced his personal independence at age 12.

He was going to stop by the neighborhood school when he came back to Salonika years later as a staff officer. He saw a gigantic lock hanging on the door and said it was good that it had been closed.

He never forgot Kaymak Hafiz his entire life. He always gave him as an example of poor education.

"He's an awful man," he would say whenever the man was mentioned. "He truly was an awful man. His rudeness and mercilessness played a major role in my leaving the civil high school, but I forgave him long ago," he said.

❈

His math teacher at the military high school was Captain Mustafa Efendi of Skopje. He changed the name of history, having said: "My boy, your name's Mustafa and my name's Mustafa. A difference should be found in between. There's a maturity to you and refinement at your young age. Your name should be Mustafa Kemal."

Kemal means mature.

He was the Kemal of Namık Kemal.

Like all the teachers at the military high school, math teacher Mustafa Efendi loved Namık Kemal.

This detail was included in the first biography of Mustafa Kemal, which was prepared by Turkish-Bulgarians in 1920.

It said: "His math teacher Mustafa Efendi gave him the name Kemal in honor of Namık Kemal."

Starting in 1921, when Istanbul newspapers started reporting on Mustafa Kemal's life story, they wrote that the name Kemal was given to him in honor of Namık Kemal.

❋

(The weekly magazine *Çocuklara Rehber* (Children's Handbook) was published in Salonika. It had articles on art, geography, health, the animal world and general culture, and also held quizzes. In April 1897, it published a list of the names of those who answered the quiz correctly. Among them was military high school student Mustafa Kemal.)

(This interesting piece of information is included in all Atatürk biographies as if photocopied. It's wrong, though, as the Mustafa Kemal we're speaking of wasn't in Salonika in 1897—he was at the Monastir Military High School in Istanbul, having graduated from junior high school two years earlier.)

(So, where did this confusion start? Well, there was another Mustafa Kemal at the Salonika Military Junior High School. He was also from Salonika and was two years younger than the Mustafa Kemal of note and, as such, was two classes his junior. This Mustafa Kemal, like Mustafa Kemal, also later attended the Monastir Military High School and then the Military Academy, where he was İsmet İnönü's classmate. Another great coincidence is that he was also sent to Damascus for his first deployment like the Mustafa Kemal who became Atatürk. He resigned from military service in 1918, moved to the civil service and retired from the Menemen Military Bureau.)

(The resemblance of the two Mustafa Kemals of Salonika was uncanny and caused confusion, as is the case with the *Children's Handbook*. Unfortunately, there are historians who have confused class notes of these two Mustafa Kemals. There have even been historians who have written books thinking the poems the other Mustafa Kemal sent to literature magazines were Atatürk's poems.)

❈

The Mustafa Kemal of this book loved mathematics with a passion and adopted it as a way of life.

He wrote a book titled *Geometry* in 1936 in which derived Turkish equivalents to Arabic and Persian geometric terms.

Mustafa Kemal coined words in Turkish for size, space, surface, radius, section, arc, circumference, tangent, angle, horizontal, vertical, perpendicular, location, triangle, square, polygon, diagonal, equilateral, isosceles, trapezoid, plus, minus, times, divided by, equal, total, ratio, proportion, derivative, area, level, line, parallel, volume, squared, square meter, cone, cube, pyramid. cylinder, pi, theory, theorem and conjecture.

Before that, all of these terms had been taken from either Arabic or Persian.

He traveled to high schools around the country after he became president. There, he would grab a piece of chalk and go to the blackboard where he would explain the Pythagorean theorem in Turkish terms.

Life was mathematics for Mustafa Kemal. "Science is mathematics," he'd say.

"The universe is written in a mathematical language and the letters of the universe are triangles, squares, circles and geometric forms," he said. "Everyone should believe mathematical knowledge is necessary. The world is absolutely incomprehensible without mathematics, and without it we wander through a dark labyrinth."

He was a real man of accounts.

Hamdullah Suphi spoke at the podium of Parliament before the Battle of Dumlupınar and praised the National Campaign as he saw it when he said, "The National Campaign is a holy madness."

Mustafa Kemal angrily jumped to his feet and yelled, "What is he saying? What does holy madness mean? The National Campaign is an account, an account!"

❋

The teachers at the military school had shaped his mentality.

He was on a trip to Samsun in 1924, when journalists accompanying him asked where he drew inspiration and from whom he found strength.

He stood up without answering, took a few steps toward the crowd, welcomed them and took a man in a fedora by the hand.

Then he turned to the journalists and gave an answer: "When we were born, we were in the destructive clutches of tyranny together with everybody in this land. People's lips had been sealed. Teachers were only obliged to cultivate one point in their students' minds—to forget the self and everything else, submit to this horrible dream and be at its beck and call. At the same time, though, one mustn't forget that under that pressure, there were true and devoted teachers who tried to cultivate us for today. Now, this is where I came across a great person. Nakiyüddin Bey was my teacher in my first year at the military junior high school. He gave me my first ideas for the future as he was still teaching the first bits of information. I want to explain this, gentlemen. The first well of information after the embrace of mother and father is the language, conscience and education from teachers at school."

Nakiyüddin Yücekök was his French teacher at the Salonika Military Junior High School. He also maintained contact after graduation. His student Mustafa Kemal personally assisted the secret organizing of the Homeland and Liberty Society against the regime of Sultan Adbülhamid II.

Mustafa Kemal said that he owed another of his teachers a debt of gratitude—his history teacher at the Monastir Military High School, Mehmet Tevfik Bilge. He learned about Turkish history and the French Revolution from this teacher. Mehmet Tevfik Bilge endeared him to the culture of history. "He opened new horizons to me," he said of his teacher.

❖

He read the books and writing of Tevfik Fikret, Namık Kemal, Ziya Gökalp, Mehmet Emin Yurdakul, Kılıçzade Hakkı, Yusuf Akçura, Abdülhak Hamit and Şehbenderzade Ahmed Hilmi of Plovdiv. He followed magazines such as *Meşveret* (Consultancy), İçtihat (Independent Reasoning) and *Mizan* (Balance). He even read line by line the old copies of the Young Turks' *Osmanlı Mecmuası* (Ottoman Journal) published in Europe.

❖

Tevfik Fikret.

Tevfik Fikret was at the forefront of those who inspired Mustafa Kemal. He read Tevfik Fikret even in the bloodiest of trench warfare and took notes.

The source for him saying "free thought, free conscience and the insight of free generations" was Tevfik Fikret. He admired the educator and poet so much that he said, "I received the spirit of revolution from him. Those who know Tevfik Fikret are those who will comprehend what it is I want to do."

He took close interest in Galatasaray High School out of respect for Tevfik Fikret after the proclamation of the republic.

For example, Mustafa Kemal allocated the building that Galatasaray University uses today.

The idea is not only in the significance. Tevfik Fikret also influenced him in his gusto for life. He took clothing as an example of pleasure.

He visited Tevfik Fikret's house in Aşiyan on the second anniversary of his death. He wrote in the commemoration book: "We are Fikret's friends who are proud to visit in his remembrance."

He examined Tevfik Fikret's belongings while he was there and years later had the same desk made for the Çankaya Mansion that he'd seen at the house in Aşiyan.

He could recite the poems such as *Sis* (Fog), *Tarih-i Kadim* (Ancient History) and *Ferda* (Tomorrow) by heart.

"Especially Tevfik Fikret's *Tarih-i Kadim* is the source of all the revolutions that have to be done in the world," he said.

Rübab-ı Şikeste (The Broken Rebab) and *Haluk'un Defteri* (The Book of Good Natured) were in his private library.

He was speaking with youngsters one day after becoming president. "I ask you, who is at the head of those who wrote, thought and sacrificed their lives so that this nation and country could live with glory and honor among the people of the civilized world?" he asked.

There were those who said Namık Kemal and those who said Ziya Gökalp.

He couldn't contain himself.

"It's Fikret, children, Fikret," he said.

"He was far ahead of us," he said. "And unfortunately, we still haven't been able to catch up."

Namık Kemal.

It wasn't just his name, Namık Kemal was also an integral part of Mustafa Kemal's intellectual world.

He came to know Namık Kemal's forbidden ideas thanks to his classmate Ömer Naci. He embraced them so much so that he reproduced his *Vatan Kasidesi* (Homeland Qasida) with a mimeograph and secretly distributed them at school.

He had a notebook in which he'd written down Namık Kemal's poems. His favorite verse was from the poet's *Hürriyet Kasidesi* (Independence Qasida) was:

May destiny gather and bestow all forms of torment
If I turn from the path of service to the nation, I am a whore

He watched the play *Vatan yahut Silistre* (The Homeland or else Silistra) while at the Monastir Military High School. He couldn't hold back his tears and shouted out excitedly at the end of the play.

"All revolutions in history are first born in the minds of intellectuals and then embrace society in time. We have

Namık Kemal and it is he who gave voice to the Turkish people for which they had waited for centuries," he said.

Works such as *Vaveyla* (Squall), İntibah (Rebirth), *Osmanlı Tarihi* (Ottoman History), Şark Meselesi (The Eastern Question) had a special place in his private library.

Namık Kemal's son, Ali Ekrem Bolayır, gave a handwritten copy of Tevfik Fikret's *Eş'ar-ı Kemal* (Poems of Maturity) in 1923, with a supplement by his father. This book is where Namık Kemal and Tevfik Fikret intersect and it held a separate, prestigious place in Mustafa Kemal's library.

He read Descartes, Kant, Durkheim, Voltaire, Jean-Jacques Rousseau and Stuart Mill while still a student. He told his classmates that "the idea that society still isn't settled busies the mind," and that "Darwin was following this theory."

He was interested in Divan poetry.

He wrote out six of Fuzuli's poems with the new script after the Turkish alphabet reform and placed it between the pages of his copy of the book *Ottoman History*.

He often recited the lines:
If my beloved desires my soul, so much the better,
What is the soul that I shouldn't sacrifice it to my lover?

He graduated from the Monastir Military High School and went to Istanbul.

His identification was recorded in the register of the Military Academy: "Mustafa Kemal Efendi, tall, fair complexion, of the Koca Kasım Paşa neighborhood of Salonika, son of late customs officer Ali Rıza Efendi."

He had a photograph taken of himself in uniform at the Military Academy. It's the oldest known photograph of Atatürk.

He had no relatives or acquaintances in Istanbul.

He needed to provide an address in order to go on leave during holidays, so he appealed to Ali Fuat Cebesoy, whom he'd met during registration.

The 16-room mansion on Kuzguncuk Nakkaşbaba Caddesi was Mustafa Kemal's first residential address in the city.

He stayed in the same room with Ali Fuat on their evenings off.

Ali Fuat's father, İsmail Fazil Pasha, was a paternalistic man. He would leave an allowance of one *mecidiye* under his son's pillow and two *mecidiye* coins under Mustafa Kemal's pillow.

Why did he give his son less?

"Count your spending so far," he said. "He's studying away from home and needs it much more than you."

Mustafa Kemal's upward twisted mustache was very stylish. Before going on weekend leave, he would put Brilliantine on his mustache, twist it up and tape it to his cheeks for a while.

❈

His days on leave were very cheerful. He and his friends usually went to the gentlemen's coffee shops, Stefan's Kiraathane at the Bab-ı Ali, as well Yani's Kiraathane in Sirkeci.

He walked around Istanbul quite a bit in his first year in the city. It reflected in his grades for his first-year courses. He was 29th out of 703 students.

He criticized himself and wrote in his notebook: "I've been captivated by the dreams of youth. I neglected my lessons. I wasn't aware of how the year passed."

In the end, he would finish eighth at the Military Academy.

❈

His French was perfect. It was the predominant language of Europe at the time and he made every effort at every opportunity to improve. For example, when he was a student at the military high school, he attended the evening classes given by priests at the missionary schools set up within the framework of capitulations.

Father Rodriguez said in an interview in 1941 how vividly he remembered Mustafa Kemal from back then: "He always had books in his hand and was a quite serious young man. He left a mark on my memory."

He chose German as a second foreign language at the Military Academy. His grades for German were even better than those for French.

He rented a place to stay from a German family while in Sofia, and took lessons from the landlady Hilda Christianus.

He reached the level where he was able to do translations.

His German got rusty since he didn't use it in his everyday life and, because of this, he considered every German he met to be an opportunity. He took lessons from a German woman who was a teacher even when he went for treatment in Carlsbad.

❋

He read French newspapers—*Le Temps, Le Matin* and *Le Figaro*.

There was an alehouse in Beyoğlu called Zeuve, which was owned by a German and had European newspapers. He often went there with his friends to drink the German beer and read the newspapers. Foreigners also frequented it. The palace secret police didn't bother it much since the owner was German, and so they could converse comfortably.

There was a three-story building in a corner to the left after leaving the Galata gate in Tünel. The first floor was a market that sold British goods. The second story was an English restaurant.

It was run by an Armenian known as John Pasha who had retired from the Directorate of Maritime Lines. He only served lunch. Mustafa Kemal and his friends would stop by the restaurant and drink scotch with English soda.

Sometimes they would go to the islands on their off days.

At that time, Thursday was a half-day, Friday was off and the week started on Saturday. He and Ali Fuat Cebesoy missed the last ferry back to the mainland on Thursday evening. They slept that night under the pines of Büyükada.

❈

He experienced the most troubling week of his life concerning his mother and siblings in July 1902.

A violent earthquake hit Salonika.

Journalists in Istanbul reported on the disaster. They wrote that there were many dead and injured, nearly no buildings remained standing, people had fled to the fields and were staying there in tents.

Telephone and telegraph services were out and he couldn't get any word from his mother and siblings. He wanted to go to Salonika, but he couldn't get permission.

It was the first time Mustafa Kemal, now 21, had felt this helpless and desperate.

The week was a nightmare. The situation was clear a week later, though. The earthquake was a magnitude 6.6. It was true that people were sleeping in the streets and that cracks had formed in the buildings, but no one had died in the city center.

Too heavy a load was put on the young man's shoulders—responsibility for his mother and siblings as the breadwinner.

He prepared a one-page, handwritten magazine called *Vatan* (Homeland) while at the Military Academy. He wrote about liberty, women's rights and nationalism. He personally handed it out in secret.

∞

After he graduated, he and his friends rented a house for themselves in Sirkeci.

They were both waiting for their assignments and having heated conversations about matters of the country while doing so.

This included criticizing the sultan.

Mustafa Kemal was taken into custody and questioned at the Yıldız Palace.

He was formally arrested and placed in the Bekirağa block.

The Bekirağa block was a two-story building in Beyazıt. Its formal name was the Istanbul Guard Office. Those who challenged Abdülhamid II were held here.

It had gotten its nickname from one of its former commanders, Bekir Ağa, who was infamous for his cruelty. It was a dreadful dungeon with torture and beatings.

The claims against Mustafa Kemal were like slander in poetry. He was charged with "publishing a secret newspaper at school and spreading harmful ideas, setting up a secret committee, being the ringleader of secret meetings held in a house in Sirkeci, planning to bomb Abdülhamid's car as he was visiting the holy mantle of Muhammad at Topkapı Palace, collecting money to establish a fund for personal benefit, and lending students money and charging interest."

He was alone in a deep, dark cell, its walls wet with damp and with no sunlight. He slept on a bed of straw that smelled strongly of mold. The nights were very cold.

This was where he first developed trouble with his kidneys.

He got a half ration once in the morning and again in the evening. It came with a few olives, as well.

He was held like this for two months.

Neither he was asked to present his defense nor was he taken to court.

They must have thought he had been sufficiently humbled and he was released after two months.

He was then assigned to Damascus as soon as he was released.

His first deployment was exile.

∞

Damascus was a forgotten corner of the empire, according to Mustafa Kemal's account. It was abandoned, left to its fate and derelict.

He boarded a ship in Istanbul and arrived at the Beirut port after an eight-day journey. There were no cars and so he crossed Lebanon on horseback. He reached Damascus after riding 22 miles. He slept for two nights in a tent. There was no bed and instead slept on two sacks stuffed with straw.

The year was 1905. The city, however, was experiencing the Middle Ages. The people lived in misery while a handful of the rich lived in houses with large gardens along the banks of the Barada River.

Having grown up in the modern cities of Salonika and Istanbul, as well as the Monastir Military High School, Mustafa Kemal came to know the Arab interpretation of Islam in this gloomy city. While there, he began to compare it with the Turkish interpretation of Islam.

He rented a two-room house.

He established the Homeland and Freedom Society together with the libertarian officers who had been exiled there like him.

He traveled through every inch of Beirut, Jaffa and Jerusalem in what is today Syria, Lebanon and Israel. He stayed four months in the Sinai Desert before he went to the Golan Heights. When he felt suffocated, he would go to Salonika without permission by means of Alexandria and Piraeus.

His life continued like this for three years. He was 26.

They had stolen three long years of his short 26 years of life in order to humble him, but then he was finally deployed to Salonika.

He had been honed by the experience.

He joined the Picardie Maneuvers in France as an observer on behalf of the Ottoman Empire. He was a captain and not included in the protocol. He attracted attention, though, due to his pointed comments and gutsy behavior. Despite his insufficient rank, the rules were stretched and he was invited to dine with the French field marshal who was the head commander of the drills.

It was these drills in which aircraft were first used as a weapon of war. The pilots made reconnaissance flights and threw down grenades and spikes.

These, however, were not spikes we're familiar with. Known as caltrops, they had four sharp, 4-inch, barbed points like a fishhook and fell to the ground points down.

They were called heel-breakers and were a sort of primitive mine. They were thrown over marching routes and were also undetectable at night.

Mustafa Kemal was the first Ottoman officer to see these caltrops that would be thrown from overhead from the planes flying over Gallipoli only four years later. He was also the first officer to understand what air superiority was and that the future of warfare was in the sky.

At the end of the Picardie Maneuvers, the French pilots gave tours in their planes to the guest officers and made a move for Mustafa Kemal to get on, but it's claimed that the head of the Ottoman delegation, Ali Rıza Pasha, grabbed him by the arm at the last moment and told him not to go.

The plane supposedly crashed and thus Mustafa Kemal averted death.

The story is stirring, but there's no document to confirm it. No plane crashed in the Picardie Maneuvers, according to French aviation statistics. What's more, no plane crash resulted in any deaths in France that year.

It's been put forward based on this story of the plane crash that Mustafa Kemal developed a fear of planes and that is why he never boarded a plane in his life.

The planes of those days, of course, were not modern passenger planes. They were made to be warplanes with space for one, maybe two people. It wasn't yet reliable technology—the wings were even made of wood. Aviation was still in its infancy.

He also wouldn't have been able to be in a plane without a pilot.

Even in 1935, the trial flights that had begun between Ankara and Istanbul only carried four passengers. There was no airport in Ankara, the flights had a transfer in Eskişehir and they landed in Güvercinlik, taking more than three hours, and only in summer. The concept of passenger planes emerged in Turkey after the 1940s.

From 1937 onward, Mustafa Kemal's ailments made it difficult for him to take even a train.

He died in 1938.

One should look at those who say Mustafa Kemal had a fear of flying and try to imagine Boeing or Airbus planes flying in Turkey in the 1930s.

One should also take note of the biographies of other leaders of the time. There is no information about whether or not they flew in an airplane. There just isn't.

While it's accepted as quite normal that other world leaders didn't fly in planes considering the insufficient conditions of the period, some say Mustafa Kemal not flying in planes is somehow abnormal.

This is unfortunately one of the main problems with books on Mustafa Kemal. While one faction with good intentions wants to aggrandize him and embraces exaggerated, fantastical stories, another with malice wants to defame him and fabricates dislocations of time, space and perception.

∞

He had stayed in Paris on his way to Picardie.

He went around to cafes and listened to music with Fethi Okyar. He danced with the French girls.

They met Abidin Daver, who was a writer for the newspaper *Tasvir-i Efkâr* (Picture of Ideas), and according to his recollection, they were in tuxedos.

He went on a 14-day trip through Switzerland, the Netherlands and Belgium, again with Fethi, before returning to the Ottoman Empire.

∞

He was then deployed to Istanbul in the days when the Italians were attacking Tripoli.

The Ottomans didn't have the power and couldn't send soldiers. They couldn't get to the Aegean or Black Sea.

They couldn't even send supplies. It was a sorrowful state of affairs.

Patriotic officers set off for Tripoli in ones and twos through Egypt. Mustafa Kemal was among them.

It was his first war.

He boarded a Russian passenger ship in Istanbul. He arrived in Alexandria under the assumed name of Mustafa Şerif with the assumed profession of journalist.

His passport was a forgery. He was supposedly a writer for the newspaper *Tanin* (Reverberation).

He was kicked in the chest by a horse as he was preparing to set out for Tripoli and was in the hospital for 15 days.

They had to cover ground in Egypt from east to west.

He and his fellow officers wore Bedouin clothes to evade British checkpoints and they crossed the parched dessert sometimes on camels and other times walking.

There were no villages or hamlets along the route. They set up their tents at nightfall and cooked their own meals. Fuat Bulca undertook the cooking and Mustafa Kemal shelled beans.

It was 122 degrees Fahrenheit in the day, which fell to 40 degrees at night. They went 410 miles grappling with sandstorms. It took eight days. Then they reached Tobruk.

They went to Tripoli and Benghazi. He organized tribal chiefs and formed the local people into a structured alliance. They did battle and employed unconventional warfare tactics.

He went to Derna. While there, he was wounded in the eye. This was his first time becoming a *gazi*—a veteran.

His friend Fuat Bulca explained what happened at that moment: "Our target was the Qasr. It was a Carthaginian ruin. It started out in full throttle. I saw Mustafa Kemal run and dive into a building in the middle of the Qasr. That's when I heard a noise in the sky. Two Italian planes were flying low and dropping grenades. There were explosions. Mustafa Kemal's face was unrecognizable when I got to him. He had a handkerchief in one hand that he was holding to his left eye and his other hand was holding his sword."

He was shot in the right arm before his eye had healed. He didn't leave his troops, despite having lost a lot of blood, until they had repelled the Eritrean battalion.

∞

The first published photographs of him.

The first published photographs of him were taken in Derna. They were published in *The Illustrated London News* magazine, which was the world's first news magazine.

He can be seen with Enver Pasha in the photographs accompanying the report introducing the Ottoman officers who organized the resistance.

A caption to a photograph said: "The commander-in-chief of the Ottoman troops in Cyrenaica; Enver Bey in conversation with Mustapha Kamel [sic], the Turkish officer who commanded the Derna division."

Another caption said: "With the Turco Arab troops at a inspection held before Enver Bey" at the camp of Ain el Mansour.

❈

One of the men serving under his command was an adventurous character worthy of being the subject of film.

He was known as Osman Efendi. His actual name, however, was John Warren Stuart Smallwood. He was an Englishman working as a correspondent for the *Daily Chronicle*. He was also a boxer and his body was covered with sailor tattoos. He had viewed and reported on many fronts of the empire on which the sun never sets.

He was probably a spy.

The tragedies he saw and massacres he witnessed, though, opened the way for him to question his country and himself, and he was driven to the other side. He converted to Islam, got circumcised, took on the name Osman and joined the Ottoman army. He came to Tripoli as a volunteer with the rank of lieutenant. He was brave and daring. In the end, he was killed while trying to infiltrate the Italian Lines.

Then the Balkan War broke out. Salonika was lost.

Mustafa Kemal returned to Istanbul after wasting 10 months of his life in what is now Libya.

∞

He was then deployed to the Dardanelles. He stayed for 10 months at Bolayır. He wrote about every inch of Gallipoli.

One could say fate had brought him here.

He wasn't aware of it himself in those days, but he found the chance to examine Gallipoli—the place that would change the track of history three years later.

He visited the places where the Trojan War took place 3,000 years ago. He compared the attack points from land and sea under modern conditions on a map. He wandered through the ruins. He read *The Iliad* and tried to discover the routes Homer wrote of in the epic.

He also visited the mound known as the tomb of Achilles.

Alexander the Great had brought his massive army of 35,000 men to the Asia Minor over the Dardanelles in 334 BCE.

He examined the crossing route and kept notes.

∞

He was then sent to Sofia as a military attaché.

He stayed at the Bulgaria Hotel across from the tsar's palace. From there he moved to the Splendid Palace Hotel and stayed there for six months. For the next nine months after that he stayed in a one-window room in a boarding house on Ferdinand Boulevard.

The owners were Hildegard and Gustav Christianus, a German couple with a 7-year-old daughter.

He took German lessons from Hilda. He learned that she loved red roses and would bring her one each lesson. He gave her a red, Turkish carpet as a gift. He also gave her a photograph as a keepsake. On the back he wrote, "Loyal and kind Madam Hilda."

They had a sentimentality that didn't overstep the bounds and exchanged letters for three or four years after he left Sofia.

She died in Germany in 1960.

He also learned enough Bulgarian to manage his daily work. He went to the opera, ballet and tea parties. He established communication in social environments very easily and Macedonian-accented Bulgarian also made him particularly sympathetic.

One of his closest friends while he was in Sofia was Şakir Zümre. He was a Turkish representative in Bulgarian Parliament, and thanks to him, Mustafa Kemal was introduced to Bulgarian lawmakers.

He became the best-loved foreigner in the country.

He was going to be collecting the fruits of his labor in Sofia when the War of Independence began. Using his friendly relationships with Bulgarians—also thanks to Şakir Zümre—he secured shipment of weapons, ammunition and food to Anatolia from across the Black Sea.

A ball was held at the Sofia Officer's Club on the occasion of the Bulgarian Education and Culture, and Slavonic Script Day in May 1914.

He wanted to make a psychological impression on the diplomats of the city. He thought about what he could do and had Uç Beylik clothing sent from the Military Museum in Istanbul.

(It's still even today vulgarly referred to as janissary dress, but it was actually Serhat Beylik and Uç Beylik clothing.)

He entered the hall and a flood of cheers erupted.

He was the favorite of the ball.

The symbolic jury of the night awarded Mustafa Kemal the prize for best-loved dress. The tsar congratulated him personally with a handshake.

The Spanish charge d'affaires in Sofia was a fan of Middle Eastern culture and had a special room in the embassy decorated with carpets from Ottoman lands. He extended an invitation to Mustafa Kemal while leaving the ball, and it was there, that night at the Spanish Embassy where the legendary photograph etched in all Turks' minds was taken.

This photograph, which is one of most important shots in Turkish history, wasn't known of until 1921.

It was published on the front page of the newspaper *Tevhid-i Efkâr* on December 20, 1921.

Everyone learned of it that day.

This is because the War of Independence wasn't only a national struggle for the Turks in Anatolia, but also the Turks in Bulgaria. Turks reproduced the photograph and hung it in their homes and shops.

It was the first poster, of sorts, of Mustafa Kemal hung on walls that pulled at people's heartstrings.

A Turk in Sofia by the name of Yasin Bey who was engaged in trade made a copy of the photograph and sent it to the owner and head writer of *Tevhid-i Efkâr*, Velid Ebuzziya, and ensured it was published in Istanbul.

World War I broke out.

He fell in love with Miti.

It was impossible for them to meet.

He packed his bags and left Sofia with a broken heart.

∞

He was then deployed to the Dardanelles.

To get there, he came to Istanbul aboard the Orient Express and then took the *Halep* steamer from Tekirdağ.

He would be the Hero of Anafartalar.

And now he stepped foot in Gallipoli.

The side-wheeler steamer normally served the ferry lines across the Bosphorus in Istanbul and nearby cities. Due to the war, however, it was used to bring supplies to the front and returned with the wounded.

A British E-11 submarine that had snuck into the Marmara Sea struck and sunk it, killing 200 people, shortly after it had delivered Mustafa Kemal.

If the *SS Halep* had been sunk with Mustafa Kemal on board, then history would have gone on a different track. A twist of fate once again, however narrowly, helped the still-as-yet-to-emerge Republic of Turkey.

The Battle of Gallipoli began.

He acted as if it were a walk in the park while he went about holding a whip along the line of fire amid bullets whizzing through the air. He would sit on a sandbag and smoke a cigarette to take courage against the infectious fear of death.

Wearing a sergeant's uniform, he would go out among those working when there was a mutual ceasefire to collect the dead. When he did so, he personally observed the enemy trenches as closely as he could.

He applied an unseen method to keep the morale of his soldiers high and break that of the enemy—he had his men eat lunch accompanied by a band.

The British were going mad, in a way. They would open heavy fire in the direction of the music every midday. The tempo of the marches would also increase along with the bombardment.

Writers from Istanbul newspapers were brought to Çanakkale—also known as Gallipoli— during the most violent time of the battle. They were taken through the trenches so they could write about what they saw. Mustafa Kemal offered them cold *ayran* (yogurt drink) and had the band play waltzes from the popular opera of the time, *Carmen*.

Photographs started appearing in *Tasvir-i Efkâr* and the journal *Servet-i Fünun* (The Wealth of the Sciences).

This due fame created great discomfort among the pashas at the Ministry of War, and so the images began to be censored.

A photograph was going to be published at the Ministry of War with the caption, "The hero of Çanakkale", but it was stopped in an instant and the photograph was pulled.

They didn't want the people to know him and they didn't want his name and distinction to be known.

Yakup Kadri Karaosmanoğlu, the editor-in-chief of the newspaper İkdam (Ahead), would explain it years later on TRT state radio and television: "Enver Pasha had given us the order not to mention Mustafa Kemal."

❉

In an irony of fate, the first oil painting of Mustafa Kemal was done in Çanakkale while they were trying to censor photographs of him back in Istanbul.

Austrian painter Victor Krausz went along the Turkish front and painted the scenes of war. He saw Mustafa Kemal by chance—his sunburnt face looked like a statue. He asked permission, took a photograph from under the hood of a camera and later used it to paint a portrait on canvas.

❉

Mustafa Kemal embraced literature to find peace and lessen the negative effects of the war on his spirit. He wrote request letters to a friend in Istanbul, Madam Corinne.

He asked her to "send novels that depict the nice and pleasant sides of life and soften the character hardened by war."

In his tent, he had nothing more than a portable iron cot with a blanket from Siirt, a portable wooden table and, on it, a sailor's lamp. The blanket had been a present from Ali Fuat.

He kept the Silver Sword Medal of Merit he was awarded at Gallipoli separate from his other medals. He wouldn't remove it from his chest.

He launched a bayonet charge to clear out Conkbayırı. Suddenly he felt something hit him. He brought his hand to his chest. His uniform was ripped and there was blood. Shrapnel had struck the watch in his right pocket.

General Otto Liman von Sanders came to the headquarters that evening.

They spoke French as a common language.

Mustafa Kemal told him the Lancashire and Wiltshire regiments had been completely annihilated. Then he took the watch from his pocket and said, "I ask you to accept it as a memory of today's success."

The German general knew about what had happened and was aware that this watch was more precious than any medal.

The general thanked him and put it in his pocket. Then he pulled out his own watch. It was gold. It had the crown of the German Empire on the back and was engraved with his initials, L.S. "I also ask you to accept this," he said.

Mustafa Kemal's watch was an Omega from Switzerland.

He had bought it for around 600 Swiss francs when he was a student at the Military Academy. He'd used it for 15 years.

Work began after Atatürk died to collect his belongings for a museum. One of the most precious pieces was the broken watch he had given Liman von Sanders.

The German general had died in 1929. His heirs were contacted, but the watch wasn't with them.

Liman von Sanders' house had been burgled and most of his medals, swords and personal belongings had been stolen. Mustafa Kemal's watch was also among the stolen items.

The Republic of Turkey's search efforts for the watch made the news in German papers in 1939. Claims began to flood in, but most of them were unfounded.

A priest came to the Turkish Embassy in Berlin with very important information. He said who had the watch and gave a name and address.

The Turkish ambassador, Hamdi Arpağ, immediately informed the Ministry of Foreign Affairs. And as they discussed the path that needed to be followed, World War II broke out. All trace of the watch was gone.

The Omega company, which had made the watch, had also stepped in while the search was still ongoing in Germany just before the outbreak of the war. They promised a reward of 250,000 Swiss francs to whomever found the watch.

At the time, 250,000 Swiss francs was equivalent to 70,000 liras. A teacher's monthly salary was 50 liras in 1939. So, the reward Omega offered was on that scale—well over a hundred years worth of a teacher's salary.

Mustafa Kemal didn't use the gold watch Liman von Sanders had given him.

There had been a young lieutenant, whose name we unfortunately don't know, next to him when he was hit. He had then taken his own Zenith watch from his wrist and given it to his commander. Mustafa Kemal used this watch for years in place of the watch from his time as a student.

It was July 1922, and the eve of the Great Offensive. British General Charles Townshend came to Konya as a representative and wanted to negotiate on behalf of the British Parliament. He met with Mustafa Kemal in Akşehir.

Mustafa Kemal took the watch from his wrist when they sat down for dinner and held it out for the British general: "It's a custom for us Turks to give guests a gift. My gift was entrusted to me. A Turkish soldier gave me this watch at Suvla Bay. He had taken it from a British soldier who'd been killed. The officer's name is on the back. We were at war, as we are now, and there was no way to find his family. So, I ask you—I would be grateful if you could find that soldier's family upon your return to England and deliver that which was entrusted to me." He handed over the watch along with another gift—his red coral *tespih*—Islamic prayer beads—which he always had in his hand.

General Townsend later recounted his memories of the night: "I conducted interviews with 15 kings and presidents. I cannot remember one single incident in which I was as excited and impressed as when I interviewed Ataturk."

∞

(There are two villages named Anafarta—small Anafarta and big Anafarta—one being at Suvla Bay, which was the breaking point of the battle. The word *Anafarta* means *upwind* or *a very windy place* in the regional dialect. It has also been included in the Turkish geographical dictionary as the place where the Hero of Anafartalar stood against the winds of imperialism.)

Medical Officer Hasan Ragıp was on duty at the Kızılay (Red Crescent) Hospital. His wife, Erica, was German and a nurse. She had come to the hospital as a volunteer. They had no house, there were no barracks, and so they lived in a tent.

Ragıp was constantly in surgery. Erica was at the bedsides of the blood-soaked wounded, dressing their wounds, caressing their heads with the compassion of a mother, strengthening their morale with the broken Turkish she'd learned and trying to make their shattered bodies hold onto life.

The wounded didn't call her nurse, though. They called her *Mrs. Mother*.

A British reconnaissance aircraft had determined the coordinates and began to hit them with artillery fire. They knowingly fired on the hospital despite the 60-foot tall red crescent on its roof.

Ragıp escaped uninjured. Erica was killed.

The soldiers held a service for *Mrs. Mother*.

She was buried in her husband's beloved country, next to the war casualties' graves in the village of Yalova. The inscription on her gravestone reads: "The lady was killed by an artillery shell while carrying out her service."

Mustafa Kemal never forgot Nurse Erica, who had followed the man she loved to Gallipoli. He later made Hasan Ragıp, this medical officer who had joined the

National Campaign, one of his personal physicians at the Çankaya Mansion.

∞

The bloodshed continued in Gallipoli. There weren't enough medical supplies. Mutilated limbs were tied off with tourniquets. Other wounds were dressed with leaves. They used leaves and mud to smear over bullet holes.

The cries of the wounded as they tried to clean their wounds with seawater tore the darkness of the nights.

There were thousands of corpses lying in a narrow field. Billions of flies had descended on them having been attracted by the smell, which was made worse by the scorching heat.

British Private Harold Boughton later wrote the flies "were all around your mouth and on any cuts or sores that you'd got, which all turned septic through it. It was a curse, really, it really was."

Major Claude Foster also kept a diary in which he wrote, "If one tries to sleep, down comes the pestilent black cloud of flies ... to harass one to the verge of insanity."

They made devices to protect themselves and distributed smocks so they could cover their heads.

A Lieutenant Herbert described the grim scene: "There was a group of dead Turks in front of me. All of their heads were lying back and I saw that their mouths were open.

Flies had filled their open mouths and then came for us. They went to the bodies before we had our meals. They would land on a piece of bread right as you brought it to your mouth. You couldn't throw the bread out since there was nothing else to eat. You had to eat it."

The latrines were not even primitive, but something beyond primitive. There were buckets in the trenches. Sanitation teams collected and emptied them wherever they could. Wide pits were excavated 6 to 9-feet deep behind the trenches. There were places to sit on planks placed over them. They squatted while trying to keep their balance and seeing to their business. There were those, too, who lost their balance or the planks broke and ended up in the filth pits.

There was an outbreak of dysentery. The diarrhea was unmanageable.

Will Cowley of the Army Service Corps described it in all its grisly detail: "Everybody felt so weak with dysentery; and all the rest of it—diarrhea—that you'd got no strength, you know, you were so weak as a kitten. You could hardly walk about at times. Well, the doctor asked me one night how many times I went out to the back, I said, 'Sixteen times, doctor.' Sixteen times. You rush out there and when you get there you couldn't do anything. Terrible."

Medical Captain Abdülkadir called the trenches sorrowful and describes them in realistic and heart wrenching detail: "There were so many of our own dead and of the enemy in front of us that it looked like a congregation prostrated for their Friday prayers at a mosque. This prostration was disorderly, though. There was a tremendous number of our dead and those slaughtered, now in eternal peace. Flies had laid eggs in the mouths and noses of the dead. The wolves of the area ate there and walked through the trenches, each of them plump and white. I took an anatomy class with cadavers at school and I'm a doctor who's conducted many autopsies, but I must confess, the smell of the front line didn't leave my nose and now I can't eat meat."

There wasn't enough drinking water, either. They had to use well water, which only brought illness. They forgot what washing was. There was also an infestation of body lice. The lice hid in the seams of their pants. The soldiers would run their lighters over the stitching to try to get rid of the parasites. There was no other choice than burning the blanket if it had gotten infested.

Then they discovered ants. Lice run from ants. They would lay their shirts on top of an ant nest and then it would be totally free of lice.

Anzac NCO Fred Haig's description of the water problem is horrifying: "I was drinking from a little creek and I thought to myself, 'This water tastes funny.' Then I went up a few yards and there were two dead bodies and the blood was coming down the creek, with the water in the creek."

This was Gallipoli.

And what did the Hero of Anafartalar have to say about Gallipoli?

Years later he explained: "I won't go any further without telling you of the *Bombasırtı* incident. There were 8 meters between us and the trenches on the other side, so it was certain death. None of the soldiers in the first trench broke through and they fell. The soldiers in the second trench replaced them. What an enviable calmness and supreme trust. A man sees his death, knows he will die in three minutes and never shows the least hesitation. He doesn't even tremble. Those who knew how to read from the Holy Quran and those who didn't recited the *shahada*. You can be certain this was the great spirit of Gallipoli."

∞

Topkapılı Mehmet.

One of the soldiers under his command was Topkapılı Mehmet. He was an old firefighter who wore a leather band around his wrist and an amulet hung from his neck—a real roughneck.

Mustafa Kemal made this rough soldier a squadron commander and always gave him the most dangerous assignments. He would say *alright, Topkapılı* and pat him on the back. He always got a result as if he had sent a company of soldiers.

He also never lost contact with Topkapılı Mehmet later. He made him the head of the National Armed Defense, also known as the Mim Mim Group, which he founded as a secret intelligence organization when he went to Samsun on May 19.

He smuggled weapons, ammunition and men into Anatolia and became famous as Sly Topkapılı Mehmet. He had dozens of men with blades and pistols, and created an incredible network of intelligence on the streets. He knew if even a leaf rustled.

He put his mark on operations that really need to be made into films. For example, he stole the official car of the commander of the occupying British forces, General Harrington, drove it away himself and presented it as a gift to Mustafa Kemal in Ankara.

Atatürk offered him to be a parliamentarian for Istanbul as an extension of thanks, but he didn't accept it: "I'm a man who can't be held back by reins," he said. "So, with your permission, let me stay free." Turkish Parliament assigned him a monthly salary of 1,500 liras, which he also didn't accept and instead donated it to the Red Crescent.

It wasn't money, office or fame that Mustafa Kemal accumulated, but people, and Sly Topkapılı Mehmet was one of these.

Mustafa Kemal collected people from Salonika to Sofia and Tripoli to Gallipoli. Nearly all of the people from the cadre that won the War of Independence were the skilled people Mustafa Kemal had accumulated throughout his life and with whom he never stopped communicating.

∞

Once he saw papers stuck to sandbags with nails as he was walking the trenches of Arıburnu. There were Quran verses written on them.

"Who wrote these," he asked.

"Istanbullu Mecid," a soldier replied.

"Call for him," he said.

Macid came running.

The commander put his hand on the man's shoulder. "These are works of art," he said. "The country doesn't raise artists like this so easily. Get out of the trenches right now and return to Istanbul; continue with your writing." He discharged the man.

This man was the famous calligrapher Macid Ayral. He was the bridge in calligraphy between the Ottoman Empire and the Republic of Turkey. He wrote for mosques in Istanbul such as Şişli, Bebek and Davutpaşa, and also for Topkapı Palace.

∞

Sergeant Bigali Mehmet was firing in battle in Seddülbahir. When he ran out of bullets, he broke his rifle and threw it at the British. When he ran out of parts of his rifle, he threw stones. Then he attacked with a pole from the fortifications.

His head was severely wounded and his hands were in pieces, but he was able to repel the British.

Mustafa Kemal heard of his heroism and gave Bigalı Mehmet a silver cigarette case as a gift. He wrote a report to Cevat Pasha, the commander of the Dardanelles, requesting Bigalı Mehmet be rewarded as an example.

He was awarded the Medal of Combat.

Istanbul newspapers were made to report it and Bigalı Mehmet became a symbol of Gallipoli.

This Sergeant Bigalı Mehmet was the man for whom the word *Mehmetçik*, or *Little Mehmet*, was coined. After this, people began calling Turkish soldiers *Mehmetçik*.

Bigalı Mehmet returned to the village of Bahçeli Köyü in Biga after the war. He never accepted the financial support offered him. He took the surname Tabak, but he was always called Sergeant Mehmet. He passed away on February 3, 1964, and is buried in his village.

Gallipoli wasn't taken. It couldn't be taken.

The British evacuated 134,000 soldiers, 14,000 horses, 400 artillery and 2,000 motor vehicles, and withdrew from Gallipoli.

Mustafa Kemal summarized those days: "They fled and only left behind a tin of preserves."

❈

These were the days when Abdülhamid II had been dethroned and was living under house arrest at the Beylerbeyi Palace. Following the victory at Gallipoli, he wrote in his diary:

"The enemy collected his bowl and comb, dumped half his soldiers in the sea and the other half on boats and left. A colonel by the name of Mustafa Kemal won this great victory. God bless those who serve the state.

"My son Abid Efendi said he's met this Mustafa Kemal Bey. He is friends with Sergeant Salih [Bozok] who is on duty at Beylerbeyi. He occasionally comes to dine with his friend and they have befriended Abid Efendi. What is more, Mustafa Kemal gave him a gift of two gazelle calves. I'm pleased with that. A pasha who had made the state proud was friendly with my son Abid Efendi, which shows that he was a man of character.

"I reminded my son to properly repay it. I was going to tell him to give a gold watch if I had the time, but I couldn't since I both held back from gossip and am in substantial economic distress.

"They informed me once when he came to Beylerbeyi. The cloak he wore was not like that of ordinary soldiers and he had a dangerous serenity about him. That is when I understood why Enver Pasha had steered clear of him.

"The armies and fleet of two great states—Britain, like France—stopped and turned back at Gallipoli. I prayed for success."

It was an exemplary transformation of fate.

Abdülhamid II was arrested when Mustafa Kemal graduated from the Military Academy and wrote this about him 12 years later.

The palace had accused Mustafa Kemal of treason, and now the same palace was hailing him for being a hero for the country. Soon, however, the same palace would once again accuse him of treason.

∞

He was deployed to Diyarbakır and promoted to the rank of pasha.

He was now 35 years old.

He started at Lake Van and went everywhere—Sason, Mutki, Silvan, Garzan, Malabadi, Kulp, Dargeçit, Midyat, Palu, Hizan, Mardin, Siirt, Bingöl and Elazığ.

He freed Bitlis and Muş from enemy occupation.

Having lost, the Russian General Staff made this evaluation of Mustafa Kemal in a report:

"Among the Turkish commanders, he is the one the people respect most. He is brave, capable, resolute and has independent ideas to the highest degree. The people respect him. He won his fame with success at Benghazi and twice saved the day in the Battle of Gallipoli."

He recorded all his experiences in his diary at the time. His daily entries from November and December 1916 reveal the deplorable state of the region where he fought.

"I saw men lying on the road as if they were dead as soon as I crossed the Batman bridge. It was from hunger. They were refugees. I saw horses dead from starvation."

"We happened upon 150 people, refugees, who were walking back to Bitlis. They had no food and were starving. They were miserable and condemned to death."

"The parents of a child of four or five had left him behind as the wife chased after her husband and the child followed in tears 100 meters behind them. I stopped them and scolded them for not keeping their child with them. They said it wasn't their child and they didn't take it."

"There were human corpses along the road. I visited the Şerefiye Mosque in Bitlis; it was ruined and full of animal carcasses. The severed heads of 10 to 15 Muslim women were found while hospital workers cleaned out the residences."

"Bitlis was reminiscent of the ruins of Pompeii."

That was the scene.

He came into possession of three children.

He found a 12-year-old boy named Ömer close to Bitlis. He couldn't find anyone to bring him to, so he kept him. He found another boy of the same age, İhsan, who had no one looking after him a few days later. He was also compelled to keep this boy with him.

According to his diary, Ömer and İhsan were housed at the headquarters for a while where he tried to teach them to read and write, and where he had them memorize Mehmet Emin Yurdakul's poem, *Yaşamak Kavgası* (The Struggle to Live).

There is unfortunately no other information about them. These were the only things he mentioned about Ömer and İhsan in his diary.

He most likely entrusted them to the orphanage in Diyarbakır at the first opportunity.

The third child without a family was Abdürrahim. He found the 3 year old in Van. He sent him to Istanbul and entrusted the boy to his mother Zübeyde.

He tried to beautify his surroundings in even the most difficult conditions. He didn't at all care for eating at tables made of overturned orange crates. During a battalion inspection, he saw that battalion Commander İsmail Şumnu had a table and tablecloth. Şumnu had commandeered them from the British at Gallipoli.

Mustafa Kemal wanted to buy them, but had no money with him.

So, what to do?

He offered to barter. He had binoculars he had captured from the Italians in Tripoli. He offered them in exchange and İsmail Şumnu accepted.

He thus gave away his keepsake from Tripoli, and in its place got a keepsake from Gallipoli.

It was at that time in 1916 when he first inspected the Ergani mine. He was very upset that it wasted its great potential due to its primitive conditions.

It wasn't actually part of Mustafa Kemal's job to investigate the economic resources of the region, but he was planning for the future. As soon as he proclaimed the republic, one of his first companies was the Ergani Copper Operation.

❋

He stayed at the Semanoğlu Mansion in Diyarbakır. It was a typical Diyarbakır house with three stories, a large room that opened to a courtyard and of alternating white and black stone.

He was sitting at the cooling, ornamented marble pool when he heard a touching voice. Young people were having a picnic in the wooded area next to the mansion and one was singing a ghazal. He sent his aides to call for the one singing the poem. They brought him.

It was Mehmet Celaleddin. He was 18 and the muezzin at the Ulu Mosque. He sat the boy at a table and asked him to sing a folksong. He listened while the boy sang—his voice, the rhythm and pitch were magnificent. He put his hand on the boy's shoulder and said, "Look Celal, our country will one day be at peace and you will record your beautiful voice in Istanbul. Then have Eastern Nightingale [*Şark Bülbülü*] written on the records. You are a true nightingale."

This sincere encouragement was a prophecy.

Mehmet Celaleddin was encouraged. He began compiling local songs and made his way to Istanbul after the proclamation of the republic. He began making records in 1931 under the name Şark Bülbülü, which Mustafa Kemal had given him 14 years earlier, and they flew off the shelves.

When the Surname Law came into effect, the young muezzin changed his name to Celal Güzelses (Beautiful Voice) and recorded such famous songs as *Esmerim Biçim Biçim* (My Brunette Is Different) and *Hele Yar Zalım Yar* (O Darling, Cruel Darling).

Mustafa Kemal stayed in Diyarbakır for 11 months.

He was then deployed to the Hejaz, where Mecca and Medina are.

Hejaz in Arabic means barrier. This deployment was in fact to get Mustafa Kemal far from Istanbul—a barrier in all senses of the word.

He didn't accept it since he saw the Hejaz was already lost.

He was sent to Damascus as if once again in exile.

He first stopped by Aleppo and set himself up at the Baron Hotel.

This was a hotel special in the history of the Middle East.

German Emperor Wilhelm II, English Princess Alice, Swedish King Gustaf V and Danish Queen Ingrid, and later Franklin Roosevelt; Charles de Gaulle; David Rockefeller; the first pilot to fly across the Atlantic Ocean, Charles Lindberg, and the first man in space, Yuri Gagarin, all stayed at this famous hotel. Agatha Christie also wrote the beginning of *Murder on the Orient Express* there.

British spy T. E. Lawrence—popularly known as Lawrence of Arabia—stayed at the hotel under the assumed profession of archaeologist. What's more, he ate, drank and skipped out on his 76 *kuruş* tab.

Mustafa Kemal stayed in room 217 for 21 days.

He had Vartan Derunyan, who was a famous photographer in Aleppo, take his portrait.

The original photograph of Mustafa Kemal in uniform was held in the archives of the Baron Hotel until the outbreak of the Syrian civil war in 2011.

He then went from Aleppo to Damascus. He didn't rent a house, as he knew he wouldn't stay long, and instead got a room at the Damascus Hotel.

He was sent back to Diyarbakır after a month and moved to the Pamuk Mansion outside the Mardin Gate.

After a month, he was sent back to Aleppo.

His deployments were mockeries. He wasn't even given time to pack his suitcases. It was a campaign to discourage the Thunderbolt Army Group commander. He was also punished as the more successful he got and the more his fame grew.

He was finally sent to Istanbul in October 1917, but he had no defined assignment. It was unclear where he would be going, and so he didn't rent a house and instead stayed at the Pera Palas hotel.

Then a surprise assignment came along. He was sent to Germany with the Crown Prince Mehmed Vahdettin.

He was asked to pay a visit before the journey and they met at the Vaniköy Mansion.

Mustafa Kemal was 36 and Mehmed was 56. It was his first close contact with the Ottoman dynasty.

It was a historic moment. The founder of the Republic of Turkey and the last sultan of the Ottoman Empire met before the proclamation of the republic.

The were sent off from the Sirkeci Railway Station to the accompaniment of a brass band. They had a special car attached to the Balkan train. They were on a route through Sofia, Belgrade, Budapest and Vienna.

The heir to the Bulgarian throne had them greeted in Sofia with a brass band, as did the Austro-Hungarian Empire's governor of Budapest when they arrived.

There was no one at the train station when they got to Vienna—no brass band or anyone to meet them.

It seems the head chamberlain of the Ottoman protocol had given the wrong date to the Ottoman Embassy in Vienna, and they thought the train would arrive a day later. The bureaucracy of the Ottoman palace was incapable of organizing for even the crown prince.

Their first stop in Germany was Munich. They got off the train for the first time and toured the city in automobiles allocated to them. They traveled by train through Frankfurt to Bad Kreuznach, where the main German headquarters were. Emperor Wilhelm II welcomed them. They stayed two days at the headquarters, which was used as a five-star hotel.

Mehmed gave the German emperor a bejeweled, gold cigarette holder. Wilhelm in turn gave the Ottoman delegation a solid gold cigarette case.

They drank red wine at dinner. After dining, they were served champagne and smoked.

The next day they were invited to the villa along the Rhine of Wilhelm's nephew, Prince Waldemar. They drank tea on the terrace and examined the prince's collection of weapons. Then, they re-boarded the train and moved on to Strasbourg.

They toured the city in cars and were hosted at Duke von Albert's palace where they toasted in honor of Mehmed.

The next morning, they went to the German western front in Alsace. They were in the line of fire. They looked out through binoculars at the French trenches.

Mehmed Vahdettin and Mustafa Kemal descended into a crucial part of the German trenches that was exposed to intense artillery fire.

Mehmed gave a short speech. He said he brought greetings from the Ottoman military.

The German soldiers shouted *hurrah* three times and applauded.

A piece of shrapnel found its way to Mehmed. He had the shrapnel tied to a small pine branch. He held it out to Mustafa Kemal and said he'd kept it as a souvenir.

They ate at the emperor's palace behind the front. They then returned to Strasburg and spent the night at the Alsace governor's villa.

The following morning, they took a private train to Mannheim, Mainz, Koblenz, Cologne and through Düsseldorf on to Essen. They toured the Krupp factory, which produced heavy weapons for the German and Ottoman militaries. They donned welding glasses and examined the artillery foundry.

That day, there were 75,000 workers at the factory. Of them, 35,000 were women. The number of women working at the factory impressed Mustafa Kemal more than the factory itself.

They dined at the mansion of the owner of Krupp, Baron Gustav Krupp von Bohlen, and then set off for Berlin at midnight.

They stayed at the Adlon Hotel right across from the Brandenburg Gate.

It was Christmas and the city was festooned in color.
All the trees were decorated.

They were extended the courtesy to visit the empress at the Bellevue Palace. Mehmed gave her a brooch decorated with jewels. They all watched an operetta in the evening from the emperor's box at the Opera Royal.

They stayed 10 days in Berlin. Cars were assigned for their use. They saw the Sanssouci Palace, the Havel River and all the other sites.

They went to the Kaiser Friedrich Museum, now the Bode Museum where they helplessly looked on the Altar of Zeus.

The construction of the Pergamon Museum was yet to finish, and so the Altar of Zeus was on display at the Kaiser Friedrich Museum. Only a section of it was there, however, as it didn't fit in the space, which is why they were building the Pergamon Museum.

The giant marble altar, at 115 feet long, 108 feet wide and 49 feet tall, was taken upon special permission from Abdülhamid II, who wasn't even aware of archaeological colonialism.

It was plucked like a flower from the Acropolis of Pergamon, loaded piece by piece into crates, pulled by hundreds of oxcarts to Dikili, and then brought to Germany aboard warships.

Mehmed looked on at his brother Abdülhamid's mistake.

Mustafa Kemal always remembered that day painfully.

When Topkapı Palace was converted into a museum seven years later, he had a chat with its first director, Tahsin Öz, and told him of what he felt when he saw the Altar of Zeus in Germany.

It was fascinating, but agonizing.

They spent New Year's Eve 1917 in Berlin, welcoming 1918 in Germany.

Gifts were distributed to the employees at the Adlon Hotel on January 1. Food and drink were bought for the return trip. Bread was rationed in Germany. They were able to get more bread with the help of the hotel administration and loaded plenty of it onto the train.

They set off back to Istanbul in the evening.

Mehmed called the entire delegation into his private car on the return journey, where they evaluated the situation.

Mustafa Kemal expressed his historic foresight at the meeting, where he said, "I am surely convinced from what I have seen personally that the Germans have lost this war. We should pull away from this war at all costs and with the least harm."

They arrived back at the Sirkeci Railway Station on January 4.

Mehmed went to Dolmabahçe Palace and Mustafa Kemal went to the Pera Palas hotel.

Their 21-day trip had come to an end.

∞

Mustafa Kemal's left kidney caused him discomfort again.

He was diagnosed with inflammation of the kidney. He rested for a month in his room at Pera Palas. The pain increased, though. They recommended he go to Vienna.

He went to Vienna, again on the Balkan train, five months after he returned from Germany, and convalesced at the Cottage Sanatorium. During examinations, he was found to have E. coli.

He was met with an unpleasant surprise when he arrived in Vienna.

His suitcases had disappeared on the train.

All he had left were the clothes on his back.

As soon as he was settled at the sanatorium, his first order of business was to go to the market and buy new items to replace what he had lost.

Professor Zuckerkandl, who oversaw his treatment in Vienna, advised he go to Carlsbad under the supervision of Professor Vermer in order to completely get rid of the disease.

It was a charming city famous for its hot springs.

He rented a two-room apartment with a salon for 140 krona a week across from a historied hot spring that is now part of a five-star hotel.

He went to the spa regularly every morning at 8:00. Recordings of classical music played in the building where he soaked in hot water pools and took steam baths.

The nurses there poured tankards of hot water over the heads of people sweating on the benches.

Professor Vermer put him on a prescription diet—no bread, no butter, no sugar, no milk. He had black coffee with a breakfast of two eggs and a little honey.

For lunch he had a serving of fish with chickpeas, lentils or beans, a serving of fruit and then some compote at the end.

For dinner he had grilled chicken breast, a small sweet, an omelet and then again compote at the end.

He drank plenty of mineral water throughout the day and especially before going to bed.

An elderly woman prepared food for the clients at the hot spring. Another woman who worked there would go to his apartment in the afternoon, apply hot compresses to his kidney and give him mud treatment.

About the mud treatment, he wrote, "God knows how useful it is. I don't understand a thing about its practice."

Sometimes he would abscond off to a restaurant, leave his diet behind and gorge on bread with a glass of brilliant wine.

He met a teacher named Paula Klemm and started taking German lessons.

He used a room in his apartment as an office. It was quite a drab room to host a woman who was his teacher.

He went to the store and bought four small vases. He stopped by a woman who had a flower stand on the corner of the hot springs and bought red and white carnations. He put them in his office and regularly replaced them every two or three days.

Paula Klemm introduced him to a Swiss-French teacher, Madame Heiniche, who was visually impaired. She had sweet blue eyes, and at first glance, he couldn't tell that the beautiful young woman was partially blind. She couldn't see, read or write, but her grammar and accent were impeccable. She spoke German, French and English.

The young woman's struggle to live deeply affected Mustafa Kemal. They agreed on 100 krona a week for him to go to her house every day for French lessons.

He also met a Mademoiselle Brandner. He flirted with the young woman for about a week.

He also met Madame Corbetie. They would go on picnics and meet in cafes in the evening.

He read, explored the city and went to concerts in his free time. He stayed in Carlsbad for a month. It was there where he learned of the death of Sultan Abdülhamid II and the ascension of Mehmed VI to the throne.

He kept a diary in Ottoman and French while he was there. It filled five notebooks and ran 158 pages. It didn't only explain his treatments, but also the people he met, how they lived and the conversations he had with the Turkish families he came across.

He first wrote his views on gender equality while in Carlsbad: "Let's be courageous about women, let's leave behind the delusion, let them open up, let their minds be embellished with true knowledge and art. Let us healthily account for modesty and science. Let's give the highest degree of importance to those with honor and dignity."

He also wrote some ruthless comparisons of what he saw around him: "Europeans are completely depraved in our view and we are completely wild in theirs."

∞

He was sent to the Sinai-Palestine front as soon as he returned to Istanbul. He went to Nablus.

There was fighting along the banks of the Jordan River, but the damage had already been done and he saw that it was futile. He included dramatic observations in the letters he sent to his friends in Istanbul.

"Syria has become pitiful," he wrote. "There's no governor, no commander, a lot of British propaganda and British intelligence organizations are operating on all sides. The locals abhor the government. They watch the British aircraft drop proclamations every day instead of bombs. The enemy is increasingly strong and all we have against it is cotton string."

He was openly critical of the German generals who ran the army. He said to their faces that their plans were wrong, but he couldn't make them listen.

The consequences were tragic. General Liman von Sanders was attacked by the British, but escaped in his nightshirt, narrowly evading capture.

Gaza and Jaffa were captured, Jerusalem was captured, Damascus fell, as did Aleppo.

He came to Istanbul. The capital was already a captive city. It had been occupied. The country was being lost. Mustafa Kemal was the pivotal point where theory and practice intersected. He had to do something.

∞

Izmir was occupied.

British, French, American, Italian and Greek battleships were anchored in the bay. Metropolitan Chrysostomos of Izmir ran with his robes flying, fell to his knees and kissed the occupying commander's boots. He raised his cross in the air and gave his famous sermon:

"My sons, you are today showing Jesus' greatest miracle. However much Turkish blood you drink for this cause, you will receive merit with God. I, too, will have my resentment and hatred calmed with a glass of Turkish blood. The saints are with you."

Then a tall and slim young man in a black suit sprang forth holding a revolver. "No way, they can't go so happily!" he cried as he pulled the trigger again and again. The standard bearer of the incantation of the procession fell from his horse like a sack of wheat. It was as if time had stopped. People's laughing faces were frozen. They quickly surrounded the area and plunged the first bayonet into his chest and then stabbed him indiscriminately. Hasan Tahsin was 30 years old.

Nearly 400 Ottoman soldiers and more than 2,000 civilians were killed in the first three days. Most of the bodies were thrown into the sea as an example. They threw corpses into the sea off Karşıyaka and Güzelyalı for weeks.

The assault particularly targeted the families of soldiers. The newspaper *Eleftheros Typos* wrote what was still to happen: "The waves of migration from Greece to the United States should be stopped. The waves of migration should be to Anatolia. The Greeks coming due to the spread of the Bolsheviks should be settled in Anatolia. We must create such a situation that even Turks should consider Greece as their country."

This was the state of affairs.
There wasn't even a second left to waste for tolerance.

Mustafa Kemal explained the situation at the time in his *Nutuk* (Address):

I landed at Samsun on May 19, 1335 [1919]. This was the general view and state of affairs:

A group of powers, including the Ottoman Empire, was defeated in the Great War. The Ottoman Army had been crushed on every front. An armistice was signed under severe conditions. The prolongation of the Great War left the people exhausted and impoverished. Those who drug the nation into a world war fled the country with the care only of saving their own lives. Mehmed Vahdettin, who sat at the head of the sultanate and caliphate, was degenerate and cowardly, searching for measures in dreams of preserving himself and his throne. The Cabinet headed by Damad Ferid was incapable, inglorious and cowardly, bowing to the will of the sultan. It was subservient to the sultan and willing to do anything to preserve him along with themselves.

Weapons and ammunition were taken from the army and that state of affairs continued.

The entente powers saw no need to respect the terms of the artistes. The navies and soldiers of the entente were in Istanbul. The French had occupied Adana and the British Urfa, Maraş and Antep. There were Italian troops in Antalya and Konya, and British soldiers in Merzifon and Samsun. Foreign officers, foreign officials and spies were operating everywhere. At last, on May 15, 1335, that is four days before the following account of events begins, the Greek military landed in İzmir with permission from the entente powers.

Christian elements were also at work everywhere the country, either openly or in secret, trying to realize their particular ambitions and thereby hasten the collapse of the state.

Certain information and authentic documents that we acquired later prove that the Mavri Mira organization established at the Greek Patriarchate in Istanbul, was forming bands, holding meetings and making propaganda in the provinces.

...

Armenian Patriarch Zave Efendi also worked in connection with the Mavri Mira. The preparations made by the Armenians progressed in step with those made by the Greeks.

The Pontus Society, having its headquarters in Istanbul, worked openly and successfully in Trabzon, Samsun and all along the Black Sea coast.

...

[I]t appears to me to be clearly evident that the possible loss of the eastern provinces to Armenia was the most important reason for the formation of the Society for the Defense of the National Rights of the Eastern Provinces.

...

[T]he was a Society for the Rise of the Kurds, which was governed from Istanbul. They aimed to establish a Kurdish state under the auspices of foreign powers.

The Society for the Rise of Islam was organized in and around Konya and governed from Istanbul.

...

There were numerous public and secret organizations in Istanbul that called themselves parties or societies, and which pursued sundry aims.

[T]he Society of the Friends of England deserves special mention.

...

At the head of this society were [Mehmed] Vahdettin carrying the titles of Ottoman sultan and caliph, Damad Ferid, Minister of Domestic Affairs Ali Kemal and Sait Mullah. Certain English adventurers also belonged to this society, for example, a Priest Frew.

...

Some notable men and women in Istanbul were convinced that the true salvation [of the country] lay in procuring an American protectorate over it.

...

Without being aware of it, the nation no longer had anyone to lead it, and rather lived in darkness and uncertainty, waiting to see what would happen.

...

In reality, the foundations of the Ottoman Empire were themselves had crumbled at that time in which we found ourselves and its life had run its course. The Ottoman Empire was completely torn asunder. All that remained was a land in which a handful of Turks had taken shelter.

...

Gentlemen, in these circumstances, there was only one resolution that was possible, and that was to create a new, autonomous Turkish state based on national independence and sovereignty unconditionally.

This was our resolution ...

...

Therefore, independence or death!

He boarded a ferry at the Galata docks and went to the *Bandırma* steamer anchored off the Maiden's Tower.

There he gave the first order of the National Campaign: "Our target is the Black Sea."

A British patrol boat around Kavaklar stopped them and searched everything before they had left the Bosporus. They were looking to see whether or not there were any weapons or ammunition.

Mustafa Kemal, just smiled.

"They think were bringing weapons. We're bringing our heads."

He only had 1,000 lira in his pocket.

(Only 1,000 liras were assigned as an allocation in exchange for a receipt from the Interior Ministry. However, those opposed Mustafa Kemal deliberately exaggerated and distorted these minor allowances given him in the books they wrote years later. One wrote he was given 300,000 liras; another wrote 50,000 pounds; yet another claimed 40,000 gold coins were given from Mehmed VI's personal fortune; and still another asserted that 400,000 gold coins were delivered to him.

The number kept rising as if it were an auction.

They are all lies, of course.

For example, 400,000 gold coins at that time are roughly equivalent to 850,000 of today's *Cumhuriyet* gold pieces, which are 7.2 grams. They would have needed trucks to load that much gold onto the *SS Bandırma* and carry it into Anatolia.

Moreover, there's a document signed by Mustafa Kemal in the state archives. The document clearly says: "This receipt shows that 1,000 Ottoman liras have been given in order to spend on public order. Army Inspector Brigadier Mustafa Kemal."

And furthermore, Mustafa Kemal sent a telegram to the offices of the grand vizier 10 days after he arrived in Samsun, giving an account of the allowance and stating how each of the 1,000 liras was spent. This telegraph is also in the state archives.)

He left Samsun 10 days later, on May 29, 1919.

It was the first time since the conquest of Istanbul in 1453 that the holiday wasn't celebrated. The commanders of the occupation forces had banned it.

Mehmed II conquered the city. Mehmed VI lost it.

This is the naked truth.

Istanbul was desperately waiting for a savior.

∞

Mustafa Kemal decided to move his headquarters to Havza, since Samsun was boiling over with the British and wasn't safe.

He and his compatriots climbed into a worn-out Benz, which they could barely get ahold of, and hit the road.

There was no asphalt and the dust blowing from fields had been turned to slick mud by the rain, so the going was rough.

He sat in the front, next to the driver. Sometimes, he couldn't help himself and grabbed hold of the steering wheel to dodge the potholes. The driver was a poor fellow—an old man who wasn't Muslim.

The car was already a jalopy and couldn't handle going for even a half hour without breaking down. There was no other choice than to get out and wait. The elderly driver would try to fix it while they waited under a tree on the side of the road to patiently bide their time.

This was never Mustafa Kemal's way of acting. Sitting and waiting went against his character.

He looked at his compatriots and asked if they could walk.

He didn't actually ask the question. He turned around and set off walking without waiting for an answer.

They were obliged to follow. The village of Karageçmiş was an hour away. That's where they were going to stay and spend the night before they got back on the road to Havza. He started to quietly sing *Dağ başını duman almış* (The Mountain Top Is Smoking) as they went with millions of silent worries about the future going through their minds.

The mountain top is smoking,
A silver stream flows unflagging,
Over the horizon the sun is rising,
Let's walk, my friends!

"Come on everybody, sing," he said enthusiastically. "It'll drive away your tiredness and give you strength.

They sang all together.

Where else is this sky, this sea?
Where else these mountains, these stones?
These trees and beautiful birds?
Let's walk, my friends!

Physical education teacher Selim Sırrı Tarcan had heard the melody in Sweden, where he had gone for higher education. It was a song called *Tre Trallade Jäntor* (Three Warbling Girls). He thought he could use it for gymnastics and so he transcribed the notes. He asked Turkish teacher and poet Ali Ulvi Elöve to write the lyrics. It was the days when World War I turned against the Ottomans and the people were in deep despair. It was with these emotions that Ali Ulvi Bey sat at the window looking out to the sea in his room at the teachers school for boys in Moda, Istanbul. He started to write in his checkered notebook in blue ink and the mountain began to smoke.

It was first sung in 1916 during physical education demonstrations at the teachers school for boys. The young people loved it so much and it was so heartening that it spread from ear to ear throughout the entire country. Among those who knew it by heart was one person who would change the fate of the people and the direction of history.

That person was Mustafa Kemal.

He sang it with a smile as they walked to the village of Karageçmiş under a light rain.

The sun crushes every night,
Our country's day is born
So what if the road is long,
Let's walk, my friends!

He was very ill 19 years later on the day of the May 19 national holiday.

He smiled and reminisced even in that state:

"I formed the habit of singing this march to my compatriots as we passed through rural Anatolia in dilapidated cars whose wheels we had filled with sacks."

∞

He settled into the Mesudiye Hotel in Havza.

He asked that a demonstration against the occupation of Izmir be organized after Friday prayers and that the memorial service be recited for those killed. The town criers announced it to the people.

There was no sugar, so they couldn't mix up halva.

Mustafa Kemal's cleverness came into play.

He found a very poignant formula and seedless raisins from Izmir were distributed at the service.

He ate the fruit of September 9 on May 19.

∞

He then moved on to Amasya.

There he came to the palace where Sultan Selim the Grim was born and settled in the barracks the people called Saraydüzü (Palace Flats).

It was a palace of sorts, but it didn't look like it.

He stayed in a room whose suspended kerosene lamps put off a weak light, the windows had no curtains and there wasn't even a bed—there was nothing more than a couch, loveseat, a tattered rug and a table. There wasn't even kerosene, so he used poppy oil in the lamps.

The table was covered with telegraphs.

Copies of *The Times* and *Le Temps* were spread around.

It was in this modest room where he wrote the Amasya Circular in which he first mentioned national sovereignty and the fundamentals of a fully independent Republic of Turkey.

One of the locals brought him some semolina halva.

It was truly an indescribable treat in that time of poverty.

He took one bite and didn't eat any more of it. Instead, he passed the plate to Abdürrahman, who was the telegraph officer who transmitted the Amasya Circular to Anatolia.

"It'll drive away your fatigue, my boy," Mustafa Kemal said.

He longed for Istanbul.

He likened the sweetly flowing Yeşilırmak river that ran in front of Saraydüzü to the Bosphorus. He would point his walking stick to the opposite bank and say it was just like Kandilli Burnu in Üsküdar.

∞

He was then off to Erzurum.

His first order of business was to go to the telegraph office.

He sat down at the telegraph machine and had the operator tap out the message word for word, informing the sultan of his resignation from the military.

Then he sat down and wrote out his letter of resignation by hand.

He reproduced it on the army corps printing press and distributed it:

"My military and official capacity has begun to be an obstacle to the free image of working with the people in order to save the blessed country and nation from the danger of breaking apart and for the sake of the National Campaign, which began in order to dispel the claims of the Greeks and Armenians. I have given my word in the name of all that is holy to work with the people until the end for this sacred cause. Therefore, today I bid farewell to and resign from my beloved and great military profession. I henceforth present and proclaim that I am about to struggle through all kinds of self-sacrifice to be found as one of the mujahidin at the heart of the nation."

The palace declared him an insurrectionist and the order was given to arrest him on sight.

Twenty-six years later, he took off the uniform he had worn since he was 12 years old.

He was now a civilian.

He didn't have any civilian clothing, though.

He called for his aide Ali Çavuş and gave him an envelope.

"Bring this to the governor," he said.

Ali Çavuş went to the governor's house and handed over the envelope.

There was a note and 50 liras in it.

The governor told him to wait. He brought out an embroidered, white bundle with a black jacket and a fez inside.

Mustafa Kemal wouldn't accept the jacket without payment despite Erzurum Governor Münir Bey's insistence.

He didn't use the fez and instead wore a kalpak.

He looked at his medals for a long while, wrapped them in a handkerchief and placed them in a trunk.

He had been able to save up 800 liras from his time in the military.

Only 800 liras.

He had spent everything in Samsun, Havza, Amasya and Erzurum.

If he wanted, he didn't have to spend any money, but he also never took anything without paying for it. Even when they were guests at the houses of patriots, he would without fail give pocket money to those who served them upon leaving the house.

All that remained of his life was a jacket.

He wrote a letter to Zübeyde:

"My venerable mother, I suppose you're curious. The man who will bring you this letter will give you all the information about me you would like. Send my clothes with him."

But would his mother only send clothes?

Two bags of dried figs came with his clothing.

Even though there was only enough for each man to have one or two, it spiced up their lives and brought a feeling of home.

Colonel Ravlenson was the representative of the British occupation forces in Erzurum. He was the nephew of Lord Curzon, who would soon take office as Britain's secretary of state for foreign affairs. He was a very showy officer.

He came to visit Mustafa Kemal and gave an arrogant warning:

"I hear you will hold a congress tomorrow. It would be more appropriate not to. My government does not authorize this congress to be held and if you don't give it up, we will be obliged to disperse it through force."

Mustafa Kemal replied calmly:

"We didn't ask you or your government if we could hold this congress for it to be a matter of concern." Then he stood up and showed the colonel to the door. "Our meeting is over!"

The Erzurum Congress convened.

The British didn't dare to intervene and their bluff ran up against Mustafa Kemal's gamble.

A festival was held in the pavilion promenade after the congress. Women and children also joined in the festivities.

∞

Mustafa Kemal and his men were about to set off for Sivas.

Again they were able to find a jalopy. The soft top was torn, so it would be hell if it rained. They prayed it wouldn't.

They were hungry on the road and took a break at a spring.

Mazhar Müfit explained that moment with the same appetite even years later:

"We were living on just enough to survive. All we had for provisions was cheese, olives and dry bread. Villagers came to us at the spring and gave us dry onions. They were so delicious."

They spent the night in the forest outside Suşehri and divided up the watch.

Mustafa Kemal didn't like taking privilege when all things were equal, and so kept watch for half the night from 3:00 to 5:00.

They got to Sivas.

Then a fight over rooms broke out.

A large, top-floor room was allocated to Mustafa Kemal in the building in which his congress was going to convene. The rest of the committee settled into other rooms. A short while later, Kazım Karabekir came. Where was he going to stay, though? Nobody wanted to give up their own room. There was a very narrow area in the coffeehouse on the ground floor nobody wanted to move to. Refik Saydam told Mazhar Müfit that his room was more suitable. Mazhar Müfit got angry, asking why he should take orders from Saydam, and the argument grew bigger from there."

Word got to Mustafa Kemal and he said he would move rooms.

He didn't change his mind despite the contrite looks from the others. He packed his things, cleaned the coffeehouse and settled in there.

The congress came to an end and Kazım Karabekir left.

They insisted, but it was futile. Mustafa Kemal didn't move back to the large room on the top floor.

He was almost assassinated while in Sivas.

They noticed a telegraph written in code from Malatya and kept watch on it.

Three people came to the city by car and got rooms at the Afyon Hotel. They also had a heavy suitcase that they carried with care.

They were stopped in the lobby and asked for their identification. At first, they were reluctant and grumbled, but were forced to produce the identification papers when the revolutionaries showed their holstered pistols. One got flustered and pulled out two different identification papers. Another said he was a civil servant and the other said he was a merchant.

The revolutionaries drew their guns. They took a knife and cut open the heavy suitcase. There were 18 hand grenades inside.

The men were interrogated and they confessed.

Their plan was to blow up the building while the congress was held.

Everything could have come to an end in Sivas.

The congress, though, went off without a hitch.

It was time for Mustafa Kemal to go to Ankara.

Again, though, he had no money.

They took out a loan of 1,000 liras from the Ottoman Bank.

It was called the Ottoman Bank, but the manager was German.

They signed a document showing the debt.

There was no gas. There also weren't any tires.

The only cars in Sivas were at the American School.

Americans had all types of financial means in the heart of Anatolia while the locals didn't even have bread to eat in their own country.

The school taught orphaned Armenian girls left behind after the forced deportation of Armenians.

They appealed to the headmaster of the school, Mary Louis Graffam.

"Of course, we'll give you whatever you need," she said. "Please accept the gift and don't insist. We won't accept any money."

They got six cans of gas and four tires.

Mustafa Kemal objected when he learned it was a gift.

"They don't take out money now," he said, "but later behind our backs they'll say we took it by force. Prepare the documents and list everything we've acquired. We should have a document that says they didn't accept any money despite our objections. Let's sign it just to be safe, and the head mistress should also sign it."

Mazhar Müfit went back to the school and both parties signed the document.

Hacı Derviş had been sent to the bazaar as soon as he got to Sivas, where he bought a large notebook. He recorded every *kuruş* for all the expenses for the congress in it.

One day, Hacı Derviş asked the question he'd had in mind for some time:

"General, who is going to ask for this account in this turmoil?"

Mustafa Kemal's answer was noteworthy:

"The day will come when the people will ask me and others to account for everything. Let's not have our accounts today be missing anything. The people should know tomorrow where the money was spent."

He was just about to head off for Ankara.

A woman came up to him.

Fatma Seher/Kara Fatma.

She had dark skin and black eyebrows over black eyes.

She was wearing a jet-black blouse. Her trousers were just as dark black. Her boots were black. Her rifle was black. She had a black dagger in her belt. She had a black riding crop. Even her horse was black as night.

She was 34 years old and from Erzurum.

Her husband was a major who had died in Sarıkamış.

She had ridden her horse three days to get to the Erzurum Congress, but wasn't able to get there in time. She had been watching the road and came up to Mustafa Kemal.

"I can ride and I can shoot," she said. "Give me a job."

This woman was Fatma Seher.

Mustafa Kemal gave her historic title when he said, "I wish all women were like you, Kara [black, strong] Fatma."

Mustafa Kemal didn't even take the sexist concept seriously such as that women should be kneading dough and not interfering in men's work. There were times in the country when women weren't even considered to be people, but as far as Mustafa Kemal was concerned, there was no distinction between men and women. He looked at her to see if she had what it would take.

He wrote out the duty roster by hand and signed it.

"Go to Istanbul," he said. "Find the revolutionary from Üsküdar, Colonel Neşet Bey, and give this roster to him."

She went to the city and found him. Neşet Bey read the roster and deployed, to the İzmit region.

She set up a militia platoon with 15 women, her own daughters among them. The number of people under her command was nearly 700 after two months. She was the commander for 43 women and around 600 men.

She was unflinching.

She was in a firefight in the İnönü area of Sakarya. Twenty-eight of her women were killed. Her daughter was shot in the hand and two of her fingers were severed. Kara Fatma's right arm was wounded.

She was at one time caught transporting crates of ammunition. She was taken prisoner and tortured for 19 days, but managed to escape.

She then joined the Great Offensive and was also among the cavalry that entered Izmir on September 9.

She started the militia with the rank of sergeant and retired as a first lieutenant. She was also awarded the Medal of Independence.

She didn't accept a salary, instead donating her pension to the Red Crescent.

She didn't pursue any personal benefits and retreated from the scene. All signs of her were lost.

It was revealed that she had fallen on hard times over the years, didn't tell anyone and had taken refuge at a Russian monastery in Galata that helped the homeless. She was forcefully persuaded and then taken to Darülaceze.

I'm certain that if this heroic woman had been American or British, Hollywood would have made a hundred films about her and she would be known to the whole world. Unfortunately, though, since there is no one and no institution in Turkey making any effort to do so, the people for whom this woman laid down her life don't even know of her.

She passed away in 1955. She had nothing other than a small bundle wrapped in a handkerchief. They opened it and found her Medal of Independence and the silver cigarette case Mustafa Kemal had given her. These were the only things she had kept.

∞

It took Mustafa Kemal nine days to reach Ankara from Sivas, going through Kayseri, Mucur, Hacıbektaş, Kırşehir and Kaman.

The population of Ankara was about 20,000. The houses were built of mud brick and the city's streets were narrow. It was a barren—a treeless, naked steppe devoid of greenery. The slightest wind would whip up a dust cloud that would engulf the city. When it rained, there were rivers of mud. There were neither hotels nor restaurants. The houses had no electricity, either. The only water was from wells. And for transportation, there used donkey and horse carts.

It's hard to believe that scheduled flights from this primitive town to Istanbul would start only 16 years later.

"I learned of Ankara from history books, not geography, and as the center of a republic," he said, referring to the republic of the Ahi Brotherhood.

"I saw the name of the Republic of Ankara when I was reading the names of the small governments in Anatolia that formed with the fragmentation of Seljuk administration. This was the first thing that compelled me to think of Ankara as the most suitable place for the center of Turkey."

There were no houses for rent.

He set himself up at the Agricultural School in Keçiören. It was a three-story, stone building with stables around it. He stayed there for 118 days.

The only fun he had while at the Agricultural School was Kadife Hanım. She was Doctor Refik Saydam's cat. Sherbet was served to everyone at the headquarters when she had kittens.

Halide Edip Adıvar lived with her husband, Doctor Adnan, in a former school called Numune Farm close to the Agricultural School. She would translate articles from foreign newspapers and present them to Mustafa Kemal.

There was an old typewriter that had been procured from the Ottoman Bank. It was frequently broken and could only type out six pages in eight hours. She asked for a new one that would be able to type in French.

They searched everywhere and finally found one that could type in French in the railway command in Eskişehir, and an order was made to send it to Ankara.

The railway commander didn't want to send it, though.

"I only have one typewriter and I communicate with more than 80 stations with it," a rail official said.

Another order was written saying that it must be sent at once.

The railway commander sent his typewriter with this order, but resigned from his position as a matter of pride.

The country had been lost. Mustafa Kemal wrestled with the world while he was forced to deal with such personal vagaries.

❈

Egos were so big that he was even challenged to a duel.

Alfred Rüstem Bey was an Ottoman citizen and the ambassador to Washington. His father was Polish and his mother was English. He was a patriot and a member of the Young Turks. He fought greatly against the allegations in the American press of the Armenian genocide. He disproved the claims with strong evidence that they didn't take kindly to and, in 1914, the U.S. government declared him *persona non grata* and asked him to leave the U.S. immediately.

He went to Anatolia as the country was being occupied where he attended the Sivas Congress and joined the National Forces.

He was one of the seven people, including Mustafa Kemal, in Sultan Mehmed VI's decree for their execution.

He was 20 years older than Mustafa Kemal and very easily offended.

One evening, they were again with a big group around a dinner table.

They ate and then Alfred Rüstem Bey lit a cigarette.

Mustafa Kemal pointed at the cigarette and said, "Don't be in such a rush, Rüstem Bey. And don't lose your appetite. There's more to eat."

Alfred Rüstem flared up. He'd taken it as an insult.

"You warn me against smoking without asking your permission as if it's lewd and offensive," he yelled. "So, you see why I don't need to ask your permission now since we smoke during meals all the time!"

He stood up enraged and stormed out of the room.

Everyone was dumbfounded.

As it were, there was always one dish every evening, enough to keep them fed, and they would leave the table only half full. That evening, though, Mustafa Kemal had made some semolina halva as a surprise for his compatriots, which was going to come after the meal, hence his remark to Alfred Rüstem Bey.

Not knowing about the halva, Alfred Rüstem flew off the handle and felt belittled. Mazhar Müfit went to him, explained about the halva and told him to come on back to the table. It was to no avail, though. He wasn't persuaded.

"A person with no manners humiliated me at a table with 15 people," he said. "This is no joke. I am obliged to challenge the Pasha to a duel in order to defend my dignity. Inform the Pasha of it."

Mazhar Müfit couldn't believe what he was hearing. "Alfred, have you gone mad? You want to kill the Pasha, do you?"

"On the contrary," Alfred Rüstem said. "I won't hurt him. I will be wounded or die, but this way I will preserve my dignity. The Pasha can choose the weapon!"

The laughter coming from the table further exasperated Alfred Rüstem and he got even angrier. He worked for the republic for the rest of his life, but his character was so stubborn that he would never again sit at a table with Mustafa Kemal.

The experiences at the National Campaign's first headquarters at the Agricultural School in Ankara, unfortunately, weren't always this amusing.

One night around midnight, Mustafa Kemal had just laid down and was about to fall asleep.

He heard a clatter on the stairs. The doorknob to his room started to turn slowly. He reached under his pillow and readied his revolver. Three people tiptoed into the room in the blind darkness. He pointed his gun at them and jumped to his feet, yelling for them to identify themselves.

They panicked when they saw the barrel of the gun pointed at their faces and hurled themselves back down the stairs.

Mustafa Kemal was yelling and shouting, and they were captured soon after.

It turned out they had tied up the guard and infiltrated the place.

They were Çerkez Ethem's hitmen.

There was always a safety concern at the Agricultural School, which was three miles outside the town, but this incident was the final straw. Mustafa Kemal had only narrowly escaped being killed in his sleep.

∞

He moved to the Ankara Train Station and set himself up in the stationmaster's building.

It was called the Steering Building.

He often went there after the foundation of the republic because the "white train" that he traveled on when touring the country would go through this station.

The train was dark blue up to the windows and white above that, so the people referred to it as the white train.

The Linke-Hofmann-Werke factory had built the train. It was 49-feet long with two cars—a food car and a sleeping car.

It had actually been built for the Baghdad Railway Company's general manager. It was the private train for Edouard Huguen of Switzerland to whom Abdülhamid II had given the title pasha, and so was known as Hügen Pasha.

Mustafa Kemal was also to make his final journey on the white train. His body was taken from Dolmabahçe Palace on November 19, 1938, to the white train waiting in İzmit, and placed on the center table in the food car to bring it to the Steering Building at the Ankara Train Station.

❈

He met with American journalist Clarence Streit at the Steering Building in 1921.

Streit was a correspondent for the *Public Ledger*. He was actually also an intelligent officer for the U.S. military.

He left the U.S. warship he'd been on in Samsun and traveled around Anatolia with a journalist's credentials for seven weeks, through Çorum, Yozgat, Eskişehir and Ankara. He made contact with the local Greeks, met with Bolshevik diplomats, visited missionary schools, went as far as the villages and spoke with the locals, and tried to learn the people's views of the revolutionaries.

He met with the "child veterans" when he came to the Steering Building for the interview.

They were Osman, Tevfik and Cemal. The three of them were 13-year-old partisans.

They had lost their parents in World War I. They had met in the orphanage they were sent to in Istanbul and had run away and joined the patriotic militias in İzmit when Istanbul was under occupation.

They had fought against the Greeks around Bursa. Nine of these young swashbucklers were killed. Tevfik and Cemal had both been shot in the arm. Osman had been shot in the face and lost an eye.

Mustafa Kemal had taken them under his protection. He had them treated and brought them to the Steering Building. They stayed with the guards and the revolutionary officers showed much respect to these young heroes.

The American intelligence officer wrote that he had been greatly impressed by these boys while he'd been taking notes.

He interviewed Mustafa Kemal and filed it with his newspaper. However, he also prepared a detailed report of what he saw. In his intelligence report, he often used the word *admiration*.

"Mustafa Kemal had none of the luster and spectacle we see with other heads of state. Very few people have affected me so much. He is the type of man people want to die for. He is a gentleman in every way. He was gentle, cultured and very elegant.

"He is a professional soldier and a sincere democrat, a man of action and instant decision maker, an organizer, practical and idealistic. Of course, these features that characterize Mustafa Kemal Pasha rarely come together in one man. The West looked at him as a dictator. Meeting this man and seeing him in his everyday life in Ankara is enough to realize that the claims of him being a dictator are nonsense.

"He is tied to the laws of parliament. He doesn't even have the veto power the U.S. president has. He uses all this power for democratic foundations. How is he a dictator? He can walk alone through the streets of Ankara. He talks and jokes with the people when he runs into them. He is calm and self-confident. "He is aware of his power, but he is not arrogant.

"After meeting with him, I understand why his compatriots believe in him so much and why what he says is so respected.

"I came to Turkey prejudiced against the Turks. I am leaving as a friend and admirer of the Turks."

Another striking observation from this American intelligence officer and journalist is related to *Hamlet*.

He watched *Hamlet* in Ankara in the midst of the War of Independence in 1921, with camels wandering the streets engulfed in dust clouds.

Kamil Rıza's traveling theater company, Otello Kamil, had come. They performed in a building of ruined stables under gaslight.

Clarence Streit couldn't believe it when he saw it.

"They're at war with the British," he noted, "yet they're staging Shakespeare to much applause. The Turks have convinced me that art has no national borders. Moreover, this is all in wartime."

American missionary schools began buying land in Anatolia, especially in the Black Sea region. They considered the conditions of the occupation as an opportunity to spread their operations. They were establishing farms under the names of orphanages. They established social clubs, which were centers for merchants. What would the consequences be, though, if the revolutionaries were to win?

The U.S. government sent intelligence officers with journalist credentials to try to find answers for American interests. Would American tobacco companies be banished? What would the capitulation agreements be? Would American aid agencies be shut down?

Mustafa Kemal knew quite well who these journalists were and why they had come. Framing his diplomatic answers in this way also served Mustafa Kemal's purposes.

They were tactical interviews.

Robert Steed Dunn was one of the American journalists he admitted to the Steering Station. He was supposedly a correspondent for the *New York Post*, but was, of course, a lieutenant with the U.S. Navy.

He didn't come alone.

He had come with a woman named Ellen who spoke fluent Turkish and who was his interpreter. It is impressive that U.S. intelligence had such a power in foreign language even in 1921.

Robert Dunn's report contained interesting observations:

"Mustafa Kemal was waiting at a table covered with a tablecloth in a room with a bay window. He stood up and welcomed us. He was nervously flicking a string of coral prayer beads with pink, silk tassels.

"He was wearing a grayish navy suit. It was quite stylish. It was obvious it hadn't been made in Ankara or Turkey. He had a white shirt on and a small, black bowtie. I didn't pay attention to his shoes or cufflinks. His light hair was combed back like that of college students. His young appearance was stunning. He had high cheekbones, slightly sunken cheeks, a small and smooth red mustache and steel blue eyes. His face was unmoving and he was always motionless.

"The feature that really explained him was his eyebrows above his darting and squinting eyes. Coming together with his sharp, projecting temples, the essence of his features came together around his eyebrows.

"The end of his nose had two large bulges. His chin was angular and sharp despite being small. He rarely blinked. Despite that, though, they gave the sense of fluttering.

"Behind it all you could feel the high concentration, intense and inexhaustible potential for energy and even cruelty in the brain behind it all. In the entirety of these features, though, was a mind with a broad perspective."

Mustafa Kemal lived at the Steering Building for two years.

It was both his headquarters and his home.

The kitchen was a serious problem. They set up a system with a fixed menu, collecting money from among everyone, buying ingredients and with an understanding between the cooks and the men. There were always three items on the menu. The soup and compote changed, but the bulgur was always the same. Breakfast was bread and olives.

They found a Jewish woman to do the laundry.

Mustafa Kemal fell asleep one night with the kerosene lamp still burning at his bedside.

It was 7:30 in the morning. He didn't leave his room, but not because he had work to do.

They waited a bit and then, not able to wait any longer, knocked on the door. They knocked harder, but there was no sound from inside. They broke the door open and went in. The room was pitch black like a cave. They yelled anxiously, *pasha, pasha*. He woke up asking what the matter was and was slightly dizzy. His face and eyes were dark from the soot from the lamp. They immediately took him out to the salon and opened the windows. They called for a doctor.

He'd been poisoned. He dodged the bullet, though. He had a cough for days and the pain in his chest and throat didn't ease for a while.

He couldn't go on like this. He needed a woman to keep the house. He arrived at this idea for this reason. He ensured the cleanliness of his home, the kitchen and its order.

∞

Mustafa Kemal also started to tidy up the country, as well. His first order of business in Ankara was to organize the National Forces.

"The National Forces are like a gun under the pillow of an honorable man," he had said, "and at the moment when there is no hope to save his honor, he at least benefits from suicide."

He wanted to issue a declaration addressing the people.

He was able to find a ramshackle print shop with missing letters that could barely print one page. There was no other option in Ankara.

The print shop said they should include a photograph of him with the declaration. It couldn't go out without one, since Mustafa Kemal was a savior, but everyone only knew his name. No one knew his face.

He turned his luggage upside down. He didn't have one. Not one photograph. There also wasn't a photographer in town.

So, what should be done?

They sent a telegraph to Yunus Nadi in Istanbul. He had taken a photograph for the *Bir Gün* newspaper of Mustafa Kemal mounted on a horse.

They asked for a stereotype of the photograph to be sent. Yunus Nadi provided it. He sent it to Ankara with a courier by horse.

This was the scale of the difficulty of the conditions. It was 10 days before the declaration was published.

∞

It was communication brilliance in those primitive conditions.

The telegraph network was used like the internet. He sent the telegraph through the capillaries of the country just as email or a WhatsApp message would be today.

News that the bird had flown was thanks to the nameless and heroic telegraph operators at a time when there were no telephones, no satellites and no electricity in most of the country's government offices.

To the question from foreign journalists about how the War of Independence was won, the answer is that it was done with the telegraph lines.

Louis Browe, a correspondent from the *Chicago Daily News* who followed the Sivas Congress, wrote, "I have not seen a telegraph network that works as well as the one I saw tonight. They were in contact with Erzurum, Erzincan, Mosul, Diyarbakir, Samsun, Trabzon, Ankara, Malatya, Harput, Konya and Bursa within half an hour. Mustafa Kemal was at one end of the line and the commanders at the other while the local authorities carried out his orders without question."

They supposedly informed London.

In reality, though, they couldn't see past their noses.

A secret telegraph center was established in the basement of the Grand Post Office in Sirkeci. A line was stealthily connected from the signal room on the second floor to the basement.

Patriotic telegraph operators would infiltrate the building at the end of the workday and work under the light of kerosene lamps until morning.

The British soldier guarding the door so that no message would be sent to Anatolia was completely unaware.

There was nonstop correspondence on vital subjects like weapons, ammunition deliveries, the forged identities of officers going to Anatolia and the list of names of British spies. On some days, over 400 coded telegraphs were wired from the Steering Building to the Mim Mim Group.

Mustafa Kemal was very interested in communication and closely followed Italian inventor Guglielmo Marconi, who had perfected wireless telegraphy and won the Noble Prize in Physics in 1909.

He sent a telegram to Marconi's family when the physicist died in 1937:

Marconi Family, Rome.

All of humanity feels the pain of your loss. I extend my condolences and sympathy to the memory of the great Marconi on the occasion of this painful tragedy.

Kemal Atatürk.

The courier was busily going between Ankara and Istanbul. Encrypted messages were delivered by hand when the lines were cut.

Mustafa Kemal's codename was Nuh (Noah). He also signed his messages as Nuh.

∞

Sean Connery (James Bond). Wilfred Dunderdale.

James Bond was in Istanbul in those times.

This fact came to light in 2010. Keith Jeffery, a professor of history at Queens University, conducted archival research on the British MI6 intelligence organization on the occasion of the centenary of its establishment. He published the book *MI6: The history of the Secret Intelligence Service.*

In the book, it says Wilfred Dunderdale was the inspiration for the character of James Bond in Ian Fleming's novels.

According to the book, Wilfred "Biffy" Dunderdale was stationed in Istanbul during the War of Independence, between 1919 and 1922.

He was a close friend of Ian Fleming and was the son of a British shipping magnate who traded at the Black Sea ports.

He was born in Odessa. He graduated from Saint Petersburg Imperial University as a marine engineer and then joined British intelligence.

He spoke fluent Russian. He was also a boxer. He dressed very sharply and wore personalized cufflinks. He was fond of luxury and women.

After his assignment in Istanbul, he went to France, where he was the station chief in Paris during World War II, working against the Nazis. Afterward, he went to Poland to work against the Soviets. He retired in 1959 and died in 1990.

His first assignment, though, was in Istanbul. He worked actively against the National Campaign. He had also infiltrated Bolshevik circles.

There were two other very influential MI6 officers who worked together.

A tailor named Mehmed Efendi, codenamed RV/5, had Ottoman officers as customers and was an informant. He was from Hereke, and his shop was in Üsküdar. Forged documents were prepared with a counterfeit seal of the Grand National Assembly, which said:

"The document of his self-sacrifice herein has been given upon decree by the Grand National Assembly in order for Herekeli Mehmet Efendi, who was involved in the National Campaign, to be seen as trustworthy in the eyes of the nationalist mujahidin."

Parliament didn't actually give any such documents to anyone, but no one in Anatolia knew that and figured it was official upon seeing the parliamentary seal. He traveled around the Black Sea with this forged document and established amicable communication with the Turkish partisans fighting against the Pontic Greeks. He then transferred all the information he had about these patriotic partisans to the British. He informed on the officers trying to smuggle the wireless equipment from the Selimiye Barracks to Anatolia. Because of him, medical students who were about to go to Anatolia were caught red-handed on the dock. He was able to go in and bring out information from the palace that he got from the informants he had gathered due to the necessities of his profession as a tailor. He was spirited off to Egypt to escape execution when his true identity was discovered.

Another spy known as JQ/6 ran a coffeehouse in Beyoğlu frequented by the revolutionaries.

British intelligence had even used an Indian woman to infiltrate the circle around Mustafa Kemal.

Her name was Bupsy Paury and she was the daughter of one of Bombay's wealthiest families. She had studies in the U.S. She stopped by Ankara while she was supposedly on the train to London. She had brought gifts of jewels. She spoke enthusiastically about Mustafa Kemal and asked to meet with him. She sent back photographs through intermediaries. She was beautiful, with dark skin, diamonds over her chest and around her arms, and in traditional Indian clothing.

Mustafa Kemal was aware of the ruse being played. He didn't even meet with her.

"Don't fall into traps and the work of intelligence services," he said.

A dentist named Ahmet İhsan emerged in Ankara. Dentists at that time were much more sought after than doctors because there were doctors around more or less but nearly no dentists in the entire country. He was suspected of using his patients to infiltrate Mustafa Kemal's circle. He was studied.

It was understood that he hadn't come from Istanbul, and rather that he came from Egypt to Antalya on a ship and then from there to Ankara. With a little more poking around, it came out that he was a British spy and had been active on behalf of the U.K. since the outbreak of World War I.

There was a military police officer named Mahmut Hamdi in Kadıköy, Istanbul. The British had captured him at Gallipoli, but subsequently released him and he returned to his post in the military. After the National Campaign began, it was understood he had leaked information to the British, was working against the Ankara government and encouraged soldiers on their way to Anatolia to desert. He had been recruited as a prisoner. When he was found out, the revolutionaries packed him off to Ankara to be tried.

An Indian in ragged clothes was captured in Malıköy, Polatlı, outside Ankara. What was an Indian doing in this tiny settlement along the Ankara-Istanbul railway, which was of strategic importance in the War of Independence? He said he had come in support of the National Campaign and was Muslim. In his first interrogation, though, it came out that he wasn't just Indian, but a

British officer. He was a spy who had come to determine points for sabotage.

The codename for the spy network British intelligence set up with Turkish collaborators and local Greeks was Black Jumbo.

It was run by Major John Bennett, who spoke perfect Turkish and enough Arabic to be able to comment on the Quran. He knew Turkish Islamic customs very well and had even been circumcised in order to appear as a Muslim in his covert assignments.

They used the Kroker Hotel near Pera Palas as their headquarters.

The basement was a center for torture.

According to reports sent to the British War Department, Black Jumbo even had extensions in the Grand National Assembly. They don't mention the names of parliamentarians who were collaborators, and instead give their codenames. They transcribed the minutes of secret sessions word for word for the British.

Colonel Nelson led the senior British spies. He was known by the pseudonym Ramiz Bey. They used an apartment in Şişli as their headquarters. Just like Bennett, he was also fluent in Turkish.

Nelson's work consisted of assassinations, sabotage and organizing insurgents.

Dunderdale was under the command of Colonel Nelson.

Britain had the most widespread and most effective intelligence service in the world and still could not overcome the wall of revolutionaries despite its efforts.

The Turks were already aware whenever they tried to make a move. They weren't ever able to infiltrate Mustafa Kemal's core cadre.

They had only one resort. A death warrant was issued for Mustafa Kemal.

∞

According to Mehmed VI's decree, Mustafa Kemal was a "seditionist and conspirator" who "collects money from the people by force ... tortures objectors ... burns and destroys cities [and] should be killed on sight."

It wasn't enough, so a fatwa for his execution was issued.

According to Sheikh ul-Islam Dürrizade Abdullah Efendi's fatwa, Mustafa Kemal "deceived the sultan's loyal subjects with lies ... material benefit contrary to Islam ... gained extorted property from innocent servants of God ... tried to weaken the power of the caliphate [and] was in rebellion against the supreme Islamic caliphate. ... Killing him is rightful and a religious obligation according to the needs of the supreme laws of Islam. ... It is necessary to gather the righteous imams of Muslims around His Excellency the Caliph Mehmed Vahdettin Khan and go to war against Mustafa Kemal."

He declared outright jihad against Mustafa Kemal.

The fatwa was duplicated tens of thousands of times and Greek and British aircraft dropped them over Anatolian cities. Sailors on British battleships distributed chests of them at the ports along the Black Sea coast.

Börekçizade Rıfat.

In response to the fatwa calling for Mustafa Kemal's death, patriotic imams under the leadership of Ankara Mufti Börekçizade Rıfat issued the Anatolian Fatwa.

According to the Anatolian Fatwa prepared by a religious delegation of 21 people, "The caliphate [was] under the occupation of enemy states ... British law [was] applied [and] İzmir, Adana, Antep, Maraş and Urfa [were] raped. ... Those who side with the enemy are committing the greatest sin." Therefore, "those who die in battle against the enemy will be considered martyrs and those who survive, *ghazis*. ... The fatwas issued under duress of enemy states are not religiously binding."

What would happen in the occupied territories with the issuance of the fatwa that said it was obligatory to kill Mustafa Kemal and the sheikh ul-Islam's declaration of jihad against the National Forces?

What happened under Greek occupation was researched by Greek investigative journalist Tasos Kostopoulos. His work turned into a book in 2007. *War and Ethnic Cleansing, the Forgotten Side of a Decade of a National Surge 1912-1922* includes personal accounts from Greek soldiers in the occupational forces:

"Turkish women, children and the elderly had shut themselves up in a mosque in a village near Uşak. The dishonorable soldiers among us gathered brush, set it on fire and threw it through the windows of the mosque. The people all ran out from the smoke. Then the vile ones started shooting at the women and children like it was target practice."

"I entered a house. I stepped over the corpse of an old Turkish man. There were voices coming from inside. Ten of our soldiers had lifted up the skirts of a Turkish girl and were making her dance. They told me to 'come and taste the meze.' I told them it was shameful. The Turkish girl ran to me, threw herself around my legs and begged me to save her. I pleaded with the soldiers and told them not to do it. One pulled out his bayonet and came toward me. I had to run away. I haven't been able to forget her screams."

"A thousand houses were on fire in Köprühisar. Prince Andrew gave the order for us to set everything on fire."

"Every place we left we set alight. It was a terrifying sight."

"Some of us were happy, like Emperor Nero burning Rome. The order was clear—burn whatever we couldn't carry. It's unknown what the elderly, sick and children did in all those villages."

"We went into the village. The girls were raped in front of their families. Our soldiers slept in the silk quilts they plundered."

"The Turks hid their families in cemeteries at night out of fear. I saved a girl two soldiers were attempting to rape. Her mother came running and started kissing my hands. Her other two daughters were lying dead a little farther away."

"I suddenly found myself in front of an old man. The greatest favor I could do for him was kill him as soon as possible. Some of them were in great pain, writhing like cows at the slaughter. The village was set on fire."

∞

A French woman, Berthe Gaulis, who was a journalist, traveled from village to village after the İnönü Victory and described her horrific observations:

"I am in Söğüt, which is a victim of the Greek withdrawal. It is very close to Bursa. It is in ruin. The rearguard battalions that were specially trained for this did the burning and destruction as the war was lost and they started to retreat."

"Söğüt resembles the towns of Roye and Lassigny after the German retreat during World War I. They used a significant amount of dynamite, firebombs and explosive cartridges."

"The Greek officers who were prisoners of war said the destruction was done under the supervision and at the directive of British officers. The wealthy of the town also explained it was done under supervision of the British officers. I was very saddened by this destruction."

"There are corpses under the ruins. The odor in the air from the corpses is so intolerable that the battlefield pales in comparison."

"Twilight has fallen on the surroundings. There is the sound of owls perched on the burned-out houses. Many of the trees have been reduced to charcoal. All the mosques have been destroyed. The orchards and gardens are all devastated. The material damage is very great and the Greeks have taken everything.

Worse than the ransacked shops, however, is that the houses were set on fire and the women, the elderly and children were affronted. The same has happened in Aydın."

"I am at the tomb of Ertuğrul Gazi. It is one of the most sacred places for Muslims to visit. It has been defiled in many ways and demolished. The gate to the tomb was broken. The granite sarcophagus in the mausoleum was opened."

"Everything I've come across on my way has been like this. When I ask the Greek officers who were captured and taken prisoner why they did this, they all gave the same answer that they didn't want to and that the British had given them the orders. The Greeks are a pawn in this."

"I came to the Bilecik Train Station. The beautiful city of Bilecik I saw 18 months ago is a skeleton of itself. It has become a land of disaster and suffering. The smell of the corpses I just mentioned here is too much to bear. Who knows how many people are buried under the heaps of stone with smoke rising from them. The destruction is terrible."

"Bilecik and Küplü have seen major catastrophes. The surviving inhabitants of the region are in deep crisis. There are no young girls or women who have not been raped. Bilecik is like Pompeii."

"Everything is in ashes and covered in soot. It is as if the earth has been turned upside down. We often come across piles of stone showing the destruction done with dynamite. There were two cute girls spinning silk thread and watching our convoy from amid the rubble. A little farther down there was a grave for an old man whose head was smashed with a rock while he tried to save his daughter."

"Each city has seen its share of the total destruction done. We walked through these ruins for hours and listened to what the people had to say."

"We are in the warzone. I looked at the corpses and piles of ammunition along the roadside. I brought my handkerchief to my nose without thinking, as if it were normal. I can now look at some of the scenes on the battlefield without looking away."

"Pazarcık was under Papulas' administration until eight days ago, and the townsfolk shudder the more they think of it. I am looking out on snowcapped Uludağ above the burning İnegöl."

This all happened in the areas under British and Greek occupation when Mehmed VI issued the decree for Mustafa Kemal to be put to death on sight for sedition.

∞

It was Friday, April 23, 1920, and a tremendous crowd had gathered at the Hacı Bayram Mosque.

Mustafa Kemal wrote an open invitation to the people and it was transmitted around the entire country that said, "God willing, the Grand National Assembly will open in Ankara after Friday prayers on April 23."

Hacı Bayram Mosque, which is a cornerstone of Turkish Parliament, was built in 1427, much before the conquest of Istanbul. It was named for Hacı Bayram-ı Veli, whose tomb is in the mosque's garden.

Hacı Bayram-ı Veli was born in Ankara in 1352 and was one of the most important representatives of Sufism, he wrote his works in Anatolian Turkish and greatly contributed to the spread of Turkish across Anatolia.

His advice has been deeply influential for centuries and has remained as fresh as if it were said today:

- Even the rancorblind eyes see reality.
- Preserve your humanity.
- Move away from evil.
- Be with those who are good
- Be good-natured.
- Be merciful.
- Be calm.
- Be earnest.
- Do not roar or shout when speaking.
- Avoid the ignorant.
- Pay attention and do not let the ignorant be found ahead of you.
- Acquire knowledge.
- Respect the knowledgeable.
- Always control your breath.
- Be careful in the work offered to you so that you are not forced to defend a view that is not your own.
- Do not be afraid to tell the truth.
- Do not join in groups of loose talk.
- Work hard.
- Gain honest earnings by working for money and wealth.
- Think—Anger and fury limit thinking and mislead.

- Justice is beautiful—Justice is more beautiful if it is in the hands of a ruler.
- Know value.
- Betrayal of trust is ugly—secure trust.

The Parliament building hadn't been completed. Construction began in 1915 and had been left half finished. There were no panes in the windows, no tiles on the roof; the interior hadn't been plastered; and there was no electricity. There was a crevice behind the presidential podium that let in the cold—Ali Fuat Pasha's prayer rug was nailed over it. Benches had been brought from a school. There was a woodstove. Kerosene lamps collected from coffeehouses were hung from the ceiling.

There were no rental houses in Ankara. There wasn't any money anyway. The parliamentarians stayed at the 25-person dormitory of the teachers' school. There weren't enough beds so they spread blankets on the floor and slept on them. There were even those who set up cloths like blankets in the open, in meadows and under trees, and most of them caught malaria.

Food was a serious problem. They collected 55 *kuruş* per person and set up a fixed menu system. They didn't take anything from the food shops or grocers or demand store credit. They didn't even get bread without paying.

The Parliament minutes were written on the backs of bills. They were even written on paper bags.

The majority of the members of Parliament had been at the fronts and came to Parliament when they had the chance.

Mustafa Kemal always sat to the left side of the door beside Diyap Ağa. He always had a notebook and pencil in hand and took notes on what was said from the podium. He would hit the bench with the top of the pencil three times when he wanted permission to speak.

He didn't only respect Diyap Ağa for his age, but for his patriotism. He'd known him since the liberation of Bitlis and they had fought together. Diyap Ağa angrily took the podium after it was proposed Parliament be moved to Kayseri when Ankara fell under the danger of occupation in August 1921.

"Did we come here to run or to fight and die?" he said. "If you want to move Parliament, go ahead and be my guest. I will stay, even if alone, and fight to the last bullet, and I'll put that last bullet in my head."

This was the type of man Diyap Ağa was—the man Mustafa Kemal always sat beside in Parliament and to whom he showed due reverence.

There was no single opinion or allegiance. There were those in the first Parliament who very much liked Mustafa Kemal as well as those who didn't. There were cutthroat battles over ideas and physical fights.

It was like this so much so that one day when they were discussing the requirement for a medical examination to be conducted in order for couples to be officially married, it was proposed that the bride and groom must be examined by a doctor. In response, a group of religious fanatical opposition shouted that their girls shouldn't be forced to be examined. Mustafa Kemal was at the podium speaking in support of the proposal of medical examinations. The lawmaker from Erzurum, Hüseyin Avni, who had been opposed to Mustafa Kemal since the first day, lost himself.

He snatched a piece of wood from the pile in front of the stove and furiously threw it at the podium. Hamdi, one of the clerks taking the minutes, was hit in the face. It broke his teeth and the poor man fainted. Mustafa Kemal didn't lose his composure and continued explaining the scientific data as if this ugly attack hadn't happened. Hüseyin Avni was embarrassed. He apologized to the chamber, sat down and remained quiet.

Mustafa Kemal was immensely tolerant of opposing ideas. He explained the criteria for honor when they complained to him about a dissident parliamentarian:

"Tolerate the dissident members because they're men of honor. Suppose you push him out and in his place comes someone who is both a dissident and has no honor. What would you do then?"

He particularly encouraged opposition in the assembly:

"Did we establish Parliament for it to be a game? On the contrary, we established it so they can express their ideas and opinions openly. Of course they will criticize—it's their duty to. Why do you get angry, or is it that you are unsure of yourselves? Are there points in your position you can't defend?"

∞

He was almost killed in the Grand National Assembly.

A team was caught red-handed in Izmir in 1926, while preparing an assassination plot. They had actually planned to carry it out in Parliament six years earlier.

Those in the assassination plot, which included parliamentarians, had brought the hitmen Laz İsmail and

Georgian Yusuf from Istanbul to Ankara. They had given them plenty of money and Lugers.

The hitmen came to Parliament on invitation and cased the room as they sat and watched the session from the spectators' benches. They gauged the distance from where they sat to Mustafa Kemal and calculated the area of effect the hand grenade would have.

They had also made a plan for an armed ambush. They studied the routes around the Çankaya Mansion Mustafa Kemal took and around the Ankara Club, which he often went to. They even determined the farm they would run to hide after the attack.

Fortunately, the revolutionaries were alert. These two odd men, having continually come to Parliament, whispering with some parliamentarians and coming and going from the same parliamentarians' homes aroused suspicion. They started to follow them. The people who were part of the assassination plot became uneasy. They understood that they would be raided and so canceled the plan. The hitmen were sent back to Istanbul.

The same team would re-enter the stage six years later. They planned an attack on Mustafa Kemal's official car in Kemeraltı, Izmir. They were to throw hand grenades from stores opposite each other, open a cross fire, escape in a car on a side street off to Urla and then onto a fishing boat to the island of Chios.

They wanted to rent the boat for 600 liras from Şevki of Crete. He had fought in the National Campaign in the mountains of the Aegean. He was the *zeybek* of Edip Bey, who was known as Sarı Efe (Blond Chief). Unfortunately, Sarı Efe was also part of the assassination plot.

It's unknown whether Şevki of Crete was an honorable man or afraid of getting caught, but either way, he didn't want to be part of the betrayal. He wrote an urgent letter to the governor of İzmir to be delivered to Mustafa Kemal in which he warned him against the plot.

That's how the assassination plot in Izmir fell apart.

∞

Another assassination attempt occurred in Ankara, in 1921. This time it was plotted by British intelligence.

An Indian by the name of Mustafa Sagir had been brought to London as a boy, educated at Oxford and trained by the British secret service. He had been taught Turkish, Arabic, German and Persian.

During his assignment in Afghanistan, he had organized the plot to assassinate Afghan Emir Habibullah Khan.

He came to Istanbul under the guise of the Khalifat Movement of India. He distributed sacks full of money to the poor and could be considered to have been loved by the people. He established communication with the revolutionaries. In order to establish trust with them, he was supposedly arrested in a British raid and imprisoned for 17 days. He went to Ankara as soon as he was released and befriended parliamentarians, saying he was a Muslim oppressed by the British. He said that India's Khalifat Movement had collected 3 million gold coins that he would bring to Ankara.

In fact, news had already arrived from the Mim Mim Group in Istanbul. Mustafa Kemal was aware of the hidden identity of this Indian who acted like a charitable Muslim. "He's an excellent spy and he should be careful," he said. They had him followed in order to determine his secret relations.

He had become friendly with Mehmet Akif Ersoy. He was going regularly to the Taceddin Lodge. He had even given the Taceddin Lodge as his address. He was writing letters to the Khalifat Movement in India, sending them with couriers to Istanbul who also brought him letters. Having first believed Mustafa Sagir to be a devout man, Mehmet Akif Ersoy in time began to have his doubts and he informed the revolutionaries about the correspondence. The letters were secretly taken and examined. They appeared to be normal, inquiring after people.

After looking at them more closely, though, there was something wrong with them. Too much paper was used for a letter of a couple of lines. The writing didn't take up even one-fifth of the page. The rest was empty.

The revolutionaries' chemist, Avni Refik Bey, warmed the letter slightly over a candle. And bingo. Invisible writing appeared on the empty page. It had been written with ammonia instead of ink.

He hadn't been sending them to the Khalifat Movement in India, but rather to Colonel Nelson, the commander of British intelligence in Istanbul.

There was reconnaissance on the places where Mustafa Kemal lived, the places he frequented, the routes he used and the homes of his close friends. He informed the network about the assassination plot.

He confessed to the assassination plot during interrogation. Then he tried to negotiate. He said he would be able to tell what he knew about the British in exchange for a pardon and release.

He was tried and hanged at the Court of Independence.

Berthe Gaulis.

The first woman to enter the building of the Grand National Assembly was French journalist Berthe Gaulis.

The first Turkish woman to set foot in the building was Latife.

Gaulis had been with the National Campaign since the beginning and supported it through her reporting.

She was writing a book about Mustafa Kemal.

She had actually lived in Istanbul for 20 years. Her husband, Georges, was also a journalist. They had embraced the land so much so that when Georges died in 1912, he was buried in the Feriköy cemetery. Their daughter was born in Istanbul.

She sent her daughter to France when the city fell under occupation and she reported from the fronts as she went to Ankara, Eskişehir, Sakarya, Afyon, Kastamonu and Konya. This French woman, this journalist, was the voice of the National Forces in Europe.

Mustafa Kemal hosted her privately in Ankara, and the Grand National Assembly thanked her with a ceremony.

She was an admirer of Mustafa Kemal and couldn't hide it.

"I suppose he is the most handsome man among world leaders and other men," she had said.

"What he explains is so clear, so evident that it is always striking," she said. "What is left in one's mind is the clarity of his proof and felicitousness of his expressions. There is no indication of violence in his vibrant voice. There is a steeliness to this vibrancy and a strange harmony. One of this man's greatest powers is his amazing conversation. He always guesses with which answer he'll be met. The sensitivity of his mind is tremendous. Nothing escapes his eye or his mind. There are three reasons for his success: perception, prudence and analysis. His talent for observation is quite advanced and he has complete self-confidence."

∞

Factions of patriots in Istanbul press had started publishing caricatures of Mustafa Kemal in 1920.

They weren't only of him armed, either.

Humor was also given to the National Campaign.

There was no possibility to publish war photographs in the papers in the primitive conditions of the time, so they opted to explain things with drawings.

In some caricatures he was a powerful wrestler pushing back the enemy, in others a boxer walloping his opponent out of the ring and still in others an athlete running in the lead.

Sometimes he was a doctor giving a diagnosis, a dentist pulling decayed teeth, a tailor measuring the enemy's neck with a tape or a cook. Where he is a cook, he is breaking a bowl labeled *Sevres* while "peace soup" boils in the pot *of the National Pact*.

Sometimes he was also a goalkeeper. The Greek occupation forces were in the form of a ball being kicked out to the Aegean Sea.

The sultan's supporters were portrayed as ridiculous. While Mustafa Kemal in a kalpak was shown as a ray of shining sunlight, Damad Ferid was drawn as a skull wearing a fez.

Mehmed VI's journalist, Ali Kemal, was portrayed as a chamber pot with the nickname "Artin Kemalidis".

King Constantine of Greece was drawn deformed, in funny outfits and with his teeth falling out.

There was also the character Con Kikirik (Beanpole John, i.e., an Englishman), who was brought to life by Aka Gündüz, a legendary satirical literature.

They were making fun of the British.

The occupation forces were trying to control and censor the newspapers but couldn't cope with the humor. The cartoonists used pseudonyms such as Crow, Tuna, Lizard, Master, Lover, Porter, Caracal, Old Horse and Steed in order not to be imprisoned.

Victory was heralded with these caricatures and humorous morale was given to the people who were hopeless in those dark days.

Occupied Izmir was depicted as a beautiful fairy waiting for Mustafa Kemal as its savior.

Postcards of Mustafa Kemal were distributed by hand in Istanbul and Izmir. Like wearing a kalpak, carrying these postcards had become a national fashion.

It was a pushback in the war of propaganda, as British intelligence distributed a headshot of Mustafa Kemal in Anatolia and dropped them from planes over villages that depicted him with a showy fez in place of his kalpak, puffy and long hair instead of his officer's shave, a frilly bowtie, chubby cheeks and dark skinned. He resembled the dancing palace jesters around the sultan more than the Hero of Anafartalar.

It was possible to muddy people's minds with this type of propaganda since there weren't any newspapers in Anatolia. The people only knew Mustafa Kemal by name since there weren't any real photographs of him, so they believed the photograph the British distributed to be true.

The prepared, fake photographs had a fake biography full of lies. They tried to fool the people to weaken the resistance and introduced Mustafa Kemal as someone not worth following. It was a win if even one person believed this rubbish or one person wavered and fell to hesitation.

The National Forces responded to the British conspiracy with patriotic printers and cartoonists.

Postcards were made of an actual headshot of Mustafa Kemal with him wearing a kalpak. Snapshots of the War of Independence were on the backside in a type of illustrated novel along with patriotic poems.

They were distributed in Istanbul and Izmir, and were carried in people's jacket pockets like identification documents. They would leave them on the tables of the restaurants and cafes frequented by British and Greek officers, place them under the glasses and plates, and paste them on the windows and walls. They would immediately replace any that were taken down and drove the occupiers mad with this national fad.

British intelligence seized these postcards of Mustafa Kemal as they were passed around in Egypt, Libya, Algeria, Yemen and even India.

British propaganda couldn't stop it. Hope in Mustafa Kemal had surpassed the borders of the country and he had become a hero around the globe.

∞

Those were the days when the concept of *Kemalism* arose.

Michel Paillares, the editor-in-chief of the newspaper *Le Bosphore*, which was published in Beyoğlu, was the first to use the term in 1919. He was a French journalist opposed to the Turks. It was supposedly an independent newspaper, although Greek banks funded it.

British intelligence used the term *Kemalists*. The press in the U.S. gave it the name the *Kemalist movement*.

The Istanbul government likened the National Forces to the Celali rebellions against the Ottoman Empire and called them *Kemali*.

Those in the Istanbul press who sided with the palace used *Kemali* while those who sided with Ankara used *Kemalici*—both meaning Kemalist, although the former was Ottoman and the latter Turkish.

Those in the West had invented and used the term Kemalism since Mustafa Kemal had left for Samsun. Yakup Kadri Karaosmanoğlu, however, was the first to use it in the Turkish press in *Hakimiyet-i Milliye* (National Sovereignty) in 1927. According to him, Kemalism didn't belong to an individual, but was rather the motto of the republic and the name of revolution.

The first book to be titled *Kemalism* was published in 1936.

Şevket Süreyya Aydemir was one of the doctrinarians of Kemalism who described its characteristics:

"He was a man of logic, not excitement. He was clear-eyed and far sighted. His talent for analysis and his power to administrate direction were marvelous. He wasn't confined to a narrow mold or those frozen in place. He did not accept the dead past or the deceased values of the past as tradition. All of his actions were dominated by a sense of legitimacy. He was a realistic humanist. He wasn't a man of adventure. His life was not quiet and retiring like a babbling brook. Hopes, dreams, disappointments, wars, revolutions, victories, defeats and still continuing denials were like the loops and knots knitting his exploits.

"He neither had a wife, place nor partner who understood him, nor children playing around him. He said to himself, 'I've kept my freedom throughout my life, not tied to my house, those close to me or even my mother'. His only tie was to himself. His true homeland was his inner world. His loneliness was as deep as his victories.

"At times he didn't even confess his melancholy to himself, but he knew that the following day or the next that the country he had rescued could be dragged into an undreamt-of crisis in sundry and worthless hands. There's no doubt he was worried."

∞

The National Holiday Law was enacted in 1921. April 23 was deigned the Day of National Sovereignty.

It wasn't yet Children's Day.

Countless children lost their mothers and fathers in the War of Independence. The Association of Child Services was established under Mustafa Kemal's personal patronage in order to take on this sacred trust. A space was given to the director of the Association of Child Services at the Day of National Sovereignty ceremony held at the Grand National Assembly on April 23, 1923, upon Mustafa Kemal's wishes. Mustafa Kemal's wife Latife represented the association at the ceremony a year later on April 23, 1924.

April 23 was associated with the Association of Children's Services. The children of those who died in battle came to mind when hearing April 23 mentioned.

Milliyet published a headline on April 23, 1926 that said "Children's Day". That is how the holiday came to be called National Sovereignty and Children's Day.

Donation campaigns were organized and people lined up in front of aid boxes every April 23.

In just six years, the Association of Children's Services managed to reach more than 300,000 children of those who died in war. Books, clothing, linens, toys and food were regularly distributed to the children and their education expenses were met.

Everyone did what was within their power—they became aunts and uncles of sorts; they held the children's hands and became relatives in time. It was with Mustafa Kemal's vision that the largest family in the world was created.

∞

The Battle of Sakarya hadn't even happened yet when the Grand National Assembly declared the holiday. Celebrating the holiday was left by the wayside and it wasn't clear if there would be a country left.

This was a daring act—the self-confidence of Mustafa Kemal having the band perform in the trenches during the bloodiest days of Gallipoli. The morale he spread was much more powerful than weapons and ammunition.

He went to Polatlı in August of 1921 for the final preparations for combat in Sakarya. His horse got spooked and he fell off onto his back straight on a rock and broke two ribs. There was pressure on his lungs and he couldn't breathe. He refused to go to the hospital and was bandaged instead.

His was a generation that had lived their lives on the front and had long ago crossed the threshold of fear. They strived to experience the beauty of life, even in life and death situations, thinking every day could be their last.

For example, Kılıç Ali's sister Naime was getting married in that critical period. Despite the pain from his broken ribs, Mustafa Kemal attended the wedding and was a deputy for the bride. He returned to the front the next day.

Halide Edip Adıvar explained about Mustafa Kemal and his broken ribs:

"An officer brought me to the headquarters. The village roads were dark and muddy. It was midnight. The guards were at the door. There was only a kerosene lamp burning in the Anatolian room, and I went in. Mustafa Kemal Pasha struggled to rise from his chair. His ribs were giving him quite a bit of pain. He said *welcome, madam*. It was he in that modest room who embodied the risk of dying so the people could live. Neither the palace, fame nor any force could come close to his greatness in that room. I approached the pasha with unconditional respect in my heart and kissed his hand."

Even if he was injured, he had no luxury to rest for even a day. He was always forced to think ahead. The morale of the soldiers in the trenches, the Grand National Assembly and Istanbul were all dependent on him.

∞

Greek intelligence knew very well the Turkish people's source of resistance and they spread lies about Mustafa Kemal to weaken the people's spirit. News was often reported that he had been captured.

What was tragic and comical about it was that they believed their own lies. The local Greeks in Izmir would pour into the street and celebrate every time they heard Mustafa Kemal had been captured.

They believed that Mustafa Kemal had actually been captured.

Greek newspapers ran headlines saying as much. Bells tolled and there were festivities even in Athens. This joy would again be stuck in their throats the next day. A Mustafa Kemal had been taken prisoner, but not the one who was the object of their derision—just a soldier named Mustafa Kemal.

∞

He commanded the Battle of Sakarya in civilian clothes instead of a military uniform.

According to Ruşen Eşref Ünaydın's recollection, "After managing and winning the war in sporting civilian clothes, he returned to the Çankaya Mansion in a battered and simple Ford one would think was a municipal taxi, wearing those civilian clothing and a pair of buckskin gloves, his chest in pain, almost struggling to proceed and not telling anyone about it and not waiting for a welcoming ceremony or applause, as if coming back from a day job."

Those who came to greet Mustafa Kemal at the entrance to the city missed him. They smiled and shook hands in congratulations with those bustling around the mansion. He mocked those who were debating the commanders, saying, "I suppose I'm not doing this military work so badly."

The Battle of Sakarya wasn't only the turning point in the War of Independence. At the same time, the continuous withdrawal that started in Vienna on September 13, 1683, was brought to an end 238 years later on September 13, 1921.

With this, there was no longer a line of defense, but rather defense of the entire country.

Parliament gave him the titles of *marshal* and *gazi (veteran)*. He hadn't worn a military uniform until that day.

∞

The Supreme Command Law was voted on. There were 177 yes votes. Eleven votes were against it. Thirteen parliamentarians abstained from the vote.

This might have been the first time in his life that he looked upset.

I was accustomed to unjust criticism and didn't even find baseless charges odd, but he was crushed by the votes against the commandership and he couldn't accept the abstentions.

He had said in response: "They say people are evil-minded by nature. Unfortunately, the meaning of this proverb was shown today in Parliament."

ص

It is called the Great Offensive in Turkey. Its actual name, though, is the *sad* operation. That is *sad*, as in the

Arabic letter ص. The letter ص was placed on the cosmically covert plans of attack.

It was the product of Mustafa Kemal's intelligence.

If the shape of the arrangement of the Turkish forces on the battlefield were drawn, then it would make the shape of the letter ص.

He had examined and analyzed military geniuses such as Alexander the Great, Attila the Hun and Hannibal. He was inspired by Hannibal's routing of a Roman army in the Battle of Cannae while he was preparing his plans for the *sad* operation. His choice wasn't to surround the enemy, but rather to give them the opportunity for retreat. Unlike Hannibal, for speedy and ruthless pursuit, he had created a cavalry to sweep through retreating forces.

(The U.S. military applied Mustafa Kemal's tactic during the Gulf War in 1990. The American documentary *Operation Desert Storm* mentions that "General Schwarzkopf used Atatürk's cavalry tactic with tanks.")

∞

The headquarters for the front was in Akşehir.

He went to Konya for inspections and visited a madrasa without giving prior notice.

It was full of 17 and 18-year-old mullahs. They were lined up with their turbaned and cloaked teachers in the yard. They bowed down to the ground while greeting him.

He was gathering a regular army for the Great Offensive. The greatest fear of those hiding in madrasas under the name of religion was to be enlisted into the army.

So, was this the reason for the surprise visit?

One of the turbaned senior men came up to Mustafa Kemal and heaped praise upon him before getting to the point and beseeching him not to enlist the madrasa students.

Mustafa Kemal could hardly hold himself back and exploded:

"The country is at war, trying to preserve its independence and existence and you spend your time here speaking Arabic. Are these madrasas more important to you than defeating the Greeks and saving the people from persecution? You feed the teenagers in perfect health here while the people are swimming in blood and the children of the nation sacrifice their lives at the front."

Then he stormed off.

There were about 5,000 madrasas in the country then. Together they were the size of an army corps, albeit unused.

Mustafa still hadn't calmed down as they drove away.

"We will put an end to this," he said. "We will definitely end this."

∞

A food shortage arose at the front. The invading forces had set fire to the fields around the villages. They didn't even leave a weed standing. The soldiers only had toasted wheat.

One night, Mustafa Kemal came to Duatepe. They sat down to a dinner the chief of staff of the army corps had had prepared. There was only a scrawny chicken and four or five slices of bread.

He turned to the chief of staff and asked, "What did you give the soldiers?"

The man hemmed and hawed. "We supplied them with toasted wheat," he finally said.

Mustafa Kemal got to his feet and left without saying a word. He didn't touch the chicken or the bread. Everyone went to bed hungry that night.

(Even fishing squads were established so the soldiers could have a little meat. They fished in the lakes of the region.)

∞

He was reading *Çalıkuşu* (The Wren) during the bloodbath.

It was being published as a serial in the *Vakit* newspaper. It hadn't yet been compiled into a book. It was a remedy to rest his mind.

He met the author, Reşat Nuri Güntekin, years later and told him: "Feride's story eased my pains."

∞

Hundreds of photographs were taken of him throughout the War of Independence. He is scowling with a hard face in all of them.

Only one was different.

He had visited the Kocaeli front before the Great Offensive. A young medical student named Muhterem approached him as he rested and introduced himself.

"Would you let me take your picture?" he asked.

Mustafa Kemal gave him permission, but then everybody was surprised by the next request. "You look rigid in photographs," Muhterem said. "Would you smile for this one if I ask?"

It felt like an icy wind.

The other commanders took the medical student's audacity as impertinence and looked over at Mustafa Kemal, wondering how he would rebuff the young man.

He quite liked it, though, and smiled.

"The boy is right, let's grant his request," he said. He even told the young man to come and sit next to him.

Etem Tem snapped the photograph. After the card was printed, he signed it and gave it to Muhterem.

This is the only photograph of him smiling during the War of Independence.

(Muhterem Gökmen graduated from medical school, did residencies in Vienna and Frankfurt, and became a professor of radiology.)

∞

It was 11:00 a.m. on August 26, 1922, in Kocatepe, Afyon.

The Great Offensive had begun at daybreak, at 5 o'clock in the morning.

Mustafa Kemal followed every step of the assault and rattled off orders over the field telephone. He left the other commanders at one point and walked by himself toward the edge of a craggy cliff. He looked at the enemy line through binoculars, pensive and contemplative. It was right as he brought his fingers to his lips as if smoking a cigarette when Etem Tem snapped the shutter.

Etem Tem was the National Forces' official photographer.

He was a reserve officer and had graduated from the civil service. He had been a photographer in Istanbul. He had fought in World War I on the Caucasian front and had gone to Anatolia with the outbreak of the War of Independence. He had a German ICA Reflex camera that took 10x15 glass negatives.

This photograph he took is etched in Turkey's history and the minds of its people, and was printed as posters and made into badges.

As for the film, he was only able to develop it eight days later in a rundown barn in Uşak.

He actually documented the Great Offensive frame by frame, but only this memorial photograph was printed as a card.

He went from front to front every day taking photographs from August 26 to September 9. He basically made a story in pictures.

There's more, though.

He entered Izmir on September 9. The sun was sinking low in the sky. He ran around in search of a photography shop. He found a local Greek photographer. He gave the man the film and filled his time walking around until the film was ready. When he returned, the Greek photographer said they were all fantastic. Etem Tem took a look. The filmstrips were still wet. He looked over them all and they were all wonderful. He needed a little more time to let them fully dry and be ready. He left and would pick them up the next morning. He went to the headquarters in Bornova.

He got back to Izmir with the first light of day. He couldn't believe his eyes. The city was engulfed in flames.

The people had poured out into the streets in chaos. It wasn't clear who was friend and who was foe.

The photography shop had burned to the ground and was in ruins. He had a few negatives left he could develop in the barn in Uşak. His photo documentary of the Great Offensive unfortunately went up in smoke with the photography shop in Izmir.

∞

Colonel Reşad Bey.

Colonel Reşad Bey was from Istanbul.

He was a heroic officer with many medals who had served under Mustafa Kemal at Gallipoli, Muş and in Syria. He went to Anatolia with no hesitation upon the start of the National Campaign and fought in İnönü and Sakarya.

It was the second day of the Great Offensive when Mustafa Kemal ordered him to drive the enemy out of Çiğiltepe. It was something that would affect the outcome of the battle and was the most strategic obstacle after Dumlupınar.

Greek General Nikolaos Trikoupis held his position in Çiğiltepe, knowing its importance.

Mustafa Kemal picked up the field telephone at 10:30 a.m.

"How much longer will it go on?" he asked.

"We've completed the encirclement and are walking around at a distance so as not to take fire," Colonel Reşad said. "I'll have the hill in half an hour."

Mustafa Kemal called again at 10:45 a.m.

"You're late, Reşad," he yelled. "Take the hill already!"

The phone rang at 11 a.m. This time Lieutenant Bozkurt Kaplangı answered.

The colonel was crying.

Colonel Reşad said, "I made a promise, but I couldn't keep it," knowing quite well the cost of his delay. These were his final words. He took his pistol from its holster, put it to his head and silently pulled the trigger.

Mustafa Kemal consoled the lieutenant: "May God be merciful—he was a great patriot. No army on earth has happened upon a sturdier soldier with a purer heart than a Turkish soldier." Then he said, "Take the hill at once!"

General Trikoupis was taken prisoner. Three hundred officers and 5,000 soldiers surrendered.

General Nikolaos Trikoupis.

They were brought to Uşak. All of them were exhausted. Mustafa Kemal came and shook their hands amicably.

"If you think you've performed your duty against your conscience, be at ease. As Napoleon said, history will record the orders of even the greatest commanders."

The Greek generals were crushed by this unexpected magnanimity. Trikoupis broke down in tears, mumbling that his aides had all abandoned him and he should have killed himself.

Mustafa Kemal spoke with a soft voice: "You are our guests and you can be certain you will be accomodated. If you have any requests, do not hesitate to notify us."

He turned to İsmet Pasha and gave the order: "They are tired. Make certain they are comfortable."

A telegraph came the next morning to Trikoupis' wife in Istanbul that said her husband was in good health and a guest of Mustafa Kemal.

This humane telegraph sent through the Red Crescent completely destroyed the already disintegrating Greek Army.

Trikoupis and other Greek officers were held for a year in camps in Kayseri and Kırşehir.

It was a Red Crescent camp, though, not a prison camp. There were almost no armed guards.

An internal feud would have started in Greece if they had been immediately sent back and they would have been hanged. They were made to wait until the war had come to a complete end and then were sent back to Greece after the waters had calmed, thus saving Trikoupis and the others' lives.

Mustafa Kemal had not only clinched victory with his intelligence and courage, but also with his conscience.

Trikoupis was still alive when Atatürk died.

He spoke to the Greek press: "I bow with respect before the greatest man of our century. He turned Turkey into one of the world's peace centers. His place will always remain empty and he will always be longed for."

He went to the Pink House in Salonika on November 10, before his death in 1956. He stood respectfully in front of a photograph of Atatürk.

Mustafa Kemal had received Gâvur Mümin in exchange for General Trikoupis.

Mümin was from Izmir. He was a 1st lieutenant. He had fought in Tripolitania. It was there where he'd met Mustafa Kemal.

Gâvur Mümin.

Having made friends at every stage of his life, Mustafa Kemal noted the name of the still young Mümin, who was a 2nd lieutenant at the time.

Mümin had been assigned in Izmir when the occupation began. He had piled up disciplinary offences and was thrown out of the army. He contacted Greek officers.

He had been dismissed from the army and appeared as a former officer angry at the state, and as such, he was thought to be a collaborator.

Having crossed over to the Greeks, the Turks of Izmir gave him the nickname *gâvur*, or infidel. He was, however, a patriot who put his life on the line as one of Mustafa Kemal's intelligence officers. It looked as though he worked for the Greeks, but he actually sent vital information to Ankara.

He was found out, though, and as a result was arrested. A Greek military court sentenced him to death.

The war had ended then and prisoner exchanges were a topic of discussion. His death sentence was reduced to life imprisonment. He was taken to Athens and imprisoned before he was sent to a prison camp.

He was brought back in 1923 in exchange for Trikoupis thanks to Mustafa Kemal's personal pursuance and he returned to the military.

He was given the Medal of Independence and took the last name Aksoy. He retired with the rank of colonel.

He died in 1948 and is buried in the Balçova cemetery in İzmir.

∞

The call to prayer rang out from minarets on September 9, 1922.

Mustafa Kemal was in Belkahve, looking out over Izmir.

He looked out over Izmir, that special city in the world where a country's War of Independence had begun on the day of the occupation. It was the city where that same war had come to an end.

He went to the garden house he had prepared for himself in Nif. It was a typical Aegean garden house—one floor, stone and with no windows.

He was tired.

They brought him food, but he didn't eat it.

He took out a cigarette.

"You know, İsmet," he said. "I feel like I'm in a dream."

It was a dream that started with a nightmare and ended with a miracle. It lasted three years, three months and 22 days. The flowers were blooming on İzmir's mountains.

He recounted that moment years later: "There was a pistol in my right hand and gallows in my left. That's how I came from Samsun to İzmir."

Falih Rıfkı Atay also described that historic day:

"We didn't know whether the city was in our full control or not when we got to the İzmir port with Yakup Kadri. The joy I felt when I saw the Turkish flag on the bastions struck me like a child's delight on a holiday morning. I wanted to go hug and shout and cry with everyone.

"We came across armed soldiers hunched in the thresholds of the doors along the dock. Everywhere smelled like victory. It was as if there hadn't been a great war. They were as simple and modest as if they had just gotten off a train.

"We left our things at the Kramer Palace Hotel.

"Ruşen Eşref appeared wearing an Anatolian kalpak and asked if we would see Mustafa Kemal Pasha and if he would introduce us to him. The headquarters was right around the corner. It was in a house of one of the old, local Greeks. The windows were open. We saw the commander-in-chief from a distance. He was dynamic, with a sharp nose and a lively, weather-beaten face.

"There were two British officers greeting him. The British officers spoke more upright than the Ottoman ministers in Istanbul and saluted the commander-in-chief as still as statues. Seeing this washed away all our anger. It cooled our desire for revenge.

"A little later, he admitted us to the hall where he was sitting at the head of a table with İsmet Pasha. He asked for the news from Istanbul and listened to every word. A large fire had broken out. Those who escaped the flames had flocked to the docks. British ships were close enough to the shore for them to make a go for it. The crowds grew there. Everyone was screaming. There were those jumping into the sea.

"The British had been taking the Greeks to İzmir under protection of their cannons and now turned their bayonets on those who wanted to go back, so they couldn't climb the ladders on the ships.

"He watched this unmatched tragedy with a trembling heart. I looked at Mustafa Kemal's rugged, unbreakable calm.

"Finally, the frightening red flames began to lick at the roof of the headquarters. The pier was chock full of Greeks. There was a truck full of soldiers in front and Mustafa Kemal got into the convertible behind it. The truck plowed through the crowd and opened the way for Mustafa Kemal to narrowly pass through the throngs of people.

"They knew who he was. They pointed and yelled out that it was him. There wouldn't have been a piece of him left if they had gone in the slowly advancing car. Everyone wanted to escape to the sea, though."

∞

He had aroused admiration around the world.

It wasn't only in oppressed Muslim countries, as he became a role model even in the heart of Europe and was looked on with admiration in the U.S.

For example, Leopoldine König, a music teacher in Vienna, was so touched that she composed a march for Mustafa Kemal:

Mustafa Kemal Pasha
Fought fiercely
And drove off the swarm of enemies.

God sent him
To win the war
And bring peace to his beautiful homeland.

The pain turned to eternal joy.
Don't cease and straight away place a laurel wreath
On the head of this great man.

Yell out with sonorous voices

And with heartfelt joy.

Ask God to give him unending happiness.

She sent the words to the march to Mustafa Kemal in a letter.

Your Excellency,

I am the daughter of an officer who was in the horrors of the Great War. We Austrians are at the edge of a cliff, with the entire world behaving as an enemy. Our unhappy country may have to wait longer for good times. In contrast, Turkey is indebted to one man for its rebirth and the happiness it has achieved.

The Turkish victory and the liberation created by your strong hand has brought sincere joy to all those who love justice. I would like to express my feelings about the glorious victory the Turkish nation won under your high command and present to Your Excellency this march I composed.

...

9.XII.1922

Leopoldine König

Mustafa Kemal wrote her a response:

Mademoiselle,

Ankara, 29.12.1922

I received your letter, which is the expression of a tender and delicate spirit, along with your march singing the praises of our nation's victory. Thank you so much. Even if late, justice will appear. May the state of your dear country not afflict you and I wish for your country's attaining its liberation and independence as soon as possible.

Grand National Assembly of Turkey
President
Commander in Chief Gazi

He aroused curiosity across continents.

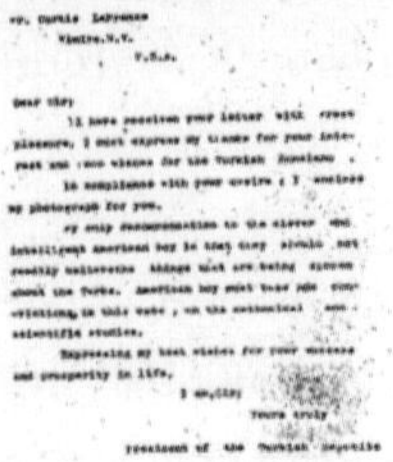

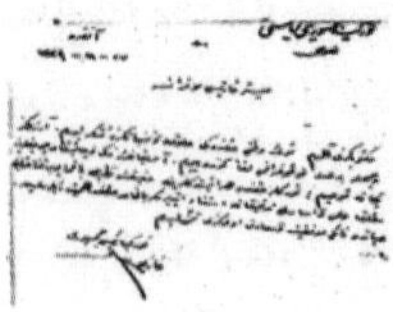

Curtis LaFrance.

Over 6,000 miles away in the town of Elmira in New York, a 10-year-old American boy wrote Mustafa Kemal a letter one day before the proclamation of the republic.

To Mustafa Kemal Pasa, Angara

Dear Sir,

I am a 10 year old American boy. I am very much interested in Turkey and the Turkish government. I read an interview with you and Mrs. Kemal recently. I have a notebook on Turkey and already collected many articles and photographs of you and Mrs. Kemal. Please send a signed photograph of you to this American boy. I hope to visit Turkey someday.

With best regards,

Curtis LaFrance

The letter reached Ankara on November 27.
Mustafa Kemal read it and wrote back.

To Mister Kurtis LaFrans [sic],

I received your letter. Thank you for your interest and thoughts on Turkey. As requested, I am enclosing a photograph of myself. My only recommendation to the hard working and intelligent youth of America is not to believe everything said about Turks as truth and to base their studies on scientific research. I wish you success and happiness in life.

President of the Republic of Turkey
Gazi Mustafa Kemal

Curtis LaFrance had kept this letter and photograph for 75 years. He came to Turkey at the age of 85 and went to Ankara as an official guest.

His voice trembled as he spoke at a ceremony at Atatürk's mausoleum, Anıtkabir:
"I was 25 in 1938 when I heard Atatürk had died. No one understood why I cried."

∞

Mustafa Kemal abolished the sultanate on November 1, 1922.

It was the most critical move of the revolution.

Not being able to twist their arm, the entente powers invited both the Istanbul government and Ankara government to the Lausanne negotiations. The two governments were equal in their minds. They made efforts to preserve the authority of the sultan.

Mustafa Kemal pounded his fist on the tale.

He climbed up on a bench in Parliament. It might have been the first time he spoke so loudly:

"Sovereignty or the sultanate, in terms of wisdom, is not given through negotiations to anyone, by anyone. Sovereignty and the sultanate are seized with strength and force. The Ottoman dynasty appropriated the sovereignty and sultanate of the Turkish people. They have sustained these attacks for six centuries. And now, by putting them in their place and rebelling, the Turkish people have actually found their sovereignty and sultanate in their own hands.

"The question is not a matter of whether or not we will give sovereignty to the people. The existing truth is already defined by law. This will certainly be the case. In my opinion, if those gathered here take it naturally, then it is appropriate. If not, the truth will still be duly stated. There is the possibility, however, that some heads will roll!"

He had never before been seen to be this angry.

Whose heads did he refer to?

The U.S. intelligence report sent from Ankara and Istanbul at the time said the Parliament was divided into three groups. The first and largest group was of the revolutionaries who carried the torch for and thought like Mustafa Kemal. The second group wanted the sultanate to continue. The third group was of parliamentarians who had no preference between democracy or the sultanate and instead were simply out for material benefit.

Mehmed VI was under the wings of the British. He was content with this, and in order to be able to sustain his existence, he used the monarchist parliamentarians as a pincher.

These were the people Mustafa Kemal spoke of. When he said it would be good if those gathered accepted it otherwise heads could roll, those heads understood it quite clearly.

It was accepted unanimously. The Ottoman Empire came to an official end.

Mehmed VI boarded a British warship anchored in the Bosphorus and went into exile.

∞

Mustafa Kemal said it was for the good of the republic: "The morality of the republic is the administration based on virtue. The sultanate was an administration based on fear and threats. The administration of the republic will raise honorable people. Being based on fear and threats, the sultanate cultivated fearful, cowardly, wretched and contemptible people. It is this composition that is the difference between the two."

The proclamation of the republic was made on October 29, 1923.

Mustafa Kemal's speech of thanks was shorter than what was expected. It was such an important decision and his speech was so short. Nobody could make any sense of it.

He explained the reason years later: "I had a new dental prosthesis. It was in the testing phase and I still hadn't gotten used to it. I heard a sound like whistling come from my mouth when I started to speak. My tongue was going around and I couldn't speak comfortably. What could I do? I cut it short."

This is how his days went. What about the evenings, though?

He felt something warm in his nose on the evening of October 29, 1923. He ran to the bathroom and the sink became covered with blood. He opened the medicine cabinet, plugged his nose with pre-prepared cotton pads and laid on his back. It had been happening for a while. His employees were alerted to it—if there were bloody towels or pillows, they were to be taken without anyone seeing and secretly washed and ironed.

He was hiding it from his aides and friends.

A doctor would mean limitations. If only he hadn't thought that way, but he did. He had much work to do. He didn't want to hear any advice like he should get some rest.

∞

The population was 13 million, with 11 million it in villages. There were 40,000 villages and 37,000 of them had no schools. There were no mosques in 30,000 of them. There were no tractors or harvesters. There was no sunflower or sugar production. Flour for bread was imported, as was rice. Only 12,400 acres of land were irrigated in the entire country. They were as hard to handle as fleas. The cattle in 5,000 villages were afflicted with rinderpest.

The animals were going to pieces, and so were the people. A million people had syphilis, 2 million had malaria and 3 million had trachoma. There were epidemics of tuberculosis, typhus and typhoid.

The infant mortality rate was over 40 percent. One out of every two babies died.

The rate of death in childbirth was 18 percent. One out of every five women giving birth died.

The average life expectancy was 40.

There were only 337 doctors in the country. There were only 60 pharmacists, and only eight of them were Turkish. There were only four nurses and only 136 midwives.

One hundred fifteen thousand buildings had burned down and 12,000 were damaged. There were over 1,000 villages that had completely burned to the ground.

The country needed to be rebuilt. There weren't even tiles.

The ports and mines belonged to foreigners. Not even a mile of railway belonged to any Turk. Turks owned only 15 percent of total equity.

There were four factories left from the Ottoman Empire—Hereke silk, Feshane wool, Bakırköy cloth and Beykoz leather.

Of all operations deemed industry, 96 percent had no machinery. There were only 280 workplaces with more than 10 employees. Two hundred fifty of these belonged to foreigners.

National per capita income was $45.

There was electricity only in Istanbul, Izmir and Tarsus. It would be more correct to say that there was supposedly electricity in these places since electric production was only at 50 kilowatt hours.

There was no highway that could be used year-round. There were only 490 automobiles. Only four cities had private cars.

Women weren't considered people. They didn't have the right to equal education, to acquire a profession, divorce, custody of children or even over inheritances left to them. They had no right to vote or be elected, they had no maternity leave, no equality in the workplace, no equal pay, no right to abortion or contraception, and they had no right to use their maiden names.

There were no theaters, no music, no paintings, no sculptures and no sports.

Archaeological artifacts had been taken abroad.

Some kept a la Turca time and considered the moment of sunset to be midnight, some kept noon time and considered noon to be when the sun was at its highest point, some based the time of sunset on sundown and still others based it on the call to prayer after the sun had completely set.

Some used the Hijri calendar and some used the Julian calendar. Some people's February coincided with others' December. Everyone lived in the same time zone but in different months.

For money there were dirhams, *oka* and çeki.

As for measurements, there were ells, fathoms and leagues.

The country's weights and measurements hadn't kept pace with the world. They remained in the Middle Ages.

A blend of Turkish with Arabic and Persian was called Ottoman for 600 years. French and Italian words invaded the language along with Levantine terms.

They tried to write Turkish with the Arabic alphabet, which doesn't have the voiced and unvoiced letter pairs Turkish requires. By the time books came to the country, 2.5 million different books had been published in Europe and 5 billion copies had been sold.

The only newspapers were in Istanbul and İzmir.

Only 7 percent of men and 0.004 percent of women were literate. The overwhelming majority of literate men were officers or non-Muslims.

Three out of every four children of school age didn't attend school. In total, there were 4,984 primary schools, only 72 middle schools and only 23 high schools. There were only 230 girls enrolled in all the high schools in the country.

One-third of the teachers had no training in education.

The country had only one university—Darülfünun—which was somewhat better than a madrasa.

Turkish was forbidden at the madrasas.

Mustafa Kemal wrote a letter to İsmet İnönü on the morning of October 30, 1923.

The first president of the republic, on the first day of the republic, said to the first prime minister of the republic:

"We have inherited a backward, indebted and sick country. We will set an example for poor and captive countries. It is a duty fate has imposed on our generation. We must form a free society. We must modernize to realize this ideal. I wanted to share the weight and honor of this duty. May God help us."

Thanks to Mustafa Kemal's vision, this poor country only 10 years later, became a center of attraction for the scientific world. German Jewish professors fleeing Nazi persecution took refuge in Atatürk's republic.

Distinguished Professor Erich Frank taught at the School of Medicine at Istanbul University and became a Turkish citizen. His casket was draped with a Turkish flag and buried with a state ceremony in Aşiyan.

Professor Clemens Emin Bosch organized the ancient coins in Turkey's archaeological museums. He converted to Islam and took the name Emin.

Carl Ebert was one of the founders of the Ankara State Conservatory and State Theater. He also brought Turkish opera up to date.

Professor Hans Gustav oversaw the Boğazköy excavations, was a pioneer in the deciphering of Hittite hieroglyphs and became an honorary member of the Turkish Historical Society.

Professor Curt Kosswigg spearheaded the establishment of the Manyas Bird Sanctuary, founded the Turkish Biological Association and laid the foundation for today's Marine Sciences Institute with the Institute of Hydrobiology. He was buried with a state ceremony in Aşiyan.

Distinguished Professor Wilhelm Peters founded the Psychology Department at Istanbul University and opened Turkey's first experimental psychology laboratory.

Ernst Reuter taught classes on urbanism in the Political Science Department of Istanbul University. After his return to Germany, he was elected mayor of Berlin.

His son, Edzard Reuter, spent 11 years of his childhood in Ankara. He became the chairman of the board for

Mercedes. He called Turkey his second country and paid his debt of loyalty to it by ensuring the establishment of Otomarsan.

Bruno Taut served as a director at the State Academy of Fine Arts in Istanbul and was the head of the Ministry of National Education's Architecture Department. He designed and made the catafalque that supported Atatürk's mortal remains. He didn't accept the 1,000 liras for the job and only wanted a thank you letter as a keepsake. He said in his will that he would stay in Turkey. The Republic of Turkey properly honored his will and he is the only non-Muslim to be buried in the Edirnekapı Martyrs' Cemetery in Istanbul.

They preferred Atatürk's republic to the United States, Britain and Canada from 1933 to 1937.

Distinguished professor and lawyer Ernst Hirsch recounted his memories on the occasion of the 10th anniversary celebrations of the republic:

"It was as if Judgment Day had come on October 29. The invitation was in a huge hall in Dolmabahçe Palace. The 600-meter pier was gleaming. And there I was, having fallen into contempt in my own country of Germany for being Jewish, having been chased from occupied land for being a member of a different race and forced to flee my home and native land to foreign countries, being presented in this magnificent palace as a respected German professor among the country's elite. This moment of good fortune laughing me in the face had been granted in only my first year in Turkey."

German-Swiss historian Emil Ludwig met with Mustafa Kemal in 1929 and described Turkey's amazing transformation with two words: "I first came to this land during the common war and now I am here for the second time. I learned two words—fast and slow. When I arrived in the old days, life was quite slow and I was obliged to tell the carriages to go fast. During my stay this time, I've seen such speed that I've been forced to tell the automobile drivers to go slow."

This was Atatürk's Turkey. It was shedding its old skin at a head spinning speed.

∞

As Mustafa Kemal elevated democracy and Parliament with the 1924 constitution, which said, "sovereignty is unconditionally the people's", Hitler had come to power in Germany; Mussolini had come to power in Italy; Franco ruled Spain; Salazar ruled Portugal; Stalin was the ruler of the Soviet Union; Piłsudski had come to power in Poland with a coup and was crushing his enemies; Admiral Horthy was regent in Hungary; there were kings in Romania and Yugoslavia; Austria had a dictator; President of Albania Ahmet Muhtar Zogolli crowned himself King Zog; General Metaksas staged a coup in Greece; and Sweden was allied with Nazi Germany.

There were no countries in Europe at that time governed by popular sovereignty other than Britain, France and Turkey.

Mustafa Kemal's vision had made Turkey one of the leaders of the modern world in the incredibly short time of three years.

∞

Reputable scientists flocked to Turkey from around the world while 150 girls and 750 boys with promising futures were sent for education abroad.

They went to Germany, France, Belgium, Switzerland, Austria, Italy, Czechoslovakia, Hungary and Sweden. The also went to the U.S. and China.

They studied at the universities in Geneva, Lausanne, the Sorbonne, Lyon, Freiburg, Heidelberg, Berlin, Charleroi, Harvard, Chicago, Cornell, Missouri, Iowa and Wisconsin.

Selahattin Reşit Alan was one of them. He returned an aircraft engineer and produced the first national aircraft, the MMV-1.

Ahmet Adnan Saygun, Ulvi Cemal Erkin, Cemal Reşit Rey, Hasan Ferit Alnar and Necil Kazım Akses were also among them. They became known as the Turkish Five and formed the backbone of polyphonic music in the country.

Ekrem Akurgal went abroad. He became an instructor of instructors in archaeology and became a distinguished professor.

Jale İnan became the first woman in Turkey to be an archaeologist. She brought the country to know the ancient cities of Perga and Side.

Cahit Arif became a distinguished professor of mathematics as well as the first chairman of the board of the Scientific and Technological Research Council of Turkey (TÜBİTAK) and theorems named for him entered the literature, such as the Arif invariant and Arif rings.

Haşim Şensoy returned an electrical engineer and signed off on the Keban Dam.

İhsan Ketin became the father of geology in Turkey and located the North Anatolian Fault.

Cevdet Arun studied abroad and became Turkey's first physical education teacher.

Sadi Irmak became a physiologist and prime minister.

There was also Hasan Tahsin Önalp, who became a mechanical engineer. He enabled the Turkish automotive industry with Otomarsan at its head. He was also the general director of highways and a minister.

Necip Tolon came back a geological engineer. He found phosphate stones used in artificial fertilizer.

Bahri Ersöz came back a metallurgical engineer. He worked for Karabük Iron and Steel.

Nüvit Arıcan returned a textile engineer and improved Sümerbank.

Adnan Erkmenol returned from his studies abroad as the country's first industrial engineer and was in charge of the General Directorate of Mineral Research and Exploration (MTA).

Bedrettin Sarp came back a mining engineer. He became the general director of the Coal Enterprises of Turkey.

Şükrü Topsakal studied abroad to become a mechanical engineer and later worked for the state railways, highways and the State Hydraulic Works (DSİ).

Seyfettin Saraçoğlu established shipyards after returning from abroad where he was trained as a naval architect.

Aziz Tanrısever returned as the country's first agricultural engineer.

Oktay Aslanapa returned as the country's first art historian.

Adnan Şener returned as the country's first chemical engineer.

Şahap Kocatopçu studied abroad and earned a doctorate in ceramics. He served as the minister of industry and director of TÜSİAD.

Sabahattin Eyüboğlu, Hamide Topçuoğlu, Refia Uğurel Şemin, Hasip Ahmet Aytuna, Vedide Baha Pars and Sabri Esat Siyavuşgil became educators and were part of the establishment of the Village Institutes.

"I send you all off as a spark and you should return as flames," Mustafa Kemal had told them.

They formed the brain team of the young republic and laid the groundwork for the construction of the country from scratch.

∞

In 1921, the Battle of Sakarya hadn't yet been fought. The occupiers were closing in on Ankara. Moving the Parliament to Kayseri was spoken of, and it was uncertain whether or not there would be a land left to call a country.

One hundred eighty teachers, 40 of them women, attended the congress at the Ankara Teachers School.

It was originally planned to run for 12 days, but was held for a week due to the beginning of the Greek offensive.

Mustafa Kemal left the front in that most critical period of the war, saying that the war against ignorance was no less important than a war against enemies. He went to Ankara and gave the opening speech at the congress:

"I advise the children of the homeland preparing for the future not to surrender to any hardship while they work with patience and maturity, and for parents to make all kinds of sacrifices for the education of their children. As with its weapons, our people must also fight with their minds, and I have absolutely no doubt that they will show as much force with the latter as with the former.

"This task falls to you, the teachers. I know our government hasn't been able to provide welfare for teachers, but I have no doubt that you will walk with fortitude as you perform the sacred duty of raising our nation. Your mission is very important and vital. I pray that God grants you success."

Distinguished teachers, such as İsmail Hakkı Tonguç, were sent for training in Germany immediately after the Education Congress. Tonguç went abroad during the middle of the War of Independence and later became the founder of the Village Institutes.

Mustafa Kemal was as relaxed as if he were watching a film. He behaved as if the War of Independence had already been won and the republic had already been declared at a time every corner of the country was occupied and the outcome was still uncertain.

There is no other leader in the history of the world who acted like this.

He was buying time while his environment was infused with self-confidence and while the foundation for the reforms that would be launched three years later were created step by step.

∞

He also didn't forget the disabled.

The republic was established in 1923, and its first school for the disabled was established in 1924.

The Organization for the Deaf, Mute and Blind opened in İzmir. It was given the İplikçizade Mansion in Karşıyaka.

(The İplikçizade Mansion had been Greek King Constantine's headquarters during the occupation. He had trampled the Turkish flag on the ground as he entered.

Mustafa Kemal came and stayed at the mansion for three nights. They laid out the Greek flag on the ground in retaliation. Mustafa Kemal had never liked this type of revenge. "A flag is the honor of a nation," he said. "It isn't possible for us to make the same mistake just because the Greek king has done it, so pick it up at once.")

(The İplikçizade Mansion had very high spiritual value and was allotted to the country's deaf and blind children. The occupiers had deemed this magnificent mansion worthy of a king and the revolutionaries deemed it worthy of Mustafa Kemal. Then it became the republic's first school for the disabled.)

Disabled children were trained in reading and speaking as well as fundamentals like mathematics and physics along with vocational lessons such as carpentry, welding, cobbling, tailoring and weaving. They were trained to be contributive and productive citizens for the republic. Music lessons were given to blind children—they were taught to play the piano, violin and flute; and a choir was established.

The first Turkish Medical Congress was held in 1925, one year after the foundation of the school.

Four disabled children were brought from the school in İzmir. They were to give a presentation about their education.

Mustafa Kemal sat in the front row. It was as if the entire hall held their breath and there wasn't a single noise. A deaf child came to the microphone. He had been taught to speak by mimicking sounds.

The name Gazi Mustafa Kemal Pasha came from his lips.

An uproarious applause erupted from the silent hall. Mustafa Kemal's eyes filled with tears. He stood up and applauded the disabled child. He hugged and kissed each one of them and congratulated them all.

He gave instructions to fill the gaps and remedy the deficiencies to further the training and education and so more children could benefit from it.

Turkey's first civil society organization for the disabled—the Support Society for the Deaf, Mute and Blind—was established, also in İzmir.

The republic had turned five years old. Mustafa Kemal changed the alphabet.

The Arabic script was loaded with religious meaning. All books written in Arabic were considered holy books. People thought that even ordinary documents printed with the Arabic script were related to Islam.

The people weren't literate. They were incapable of writing even the simplest petition or letter. Those who could write Arabic were perceived as men of God and those who could write a two-line letter were treated as if they were Islamic scholars. They turned this dark ignorance into opportunity and manipulated people as they wanted.

Mustafa Kemal had actually started thinking about the script while in Damascus in 1905. He had told Halide Edip Adıvar that the script needed changing while the War of Independence was still ongoing.

He had said that a Turkish alphabet was the key to reading and writing easily. "Our minds have been in an iron frame for centuries and we should save ourselves from these incoherent symbols we don't understand," he said about the Ottoman script. "We'll either do it in three months or not at all."

A campaign began in the entire country. The new alphabet with Latin letters was written on blackboards in parks and squares. There were no longer Arabic letters to confuse them; and it was so easy to learn, especially for children, that parents who never went to school taught it to their children.

Mustafa Kemal explained the situation:

"If those who know teach those who don't, then it will be an incredible value for the nation."

The population then was 13 million. In just a year, an unbelievable number of people, arround two million, learned how to read and write.

The new Turkish alphabet didn't only ensure that Turkish citizens were literate, it also made it possible for foreigners who already used the Latin alphabet to learn Turkish without encountering difficulties of an unfamiliar alphabet.

This universal aspect of the Alphabet Reform is not often addressed. While those who knew Ottoman Turkish around the world could barely be counted on one hand, there was a virtual explosion of foreigners who were literate in Turkish afterward due to the ease of learning the language with the new alphabet.

∞

It was Fikriye who chose the Çankaya Mansion.

There were three options. One was in Etlik, another in Keçiören and the other in Çankaya. Mustafa Kemal didn't have time to visit them. He sent Fikriye along with Ruşen Eşref. The one in Çankaya was a vineyard estate with two floors and a basement. It was rustic and built of stone. The floors and roof were made of wood and tiled. The windows had wooden shutters. There were two bedrooms each on the upper and lower floors. There was also a fountain with an ornamental pool in the middle of the ground floor. The grounds were covered with poplars and fruit trees. It was better cared for than the others and Fikriye liked it.

The mufti of Ankara, Börekçizade Rıfat, collected donations from the people. He bought the mansion for 4,500 liras and presented it as a gift.

Mustafa Kemal didn't accept it on his own behalf. He had the deed registered in the name of the Turkish Army.

There was no road; and horses were used to get there. A road was later paved through a field.

It had no electricity when it was bought. It was instead lit by kerosene lamps.

It was simple and far from ostentatious. It was, however, a spiritual jewelry box of sorts. There was a portrait in pencil of Osman Gazi—the founder of the Ottoman dynasty—hung in the study. Timur's 530-year-old Quran, which had been a gift from Persia, was in the library. There was an engraved, gold dagger on the table. A large, white bearskin rug was spread out on the floor that Russian Ambassador Semyon Aralov had brought.

Now, if you'd like, let me take you to 1930, and let's take a tour of Mustafa Kemal's Çankaya Mansion.

There was a Hereke carpet in the study. It was indigo with almond blossoms in the corners. The Ericson telephone on the table was white. The armchair was black, Moroccan leather. The writing set was bronze. There was a Telefunken radio and an RSA film projector. He had set up a portable film curtain on stands. He used a General Electric mini refrigerator. A crude generator called a *Lokomobil* had been connected. An electric stove heated the house. One coffee table had a bronze bust of Wagner and another had one of Shakespeare.

The dining room table was lacquered mahogany. It had three collapsible pieces and sat 10 people. The chairs had red upholstery. The utensils were gilded silver. The napkins were monogramed with *G.M.K.* There were six-candle, silver candelabras. The buffet was lacquered mahogany, like the table. There was a Longines clock in the shape of a mine sitting on the buffet along with seashells as ornaments. The curtains were beige. The carpet in the dining room was also from Hereke. It was cream colored and covered with pink flowers. There was a gramophone. The service cart in the shape of a gun carriage with three wheels was used for drink service.

The bedroom floor was covered from wall to wall with felt. It kept the room warm like a floor heater. On top of the felt was another Hereke carpet, this one red and covered with flowers. A chandelier with six arms and light bulbs lit the room. The bedstead was wood with yellow lacquer. There was a chaise longue. He never stretched out on the bed or couch when he felt tired during the day, and instead used the cream-colored, velvet chaise longue. The drapes were of the same velvet. The wardrobe had double doors. It was where he put his accessories like ties and hats. There was also a dressing room with a full-length mirror, which was where he kept his clothes.

There was a buff-colored prayer rug with flowers along the border.

The only safe in the Çankaya Mansion was in Mustafa Kemal's bedroom. He kept his medals and the gifts he received, such as a gold pen, gold watch, pearl cufflinks and a diamond tiepin in it. He never wore accessories or extravagant clothing in his daily life. He graciously accepted the gifts and kept them in trust of the people.

❋

He had also kept a 5 *kuruş* coin.

It was the first money struck in the republic. It had begun to circulate in 1924.

The 5 *kuruş* coin was designed by Mesrur İzzet Bey, who also designed the Medal of Independence. It was struck with Ottoman letters.

One face gave the value and Republic of Turkey was the obverse side. Ears of grain ran along the edge as a symbol of agricultural development.

Mustafa Kemal put the first coin the republic minted, and whose memory is priceless, into his safe as if it were a jewel.

It unfortunately has a sad story. The safe was opened after Mustafa Kemal passed away and the 5 *kuruş* coin found among the jewels was sent to the central bank to take it out of circulation and it disappeared.

❉

(The same happened to many of Mustafa Kemal's belongings after 1938. Most of the chairs for the tables at the Çankaya Mansion were distributed to schools and used as normal chairs around tables, going to waste without their value known.

The carpets on the list of his effects rotted in dank warehouses. They were destroyed in the 1960 and 1970s on the pretext they'd been abandoned and they were lost to history. Some were given to public institutions. They weren't registered and went to waste.

The carpets, armchairs, coffee tables, table clocks, chandeliers, lampshades and even sculptures Mustafa Kemal personally used were considered old and sold. There is no list of who bought what and for how much. What there is on display at Anıtkabir and Çankaya today isn't even half of Mustafa Kemal's personal effects. The rest went to waste.

It's unknown what happened to the gold watch and chain and clock from the dining room on the list of his belongings.

Among his missing effects are his shirts, shoes, hats and glasses.

The bathing suit he was wearing in the famous photograph taken of him swimming in Florya is lost. The silverware, pans and ladles from the kitchen are nearly all lost. Even Atatürk's dentures are missing. It's hard to believe, but even his pistols are missing.)

(He carried two pistols—a Smith & Wesson and a Colt. He always had them at his waist, especially when he was traveling. He even kept them under his pillow as he slept during the National Campaign. He carried these pistols since his youth, compulsory in his way of life, and continued to do so after he became president. When he wore a formal outfit for meals on hot summer nights or at outings, he gave them to his aide and took them back right after the event ended.

He was also a sharpshooter. He would stop the automobile in suitable terrain for target practice, saying they shouldn't let their marksmanship skill get rusty.

They had a conversation about pistols one night in Çankaya. "It's difficult to take aim at light bulbs," the interior minister, Şükrü Kaya, said. "The light throws you off." Then they put down bets. Mustafa Kemal drew his Smith & Wesson, held it with both hands and opened fire from where he was sitting, shot out two light bulbs in the chandelier. The bullets passed through the ceiling and lodged in the wardrobe in the bedroom on the upper floor. But let's keep moving.)

The poker room had felt from wall to wall. The table was round, the top was marble and it sat four people. There was a backgammon board inlaid with mother of pearl. A 21-light, crystal chandelier hung from the ceiling.

There was also wall to wall felt in the billiards room. The billiards table was mahogany. It was sold in 1960. It didn't have pockets and he played with three balls. The balls were ivory and the cues had inlaid mother of pearl. A two-part chandelier with six lights shone overhead. There was also a poker table in the billiards room. It was covered in green felt and had five corners and five drawers. Every corner had a place for the chips.

There was a cubic, Hereke carpet in the bath. The bathtub also had a shaving seat. The bathroom was covered with linoleum. There was a portable bidet that he brought along while traveling. There were instruments for measuring weight and height. The medicine cabinet had three shelves. The mirror on the wall was small and oval. There was a full-length mirror screwed to the door. There was a bronze figurine of a nude woman on a small, low table. He used soap from Edirne. The Edirne soap was in the shape of fruit and mixed with traditional fragrances like amber, rose and musk. They were very popular in Istanbul and he had them brought to Ankara.

It is striking how he presented himself while living under such large threats. If he had to, in order to protect himself, he would keep bullets on hand in his shaving soap case as he went from the bedroom to the bathroom.

There was a Hereke rug in the hallway that led to the rooms on the upper floor. The stairs leading to the second floor were covered with a Hereke runner.

❖

The guestroom where he hosted foreign visitors such as diplomats and journalists was fascinating. There were unique paintings hung on the walls.

There was *A Rough Sea* by the French painter Jean Baptiste Henri Durand-Brager, whose many works are found at the Palace of Versailles.

There were the paintings *Girls walking in fields* and *A young girl standing barefoot, wrapped in a shawl* by the Austrian painter Leopold Müller.

There was also *Arab Cavalry in Retreat* by the German painter Adolf Schreyer, most of whose pieces are with the Rockefeller family.

The French painter Ferdinand Humbert's *Tariq ibn Ziyad on horseback* was quite impressive.

The French painter Eduard Becher's *A bedouin* also hung there.

And of course, there was the Russian painter Ivan Konstantinovich Aivazovsky's *Ship in the stormy sea, Moonlight* and *Fishermen*.

❖

There was a grand piano in the guest room.

The rug was from Hereke. It was cream colored with floral designs in the corners. There was a glass-topped, oval table that sat eight people.

The armchairs and chairs at the table were upholstered with fabric with arboreal designs. The curtains were of the same fabric. There was also a showcase with a glass cover.

❈

His sword collection was also displayed in addition to the paintings.

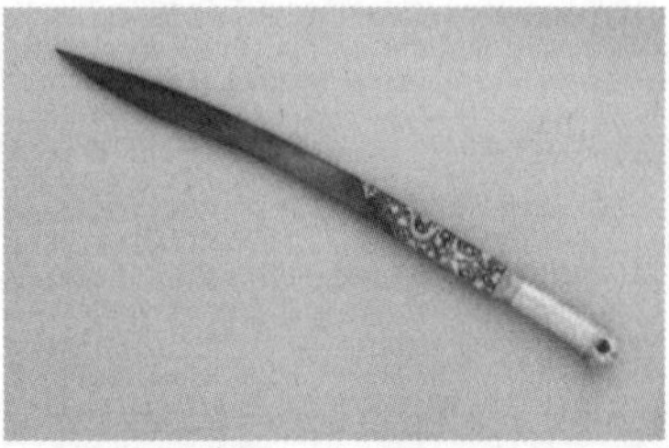

Foreign guests virtually quaked with excitement.

There was a scimitar with stone enamel and a leather scabbard. A Russian sword there had a gold hilt and was inlaid with diamonds. There was a dagger with gold inlay that was a gift from Azerbaijan. He had a shorter dagger with an ivory handle. There was a Persian sword with a hilt studded with diamonds. Another's hilt had a crescent and star and was inlaid with diamonds. There was a Japanese sword in a wooden sheath. There was Libyan mujahed Sheikh Ahmed Sharif as-Senussi's jeweled sword and also a scimitar from 1241.

The most important one was Sultan Süleyman the Magnificent's scimitar. It's now at Anıtkabir.

There was his bayonet and sheath from the War of Independence, a stone ax and a flintlock rifle.

❈

The table and chairs on the terrace were wicker.

A cave in the basement held a considerably rich collection of mostly French and German wines.

There was a compass in the library. There was a round magnifying glass called a loupe. A globe sat on a wooden pedestal. A coffee table also had a map on it.

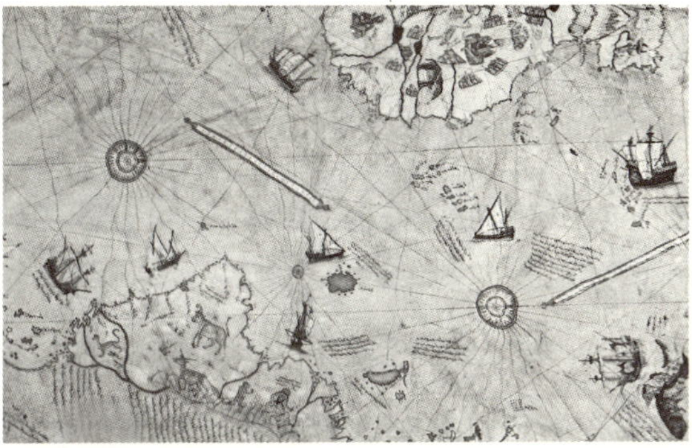

A map by Piri Reis was found in the inventory work done at Topkapı Palace as it was being turned into a museum. He had the map brought to Ankara in 1929, where he examined it and had it reproduced at the state printing houses. He placed one of the copies in his own library.

There was an ash-colored carpet from Isparta on the floor. Over that was a Hereke runner with brown bands. The table held 10 people and was covered with green cloth. There was also a writing desk with six drawers. The armchairs were of black leather. There was also a portable ladder to reach books, which went up to the ceiling.

One of his most remarkable ornamental objects was placed in the display case—a small box inlaid with mother of pearl and images of Hacivat and Karagöz on its sides.

The curtains were made of grey velvet. The clock on the wall was in the shape of a lion. An eight-bulb chandelier lit the room. There were lamps at the tables. There was also Hüseyin Avni Lifij's painting *Nude woman*.

The mansion's garage had five Chevrolet cars and a Ford truck that his aides and other personnel used.

(Architect Vedat Tek designed a project in 1924, and the mansion was enlarged. A new, two story section was added as an octagonal tower adjacent to the building. The heating system was installed in 1926. The German architect Holzmeister designed and built the Pink Pavilion next to it in 1932.)

He got bored in Çankaya. and would complain to his friends about it.

"You've imprisoned me in the rocks of Çankaya, saying I'm the president of the republic," he protested. "You all stroll along as you like, but look at me. My freedom is limited, but you go have fun. I'll console myself in fantasies."

He didn't like living in isolation from the people in the Çankaya Mansion and feared he'd become desensitized over time.

He used an example from his years at the Military Academy when expressing this concern:

"The stoves wouldn't light at the Military Academy when we were students and we shivered all winter. Then one day my friends chose me as the representative to go to the director. We got permission and came before the director, Zülüflü İsmail Pasha, who was a man of the palace. First, we extended our prayers to the sultan and then the director, and then we got to the point.

We wanted to explain, but with the first sentence the director roared, 'What cold, you ingrates? Shame on you, what with the blessings from the sultan. Don't you see the heating stoves burning away? Now clear out.' The stoves in the director's room truly burned brightly and he sweated away, thinking all the school's stoves were like that. I suppose that we here at the Çankaya Mansion delude ourselves sometimes the same way Zülüflü İsmail Pasha did."

∞

From 1881 to 1893 he was only Mustafa. Then he was Mustafa Kemal until 1916. From then on, he was Mustafa Kemal Pasha until 1921. Then, until 1934, he was Gazi Mustafa Kemal. He became Atatürk in 1934.

He took Atatürk as his surname.

A meeting was held with linguists and historians. They came up with the names

Etealp (Great Hero),
Etel-Etil (variant of Attila),
Korkut (Resolute),
Araz (Good Fortune—name of historical Turkic figure),
Ulaş (Exaltedness—name of historical Turkic figure),
Yazır (Virtuous—name of historical Turkic figure),
Emen (Spirit, Life—name of historical Turkic figure),
Çoğaş (Splendor, Light),
Salır (name of historical Turkic figure),
Begit (Powerful),
Ergin (Wisdom),
Tokuş (Resistance—name of historical Turkic figure)
Beşe (Estimable, Distinguished).

They presented the list to Mustafa Kemal. He said they should hold consultations. It was a polite way to say he didn't like them.

A meeting was held again. Erzincan parliamentarian Saffet Arıkan suggested Türkata. Konya parliamentarian Naim Hazım Onat said that it sounded strange and switched the words around to Atatürk

It was done.

He started using it before it became law.

The first time he used his surname was when he wrote it in the guest book of an exhibition opened by Sümerbank on November 8, 1934, 16 days before it was officially accepted in the Grand National Assembly of Turkey.

Sycophants entered the circle. They suggested changing Ankara's name to Atatürk. They had even prepared a draft law. He emphatically rejected it.

"History is a delicate fairy that does not like being forced," he said. "Look, Istanbul's name is Istanbul, but when we think of Istanbul, we immediately remember Mehmed the Conqueror. There is no need to take refuge in the foundations of the city for a word to remain in a language."

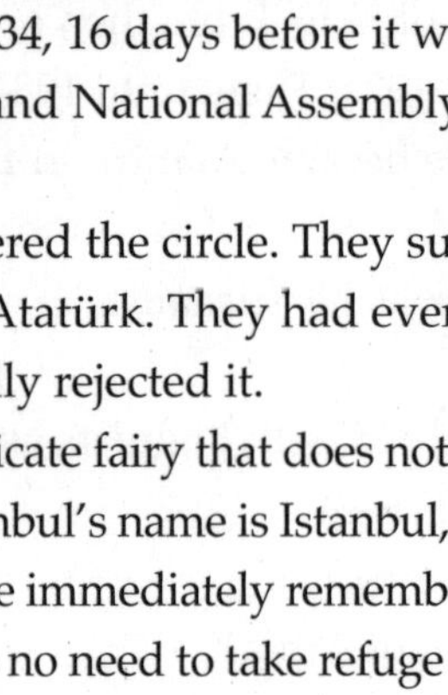

He changed his signature twice throughout his life. He did it once when the alphabet changed and again with the Surname Law.

In the Ottoman period, his signature was in a form that read *M. Kemal* in both Arabic and Latin script. It was the product of wit.

In Ottoman Turkish, read from right to left, it reads *M. Kemal*. The same signature reads his initials, *M.K*, in Latin letters from left to right. It had three hooks and looked like a bird of prey's talons.

With the Alphabet Reform, he changed it to *gazi m. kemal*.

He started using *k. atatürk* when he took the surname.

Hagop Vahram Çerçiyan designed the signature. He was a mathematics and geography teacher at Robert College. He had also studied calligraphy in the U.S. He prepared five different examples upon Mustafa Kemal's request. He presented them one by one. Mustafa Kemal chose *k. atatürk*.

He was registered in three cities—Göztepe, İzmir; Hacıbayram, Ankara; and Bey, Gaziantep.

∞

Eleftherios Venizelos.

He was nominated for a Nobel Peace Prize.

The prime minister of Greece, Eleftherios Venizelos, sent a letter to the Nobel Committee in 1934, that said:

Dear president,

The Near East and Central Europe has been the scene for bloody warfare for nearly seven centuries. The Republic of Turkey that was founded with Mustafa Kemal Pasha's national movement's victory over their rivals has put an end to this environment of uncertainty and intolerance.

Such radical change in the lives of a people over such a short time indeed rarely comes to pass.

An empire in decline that lived under a theocratic regime and mixed the concepts of law and religion was turned into a modern nation-state brimming with life and vitality.

The Near East has the foundation of peace.

We Greeks were dragged into bloody wars as a result of the ongoing conflicts with Turkey and were the first to feel the effects of the profound changes taking place in this country as the successor to the Ottoman Empire.

Turkey emerged from the war and was reborn as a nation-state immediately after the catastrophe of Asia Minor. It's to that Turkey to which we extended our hand with a sincere desire for peace, and it responded sincerely.

The man performing this invaluable contribution to peace is, of course, the president of the Republic of Turkey, Mustafa Kemal Pasha.

Therefore, as the leader of the Greek government of 1933, I am honored to propose Mustafa Kemal Pasha to be awarded the distinguished Nobel Peace Prize.

His humanitarian values along with his charisma even inspired Greece—and this is the Greece with which Turkey had gone into war and cast into the sea.

A Greek poet, Menelaos Nomdis, wrote a poem the same year titled *To Atatürk*.

It is you who shows what valor in battle is
And you again who delivers the power politics
Praise from the entire world falls on you
Do what you can in your beautiful homeland
Admiration is upon you and greetings

He was on the cover of *Time* magazine.

American newspapers used very severe words for the revolutionaries during the War of Independence, calling them barbarians, wild men, slaughterers and plunderers, and said Turks were a people incapable of managing themselves.

The New York Times conducted glowing interviews with the Greek King Constantine. They said Mustafa Kemal was a "brigand [who] will be wiped from the map like a fly."

They gave in. He was put on the cover in 1923. They used a photograph of him in which he wears his kalpak.

"He proved by a personal demonstration that a Turk can be his own master in Anatolia without having to wait for a better world," the article quoted from Professor Arnold J. Toynbee's book, *The Western Question in Greece and Turkey*. It also refers to Mustafa Kemal as "the Emancipator of Turkey".

Time put him on the cover again in 1927. It used a photograph of him as a civilian. This time the article explained the miracle of development and democracy. It said the young Republic of Turkey was breaking economic records and that while dictatorships were on the rise in Europe, Mustafa Kemal's democratic character was a role model for the entire world.

∞

The name of Mustafa Kemal was so prestigious around the world that scoundrels appeared to make a profit off of him.

Some advertised a normal, 100-franc sword for 10,000 francs with the claim that Mustafa Kemal had used it in Damascus.

Of those deceiving the Turks, there was someone in the U.S. who made up the story that he was Mustafa Kemal's aide and had been sent on a secret mission.

Another trying to con bankers and enter New York high society claimed he was Mustafa Kemal's nephew.

There were even those who bought an advertisement in Vienna newspapers that ran with the line: "Kemal Pasha and His Partners". They claimed to be an import-export company from central Turkey. The head of the firm was Ali Kemal—somehow Mustafa Kemal's brother.

Mustafa Kemal, little Ülkü, Nuri Conker.

He didn't have a brother.
He did, however, have friends who were more than siblings.

One was Nuri Conker.

They were childhood friends from the neighborhood and school, and they were brothers in arms.

He was the only person other than his mother and wife who could address him as Kemal.

He was one year younger.
He was a comrade and a confidant.

He was always there for with Mustafa Kemal in Conkbayır, as he had been his entire life, when he was seriously wounded in the temple. Mustafa Kemal gave him the surname Conker.

(The *conk* in Conkbayır has the meaning *to get together, chat and laugh*. They used the verbs *conguldaşmak* and *conklaşmak*—both meaning to sit, talk and have fun—in Gallipoli and Balıkesir.

Nuri Conker showed great heroism at the Battle of Conkbayır (Chunuk Bair), which was one of the bloodiest at Gallipoli, and, of course, was far from anything one could describe as enjoying oneself. It aptly fit Conker's character, as he was always cheerful and talkative.)

Whether with the Action Army, at Tripoli, Gallipoli, the Muş front or the War of Independence, if Mustafa Kemal was there, so was Nuri Conker.

He could have been a pasha himself. He could have been a minister. He could have been the speaker of Parliament. He didn't want any of it, though. He preferred to remain a friend. He never abused or misused their friendship.

There was always the same sight when the lights came back on after a power cut. There was Conker, standing with gun in hand, ready to use his body to shield Mustafa Kemal.

A knock came at the door the evening of his 50th birthday—it was Mustafa Kemal. It was a surprise, as he hadn't given notice beforehand. "I came to wish you a happy birthday," he said and sat down. Then he drove Conker mad all night by saying that he doesn't have anything to do with the elderly and that he no longer speaks with them. He cheerfully chatted with Conker's family and they cracked up laughing. He didn't say a word to Conker, not even when the man asked him a question, and left chuckling, as he had arrived.

He loved making Conker mad.

He never took anyone's money when they played poker, but if Conker lost, he would take every single *kuruş* and then poke fun at him.

Conker came home one night wearing a black overcoat, its sleeves were very tight around the elbows and shoulders. His wife asked what was wrong. It turns out they had been playing poker and Conker had lost again.

He had paid up and as he left the Çankaya Mansion to Mustafa Kemal's laughter, had said, "I'll take your overcoat and we'll be even." There was a difference in weight and size of belly between them, hence the tightness.

Mustafa Kemal wouldn't sit at the table without Conker. He only ever put up with Conker's whims. Only Conker had the privilege to raise his voice. His voice was already quite low and he would shout loudly. He would also pound his fist on the table as he talked when he was very angry.

They drank together and they sang together.

To tease his opponents, he would sometimes say that he would resign and nominate Conker as a candidate, saying he would make a splendid president. Conker would say that he was ready for duty, and moreover, would take half the salary as Mustafa Kemal.

Mustafa Kemal was often asked questions about his childhood. "Who knows what an exceptional person you were as a child and who knows what extraordinary and wondrous memories you have," he would say to their wonderment.

At times like this, he would point to Conker and say, "Nuri will explain."

As always, Conker would wryly say: "He herded crows in the bean field."

It was a code they had between themselves.

People would grumble when they heard Conker mention a "crowherd" and attempt to protest, but Mustafa Kemal would jump back in and tell them not to try to make his childhood seem superhuman, saying that he'd had a childhood like the rest of them.

This is the source for the cliché found in nearly all Atatürk biographies that says they would chase crows in the bean fields.

It was a result of Conker and Mustafa Kemal's setup.

They didn't mean to say that Mustafa Kemal was actually chasing crows, but that he was a child like everyone else. They tried to explain that there was no need to exaggerate and butter up the story.

This wry expression from Conker has been turned around on itself and entered Atatürk biographies as if it were a cold, hard fact.

Nuri Conker died of a heart attack in 1937. Mustafa Kemal was devastated.

He didn't attend the funeral. He didn't even give his condolences so he wouldn't have to see his friend's house. He never even stepped foot again in the district where Conker had lived and tried to avoid everything that reminded him of his friend.

He was in thought one evening as he ate his dinner. He suddenly jumped up, got into his car and gave directions to his driver without saying where he was going. They got to Cebeci, where he told his driver to stop. He had come to Conker's grave. He walked to the gravestone and stood there in silence.

Then he said one thing: "Why have you left me alone?"

He stood silently for a while longer and, exhausted, returned to the car. He never returned to the grave.

According to Mustafa Kemal, Conker was a brother whose memory would never leave his heart or mind.

All his friends married young. Mustafa Kemal had no intention to do the same.

He sent a letter of congratulations to Fuat Bulca upon his marriage:

"My brother Fuat, I wish you happiness. Marriage is a level of maturity in life. My name may be Kemal [which means maturity], but I haven't reached that level yet."

He translated the poem *Peu de Chose et Presque Trop* by Belgian poet Léon Montenaeken in a letter he wrote to Salih Bozok:

Life is futile:
A little love,
A bit of hate—
And then—good day!

Life is short:
A little hope,
A little dream—
And then—good evening!

Life is such
That God has made,
And, as it is,
It is enough!

He finished it by saying: "My brother Salih, remember these lines and embrace them in how you understand life."

The idea of establishing a family didn't fit his temprament.

"I've had a certain nature since I was a child," he once said. "I didn't like being at home with my mother, sister or pals. I have always preferred being alone and untethered, and I've always lived as such. There's another strange thing about me. My father died very young, and I had no tolerance for the advice my mother, sister and close relatives would give in one way or another according to their own mindsets. Those who lived with family knew well enough they couldn't be saved from the very pure and sincere remarks and warnings."

Sabiha Sultan.

He had just returned from his trip to Germany with the then Crown Prince Mehmed. He was about to go to Carlsbad for treatment when there was a surprise. Mehmed's attendant in charge of his prayer rug, İbrahim Efendi, came and started talking about it with Mustafa Kemal's aide Cevat Abbas.

He said the crown prince wanted to see Mustafa Kemal married and was thinking about giving his daughter Sabiha Sultan's hand to him in marriage.

Mustafa Kemal heard it. He postponed his answer until after his treatment.

Mehmed VI ascended to the throne while he was in Carlsbad.

The new sultan's sister Münibe Sultan went to Salih Fansa's house on İstiklal Caddesi.

Salih Fansa and Mustafa Kemal had been friends since they were in Aleppo. He often went to the Fansas for dinner and would stay overnight. Salih Fansa's wife, Selma, was a close friend of Münibe Sultan.

"His Highness sent me here," she said. "He wishes that his daughter Sabiha Sultan marry Mustafa Kemal. You tell him of the matter and I'll get word from you in two days."

Sabiha Sultan was one of Mehmed VI's two daughters. She was 24 years old.

Doctor Rasim Ferid was the best eyewitness as to what happened afterward. Mustafa Kemal valued his friend's views, and took him aside one night on the way back from a party. He mentioned the matter concerning Sabiha Sultan and asked Ferid what he thought about it.

Ferid didn't mince his words: "You would be subject to the ceremonies weighing on you in married life to the sultan's daughter. You would have to ask permission just to see her. You would grow tired of such a marriage and be fed up in two months."

Mustafa Kemal burst out laughing: "You're my one true friend, doctor. Everyone else pushes me to do it."

He sent back word with Münibe Sultan's intermediary: "Let Sabiha Sultan do the honor and grace us with a meeting."

Of course, it wasn't going to happen. It was unimaginable for a sultan's daughter to leave the palace to go to her prospective husband's house. This impossible offer signaled the intended meaning without saying outright that he didn't want to marry her.

Another night around the same time, he was going down the Akaretler hill with Rasim Ferid. Mustafa Kemal stooped over slightly when they got to the corner of the Vişnezade Mosque. "Doctor, there's a pistol in my left jacket pocket," he said. "Take it now and cock it." With this, he pulled his other pistol from his right pocket, turned around to the man following them and yelled for him to freeze.

The man following behind them was named İdris. He was a stout sergeant. He panicked with Mustafa Kemal's sudden movement and dropped his pistol as he tried to draw it. Rasim Ferid picked up the would-be assassin's pistol from the ground and drove the man in front of them to the house in Akaretler.

He admitted that he'd been assigned to kill Mustafa Kemal.

Mustafa Kemal was targeted because he had a great reputation in Mehmed VI's view, and he wanted him to marry one of the princesses at the palace. In particular, Enver Pasha, who had married one of the princesses, was enraged with him.

They didn't know of Mustafa Kemal's patriotic ideals and, like themselves, thought he was out for personal gain.

Sabiha Sultan married Prince Ömer Faruk Efendi, son of the last caliph, Abdülmecid II. They had three daughters. She was sent into exile in 1924. She lived in Switzerland, France and Egypt, and got divorced in 1948. She settled in Istanbul and became a Turkish citizen, taking the surname Osmanoğlu in 1952, when the women from the Ottoman dynasty were allowed to enter Turkey. She passed away in Yeniköy in 1971, and is buried in the Aşiyan cemetery.

Münibe Sultan brought the one photograph Mustafa Kemal saw of Sabiha Sultan.

Sabiha Sultan, though, had seen Mustafa Kemal in person. She explained those days to her close friends years later: "I saw him once and liked him. He was very handsome. His eyes were like fire, burning with flames, but I loved Faruk."

Those who wanted to belittle Mustafa Kemal distorted the whole matter of marriage between him and Sabiha Sultan in the books they wrote years later. They intentionally created confusion and spoke as if it had been Mustafa Kemal who had proposed the marriage and not Mehmed VI. Anyone who knows a bit of Ottoman history would know quite well that no one could ask for the sultan's daughter's hand in marriage without first receiving the sultan's blessing.

∞

Latife.

He married Latife five years later.

He was 42. Latife was 24.

There wasn't a ceremony where he would ask for her hand. He proposed in person. He didn't meet his father-in-law until the day of the wedding.

The mufti of Izmir was called in his capacity as a *qadi* (Islamic judge). They didn't kneel. They sat at a table.

Latife wore a plain, dark grey dress she had bought in Paris. She had a white, silk veil over her head. Of course, she had wanted to wear a white wedding dress, but it was the period of mourning for Zübeyde. She had to compromise on, the happiest day of her life.

Mustafa Kemal wore a three-piece, navy suit. He had picked out a red tie. He had a white, linen handkerchief in his breast pocket. He also wore an Astragan kalpak.

The witnesses for the bride were Salih Bozok and the governor of Izmir, Abdülhalik Renda. The groom's witnesses were Fevzi Çakmak and Kazım Karabekir.

Weddings were traditionally held on Thursdays at the time. They got married on Monday. Traditionally, there weren't women at weddings and there would be a representative in place of the bride.

They broke that practice, too. Latife was present at her own wedding.

Mustafa Kemal gave his wife a handwritten Quran in a gold case the size of a matchbox and an agate brooch. Latife gave her husband a silver cigarette case and a silver tiepin.

They organized a tea party for after the wedding. There were about 50 guests. Sweets were served and food was distributed to the poor.

Latife had been born in Izmir in 1899. Her name at birth was Fatma Zehra. She was the daughter of Muammer Bey, who was an arbiter of tobacco and cotton on the American and British stock exchanges, mayor of Izmir and the richest merchant in the city. Her primary education was given at home by British and German tutors. She attended junior high and high school at the American College for Girls in Arnavutköy, Istanbul.

She furthered her schooling at the Tudor Hall School in Oxfordshire, England. She was a student of Halide Edip Adıvar and had classes from Tevfik Fikret and Halit Ziya Uşaklıgil.

She spoke English at a native level and was advanced in German, French and Persian. She also knew Greek and Italian.

She was a pianist. She was an excellent rider and sat on the saddle like a cavalryman. She also later studied politics and law at the Sorbonne.

Her family had moved to France when the country was under occupation. They lived on the coastal paradise of Biarritz along the Atlantic. She was far from danger, but it grieved this free, 23 year old to be living abroad while her home country was being battered. She threw in everything and told her father she couldn't stay there any longer. She left university as soon as she found out the Battle of Sakarya had been won and returned to Izmir by ship from Marseille. Her grandfather Sadık Bey had had a summer mansion built in Göztepe, which is where she stayed once she got back.

The medallion on her chest bore a photograph of Mustafa Kemal wearing a kalpak that she had cut out from a French newspaper.

The flowers bloomed on the mountains of Izmir on September 9.

A fire started in the Armenian neighborhood, which is now the culture park. Those who inflicted this last evil on Izmir predicted the fire would spread to the Turkish neighborhood with the offshore winds. However it blew in the opposite direction. It an that up in the Levantine neighborhood, Punta, all the way to Kordon after Alsancak was destroyed.

Salih Bozok traveled around Güzelyalı with a small cavalry troop looking for a building that hadn't been touched by fire to use as a headquarters for the chief command.

He found the summer mansion in Göztepe.

It was as if Latife's heart skipped a beat. She chased her dream Mustafa Kemal to Izmir. And now Mustafa Kemal came to Izmir.

Beautiful İzmir, later rebuilt from its ashes, burned like a torch in the dark evening.

The car carrying Mustafa Kemal entered the mansion's yard, which had purple wisteria and smelled of sweet violets.

Latife greeted him at the door. "The Turkish nation has attained its desire with your arrival in İzmir," she said. "I also find I've attained my desire with you honoring my house. I am grateful. Welcome, Pasha."

A table was prepared on the terrace. There was Mustafa Kemal, İsmet Pasha, Fevzi Pasha, Ruşen Eşref, Falih Rıfkı and Yakup Kadri. The food was delicious. None of them would forget the calamari, above all else, so etched in their memory. Everyone filled their glasses, except Fevzi Pasha.

As soon as Mustafa Kemal returned, he sent the Arabian horse he had used throughout the National Campaign to Latife in Sakarya as a wedding present.

At the same time, it was also a thank you, since he had sent his mother to Izmir and entrusted her to Latife.

Zübeyde didn't much like the future bride and made it known quite clearly, although Latife didn't resent her and treated her like her own mother.

They held the wedding ceremony on January 29, 1923. They didn't go on a honeymoon afterward.

Mustafa Kemal made his decision to get married with his heart, but he determined the date of the marriage with his mind.

The negotiations in Lausanne were ongoing.

Latife was covered widely in European newspapers due to her having a much more advanced level of education than Western women and being a role model for Turkish Muslim women. She amused sympathy. She was the face of modern Turkey. She changed the perception of Ankara. She both strengthened Turkey's image and the Turkish delegation in Lausanne. It was in this sense that the date of their marriage was so important.

Mustafa Kemal didn't call her Latife. He would say Latif instead. And with that, called her his female aide-de-camp.

He would make pretexts to honor her in crowded places. In such environments, he would ask her to recite some Byron or Hugo. He was proud of his wife's cultured background.

Latife would rise early and take notes as she read the local, foreign-language newspapers and summarized the news from the agencies. Then at breakfast, she would report on them to Mustafa Kemal.

She accompanied her husband on trips throughout the country, emboldened women in Anatolia against bigotry, watched sessions of Parliament from the area set aside for foreign diplomats, and played the piano and sang Mustafa Kemal's favorite songs on some jovial evenings.

She addressed him as Kemal.

She never called him Gazi or president of the republic when she spoke with people when her husband wasn't there. Instead she would say that Kemal made such a decision or Kemal has gone off to some place—always Kemal.

She wasn't just his partner. She was his equal. The first vote for a woman was for her even before women had the right to vote and be elected. The first general election in Turkey was held in June 1923. She received votes in Izmir and Konya even though she wasn't a candidate and, according to the law, there was no possibility for her to be one.

She sent a telegram of thanks in which she said, "I would like to express my enthusiasm and gratitude for the votes for me in the parliamentary election, not for myself, but in appreciation of Turkish women."

She was a signal flare for women's rights.

She brought her nanny and cook to Ankara. She started refurnishing the Çankaya Mansion to her liking with the furniture and domestic items she'd had brought from Izmir. The bed set, for example, was in Louis XV style, which was a work of art in itself. All the bedding, from sheets to pillows, was yellow. The bathroom was covered in white marble. She had the armchairs removed from the guestroom and had them replaced with blue armchairs she had brought back from France.

She would host the wives of the pashas, parliamentarians and journalists on Saturday afternoons. She would prepare tables of pastries and cookies and tea was served standing. These were all things previously unheard of in Ankara. The items she pulled from her dowry chest were mesmerizing—crystal glasses, silver cutlery and embroidered tablecloths.

Her wardrobe had clothing from Paris and Milan. The women who came to visit couldn't take their eyes off her dresses, shoes and especially the four-karat ring with one stone her father, Muammer Bey, had given her. Her grace and hosting were superb.

She was happy. The vineyard estate that she found quite boring and felt lonely in when she first saw, she now looked upon as her nest.

The good days didn't last long, unfortunately. Domestic tranquility faded with two dominant characters and two free spirits.

The dog Mustafa Kemal had by his side since the War of Independence, Alber, gave birth one late afternoon and he looked cheerfully on the lovable puppies. He lost himself in it so much he said, "Look, Fikriye, how wonderfully they play."

Then a severe crisis arose.

Latife felt faint hearing Mustafa Kemal refer to her as Fikriye. She wired her father to come get her at once. Muammer Bey came right away. He managed to calm his daughter, but it was the beginning of the end.

She began to be intrusive, thinking she would bring order to Mustafa Kemal's life. She tried to impose bans.

The rules she imposed bothered Mustafa Kemal. As a young, social woman who grew up in the Levantine culture of Izmir and then in London and Paris, Latife felt constricted in the steppe town of Ankara and got ill-tempered.

Fikriye's tragic death was the kicker. Mustafa Kemal and Latife's marriage, which had been shaken to its foundations, couldn't recover after Fikriye's suicide.

They started to fight. Their discord had become so unpalatable that once, Mustafa Kemal angrily stepped out of the Çankaya Mansion and yelled, "I'll either leave this house or pour gasoline on it and burn it down!"

There were nearly no more quiet and peaceful evenings. They couldn't stand it any longer.

Mustafa Kemal would often throw himself out the door, running to his official car and calling out to his driver to take him to Yozgat.

Going to Yozgat meant going to the Marmara Mansion. It was his house in the Forest Farm.

The nights he spent out increased.

They got divorced. Their marriage lasted two years, six months and four days.

The *One Thousand and One Nights* since they met had come to an end.

She had left Izmir as Latife Gazi Mustafa Kemal and came back as Latife.

In his last letter to her, Mustafa Kemal wrote:

To Mrs. Uşakizade Latife,

According to the certain perception I have had in the two and a half years of our common life, I have realized for certain and without a doubt that there will be no opportunity to find happiness, especially for you, if we continue with this life and I have found it appropriate to let you go free. I present you with the divorce papers, madam.

President of Turkey Gazi M. Kemal

He also wrote a letter to Latife's family:

To Mr. Uşakzade Muammer and Mrs. Adeviye,

According to the certain impression that has grown within me during the two and a half years of our shared life together in wedlock with your respectable daughter, Mrs. Latife, it is my deep conviction that continuing with this life will make it impossible, particularly for your respectable daughter, to find happiness. With this, I have seen it as appropriate to free the aforementioned person.

I extend my very special respects and have sent the divorce papers to her.

President of Turkey Gazi M. Kemal

His father-in-law Muammer had the most poignant remark on it all: "My daughter thought she married the president of the republic. She wasn't aware she'd married Mustafa Kemal."

When Latife's sisters came to the Çankaya Mansion to collect her personal belongings, Mustafa Kemal had a request for them. He asked, if she didn't mind, whether he could keep some of Latife's books in the mansion's library and he gave them a list. They asked Latife and she agreed.

He asked for her 13-volum set of Voltaire; Victor Hugo's *Les Misérables*; a biography of Napoleon; books on world history, the British Isles, the Roman Empire; a book on theater; and one on the people of the world. They were all in French.

Only the books they had both read remained as a memory of the happy days at the Çankaya Mansion.

It was November 10, 1938. Latife was in Switzerland. She was at a hospital in Bern, undergoing treatment for pneumonia. She was reading a newspaper. She later described that moment: It felt like "I was shot in the head. ... I've died twice—once in 1925 and again in 1938."

She never remarried. She had offers. She didn't even consider them.

She asked to be employed at a Turkish embassy in any country. She was respectfully declined. She was told that Atatürk didn't want family members to be employed in the state, and she dropped the request.

The brutal order of the male-dominated society came into play. If one were to get divorced, then the blame always fell on the woman and never the man. And if this man was Mustafa Kemal, then the woman stood no chance.

Latife was all of a sudden left alone. She started to get a bad name. Even her close friends stopped calling and asking about her. She heard unjust remarks said behind her back, which increased her sadness.

She wanted to run far away. She went to what is now Slovakia and rested at a sanatorium in the Tatra Mountains. She also lived in Nice, France, for nearly two years.

She eventually settled in Istanbul. She stayed for a short while in a mansion in Ayaspaşa that belonged to her family. In 1965, she moved to the Safir Apartments in Harbiye.

She had lived in mansions her entire life and was accustomed to large gardens, so why did she choose to live in an apartment?

She pointed from the window as if to say to look. Right across from the window was the Harbiye Officer's Club with a statue of Atatürk standing in front of it.

"This statue is the most faithful of them all in its depiction and looks very much like him," she explained once. "I watch him from here. If I didn't, why would I live in an apartment?"

She didn't put out the photographs of her and Atatürk together. There were only pictures of Atatürk on the wall and coffee table. She didn't present even one item from their marriage.

It was asked for 50 years and she always refused. She didn't write her memoirs or explain anything.

She was a close friend of the İnönü family. She very much loved Mevhibe.

After İsmet İnönü became president, she was often invited to dinner at Dolmabahçe Palace and would sometimes stay the night. She would kiss İsmet İnönü's forehead whenever they saw each other.

She was always stylish. Her favorite color was black. She never removed the ring with a single diamond her father had given her.

She didn't shut herself off at home. She never gave up traveling and going abroad. A passport was arranged for her under the name Fatma Sadık—a request from Atatürk so she wouldn't be recognized or disturbed. She used the identity Fatma Sadık instead of Latife Uşaki while she was abroad.

She wouldn't miss concerts or the theater. She bought a season seat for the Kenter Theater. She also would go to the cinema in Beyoğlu.

She minded what she ate and drank and didn't gain weight.

She never dyed her hair and it shone a brilliant white. She wore it in a bun and always held it in place with an ivory comb.

She had a fabulous library. She read Shakespeare, Goethe, Schiller and Corneille in their original languages. She knew Tevfik Fikret, Ahmet Haşim and Yahya Kemal by heart.

After she turned 50, she learned Russian. She adored Pushkin.

She loved giving gifts, as well. Her personal problems, though, were something she never spoke of to those around her.

She had an old, local Greek woman as a servant. Her cook was İrfan Hanım. She didn't have a driver and instead used taxis.

She got breast cancer in later life. She passed away in 1975, at the age of 76.

There was a notice of her passing in *Milliyet* and *Cumhuriyet* newspapers. It mentioned her grandfather, father, mother and siblings.

There was no mention of Atatürk.

She didn't have a state funeral. No one from the government attended, either.

He family draped a Turkish flag over her coffin. The funeral prayer was done at the Teşvikiye Mosque. She was then buried at the Martyrs Cemetery in Edirnekapı.

She had two safe deposit boxes, one at Ziraat Bank and one at the Ottoman Bank. Due to a court case among her family members over the inheritance, the boxes were only opened by court decision four years after her death. The heirs gave the documents related to the history of the republic to the Turkish Historical Society.

Her wedding ring was among her personal belongings. It was platinum. On the inside, it was inscribed in Ottoman Turkish: "Latife 1339".

In addition to the ring were 10 silver *para* coins Mustafa Kemal had given her as *mahr*—a mandatory payment in Islam by the groom to the bride—at the time of their wedding. The ring and silver coins were wrapped in a sheet of pink paper, placed in her jewelry box and then that was wrapped in muslin.

A very thin platinum ring had also been found among Atatürk's personal effects after he passed away. On the inside, it was inscribed in Ottoman Turkish: "Gazi M. Kemal 1339".

They had returned each other's rings when they got divorced.

These wedding rings they had kept until the end of their lives had been a gift from İsmet İnönü. He had brought them from Lausanne.

Latife's jewelry was worth a fortune. She also owned three properties: an apartment in Istanbul and a mansion in İzmir, as an office building in the city. She had inherited all of them from her father.

Vienna University—one of the oldest in Europe—opened an exhibition on the subject of gender equality. Thirty-six pioneering women were selected as role models in a worldwide assessment.

Busts of them were placed in a courtyard at the university.

Latife was one of those 36 women from around the world.

Among them were Mary Magdalene, Marie Curie, Mileva Einstein, Frida Kahlo, Elisabeth Oppenheim, Sylvia Plath, Virginia Woolf, Josephine Baker, Maria Callas, Sara Baartman, Ana Mendieta, Hatshepsut, Janis Joplin, Sappho, Maria Montessori, Pope Joan, Gertrude Stein, Susan Sontag and Latife.

Turkey virtually brushed Latife to the side. For the wider world, though, she was esteemed as a role model.

∞

Fikriye.

Fikriye was born in 1887

She was a niece of Zübeyde's second husband, Ragıp Bey. She had known Mustafa Kemal since she was 9.

Both of her parents were deceased. She had a brother and a sister. They migrated to Istanbul when Salonika was lost. They lived on Büyükada—one of the Princes' Islands. Her older brother Enver went to Anatolia to join the National Campaign and her younger sister Jülide died of tuberculosis. She was alone and petrified.

Cevat Abbas was Mustafa Kemal's aide. Fikriye had an intimate friendship with Cevat Abbas' wife, Memduha, and moved in with her.

She often went to Akaretler in Beşiktaş. She would go to visit Makbule with Zübeyde.

Mustafa Kemal was friends with Fuat Bulca, who was Fikriye's cousin. She wrote a letter to Fuat in which she said she wanted to come to Ankara.

The Steering Building needed a woman's touch.

Mustafa Kemal approved it with support from Fuat Bulca and Cevat Abbas.

She went to İnebolu on a motorized fishing boat. From there, she went by horse-drawn carriage to Ankara.

She was tall, delicate and had dark hair and eyes.

Halide Edip, Salih Bozok, Kılıç Ali and Sabiha Gökçen all recalled her as being very beautiful.

Her father was a colonel and a modern-minded man. He employed private tutors for his daughters, and as such, they knew French and Russian.

She was a bookworm who particularly loved to read history. She also played piano and ud and would sing folksongs from Rumelia.

She gleamed when she wanted to in the most crowded of places, radiant and drawing everyone to her like a magnet. She could also be transparent when she wanted and her presence wouldn't even be felt in an empty room.

I have read thousands of pages about the people in Mustafa Kemal's close circle. I haven't seen any one of them not liking Fikriye, saying something negative about her or even not completely admiring her.

She had been married. She was married when she was 16 to an Egyptian merchant. Before a year passed, though, she had already returned to her father's house.

Her thin body carried a warrior's spirit. She rode horses and shot guns. In the uncertain, final days of the National Campaign, she had the courage to go to Anatolia amid the most difficult of wartime conditions.

She was in love.

She had Mustafa Kemal's amber *tespih* made into a necklace. She never removed it.

He had brought it back from his first assignment in Damascus as a gift for her and she had set it safely aside as if it were precious stone.

Her hair was uncovered in photographs from even before the foundation of the republic. She didn't wear a headscarf even when she was around the aides and soldiers. On the streets, she generally wore a beret that didn't even cover all of her hair. It was considered an obscenity in that period, but she wore trousers without a care.

Her room in the Steering Building was on the second floor. There was only a kerosene lamp, an armchair and a school bedstead with a straw mattress laid out. It was empty, with nothing else. There wasn't even a rug.

There was one toilet in the building. The commanders and aides used it throughout the day. She was forced to wait until midnight, after they'd all left, to use it.

She lived like this for two and a half years.

After her time at the Steering Building, she spent a year at the Çankaya Mansion.

There are many photographs of her taken by military photographer Esat Nedim Tengizman, but not even one with Mustafa Kemal. She was the only person who was near Mustafa Kemal for such a long time and not have an image to show for.

She organized the kitchen, laundry and cleaning while she was there. The semolina halva she distributed among the guards was famous. She bought drapery fabric and sewed them herself. She also planted flowers in the garden.

She was the first hostess for the dinner table at the Çankaya Mansion.

She built a family environment. The commanders who would come to the mansion for meetings began to come with their wives, as if they were coming as guests.

She called Zübeyde auntie and looked on her as if she were her own mother.

She rode over the hillcrests and along the ridges of Çankaya on the horse, Zafer (Victory), that Mustafa Kemal had given her. She wouldn't take a security detail and instead would bring along a rifle.

Her health was failing, though. She was diagnosed with tuberculosis. Unfortunately, she was also a heavy smoker. A decision was made to send her to Europe for treatment.

In fact, the treatment process was a pretext, as Mustafa Kemal had decided to get married. Latife was going to come and it wouldn't be right for her and Fikriye to be under the same roof.

Mustafa Kemal brought her to the train station. She by chance ran into Halide Edip Adıvar, who later described the parting: "She looked very weak and sick in her fur coat. She even had difficulty mustering the strength to smile and her face was masked with anguish."

She headed to the sanatorium in Munich by way of Paris. "I didn't want to go, but the pasha insisted," she said.

She learned Mustafa Kemal got married while she was in Munich. She wept and was inconsolable. She left the treatment halfway through and returned to Istanbul at once.

She found a totally different atmosphere when she returned. The women who had until recently whirled around her and entertained her at tea parties as if they were ceremonies, suddenly wouldn't even turn to look at her. There was no one calling on her or asking about her.

Latife was in fashion now.

Fikriye was isolated. The disloyalty and hypocrisy had sent her already sensitive emotions flying.

She stayed with relatives for 14 months. They reckoned she'd accepted reality. She got a ticket without anyone knowing and took the train to Ankara. She went to the door of the Çankaya Mansion.

Latife was home.

The rumors had already been pushing her limit of tolerance.

Latife yelled that she didn't want to ever see her.

Fikriye wasn't allowed to see Mustafa Kemal.

She turned to the waiting coach at the door. Her grief could be seen in her eyes—she'd broken down. The coach pulled away from the door. She pulled out the Browning pistol with the mother of pearl handle that had been a gift from Mustafa Kemal. She pointed it at her heart and pulled the trigger.

She fell bleeding from the coach.

She was still alive.

They took her to Numune Hospital. According to the head physician, Ömer Aybat, the bullet had perforated her left lung and damaged the outer membrane of her heart.

She had difficulty breathing, but it was taken for granted that she would survive.

She pulled through for a week. Everything returned to normal. Then, unfortunately, she got a high fever. Her pneumonia returned and she fell into a coma. She was able to hold on for two days. She died nine days after pulling the trigger.

She was 37.

Hakimiyet-i Milliye and *Vatan* newspapers of the time published that a woman named Zeynep Fikriye had committed suicide.

One reported: "She was a distant relative to his Highness the President. Due to her lack of close family and her illness, she enjoyed two and a half years of Gazi Pasha's patronage and assistance as an object of honor."

It was one column on the third page. That was all.

It's unknown where her grave is.

She was buried at the foot of a willow tree beside a stream that flowed through Çankaya, close to where Kuğulu Park stands today.

Salih Bozok—Mustafa Kemal's black box of sorts—prepared the burial. The burial area was confirmed by Bozok's relatives, according to the details they had heard.

Latife also told her close friends about what she had heard that the grave was beside the stream running through Çankaya.

According to Mustafa Kemal's sister Makbule, Latife loved Atatürk, but Fikriye loved Mustafa Kemal. One was in love with the result and the other with the reason.

Sabiha Gökçen spoke more openly:

"There are things I've heard and witnessed while he spoke with friends. There's absolutely no doubt Atatürk was interested in Fikriye Hanım, but he didn't think of marriage. If he had, he would have married her instead of keeping her. In my own way, I always wish he had married Fikriye Hanım."

Latife, though, was realistic as usual. About Fikriye's suicide, she said, "It was the power of madness of a woman in love."

∞

Dimitrina Kovacheva.

Mustafa Kemal was between two women.

Actually, though, his heart had been left in Sofia a very long time ago.

It was 1914, and Mustafa Kemal was a strapping young man.

He was a military attaché, had just moved, and had no friends. He would sit alone in the pastry shops of Bulgaria and in the evenings go to the opera or theater.

He got an invitation to the City Club. That's where he met Dimitrina Kovacheva.

They called her Miti for short. She was gorgeous. She'd studied music in Switzerland and knew three languages. She was also high society's most prized bachelorette.

The Blue Danube was played in the background. Mustafa Kemal walked straight to her without hesitating, as if he were parting the hall in two with his sword, and asked her if she would grant him a dance.

They went to the dance floor to jealous looks shooting lightning bolts at them. Everyone murmured something about them, although they didn't say a word, and instead looked into each other's smiling faces as they danced.

The next day, Miti's mother invited him over to the house for tea. The invitation had the meaning of officially allowing the young man and woman to see each other.

Then, they did start to see each other. They would wander through Borisova Park, go ice-skating and attend the theater.

First, there was rampant gossip, and then unpleasantness started. That was because Miti's father was one of the Bulgarian tsar's important men, a general who was a war hero and the defense minister. Such a man's daughter being with an Ottoman officer was beyond belief.

Mustafa Kemal didn't care one bit. He chose the right time at a ball at the Officer's Club, and as if out of spite, danced with Miti in front of the tsar. He defied everything in front of everyone. It was the last straw.

Miti's father went to visit Mustafa Kemal. He said he would be happy if he no longer saw his daughter. They engaged Miti to an engineer before the week was out.

Mustafa Kemal's world was destroyed.

World War I had already exploded on the scene. He angrily packed his suitcases and went back to Istanbul.

There hadn't been an engagement or anything like it, though. Miti had refused a proposal and thrown off the ring forced on her finger.

Mustafa Kemal, however, got no word of this.

He didn't forget, though.

He spoke with the actors of the Bulgarian Cooperative Theater in Ankara in 1931. "I left a part of my youth in Sofia," he said. "I loved a beautiful girl there, but they didn't give her to me."

He lived with a broken heart and passed away with a lonely heart.

Miti, though, had met Mustafa Kemal when she was 21. She waited until she was 30. Maybe a letter would come one day or the next and then he would come. She waited and didn't get married.

Unfortunately, nothing came.

She finally agreed to marry a lawyer under pressure from her family. It was a respectable but loveless marriage. They had two daughters. She tried to fill the emptiness in her heart with her children.

A bomb exploded in an assassination attempt on the Bulgarian tsar in 1925. Miti was wounded in the explosion. The Ottoman Embassy that had been shut in 1918 had yet to open as a Turkish embassy. Mustafa Kemal got in touch with his friends in Sofia and asked about Miti's well being. She had been slightly injured and was recovering.

Miti endured difficult times in her final days. The communist regime confiscated her family's property and she was exiled to Ludogorie.

It was August 1966, and she was seriously ill. She had difficulty speaking. She mumbled to her sister Olga who was waiting beside her.

"You know what?" she said. "I had him in a dream. I guess I'm finally getting back together with Mustafa Kemal."

She was 73.

A documentary about her was made in Bulgaria, and a book was published. Her daughter, Anna Deyanova, explained that her mother had experienced a woeful love life until her death, that she had never gone to Turkey and that she learned of Atatürk's death from the radio.

"She very much wanted to marry Mustafa Kemal," she said, "but it was impossible. She didn't mention him, choosing rather to forget."

Emine.

What about Mustafa Kemal's childhood adventures?

He and Emine, the daughter of Salonika Central Commander Şevki Pasha, were quite taken with each other when he was a student at the Military Academy.

Sixty-two years had passed since then. Yılmaz Çetiner from *Cumhuriyet* tracked Emine down. She was 77 and never got married. She lived in Teşvikiye, Istanbul. She had a photograph of Atatürk hanging in the living room. She told him with teary eyes:

"I didn't love the Gazi because he would marry me. He was an inaccessible entity for me, an unrequited love. For years, I was behind the lattice and he was at the school. We would say a couple of words to each other when we met, when our families would have gatherings from time to time. I would have dreams of him as I slept. My father was quite fanatical and so it was impossible for us to see each other any other way.

"He had finished at the Monastir Military High School and was readying to go to the Military Academy in Harbiye, Istanbul. I sent a message through his close friends and asked when he was going. He sent me a handwritten response. He wrote, 'I'm boarding the ferry this minute. This inauspicious moment will make us feel dejected. I swear in all conscience that I will not forget you and expect from you the same faithfulness. Farewell, Mustafa Kemal.' I can't explain how I shook when I got this letter. I was in a ghastly state. But at the same time, I was glad he was finally going to the Military Academy.

"Years passed in between, there were events, he would come to visit his mother and siblings when he was on leave. We were very rarely able to see each other. But this time I understood he had wrapped his entire being around the matters of the country and troubles of the nation. I heard that he'd been constantly meeting with his friends about it. I learned from Mrs. Makbule of something he said that delighted me as much as if I owned the world. He asked my mother about me as soon as he came and asked about whether or not I got married.

"We moved as a family to Istanbul years later. I saw Mrs. Makbule every once in a while. They invited me to balls at Dolmabahçe a few times, but I couldn't ever go due to my excitement. I also spoke with Mr. Salih Bozok a few times.

"The most painful moments in my life were when the Gazi was ill. I still have newspapers from that day. My growing misery continued since I went to the Gazi's yacht, the *Savarona*. Days pass and I sit and watch as if I see him.

"I was shaken as if I'd been struck by lightning one morning when I saw the flag of the presidency at half staff. He passed away, but he had succeeded in saving the country and making great reforms. I now collect all the newspapers on the anniversary of his death. Life's not the same for me. I have no family or children, so who knows what will happen to these newspapers after I die.

"The great intervening incidents didn't lead us to marriage. He had no time to deal with matters of the heart. It was essentially unrequited love."

At the end of her sad account, Emine said, "He was a fantasy, my dear. He was a dream."

The love that wasn't lived was a tragedy.

∞

Zsa Zsa Gabor.

There were no paparazzi yet in the founding years of the republic, but Mustafa Kemal being the most prized bachelor whipped up gossip and rumors.

There was Zsa Zsa Gabor, for example. She was crowned Miss Hungary in 1936. She married journalist Burhan Asaf Belge in 1937. She came to Turkey and danced with Atatürk at a ball.

She and Burhan Asaf Belge got divorced, then she went to the U.S. and became a Hollywood star. She married Conrad Hilton, the owner of the Hilton Hotels. Later she married Prince Frederick von Anhalt and became a princess. There were scandals throughout her life. She got married nine times and got divorced eight times.

She said in her autobiography, *One Lifetime Is Not Enough*, that she had relations with Atatürk, that she'd given him her virginity at age 15; and that Atatürk; gave her gifts of jewelry encrusted with rubies.

She claimed that on the night she gave her virginity to Atatürk, he had her smoke a hookah, drink *rakı* and that she felt as if she were in a dream in her smoky drunkenness. She said that he was a professional lover with his devilish charm and that girls danced as the deed was done.

A cavalry officer came to her as 15-year-old Zsa Zsa Gabor walked alone in the meadows. He gave her a key with a note and an address. Not being able to restrain her curiosity, she went to the address, and after she opened the door with the key, she found Mustafa Kemal smoking a hookah as he watched the dancing girls.

This, however, is a tempest of erotic fancy more than anything real from her life. All it's missing is a flying carpet.

People in the circles on the lookout to besmirch Atatürk with attacks virtually flew at him. No one questioned whether what is explained in this book is true or not.

Even what some less-than-stellar journalists known to be Kemalists said was accepted as truth. There's even one writer who unabashedly said that Mustafa Kemal and Zsa Zsa Gabor were together for six months.

Someone in the Turkish press wrote when Zsa Zsa Gabor was 85 years old that Mustafa Kemal had said she was gorgeous and he had been enamored. This writer didn't have the slightest knowledge, explain a single thing specific to Atatürk or present any witnesses.

Journalists returning empty handed from interviews with Zsa Zsa Gabor tried to put on mysterious airs with fabrications, with one saying: "She entrusted me with a big secret and asked me to write about it after her death." Zsa Zsa Gabor died in 2016 and none of those supposed secrets have ever come to light.

So, what was it?

This particular book, published in 1991, is by British writer Wendy Leigh, who was known for her tall tales of the boudoir. She was a sensationalist writer who is just as well known for being sued for millions in damages as she is for being a best-selling author. Her own life was full of scandals. She had a forbidden affair with British media mogul Robert Maxwell, who died under dubious circumstances. Her own death was also suspicious—she fell from the balcony of her London apartment. It remains unsolved, though, whether it was suicide or murder.

Zsa Zsa Gabor claimed she'd given Atatürk her virginity when she was 15, although when they first met, she was 20 years old, already married and was working as a showgirl at the Femina revue-theater in Vienna.

Would it even be possible for Mustafa Kemal, who lived very openly every second of his life with his aides, friends and servants to be together with a teenage girl, have a six-month affair and keep it all secret? This episode doesn't exist in anybody's memories or attestations. There were people in Ankara and Istanbul at the time who didn't care for Mustafa Kemal. They all wrote down their recollections. If there were even the smallest trace of Zsa Zsa Gabor, wouldn't they have mentioned it in order to injure Mustafa Kemal?

What's more, Burhan Asaf Belge's relatives refuted the ugly claims in the book. Everyone knew very clearly that she had only met Mustafa Kemal once when her husband introduced them at a ball.

The rest was just flights of imagination to sell books.

Someone else who was material for the magazines was Madam Bauer.

She was a governess and 50 years old. She had been brought from Switzerland with a reference from Ruşen Eşref to tutor Atatürk's adopted daughters. She taught French, piano, dance and table manners.

She wasn't treated as a staff member—she was with the girls throughout the day and was treated like a member of the household. She would sit at the dinner table in colorful housecoats and if she played records on the gramophone after the meal, she'd waltz with Atatürk or the guests.

Madam Bauer had been asked to instill discipline in the housework after Latife left and there was a hitch in the oversight of the Çankaya Mansion.

She exaggerated the degree of discomfort.

The waiters wore gloves and tailcoats. She started going on return visits as if she were the lady of the house. She started to take appointments and accept guests. She loved speaking in commands. Rumors and gossip were already running rampant and tried their patience. They put her on a train and sent her off.

She lived at the Çankaya Mansion for a total of 10 months.

Corinne Lütfü.

There are many women mentioned in Mustafa Kemal's life. There were only two women in his life, though, with whom he got on.

These two women listened to the same music and read the same writers. Mustafa Kemal greatly enjoyed talking with them about life, making chitchat while walking together and spending time together.

It wouldn't be wrong to call them twin spirits.

One of them was Corinne Lütfü.

She was of Italian descent. Her family, though, had lived in Istanbul for three generations. Her grandfather Gregoire had been one of the sultan's interpreters. Her father Luigi had been an Ottoman pasha's physician. Corinne, herself, was born in Istanbul in 1883. She studied at a conservatory in Paris and knew five languages.

She was married to Ömer Lütfü, who was a friend of Mustafa Kemal from the Military Academy. The house where they lived in Beyoğlu was on what is today Sadri Alışık Sokak. It was a splendid residence with four stories and 36 rooms. It was also a virtual cultural center.

There was music entertainment every Saturday evening. Songs were sung to piano accompaniment and poems were recited. There were discussions on literature.

Intellectuals like Halide Edip Adıvar, Abdülhak Hamit Tarhan and Selim Sırrı Tarcan were often found there.

Mustafa Kemal was also among the regular guests.

Ömer Lütfü had been killed in the First Balkan War. Mustafa Kemal didn't cut off his friendship with Corinne afterward. It was a platonic friendship that never overstepped the bounds.

They exchanged letters constantly from 1913 to 1917. They always wrote wherever they were—Sophia, Gallipoli and Diyarbakır.

He addressed her as, "Dear Corrine, my dear friend and lady." He would also sign his letters, "Your sincere and true friend".

He wrote about his daily life. In return, he got news about her daily life in Istanbul. They corresponded about their worries, their passions and their troubles, but were careful to avoid words that would evoke love.

Corinne's son, Reşat Ersu, gave these correspondences to Peyami Safa and they were published in *Milliyet* in 1954. In total, there were 15 lettes, five postcards and two telegraphs.

Corinne was a progressive and liberal woman. Her ideas overlapped with those of Mustafa Kemal. She was a member of the executive board of the Ottoman Women's Association and worked for the inclusion of women in the workforce.

Years later, Mustafa Kemal spoke of Corinne to Fatin Rüştü's mother, Güzide Hanım:

"Madam, sometimes you remind me of Corinne. She had common sense, was brave and delightful. I used to tell or write her of my hardships in the moments when I felt lonely. She was very precious to me and she inspired me."

There have been many claims suggesting what was said. This, though, is the most truthful account of the friendship between Mustafa Kemal and Corinne.

When he spoke of her to his friends he would refer to her as the country's most intellectual woman and that he'd learned much from her.

Their friendship continued until he boarded the *SS Bandırma*.

Corinne was under great pressure when the National Campaign began. The occupation forces constantly disturbed her due to her closeness to Mustafa Kemal. Her house was raided and denounced, it was searched and her father was even detained. She was forced to move to Italy.

They never saw each other again.

She returned to Turkey in 1941, three years after Atatürk's death.

She died at 63 in 1946.

∞

Princess Mevhibe Celaleddin was the other deeply influential woman in Mustafa Kemal's life. She was the first and only woman in his life he had told to come with him.

Princess Mevhibe Celaleddin.

It's truly dumbfounding that as of today there has been no film made of her life or book written about her. She has been so ignored. She was a colorful character with a life full of incredible adventures.

She was Cemile Sultan's granddaughter. Cemile Sultan was Sultan Abdülmecid I's daughter and sister to Abdülhamid II and Mehmed VI.

Mevhibe Celaleddin was born in the Fındıklı Palace, which had been built for Cemile Sultan as a wedding gift in 1887. She lived in both the Fındıklı Palace and Kandilli Palace until she got married.

Her grandfather, Mahmud Celaleddin Pasha, was executed along with Midhat Pasha in the dungeons of Ta'if on orders from Abdülhamid II.

Cemile Sultan never forgave her brother Abdülhamid II for having her husband drowned and lived in mourning until her final breath. It's also how she raised her children and grandchildren. Sharing her grandfather's name, these are the emotions with which Mevhibe Celaleddin grew up.

She knew three languages and played the piano. She was an independent and free-spirited woman.

She was married and had one son. She fell in love with another man while she was married. She got divorced and married her forbidden love. Her husband was close to the Young Turks and was arrested. Mevhibe implored the pashas she knew and secured his release on condition they leave the country. They first went to Egypt, then they moved to France and lived in Paris.

She suffered from asthma. Doctors gave her morphine for her asthma attacks, which only made things worse. She used a little more each time and got hooked. She went to Switzerland and convalesced in a sanatorium in Geneva, where she received treatment for two months and kicked her addiction.

She lost her mother and father one after the other. She and her husband fell on hard times before her father died when the regular salary he received from the palace was cut. They had no other income and were compelled to start selling their property. Nothing they experienced in the empire nor semblance of pageantry remained when they sold their mansion and residence.

She also divorced her second husband. She went back to Istanbul and rented an apartment in Nişantaşı. Her palace life was over and she moved
into a modest home. Her husband was actually quite affluent and she could have continued her high living if she hadn't gotten divorced, but she favored freedom over money.

The empire was collapsing with a crash. The sons of the country were falling at Gallipoli, Galicia and in the Arabian desert while those in the palace continued to dole out orders. This disgraceful situation made Mevhibe unable to tolerate the environment in which she grew up. She drew away from her relatives and palace friends and started not seeing any of them.

Istanbul was under occupation. Enemy battleships were anchored in the Bosphorus. The streets were filled with Senegalese and Indian soldiers in British, French and Italian uniforms. They were arrogant. They accosted the women, slapped people and insulted them.

Mevhibe recounted her memories years later, saying that she had never forgotten those days, what she called "the darkest days for the country".

This was the atmosphere in which she lived.

She attended a party at the Karlo Apartments in Şişli, which is where she met Mustafa Kemal.

The night didn't stop there. A large group went to Mevhibe's house as the party was letting out and they kept talking until light of day.

She didn't sleep after sending off the guests. She sat in an armchair beside the window. There was a sweet smile on her face as she sat and thought of Mustafa Kemal.

They started seeing each other nearly every evening. It wasn't, however, only limited to fun dinners with musical entertainment. Mevhibe also attended political meetings at Mustafa Kemal's house.

On Mustafa Kemal's instructions, she attended a ball for the commanders of the British and Italian occupation forces with her ears pricked. She got into the circles the Mim Mim Group couldn't and collected intelligence. This princess of the palace became a spy for the National Forces.

Mustafa Kemal had terrific stomach discomfort at the time. He would experience painful bouts with high fever.

He was in bed for 17 days. Mevhibe didn't leave his bedside for those 17 days.

It was May 1919, and a packed meeting was going on in Mustafa Kemal's house. His aide Cevat Abbas was looking for the right time and called Mevhibe to the dining room. "The pasha has made his decision," he said. "He's going to Anatolia. The preparations are complete. Would you also like to come?"

Mevhibe was astonished. She never expected this. She could only say she needed to think about it.

Two days later, she sat across from Mustafa Kemal himself.

"I'm going. You come with me, too," he said. He tried to convince her so she wouldn't refuse: "You'd be very useful to us. Halide Edip Hanım is also going to Anatolia, so you wouldn't be lonely."

That was the first and only time he asked a woman to come with him.

There was a long silence. Mevhibe's heart was saying run. Her mind, however, was tugging at her arm.

"If you permit, let me think about it for a bit," she said.

Mustafa Kemal's disappointment could be seen on his face. He never broached the subject again, ever.

He went to Samsun. Mevhibe went to Milan.

She lived there for a while and then for a spell in Vienna. Then she moved on to Dresden. Her money had been thoroughly depleted. She rented a cheap room in a boarding house. She wrote to the conservatory and studied piano and singing. It was her wounded spirit, though, that she was dressing with music.

She lived abroad for four years. Materially, she had nothing left. She returned to Istanbul in February 1923.

She had no home of her own and stayed with friends.

Mustafa Kemal declared the foundation of the republic. Members of the Ottoman dynasty were to be exiled abroad. Mevhibe panicked for the first time in her life. She had nowhere to go, no money and no family with which to take refuge.

Law No. 431 abolished the caliphate. One hundred fifty-five men, women and children were expelled from the country. The rest were excluded from the law.

Mevhibe was rescued. In order to live, though, she had to work.

She mulled over what she could do and made a move. She went to Muhsin Ertuğrul and asked for help. They gave her a piece of paper with a text on it, and told her to memorize and rehearse it. She was a natural talent and they loved her.

She joined Muhsin Ertuğrul's troupe. She began to get roles at the Ferah Theater. She shared the stage with legends such as Muhsin Ertuğrul, Neyire Neyir, Muammer Karaca, Vasfi Rıza Zobu and Hazım Körmükçü. She acted in productions of *Renkli Fener* (Colorful Torch), İşsizler (The Unemployed), *Sırat Köprüsü* (The Straight Path), *Bir Zaid Bir Baskın* (A Zaid and a Raid), *Taş Parçası* (Stone Fragment), *Cehennem* (Hell), *Donanma Gecesi* (Night of the Fleet).

She was billed as Princess Mevhibe. The press called her the theater princess. She even joined a tour through Anatolia.

The entire troupe was left unemployed when Muhsin Ertuğrul went to Europe. They joined Şadi Bey's theater group. There was no steady theater space, though, so they put on productions wherever they could find space. She was able to endure it for three months before she left.

She couldn't take care of her son properly due to her stormy life and so entrusted him to her mother, Cemile Sultan, thus losing her only child.

She received a blow after blow. She couldn't carry the trauma of giving up her son. She retreated deep within herself, racked with feelings of guilt.

She became an operator at the Galata Port Company. A week hadn't even passed before she had an argument with the manager. She threw a chair at his head, picked up and left.

Monsieur Cormier was the husband of her childhood friend Odette and was the director of the Ottoman Bank. He told her to come work with him. Without any other option, she became an operator at the Ottoman Bank's central branch.

Once upon a time, she had been one of the Ottoman Bank's most affluent customers, but now she was an operator at the same bank.

She was 41. She'd lost everything, but her pride stood tall as a tower. She didn't call Mustafa Kemal for help.

Her great grandfather had been sultan. Her great uncle had been sultan. Her uncle had been sultan. She was an operator.

She began working at the Ottoman bank in 1928, and stayed there until her death in 1952 from pneumonia.

This, the second woman Mustafa Kemal told to come with him, is one of the maddest, most honorable and most tragic stories in Turkish history.

❋

Women were a focal point for Mustafa Kemal's enlightenment.

The Civil Law was enacted, ushering in official, civil marriage. At the same time, it nullified polygamy. An age limit was set to prevent marriage at a young age. Gender distinction was removed from inheritance law. People were granted political rights and the right to vote in elections. The people were given the right to equal education. They were also given the right to acquire a profession.

Women hadn't been considered people. They weren't counted in the census. Cattle were counted, but women weren't.

They were now equal individuals.

Mustafa Kemal went on a tour of the country with Latife in 1923. A group of women in Adana sent word with their husbands that they wanted to host Latife. Mustafa Kemal objected to the invitation as to how it was extended: "My wife can't be anywhere I, too, can't go. The concept of the *harem and selamlık*—segregated areas for women and men—was dead and buried in its application.

The Ankara Cinema was in İkiçeşmelik, Izmir, in 1923. Turkey's first filmmaker, Cemil Filmer, operated it. Mustafa Kemal attended a screening with Latife. They were seated in a box. He looked out over the hall—it was jam packed, but only with men.

He asked Cemil why there were no women. Cemil answered that the cinema was only open to women on Tuesdays. With this, Mustafa Kemal turned to his aide and said, "Empty half the hall and invite the women gathered outside in so there's just as many of them as there is of us."

He filled the hall with women who applauded and cried. Even the hallways teemed with women. Then, they all watched Charlie Chaplin's *The Pilgrim* together. It was a milestone. It was the first time in Turkey's history men and women watched a film together.

He wanted to extend his joy from this revolutionary event. "I don't remember having ever laughed so much in my life," he said. "What if we watch it again?" Then they watched it again amid fits of laughter.

Bedia Muvahhit.

The Darülbedayi Theater came to Izmir in 1923. It was going to stage the play *Ceza Kanunu* (Penal Code). They invited Mustafa Kemal. He asked if Muslim Turkish women would be acting in it and then, without waiting for an answer, turned to Ahmet Refet Muvahhit and said, "I watched your wife in *Ateşten Gömlek* [The Shirt of Flame] and I quite enjoyed it. Why don't you give her any roles in the theater?"

Afife Jale was a pioneer, the first Muslim woman to act on stage in the Ottoman period, albeit illicitly. She was continually hauled off to the police station and questioned, as it was illegal for Muslim women to be on stage.

That night, Bedia Hanım was made to memorize and rehearse until morning. Mustafa Kemal and Latife went to the Kordon Palas Hotel and settled in their room. Bedia Muvahhit was the first Muslim Turkish woman in the republican period to go on stage—freely, so to say.

Süreyya Ağaoğlu.

Süreyya was, in 1925, the first female student to graduate from a school of law. She was Mustafa Kemal's friend Ahmet Ağaoğlu's daughter. She worked at the General Directorate of Penal Affairs in Ankara.

She went for lunch one day with her friend Melahat at the Istanbul Lokantası. It was the only restaurant in the capital and only parliamentarians went there. Süreyya and Melahat entered abashedly and sat at a tiny table beside a sink.

Her distressed father sat her across from him when she got home in the evening. He told her not to go to the restaurant again because people gossiped.

The next day, Mustafa Kemal and Latife came as guests by chance. Süreyya couldn't hold her tongue once they began chatting. "We have a big problem," she said. "We want to go to the restaurant and it's become an issue."

The day after that, Justice Minister Mustafa Necati Bey walked into the room while Süreyya was working. "Get ready. The pasha's taking you to dinner," he said. She ran down to Mustafa Kemal's official car, where he said Latife was waiting at dinner and told her to get in.

They passed by the Istanbul Lokantası as they went toward Çankaya. Mustafa Kemal told the driver to stop. All of the parliamentarians in the restaurant rushed outside. He addressed them all: "Süreyya is coming to this restaurant tomorrow."

The issue was over.

Süreyya and Melahat went to the restaurant the next day. They went the next day, as well, but this time there were also the wives of the representatives for Istanbul, Hamdullah Suphi Bey and Ali Rıza Bey. Turkish women had won the freedom to go to a restaurant without being accompanied by a man.

Among the guests one evening in 1925 were Abdülhak Hamit Tarhan and his wife, Lucienne, who was 42 years his junior.

Lucienne was Belgian.

It seemed Abdülhak Hamit Tarhan had lost himself after a few glasses. With the other guests—women as well—he presented his wife and said, "Is there any Turkish woman like this?"

The room went cold.

Mustafa Kemal barely contained himself. His face had gone bright red. He pretended as though he hadn't heard so the man could correct himself. "What was that you said, sir?" he asked.

Abdülhak Hamit babbled: "Please don't call me sir, just call me man."

Mustafa Kemal shut him down: "There you have it—I say sir because I can't say man."

Things started brewing at the balls women attended, as well. Women would gather on one side of the hall and all sat as a group. They wouldn't even budge to go get food from the buffet, being very shy and timid, as if it would be shameful if they did anything.

Mustafa Kemal showed men the way to encourage women. "Honor and give credit to the standing women," he said. "Serve them, and then, slowly, those sitting will also stand up." And that's what happened. It was enviable.

The evenings that had started with just men finally became a place where women and men stood together and chatted.

In 1923, in Istanbul, there were curtains on public transit like ferries and trams. Women sat behind the curtain and couldn't even sit with their husbands.

Mustafa Kemal had the curtains lifted.

It was such a radical decision that not only conservative men, but also Halide Edip Adıvar—an enlightened woman of Istanbul educated at the American Academy for Girls in Üsküdar—objected to it, saying: "What business of yours is our curtain for you to mess with?"

He lifted the curtains on the ferries and trams, but it wasn't so easy to lift the curtains of the mind.

He even found it rude to address a woman as "woman".

One night, for example, Selahattin Pınar sang a new composition:

Come, don't go, woman; don't burn my spirit with separation
Make me groan, kill me; don't leave me to strangers
I'm a prisoner across from you; don't look on me as an enemy

The song ended and Mustafa Kemal made a suggestion as he clapped: "It's very nice, but doesn't this word, woman, fall a little bristly on the ears? Wouldn't it work if you used a word that better expresses the woman's grace and kindness? Let's say, my dear."

Selahattin Pınar hadn't written the lyrics, but argued, "I'd say the word woman fits because you could say my dear to a man, too." The lyrics to the song remained unchanged.

He knew the value of love.

King of Britain Edward VIII came to the city now officially named Istanbul in 1936.

They watched the paddle and sailing races off Moda. There was an American woman in the king's retinue. Mustafa Kemal's sharp eyes didn't miss this detail.

Wallis Simpson.

And what happened?

Wallis Simpson was a radiant woman. She was married and had a secret affair with the king, which wasn't known at the time they came to Istanbul.

She got divorced upon their return to Britain. It was against everything—the laws of the monarchy, tradition, the Anglican church. There was only one option. Three months after his visit to Turkey, British people who gathered around their radios were stunned to hear that King Edward VIII abdicated the throne so he could marry his lover, leaving the crown to his brother.

Feriha Tevfik.

Cumhuriyet organized the country's first official beauty pageant in 1929 at the directive of Mustafa Kemal.

There were publicity announcements. The conditions to participate were as follows: "No distinction for race, religion or sect. It is not only a competition for the beauty of the face. The symmetry and proportions of the body are also judged."

One hundred twenty-five contestants participated. Sitting on the panel of judges was Halit Ziya Uşaklıgil, Peyami Safa, Cenap Şahabettin, Hüseyin Rahmi Gürpınar, Abdülhak Hamit Tarhan, painter İbrahim Çallı, architect Vedat Tek, actors Vasfi Rıza Zobu and Bedia Muvahhit, and journalists Zekeriya Sertel, Sabiha Sertel, Vâlâ Nureddin and Yusuf Ziya Ortaç.

Feriha Tevfik was chosen as Turkey's first beauty queen.

According to an article in *Cumhuriyet*, "She is of medium height with curly, flaxen hair, golden eyes, white skin and has an elegant figure." She had worn a white satin dress.

Mübeccel Namık won in 1930.
Naşide Saffet was the beauty queen for 1931.

∞

Keriman Halis was chosen as Miss Turkey in 1932.

She competed in the international beauty pageant finals in Belgium against contestants from 27 other countries and won the International Pageant of Pulchritude to become Miss Universe.

Keriman Halis.

Mustafa Kemal was very happy. A Turkish woman who didn't have a place as a person before the republic had now been saved from the chador, veil and cage she was now the world's most beautiful woman, too.

A stage was set up in Taksim, and there, Miss Universe from Turkey was introduced to the public.

Mustafa Kemal had a ball held in honor of Keriman Halis and the two danced together.

He gave her the surname Ece, meaning *queen*.

∞

He didn't like makeup and preferred the natural look.

None of the women around him used lipstick or nail polish. He called women with a lot of makeup vats of paint.

He read books about women. He couldn't put down Enis Behiç's *Tarihte Güzel Kadınlar* (Beautiful Women in History) and read it over a night, finishing it the morning.

He took note of all the striking information he found about women. He studied Sappho, the poetess born on Lesbos in the 600s BCE with interest, while he was looking into ancient Greek history. He also studied the women who were heroes in the French Revolution.

In Hittite culture, men and women were equal individuals. Women had a political identity and a say in the administration of their lands. They were active in every field, as priestesses, physicians and musicians, just to name a few.

Women were one point of focus for Mustafa Kemal concerning the Hittites.

He carried the rights granted to women to the global platform.

In 1935, he invited the International Association of Women to the country. He played host to the International Women's Congress.

It was a congress on feminism.

Thirty-six countries sent 360 delegates, all of whom were women. They came from the U.S., the U.K., the Netherlands, Switzerland, Australia, Egypt, India, Bulgaria, Czechoslovakia, New Zealand, Romania, France,

Norway, Yugoslavia, Prtugal, Jamaica, Iran, Poland, Greece, Estonia, Syria, Denmark, Belgium, the Bermuda Islands, Finland, Ireland, Iceland, Spain, Sweden, Italy, Luxemburg, Hungary, Sri Lanka and. Uruguay. All of them either fought for women's rights in their own countries, were professionals, or parliamentarians.

Turkey was represented by 24 delegates. One was the president of the Turkish Women's Association, Latife Bekir. Her assistants were Aliye Esad, Lamia Refik and Nermin Muvaffak.

The first women to enter the Grand National Assembly of Turkey as parliamentarians with the 1935 elections were also there.

It was held at the Yıldız Palace and lasted one week.

There were two large Turkish flags behind the podium. Between the flags was a banner with the words *Justice–(Adalet)* on it.

Speeches were given in French, German and English.

They focused on gender equality before the law and the rights to equal education, equal employment and economic freedom. The problem of child brides attracted attention.

It was emphasized that war was not the problem of any individual country, but a common problem for the women of the world since it's their sons who died.

Turkish Women's Association President Latife Bekir gave her speech in French. She said, "We owe a debt of gratitude to Mustafa Kemal, who freed Turkish women from the cage of the harem, brought us to the podium in Parliament and gave Turkish women the right to stand equal next to men."

The president of the International Women's Association, Margery Corbett Ashby said, "The most important event at this feminism congress is meeting with Mustafa Kemal Atatürk."

Australian delegate Kardel Oliver traveled for weeks and over 17,400 miles in order to attend. While there, she said, "Next to the respect I have for Turkish women and this great man, I can't even speak of my tiredness."

"Siz Büyük Şefinize Atatürk diyorsunuz. Biz onu Ataşark diye anarız!„

Dünya kadınları Ulu Halâskâra derin hayranlıklarını heyecanla ifade ediyorlar!

Ankaraya Atatürkü ziyarete giden Arsıulusal Kadınlar Birliği kongresi murahhaslarından mürekkep 30 kişilik heyet dün sabah Haydarpaşaya gelmiştir. Murahhaslarla trende konuşmak için Pendiğe giden bir muharririmiz yolda, murahhas heyetleri başkanlarile konuşmuştur.

Ladey Asthorun sözleri

«— Türkiyeye gelirken Ankarayı da görebileceğimi zannetmiyordum. Bu itibarla Ankara yolculuğu benim için hakiki bir sürpriz oldu. Ben uzun söz söylemesini sevmem. Düşündüklerimi kısaca ve açıkça söylerim. Ankarayı çok beğendim ve on yıl gibi kısa bir müddet zarfında vücude getirilen eserleri takdire şayan buldum.

The president of the Egyptian Feminist Union, Howda Shaarawi, said, "This congress is a holiday for us. Turkey is the first country in the Orient where women know their rights. There's a debt owed to Atatürk that women have been liberated in Islam. The Turks call him Atatürk, but that's not enough for us—for us he is *Ataşark* [father of the Orient]."

The guest delegates wore the national dress from their respective countries.

They were hosted at the hotels in Taksim. A liaison office was established in the Pera Palas Hotel. Buses were also allocated so they could tour Istanbul.

There was teatime every late afternoon at Dolmabahçe Palace. They ate lunch at the Beylerbeyi Palace. A special ferry was prepared and fitted with the flags of the delegates' countries. They sailed up and down the Bosphorus on it.

A special law was enacted in Parliament.
Marie Curie was the first woman to win a Nobel Prize.
Norwegian author Sigrid Undset had won it.
American social reformer Jane Addams had won it.
Italian writer Grazie Deledda had won one.
Swedish author Selma Lagerlöf had won one.
Austrian writer Bertha von Suttner had won one.
French scientist Irene Joliot Curie had also won one.

Stamps were printed using photographs of these legendary women along with the logo of the International Women's Association in order to honor the International Women's Congress.

They printed 1.5 million copies.

Turkey had fabulous publicity. It was written about extensively in newspapers from the United States to Australia, Egypt to Finland and everywhere in between.

The newspapers in Greece were amazed, a little jealous and full of respect. The *Akropolis* newspaper published in its lead article: "Who could have guessed? Who would have believed 15 years ago if they had been told? These women who were prisoners, and who were off-limits, these Turkish women now wear the feminist crown of the world."

The congress came to an end and the International Women's Association delegation went to Ankara.

Mustafa Kemal met them at the door to the Çankaya Mansion.

There he gave a historic speech addressed to the women of the world:

"I thank you for doing us the favor, coming to Turkey, and accepting to hold your international congress in Istanbul.

"Turkish women will not fall behind men in any field. Turkish women will not fall behind European women in any field. Turkish women are capable of producing greater generations.

"The real area of struggle for the women of this country, the true area where victory must be won, is to have them brought up to date and adorned with knowledge, culture and true virtues rather than being successful with clothing and dress. You can be certain that Turkish women will work with the women of the world hand in hand for world peace and serenity."

Rukiye Erkin, Sabiha Gökçen, Afet İnan and Zehra Aylin.

Mustafa Kemal had eight adopted children—Sabiha Gökçen, Afet İnan, Ülkü, Abdürrahim, Rukiye, Nebile, Mustafa and Zehra.

He would sit at the table with his daughters—he called them his diamonds—and the girls would go to their rooms after eating. The conversations would continue at the table afterward with the other guests.

He didn't want his children to be treated differently.

One day Sabiha and Zehra were playing rope in the schoolyard. Recess ended and class started again, but they kept on playing rope. Their teachers were women. One opened the door and called out for them. They didn't listen and kept on laughing and playing. The teachers couldn't abide their being so bratty.

The girls were floored by what happened next. It was the first time they'd seen such a reaction. They were

Atatürk's daughters. Who did the teachers think they were to be able to yell at them? They ran home in tears. They went into Mustafa Kemal's study and complained to him that the teacher had chased them from school and they didn't like her.

"Let's have a look at this teacher," he said.

Smiles spread across the girls' faces.

He called his aide.

"Take these two back to school right away," he said. "Make known my appreciation and let the teacher teach my daughters as she sees fit."

Then he turned to the girls. He was harsh: "You will kiss your teacher's hand and ask for forgiveness. If she forgives you, then I'll forgive you."

He closely followed the grades of his daughters, Abdürrahman and Mustafa's. He would make a special trip to their teachers when they got high scores and ask if they did his children a favor. He would take the tests himself sometimes to be certain and be able to personally determine if they knew enough about the course or not.

Mustafa Kemal's children went to the same elementary school as the children of his cook, driver, waiter, barber and other attendants at the Çankaya Mansion.

"You will never lie," he warned them. "Never forget, I'm not angry when you do wrong, but when you lie."

He wanted his children to be free individuals in the family.

On the topic of children, he said: "For all time there has been a very bad habit among most families. They don't let their children speak and they don't listen to them. When the poor things interrupt, they tell them not to interfere when those older than them are talking and they silence them. This is a very wrong thing to do and, what's more, it's harmful. Children should be encouraged to speak freely and express themselves just as they are to think and listen. That way, there is both the possibility to correct their mistakes and prevent them from lying and being hypocritical in the future. We must grow accustomed to our children expressing their thoughts without hesitation and defending their sincere beliefs while instilling in them respect for other people's sincere opinions. We must strive to awaken in their pure hearts love for the country, nation, family and fellow citizens along with love for and interest in what is correct and good and beautiful things. In my opinion, these are the important points children's education will always rest on everywhere, from the mother's lap to the halls of the highest education. In this way, each of our children will be useful to the country and be complete people."

He never said they couldn't go to the cinema or shopping.

There was a black servant, Nesip Efendi, at the mansion. Mustafa Kemal had great trust in him. The girls would address him as *baba*, meaning father. Nesip Efendi would accompany them when they went out.

General Secretary Hasan Rıza Soyak would give them their pocket money.

In later years, the political parties made proposal after proposal for Mustafa Kemal's adopted children to run as candidates for them. The answer was no every time, including for the Republican People's Party (CHP). He stipulated in his will for them not to enter politics.

∞

Sabiha Gökçen.

Sabiha was born in Bursa, in 1913.

Her father was the head of the provincial treasury. He was also a Young Turk. Because of that, they were exiled from Edirne to Bursa.

She had lost her mother and father and lived with her older brothers and sisters.

She stood up straight in front of Mustafa Kemal when he went to visit Bursa in 1925. She said she wanted to study.

This courageous girl, still only 12 years old, greatly impressed Mustafa Kemal. His eyes filled with tears. He asked her brothers and sisters for permission, took her by the hand and brought her to Ankara.

She went to elementary school there and then high school at the American Academy for Girls in Üsküdar.

She wanted to join the operation on Dersim. Mustafa Kemal was worried.

"If you fall into the hands of those you fight against, they'll treat you very badly," he warned her. "Without it happening to you, you have no idea what this means."

Sabiha was determined. "You're right. Ultimately, there's an aircraft under us," she said. "It could fail, it could get hit, it could crash. Say there's some such misfortune—you can be sure I won't fall into anyone's hands alive."

A flash of pride passed over Mustafa Kemal's deep, blue eyes. He got up from his seat and opened the drawer to his desk. He took out his Smith & Wesson in a leather holster and handed it to Sabiha. "If you find yourself in a situation that will harm your honor or dignity," he said, "don't hesitate to first shoot your attacker and then yourself."

Sabiha was a sharp shooter with a pistol. She first kissed Mustafa Kemal's hand and then the gift of trust.

It was around 5 o'clock the next morning. Dawn was just over the horizon. Mustafa Kemal woke Sabiha up by stroking her hair.

He was nervous about the responsibility his 24-year-old, courageous daughter had taken upon herself. He didn't sleep that night—he didn't even blink.

He told her it was time. He took her to the airport in his own car. He didn't speak with anyone for four days until she got back.

Sabiha won the title of being the world's first woman to pilot a warplane. She received a Medal of Commendation.

She always carried the pistol Mustafa Kemal had given her in her bag. She donated it to the Anıtkabir Museum in 1960.

She flew 22 different types of aircraft, including bombers and acrobatic planes, and had more than 8,000 flight hours. She became the head instructor at the Türkkuşu Flight School. She was awarded the world's most prestigious aviation honor when the U.S. Air Force Academy named her one of "The 20 Greatest Aviators in History". She is the first and only woman to be awarded this honor. She would even take a seat in the cockpit and fly solo when she was in her 70s. Her last flight was when she was 83, with a French copilot, in a Falcon 2000 jet while she was in the skies of Ankara.

She was one of the strongest female role models Turkish women had.

Mustafa Kemal gave her the surname Gökçen.

She married a pilot, Captain Kemal Esiner, in 1940. She didn't take his name and instead gave her own. This was also a first, in a sense.

She didn't have any children. Unfortunately, she lost her husband after three years. She never remarried and lived 58 years alone.

She passed away at 88 and is buried in the Ankara Cebeci Martyr's Cemetery.

An article in *Agos*—an Istanbul-based, Armenian-language newspaper—in 2004, claimed Sabiha Gökçen was ethnically Armenian. While there had been no hint of it throughout her 88 years of life, such a claim sprang up three years after her death. Hripsime Gazalyan, a citizen of Armenia, claimed to be Sabiha's aunt and that she had left her at an orphanage in Şanlıurfa when she was a baby.

Of course, Sabiha Gökçen's ethnic origin is of no importance one way or another, but those who suggested this claim have forgotten a few snags.

Information on Sabiha's parents isn't unknown. Her father was İzzet Bey, who was a civil servant and head of the provincial treasury. As such, her genealogy is in the Ottoman archives. Her mother was Hayriye Hanım, who was born in Sarajevo. Her older brother Neşet had been Mustafa Kemal's bodyguard for a while. She also had a sister named Saime. There is also no mention of an orphanage or Şanlıurfa in any of it.

Mustafa Kemal's youngest adopted daughter, Ülkü, was first married to Sabiha's cousin Fethi Doğançay, providing further evidence of her genealogy. Her father-in-law, Vural Arıkan, who was a finance minister, was Sabiha's second cousin and confirmed that her mother was born in Sarajevo.

So, what was it all about?

Those who put this assertion forward wanted to support the claims of the alleged genocide against Armenians.

It wouldn't be news if it were just any child victim of forced relocation, but if it were Mustafa Kemal's daughter, then it would be a topic of interest around the world.

And that's what happened. There were heated discussions for two or three years. As a result, the previously given evidence was refuted. The alleged Armenian genocide, however, continued as a topic of discussion in the meantime. The intention behind the claim had emerged.

∞

Afet İnan.

Afet was born in Salonika, in 1908.

She was a primary school teacher. It was 1925 when she met Mustafa Kemal while he was on assignment in Izmir—now officially renamed İzmir.

She said she wanted a higher education. For that she was sent to Lausanne, Switzerland.

She studied French for two years at the Rochemont school. She returned to Turkey and later graduated from Notre Dame de Sion High School in Istanbul. She went back to Switzerland, this time to the University of Geneva, where she graduated with a degree in history. She completed her doctorate at the same university. Her dissertation was titled "The Anthropological Character of the Turkish People and Turkish History". She rose the ranks from lecturer to professor in the Faculty of Languages, History and Geography at Ankara University. She became the vice president of the Turkish Historical Society. She taught at Ankara University, Hacettepe University and Ege University, as well as at the Turkish Military Academy. Her books on the history of revolution and women's rights have been translated into nine languages.

She lived at the Çankaya Mansion, like the other adopted girls. Sabiha, Zehra and Rukiye were her older sisters. She also personally contributed to the education of her younger siblings.

She lived her life as a professor of history with paper, pens and books, but she wielded formidable weapons. She always kept the Browning pistol Mustafa Kemal had given her in her handbag.

Afet and Sabiha were models of the modern, Turkish woman, raised as educated, republican girls. They took social responsibility and were pioneers of women's rights. They were also targeted because of these qualities. They were an easy target for Mustafa Kemal's enemies who couldn't strike out at him. Their lives and safety were always under threat. This is why both Sabiha and

Afet were given firearms training, so they could protect themselves if need be.

Afet married Doctor Rıfat İnan in 1940, and had two children.

She lived an exemplary life. She always avoided ostentation. Her only accessories were the pearl earrings she bought with her first paycheck.

She passed away at 77 and is buried at the Ankara Cebeci Cemetery.

∞

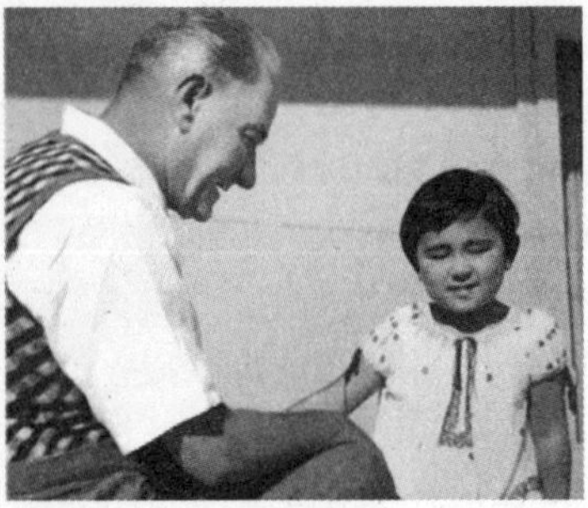

Mustafa Kemal with little Ülkü.

Ülkü was born in 1932.

Zübeyde Hanım had raised her mother, Vasfiye Hanım, as an adopted child in Salonika. She married Mehmet Tahsin Bey, who was the station chief at the Gazi Forest Farm. Ülkü was the product of their marriage.

Mustafa Kemal adopted her when she was only 9 months old. This little baby experienced virtual grandchild worship.

Ülkü gave names to everybody around her. She called her older sister Rukiye Auntie Istanbulite. She called Sabiha Gökçen Auntie Airplane. Ferahşan Hanım, who was black, she called Auntie Chocolate.

She didn't come up with additional names for Mustafa Kemal, though. She addressed him as "my dear Atatürk".

She was six years old when Mustafa Kemal died.

She attended the American Academy for Girls in Üsküdar.

Rather than realizing her adoptive father's ideal and continuing on to higher studies, unfortunately, she got married before she was even an adult. Her first marriage was to Kastamonu Representative Fethi Doğançay, her second was to Yeşua Bensusen and her third was to Öke Adatepe.

Her second husband was Jewish, which whipped up a storm in the country. The National Turkish Students Union and Mustafa Kemal Association held protests. They wanted the rights passed to her from Atatürk rescinded and all mention of Ülkü removed from textbooks. They even wanted her to be stripped of her citizenship.

The press attacked her as if marrying a Jewish man or being Jewish were crimes.

Yeşua Bensusen was an Istanbul businessman in the cooking oil trade. He bent over backward to explain himself:

"I am a Turkish citizen, I performed my national service in the honorable Turkish military, I would give my life for my country and I am committed to Atatürk to the utmost."

He even changed his name to Yaşar Bensu so it would sound more Turkish. It was futile.

They couldn't save him from the attacks. They were able to stand the terrible neighborhood pressure for six years and then they got divorced.

Ülkü grew up as the happiest child in Turkey, but became an unhappy adult. Her 80-year life was also punctuated with an unfortunate end. She died in a traffic accident in 2012 while on the road from Istanbul to Ankara.

She is buried in Zincirlikuyu.

∞

Mustafa Kemal with little Abdürrahim.

Officers tried to look out for the many orphans left at what had been the Caucasian front after the Caucasus Campaign of World War I.

Abdürrahim was one of them.

He was 3 years old and had lost both his parents. Mustafa Kemal adopted him in 1916 when he was the commander of the 2nd Army in Van.

He had Zübeyde and Makbule raise the boy in Istanbul.

Abdürrahim was there when Mustafa Kemal was about to leave the house in Şişli for Samsun. He splashed water from a small jug on the ground behind Mustafa Kemal as he left, as was custom.

Abdürrahim was there in Izmir when Mustafa Kemal and Latife got married. He had come to Izmir with Zübeyde and stayed with Latife after Zübeyde's death. He had the chance to be one of the 50 special guests at the historic wedding ceremony.

He went to primary school in Ankara. Then, he was sent to İzmir. He got a diploma from the Mithatpaşa Vocational High School. Then, he was sent to Germany.

He graduated as an electrical engineer from the Technical University of Berlin. He interned at the German firm AEG.

He knew German and French and was the interpreter during the procurement of the *MV Savarona*. He later got a job operating the Ankara electricity and gas plant.

He retired from the Central Bank.

"I don't know my mother and I don't know my father," he once said. "When I knew myself, I accepted Zübeyde as my mother and Makbule Hanım as my aunt. I also knew the Pasha. This family is my family. I have always considered myself a child of this family, and that's how I've always been. We searched extensively for my real mother and father, but we couldn't find them for certain. What I do know for certain is that I was at Mustafa Kemal Pasha's house when I was 3. The greatest fortune I've been able to receive as a living being is the pride and honor of having been raised by the mother who raised Atatürk and having received the upbringing he did."

He got married and had three children.

He always lived a modest, peaceful life.

He passed away at 90 in Ankara, and is buried at the Ortaköy Cemetery in Istanbul.

∞

Mustafa Kemal with Rukiye.

Rukiye was born in Seydişehir, Konya, in 1914.

Her father had joined in the War of Independence. He was an aide at the main headquarters. He went to Mustafa Kemal to ask for help after the declaration of the republic. "I have three daughters," he said. "I can't get them educated. You take the youngest of them."

Rukiye was 9 when she was adopted.

She grew up like one of a set of triplets along with Sabiha and Zehra.

She would fast during Ramadan. They ate dinner according to the times of *iftar* during Ramadan so she wouldn't be left to eat alone. Everyone sat to eat *iftar* with Rukiye whether or not they themselves were fasting.

It was during one of these Ramadans when Mustafa Kemal gave her a small, silver case containing a tiny, handwritten Quran. Rukiye carried it with her in her handbag for the rest of her life.

She attended primary school in Ankara. She graduated from the Notre Dame de Sion High School in Istanbul.

She married Captain Hüsnü Erkin, who was the commander of the Gazi Forest Farm guard unit. The signing ceremony for the marriage was done at the Ankara Municipality building and the wedding ceremony was held at Dolmabahçe Palace. She had one son.

She died in Istanbul at the age of 84.

∞

Nebile was born in Istanbul, in 1910.

She was an orphan.

Nebile.

She was a student at the Çapa Teachers School. A brother of hers studied at Darüşşafaka. She had no one else.

She went to Dolmabahçe Palace with great courage and said she wanted to work under Mustafa Kemal's command whether it be as a maid or anything else. Mustafa Kemal heard of her from Yaver Cevat Abbas and adopted her when she was 17.

She attended the American Academy for Girls in Üsküdar. She adored dancing and singing, though, and didn't have much of an intention to study. During the hours she should have been studying, she would instead stroll around.

She would benefit from marriage. She was 19. She married Raşit Bey, the first secretary of the embassy in Vienna. She danced with Mustafa Kemal at her wedding at the Ankara Palas.

The photograph of the founder of the Republic of Turkey dancing with his adopted daughter made the cover of *The Illustrated London News* and received worldwide attention. It was a photograph of the transformation of the Ottoman Empire into a republic in women's favor.

She got divorced three years later and went back to Ankara.

In 1937, she married engineer Sabahattin İrdelp. A simple wedding ceremony was held at Dolmabahçe Palace. She couldn't find happiness and got divorced again after four years.

Troubles came one on top of another. She lost her sight when she was 29 when she got meningitis.

She never forgot the financial difficulties from her childhood and used every *kuruş* she got for charity, never forgetting that her brother had a profession thanks to Darüşşafaka.

She donated 34,000 liras to Darüşşafaka throughout her years of marriages. It was an incredible amount of money at that time.

She also donated the allowance she was granted in Mustafa Kemal's will to Darüşşafaka. She had no other income. She was left completely broke when she divorced her second husband.

She didn't even have a roof over her head. Being visually impaired, it was impossible for her to live alone. Her friends sent her to a sanatorium in Yakacık, Istanbul.

She stayed there without any complaints.

She could have set Ankara on fire if she wanted to, but she never asked for help. Then President İsmet İnönü got word of her. He persuaded her, albeit forcibly, and she was taken to the French La Paix Hospital. She held on for four years. She was only 33 when she passed away. Her grave is in the Feriköy Cemetery.

Her honorable story had a sparkling beginning and a tragic end.

∞

"Sığırtmaç" Mustafa with Mustafa Kemal.

Mustafa was born in Varna.

He and his family emigrated from Bulgaria to Yalova.

He couldn't read or write. He was a shepherd boy.

He met Mustafa Kemal by coincidence when he was 11. He changed the trajectory of this honorable boy's life.

Mustafa Kemal was horseback riding around the Yalova farm in 1929, when he came across a poverty-stricken child dressed in tatters and grazing a flock. He dismounted and chatted with the boy. He liked the boy's confident answers. He wanted to give the boy some pocket money and said, "We've got the same name." The boy didn't accept the money. Mustafa Kemal pulled some walnuts from his pocket as he tried to persuade the boy and offered them to him. The boy didn't take the money he couldn't pay back.

This dignity in self was a character Mustafa Kemal admired. He hugged and kissed this boy who didn't want money.

He told the boy to introduce him to his family. He asked the boy's parents for permission. Then he took him by the hand and brought him to Istanbul.

This boy who shared his name was in very bad health. He was admitted to the Şişli Children's Hospital and received treatment there for four months.

He went to elementary school in Beşiktaş, Istanbul. Afterward, he went to the Kuleli Military High School. He graduated from the Turkish Military Academy.

He was known by the nickname "Sığırtmaç", or Wrangler, and he took the surname Demir.

He got married and had two daughters.

He died at 70 and is buried in Yalova.

The symbol of the revolution in education was the equal opportunity. It was proof that every citizen given the chance to study could attain a profession and rise economically.

∞

Zehra Aylin.

Zehra had no one.

She was born in 1912, in Amasya. She was four when she lost her father.

At five, she lost her mother. She was left alone in a very large world.

Mustafa Kemal and Latife went to Amasya together in 1924. They met Zehra when they went to the Darüleytam orphanage dormitory.

She was the first girl they adopted.

She completed elementary school in Ankara. Then she studied at the American Academy for Girls in Üsküdar. She was then sent to England. There she attended Saint

Hilda College at Oxford University where she started to study literature.

She had full possibilities open to her, but Zehra had difficulty. She was an introverted girl and couldn't socialize. She couldn't adapt. She didn't make any friends.

Before the semester was even out, she'd already become depressed. She thought she didn't uphold her responsibilities since she wasn't good enough in her classes. She felt like a failure and sunk into depression.

She often wrote letters with her complaints to Sabiha and Rukiye. She explained the storms of her inner world.

"I'm wavering," she wrote. "I don't want to leave school half done, but I also don't want to stay here."

She felt she was alone and lost. She went to the Turkish Embassy in London at every chance she had and passed her time there.

Mustafa Kemal got word of it. He saw it would be pointless to insist. Instead, he said, "Let her leave and we'll find a different school."

It was November 1935. The Turkish ambassador in London, Fethi Okyar, brought her to France by ship. She boarded a train for Paris accompanied by an escort.

The trip was 10 hours. It was nearly 4 in the morning. She couldn't sleep. She didn't feel well and left her compartment to go get some air at the window.

Nobody knows how it happened.

An article in *Le Figaro* reported the incident:

"A young woman fell from a train from Calais to Paris. The alarm was given and she was found lying on the rocks beside the tracks. She was taken to the Amiens Hospital but succumbed to her injuries. He identification was found in her passport. She was the president of Turkey's adopted daughter Miss Zehra. She was coming from Britain."

She was 23.

Her funeral was at the Amiens Cathedral. Her body was then given to the Turkish Embassy in Paris. She was brought in a private wagon to Marseilles. Then she was sent by ship to Istanbul. The press wasn't informed of it, which intentional.

The funeral prayer was performed at Teşvikiye Mosque and she is buried at the Maçka Cemetery.

Mustafa Kemal was an emotional mess. He didn't attend the funeral. Instead, he sent Hasan Rıza Soyak to represent him.

Hasan Rıza had thought he'd seen every kind of drama throughout the National Campaign, but he was mistaken. He had watched Zehra grow up since she was 12, and he experienced the hardest day of his life throwing dirt onto her coffin.

This child was born unfortunate, then had fortune smile on her and then died as unfortunately as her life began.

∞

Mustafa Kemal would adopt another daughter.
Illicit love prevented it.

The captain of the *Ertuğrul* yacht, Kemal Bey, had a sister named Bülent who attended the American Academy for Girls in Üsküdar.

Mustafa Kemal was very fond of Captain Kemal, who was also from Salonika. He took Bülent into the fold of his adopted children on Captain Kemal's wishes and then sent her abroad for her higher education.

However, Bülent had a premarital affair with a young, non-Muslim man. It was understood that they met in secret. They couldn't get married, according to the conditions of the time, and they definitely couldn't continue like this. She was removed from around Mustafa Kemal when rumors started to emerge.

Bülent dropped out of school and ran away from home, leaving the city with the young man. Unfortunately, she fell ill and died at 20. She is buried in the Rumelihisarı Cemetery.

∞

Makbule.

Mustafa Kemal's only surviving sibling was Makbule.

She was four years his younger. He affectionately called her Makbuş. When he spoke of her to others, he'd call her his nurse. He kept her under his wing his entire life, even in the most difficult conditions, but they couldn't be said to be too close.

She got married, even though her older brother objected to it. This was the incident that broke the emotional bond between brother and sister.

He gave Fikriye as an example when describing Makbule:

"When I went to Samsun and they issued the death warrant for me with the story that I'm a killer, she married a good-for-nothing buffalo I didn't approve of. Fikriye, however, followed me, stood up to all kinds of danger and reached me in Ankara."

And who was this good-for-nothing man Makbule married? It has remained uncertain. Only his name is known—Lütfü Efendi.

While in Sofia, Mustafa Kemal wrote in a letter to Cemal Pasha: "As the sole refuge for my family, I am truly embarrassed to ask you to help my brother-in-law Lütfü. I had decided to absolutely not disturb you if your last letter of courtesy hadn't come. The nurse is bending over backward in Salonika with our mother while my brother-in-law grovels miserably in Istanbul."

Since Mustafa Kemal had asked for help from Cemal Pasha, who was a powerful member of the Committee of Union and Progress, Lütfü was most likely a retired soldier looking for work in Istanbul.

Mustafa Kemal's brother in law had visited him while he was in Gallipoli.

Mustafa Kemal never mentioned a word about it, but there's a short line written in the Chief of Staff İzzettin Çalışlar's Gallipoli logbook from 1915: "Mustafa Kemal's brother-in-law Lütfü Efendi came as a guest."

Lütfü Efendi wasn't around when Mustafa Kemal was about to leave the house in Şişli for Samsun on May 16, 1919. He did, however, move into the house immediately afterward, as Makbule explained in her memoirs what happened a few days after her brother left: "A knock came at the door and I looked out from the window. There were people I didn't know. I came down and asked what they wanted. They said they were going to search the house. I excitedly ran up the stairs and told my husband. He put on his boots."

These are all the crumbs of information we have about his brother-in-law Lütfü. None of the journalists of the period took interest in Makbule's private life. Lütfü was like a phantom. There isn't even the slightest trace of him in the news, memoirs or any records. They probably didn't want people to wonder, knowing that Mustafa Kemal didn't care for him and couldn't even tolerate hearing his name.

What we do know, however, is that his sister had no husband and was single when Mustafa Kemal returned to Istanbul eight years later.

Makbule got married for the second time in 1935, when she was 50, to Mecdi Boysan. There was no wedding ceremony. No wedding photographs were published in the papers. Unfortunately, it was another unsuccessful, expediency-oriented marriage.

Mecdi Boysan owned a factory in Mecidiyeköy, Istanbul. He became successful as soon as he married Makbule. He was elected as a parliamentarian for Edirne in the elections that year. He became a member of the İş Bank board of directors. It wasn't enough and he started a construction business. He grew wealthier remarkably fast.

Mustafa Kemal heard of some unpleasantness.

One evening, he sat the finance minister, Abdülhalik Renda, next to him at the dinner table. "Obstruct favoritism for my brother-in-law by any possible means. It might be thought the work he does is on my behalf. They'll think that even though he has no such intention."

He euphemistically told them to put an end to it.

The factory soon closed. It was heard that Mecdi Boysan had gone bankrupt. His term in Parliament ended in 1939. He and Makbule got divorced the same year.

The mortar had crumbled and the structure gave up the ghost.

They went up against each other at the divorce hearing. Makbule said her husband had forcibly seized her house. She said he had removed what belonged to her. Witnesses for Mecdi said the exact opposite and condemned Makbule. The divorce case got ugly and entangled. It lasted seven years. It finally reached a conclusion at the Court of Cassation in 1946.

Makbule liked to use her brother's power and influence. She lived at Dolmabahçe Palace while her brother was alive. She bought a farm in Alibeyköy.

This was the behavior Mustafa Kemal most disliked. He got angry and warned her, but Makbule didn't care.

The municipality of Salonika, now Thessaloniki, expropriated the Pink House Mustafa Kemal was born in and gave it to him as a gift.

It was to be preserved as a museum. Makbule wasn't even able to comprehend this symbolic gesture.

"The room painted pink on the upper floor was mine. Let it be mine again," she said.

Mustafa Kemal would often explain it around the dinner table. He would ask if it was money that she needed.

Makbule took her husband's name when she was married, but took the surname Atadan after her divorce. It had the significance of being a memento, so to speak, of Atatürk.

She didn't have any children of her own. She did have adopted children, though. She adopted Mustafa Kemal's adopted children.

She adopted Mustafa the cowherd with a court decision in 1954 along with Abdürrahim's wife, Hatice. She had raised Abdürrahim with Zübeyde and had personally married him off. She looked on his wife Hatice, as if she were her own daughter.

She was Mustafa Kemal's legal heir, as his younger sister. It would seem there was no inheritance at first glance, since Mustafa Kemal donated all his wealth to the people.

There were, however, houses and real estate in Ankara, İzmir, Bursa, Samsun, Diyarbakır, Erzurum, Konya, Trabzon and Antalya that had been given to Mustafa Kemal. He had left these out of his will. He had in fact decided to grant these houses given to him as gifts to the municipalities of the cities they were in.

While on his last visit to Bursa, he officially donated his house there and his shares in the Çelik Palace Hotel to the municipality. He officially left the houses, hotel, land and shops he had received as gifts in Ankara to the municipality. He wasn't around that long to bequeath the others.

Therefore, the titles of the houses he'd gotten as gifts had to be transferred to Makbule. They were registered in her name in 1939.

She didn't say, "These houses that were given to my brother as gifts have nothing to do with me. They are Atatürk's spiritual legacy." She had no qualms about receiving them.

The government couldn't find another solution.

The houses from his life were expropriated one by one to be used as museums. Makbule, for her part, was paid compensation.

She took gifts the people gave to Mustafa Kemal and those he returned to the people and turned them into cash.

Mustafa Kemal's will also provoked quarrels. Makbule said she didn't believe his will and insinuated that he might not have written it.

Even though, her brother had taken the pen in his hand and written it, she said, "My brother didn't even have the strength to break bread at that time."

She also implied that someone else had written it.

She didn't want to sign the official record when Mustafa Kemal's will was opened and read in court 18 days after his death. She said she wanted to consult her lawyers.

She was haggling in order to accept the will. She said her monthly expenses were around 700 liras and would need to be given 10 times that amount.

She found it in her heart to accept the will when the title deeds to the previously mentioned houses passed to her, and she kept quiet.

Nine years later, though, she experienced another crisis with money.

She wrote a letter in 1947 to the Republican People's Party in which she asked for her allowance to be increased:

"Because I cannot support myself with the salary paid, which is not even enough to cover rent, because I cannot cover the expenses of a driver and maid and because there is no one to care for me after my divorce from my husband, as Mustafa Kemal Atatürk's sister, it behoovers that I live comfortably."

She got an answer in a letter from the Republican People's Party, which said:

"Your allowance is based on Mustafa Kemal Atatürk's will and it is not in the party's authority to raise it."

Makbule got angry and wrote another letter. This time, though, she sent it to the presidency, the Office of the Speaker of Parliament, the Prime Ministry and the office of the chairman of the Democrat Party.

"It has become impossible for me to get by with the salary allocated me in Mustafa Kemal Atatürk's will, which covers automobile expenses and half those of a driver. I have no house in Istanbul. I pay 200 liras for rent. Considering my brother's service to the country, I would like to be allotted a monthly allowance based on that service to the country."

They took a look—it was impossible. They drafted a law for Parliament to pay in surplus of 1,000 liras. It was discussed in Parliament in February 1948.

Some spoke pitiably from the podium.

There was the question of how quickly the money from Atatürk's houses was used up.

One asked, "The families of those who have given their lives for the country are only given a salary of 60 liras. Why would we give Makbule Boysan a thousand?"

Another said, "After his death, Makbule Boysan sold some of the valuable belongings Mustafa Kemal had received as gifts."

Examples were given one by one. She had sold Mustafa Kemal's clothing. She had even sold Mustafa Kemal's *tespih*. Unfortunately, this was all true.

It came out that she had sold Mustafa Kemal's gold cigarette case engraved with his initials to a goldsmith. The goldsmith didn't buy it to make a profit, though. He paid Makbule much more than its weight in gold so Atatürk's belongings wouldn't go to someone else. He later gave it as a gift to the CHP.

Her brother's will had allocated her the Camlı Mansion in Çankaya for her lifetime. It was disclosed that she even wanted to rent it out.

İsmet İnönü intervened so it wouldn't be given to just anyone and paid 20,000 liras. For this amount, Makbule also transferred the right to use the Camlı Mansion to the Republican People's Party.

It was said that if Mustafa Kemal Atatürk had been alive, he would have been tortured by the negotiations in Parliament because of his sister.

The law was passed as a result of it all. Makbule began to get paid 1,000 liras more a month.

She even said the money paid to her shouldn't be taxed. She couldn't get that accepted, however.

Right before a museum was to be opened, she opened court cases against the Treasury concerning the houses, the money paid for their value and their expropriation. She said she'd been defrauded and that more money should have been paid. She didn't win the cases.

She was busy with the courts for the rest of her life.

She lived in Moda, Istanbul. She died at 71 in Gata, Ankara. Her grave is in the Cebeci Cemetery.

The crises with money continued even after her death.

She had her will prepared at the Istanbul 4th Notary in 1949. In it she said, "I donate my inheritance from Atatürk, all of my belongings, stocks and bonds to Darüşşafaka."

However, she had sold the houses her brother had left her and the money was all gone. All of Mustafa Kemal's remaining assets were donated to the Republican People's

Party. There were no other real estate, stocks or bonds remaining from Makbule.

Members of the Democrat Party said all of Mustafa Kemal's assets that passed to the Republican People's Party should be transferred to Darüşşafaka. There was word Darüşşafaka would sue the CHP.

These heart-wrenching debates about money made headlines for days. It was a new day for those insidiously on the lookout for an opportunity to attack Mustafa Kemal.

Makbule's unending demands for money were an affront to Atatürk's legacy.

∞

He had relatives from his father's side. His cousins lived in Istanbul.

He didn't neglect his cousins in between the dozens of things he had to do and took close interest in them. He would get word from Makbule if they had need of anything.

His cousin Necati Erbatur got married in 1927. The ceremony was held at Dolmabahçe Palace. He personally had Necati and Zeliha's invitations prepared.

He very much loved his female cousins, Vüsat, Naifa and Zeynep. He had a special place for Vüsat, as her husband had been a captain who had been killed in the National Campaign. He felt twice as responsible to her because of this.

He covered all the expenses when Vüsat's daughter, Nesrin, got married in 1937. He attended the wedding at the Park Hotel and danced with the bride.

Mustafa Kemal's relatives lived lives worthy of him. They didn't demand benefit or strive for fame. They lived modest lives as ordinary people and citizens.

The fourth and fifth generations of these families still do the same today.

∞

Mustafa Kemal never favored men. As in the example of his brother-in-law, he didn't even pull strings for a sibling's benefit.

He loathed sycophancy, flattery and toadyism, saying: "The worst thing in life is hypocrisy."

He was candid. He also liked straight answers.

"We will always tell each other the truth," he said, "whether it brings disaster or felicity, be it good or bad, we will never depart from the truth. The truth must be looked right in the eye."

He didn't like to be glorified and would change the subject. He stayed clear of the simpering flatterers around him. He warned once: "Don't bring these people near me or I'll mistreat them."

Charles de Chambrun, who was the French ambassador in Ankara from 1928 to 1933, described the man he called a humble leader: "Mustafa Kemal could have been a monarch, the caliph and a dictator. But he didn't need shiny titles in order to be a great man. There's no doubt he could have ascended to the throne, but his foresight prevented it. He was devoid of conceit. He did not like pretention and he did not know boasting. He knew how to limit ambitions. He became a little more philosophical every day and he became more valuable among the people. He was a genuine man."

He didn't like informants.

When someone gossiped to him about someone else and laid a charge on them, he would bring the one spoken about and the gossiper together before him and tell the latter to say it to the person's face.

Unsigned letters of denunciation angered him greatly. About them he said, "Sincere and honest people also have courage. They don't sink to hiding their signatures. Those who write letters and don't sign them are without fail immoral liars."

He would never start an investigation when an unsigned letter came, and instead would send the letter on to the person who was denounced so they would know of it.

"I can't say a thing to those who oppose me," he said. "They are free to have their own opinions and thoughts, and I even appreciate them. But I cannot tolerate the hypocritical politics of those who, without support of any idea, pretend to be with me and are against the people who love me.

"There is nothing but benefit in us criticizing each other. It never hurts. It is unchanging, though, with experience that it would be very harmful if it were not to happen."

Charles Sherrill, the American ambassador in Ankara in 1932 and 1933, explained Mustafa Kemal's tolerance of dissent: "Mustafa Kemal acted with reason, logic and equity. When you didn't share his opinions, he would look for the reason. He wanted to know you and what made you think in a different way than him."

In 1923, some meddlesome parliamentarians tried to reward themselves with money on the strength of their service to the country. They even prepared a law that said, "For his service to the country, 1 million liras have been set for His Excellency Gazi Mustafa Kemal Pasha." It was opened for signatures. Mustafa Kemal called it arrogant and shameful when he got word of it. He had the proposed law brought to him, whereupon he ripped it up and threw it out.

It was 1924 and Sinop Representative Recep Zühtü was a hero of the National Campaign. He was stingy, though. He owned a printing house. He began to produce quality cigarette paper, which he brought to market under the brand name Gazi Mustafa Kemal. There wasn't only Mustafa Kemal's name on the cigarette paper; they even had a photograph of him printed on them, too. There were many trying to do business by using him in one way or another, but this was the first instance of such exploitation. Production was stopped immediately on order from Mustafa Kemal.

He made a striking analogy once about those whose sycophancy he had grown tired of: "All types of rubbish are thrown in a trash can, but no matter how much you empty it, there's always some bits stuck to the bottom, and that is what these people are."

Even his passion for books was used as an opportunity for sycophancy. Those who wanted to curry favor with him installed huge libraries in their homes and bought leather-bound books that they never cracked open.

Mustafa Kemal knew quite well how to see what someone was made of. He would take out any random book from the library when he was a guest at someone's house and ask questions about it, which would make the dishonest hosts sweat bullets.

A ball was held on the *Gülcemal* steamer in 1926. Everyone boarded together at the Mudanya pier. There were some high society women among the guests who curtsied exaggeratedly as if they were before a king or sultan. Mustafa Kemal gave a silent message to his aide with a scowl and the women were brought back to the pier.

He sat down and chatted at a coffeehouse while on an excursion around Ankara in 1932. The coffeehouse had the CHP flag with six arrows hung on its door. One of the villagers wanted to get on Mustafa Kemal's good side, as he saw it. He pointed to the flag on the door and said, "Pasha, thanks to you, we'll hopefully make these six arrows 16." Mustafa Kemal got up and left without saying a word.

He turned to the CHP general secretary, Recep Peker, and, with an extremely terse look, said, "Very good, sir. It seems you've taught the citizens very well the principles of the party. I'm very pleased with what I've heard."

In 1935, banners were prepared for the anniversary of the founding of the republic. Printed on them were things such as, "Atatürk is the greatest of us" and Atatürk is the highest in this nation".

Mustafa Kemal asked for a piece of notepaper. "Atatürk is one of us," he wrote.

"If they're going to write something, have them write this," he said.

He went to Büyükada of the Princes' Islands on a fine summer evening in 1936. He was going to walk a bit and dine at the Splendid Hotel. He got off the ferry at the pier and a cabriolet pulled up. A car had been brought with the ferry for him to more comfortably get around the island. "Aren't motor vehicles banned on the island?" he asked. "Get rid of it right away." Then he walked off.

His adopted daughter Nebile got married in 1937, to Sabahatin İrdelp, who was an engineer working at a paper factory in İzmit. One day, they all met with the manager of the factory. There, Mustafa Kemal cautioned the manager in no uncertain terms: "These are my children, but always do what is necessary for how the work must be done." He was even against bestowing privileges on his adopted children.

"I am in love with competence," he said.

He gave work to those who were qualified.

Those around him were split in two groups. One was of those who were useful. The other was of those who were pleasurable.

He never hesitated to give the highest positions in state affairs to those who were useful even though he didn't care for them.

There were also those whom, despite liking them very much, he never gave positions to. These were the pleasurable ones, or the "tasties", as he called them.

He often mentioned in conversations the statesmen he liked and the historical personalities who should be taken as examples.

He called Sultan Mehmed the Conqueror a great man.

"The many times I've thought about the issues Mehmed faced," he said, "I arrive at the same solution. I always wonder, though, how he would handle what I have faced."

According to Afet İnan, Mustafa Kemal had a statue of Mehmed the Conqueror planned for the Maiden's Tower. Mustafa Kemal had said that whenever he passed by the Maiden's Tower, he wanted to see such a monument.

Bayezid I was his favorite of the sultans. Of the sultan, he said, "If one day painters lose the face of heroism, they can take Bayezid and conjure it back."

Among the grand viziers, his most highly regarded was Alemdar Mustafa Pasha, who had installed Mahmud II on the throne. He remarked that the first constitutional document in Turkish history was the materialization of the *Sened-i İttifak* (Charter of Alliance). "If he'd had a bit of culture, he would have declared a republic," he said of the man.

One evening, Mustafa Kemal dined with the French ambassador. They had a meandering conversation that eventually came to Alexander the Great. He put his hand up to stop the conversation as the French ambassador likened Mustafa Kemal and Alexander's military abilities to each other.

"The comparison ends here," he said. "Alexander conquered the world. I've done no such thing. Alexander overran the world and forgot his own land. I will never forget my country."

It was said that after conquering Roman territory, Attila the Hun supposedly addressed the gaudily dressed Roman dignitaries who had come before him and said, "I am not rich and noble like you all, but my people are."

Mustafa Kemal made these words from Attila his rallying cry and gave it as an example of the concept of a people as a nation.

Accepted as the father of strategy, Mustafa Kemal held Hannibal's military genius in high regard. He made use of the legendary Carthaginian commander's tactics while preparing the plans for the Great Offensive. He thought that because of that, Hannibal should unconditionally be held in high esteem in Turkey.

Hannibal killed himself in 182 BCE in the area around Libyssa, in modern-day Gebze. Mustafa Kemal ordered an archaeological dig for the area to find Hannibal's tomb in Gebze, and for it to be turned into a park, including a monument.

They conducted intensive research, but couldn't locate the grave. Mustafa Kemal's desire was fulfilled in 1981.

No tomb was found, but a monument to Hannibal was erected on land owned by the Scientific and Technological Research Council of Turkey (TÜBİTAK).

He would recommend Gazi Osman Pasha—the hero of Pleven—as a role model to everyone falling into pessimism. When speaking with Turkish youth while he was serving as an attaché in Sofia, he said, "I chose

Gazi Osman Pasha as my guide. The Turkish spirit is the national spirit in him. We will think of Pleven and Gazi Osman Pasha in days of tribulation; let him be a symbol for you."

❉

He was a great admirer of the architect Mimar Sinan.

He instructed the Turkish Historical Society to conduct scientific research to determine the most appropriate body and facial features for a statue of Mimar Sinan.

The renowned architect's tomb in the Süleymaniye complex was opened. His skull and bones were measured and his height was determined.

His remains were sent to the village of Ağırnas in Kayseri, where he was born. Photographs of typical people born and raised in the region were taken. Anecdotes that had passed down from generation to generation were also collected.

The findings were presented to Mustafa Kemal and he approved them.

Today, every one of the statues of Mimar Sinan found throughout Turkey was designed from the medallion made from those first findings.

❉

In addition to Mimar Sinan, Mustafa Kemal also wanted statues made of Süleyman the Magnificent,

Hayreddin Barbarossa and ibn Sina. The monument to Barbarossa, for example, was opened in 1944, by İsmet İnönü. The construction of the monument had begun in Mustafa Kemal's lifetime.

He had Topkapı Palace turned into a museum and opened to the public. He visited the holy relics in the Chamber of the Holy Mantle. He wanted to see the Holy Banner. They took it from its chest and spread it over a table. While everyone else looked on as if they were enchanted, Mustafa Kemal said, "This isn't the Holy Banner; where's the real one?"

It was like a bomb had fallen on Topkapı. There was a panic and the situation was soon understood.

The original, black Holy Banner had moldered to pieces and in its place, they'd put a green copy. The tatters of the original were in a bag at the bottom of the chest.

It was impossible to fool Mustafa Kemal, especially concerning history. He didn't get information by word of mouth; it was always based on knowledge.

His appetite for learning was insatiable. Reading was like breathing to him.

Even in Tripoli, Gallipoli, the War of Independence and the bloodiest battles and most critical days, he never dropped what he was reading.

In 1922, for example, shortly before the Battle of Dumlupınar, the entries in his diary included:

"I got up early in the morning and read a book for a while."

"İsmet Pasha left. I'll read a little and then go to bed."

"I took a bath and then got ready after reading a book in bed."

"I'm alone. I'll read a book for a while."

Halide Edip Adıvar said that Mustafa Kemal was going through the battle plans on his desk while also reading a book on the history of Islam. "I attest that the first 24 years of Islamic history in particular were its most democratic," he said.

Fahrettin Altay explained how Mustafa Kemal would read the book *Islamic Religion and Tasfir* in his tent at night.

He was reading Namık Kemal's *Tarih-i Osmani* (Ottoman History), Mehmet Yurdakul's poems, Tevfik Fikret's *Rübab-ı Şikeste* (Broken Rebab) and *Sappho* by Alphonse Daudet as he rescued Bitlis from enemy occupation in 1916.

He read Balzac while he received treatment in Carlsbad in 1918. He also followed the criticism of Karl Marx's *Das Kapital*.

He wrote the book *Zabit ve Kumandan ile Hasbihal* (Reflections Upon the Officer and Commander). He had 1,000 copies made at the Minber Printing House. The price tag was 7.50 *kuruş*. When he went to Anatolia in 1919, even reading the book was criminal.

Damad Ferid's government had copies of it collected and burned, and then they banned it again.

He was speaking at the podium of the Grand National Assembly when he took the Ottoman Basic Law, held it in the air and said, "Gentlemen, Sultan Hamid used the people like slaves for the past 33 years by leaning on this book and the law in it and by distributing it to gullible representatives."

Then he lifted up Jean Jacques Rousseau's *The Social Contract* and said, "Gentlemen, read Jean Jacques Rousseau from beginning to end—I have."

The republic had yet to be declared in 1922. Upon suggestion from Yahya Kemal Beyatlı, Istanbul University Department of Literature bestowed on Mustafa Kemal the title of honorary professor.

An earthquake struck Erzurum in 1924. Sixty people lost their lives. There was massive destruction. Aid campaigns were launched across the country to collect food, clothing and money.

A bookseller from Istanbul provided unprecedented help. He sent 1,000 liras worth of books to children affected by the earthquake. As soon as he heard of it, Mustafa Kemal sent the man a telegram of thanks:

Istanbul, Babıali Street

To bookseller Hilmi Bey,

My many thanks to you for sending the gift of books to children who survived the earthquake. I find it valuable what you have done for the learning and wisdom of the country. This type of contribution has significance to show that a people equipped with knowledge and wisdom can cope with all types of disaster, even natural disasters, and is praiseworthy for the entire nation.

President of the Republic

Gazi Mustafa Kemal

He wrote the *Nutuk* (Address to the Notion) in 1927.

He put pen to paper to write the documentary of the Republic of Turkey since the beginning of the War of Independence. It took him three months to complete. It covered from May 19, 1919 to October 20, 1927. It ran 534 pages. There were also 308 pages of documents such as letters and telegraphs.

He was both the writer and speaker. He read it aloud from the podium of the Grand National Assembly.

He read for six hours every day for six days. It took 36 hours and 31 minutes in total.

It was an unprecedented event in the world. It became known as the marathon address.

His writing was emotional, both to give the official record of the National Campaign and also to account to the people.

He started his historic speech with: "I am of the opinion that it is my duty to account to our people concerning our obligations and activities that have been ongoing for years."

He finished this, his political testament, with his *Address to the Turkish Youth.*

Honorable gentlemen, this long and exhaustive speech of mine, which has occupied you for so many days, is a narrative of a time that henceforth belongs to the past.

I consider myself fortunate if I have been able to express in this address some truths calculated to draw attention and vigilance for my nation and our future generations.

Gentlemen, I have tried to show in this address how a great people whose national existence was considered to have ended won its independence and how it created a national and modern state founded on the principles of the most recent science and technology.

The result we have reached today is the product of vigilance created by centuries of national disasters and the price of the blood that has soaked every corner of the soil of the homeland.

I lay this result in the hands of the Turkish youth.

O Turkish youth!

Your first duty is to forever preserve and defend Turkish independence and that of the Turkish Republic.

This is the very foundation of your existence and your future.

This foundation is your most precious treasure.

You will also see malicious people in the future, at home and abroad, who want to deprive you of this treasure.

If you are one day compelled to defend your independence and the republic, you must not wait to weigh the possibilities and circumstances of the situation before taking up your duty.

These possibilities and circumstances appear to be extremely unfavorable.

It could be that these enemies who conspire against your freedom and the republic are the representative of a victory unprecedented the world over.

It may be that by violence and deceit, all the fortresses of the beloved homeland are captured, all its shipyards entered, all its armies dispersed and every corner of the country under active occupation.

More deplorable and perilous than all these circumstances is that those who hold power within the country may be careless or misguided, or might even be traitorous.

Furthermore, they may identify their personal interests with the political aims of the invaders. The country may fall into abject poverty, be ruined and exhausted.

O sons and daughters of the Turkish future!

It is your duty to save Turkish Independence and the republic even in such circumstances.

The strength you need is the noble blood coursing through your veins.

The same sight imprinted in the memories of all the local and foreign observers in the Grand National Assembly—the sight of Mustafa Kemal's eyes filling with tears as he read his *Address to the Turkish Youth*.

Mustafa Kemal's original, handwritten notes for the *Nutuk* were placed in the Ziraat Bank vault after his death. They were transferred to the archive of the General Staff upon completion of carrying out his will.

It was printed in Ottoman Turkish in 1927. It's been published in modern Turkish since 1934. On average, between 100,000 and 150,000 copies are sold per year. As of 2018, it is still on the list of Turkey's best-selling books.

❉

The *Nutuk* is the most practical way to determine whether the many rumors concerning the National Campaign that later came into existence are true or not. It is the ultimate litmus test for the lies created to muddy the waters, and it is these lies that the words from Mustafa Kemal's own mouth have rebuffed.

∞

In 1931, he had a plot of land allocated to create the İzmir National Library—the country's first national library. A budget was allocated for its construction. He came in person twice to supervise its construction. It opened on October 29, 1933, on the 10th anniversary of the founding of the republic.

The shah of Iran visited Turkey in 1934, and Mustafa Kemal brought him to İzmir, where he showed the shah around the İzmir National Library. Mustafa Kemal was the first and only head of state to lead a visiting head of state on a tour of a library.

Mustafa Kemal was in his study when the Turkish ambassador in Moscow, Vasıf Çınar, came to Çankaya in 1935. He was pensive and reading a book.

Çınar started to babble: "Pasha, you exhaust yourself reading such a book. Were you reading a book like this when you set off for Samsun?"

Mustafa Kemal smiled and said, "I hear this kind of talk quite often. They gossip about me, saying I have no power for work and spend my time with books. It's been like that since I was a child. If I got a few *kuruş,* I would certainly spend half of it on books. If I hadn't done so, I wouldn't be Atatürk."

He called those who didn't read straw heads in addition to calling them half-headed.

The world's most prestigious literary organization, the International Mark Twain Society, invited him to be an honorary member in 1938.

The letter of invitation sent to Çankaya said:

"You have left a more glorious name in history than that of Alexander the Great, Julius Cesar and Napoleon. Your military and civilian genius has deeply affected human history."

Grigory S. Petrov

Finland: The Country of White Lilies comes at the forefront of books that have left deep marks on the intellectual world.

It was written by the Russian man of letters Grigory Spiridonovich Petrov.

It explains how in the 1800s, a handful of patriotic intellectuals turned Finland from a miserable country stuck in a swamp to the country of white lilies. It was an example of economic, political and cultural revolution, and a complete model for development based on science and the concept of the nation-state.

It was in lock step with the Turkish revolution. It was this similarity that excited Mustafa Kemal.

He would quote from the book, including, "A healthy mind is found on a healthy body".

There were also striking coincidences. The protagonist of *Finland: The Country of White Lilies*, Johan Snelman, died in 1881, the year of Mustafa Kemal's birth. The book was also written in 1923, or the founding year of the republic.

Mustafa Kemal had the book added to the curriculum of military schools. It was the best-selling foreign book in Turkey until the 1970s.

H. G. Wells.

He also read H. G. Wells.

This pioneer of science fiction wrote such legendary novels as *The Island of Doctor Moreau, The Invisible Man* and *The Time Machine*.

He read the English futurist's book, *The Outline of History*, in its French translation and was very impressed. He even mentioned it in the *Nutuk*.

Mustafa Kemal had the book, which explains the concept of a united world government for lasting peace, translated into Turkish.

He read the books on theoretical physics by Sorbonne professor Henri Poincaré. He was aware of Albert Einstein's theories of relativity and spacetime. These scientists had influenced the early foundations of aviation and space exploration.

He found Alfred Fouillée's *A Psychological Sketch of the European Peoples* to be very interesting. He wrote a note on the last page of the book: "I read it in one night, September 4-5."

He read the book in 1923 and underlined these passages:

- *Every nation has its own peculiar sense.*
- *Every nation devises its religion for itself.*
- *Its philosophy of religion shows how a nation looks at life and how it values life and the universe, and affects its happiness and disasters.*

• *A poor nation is in need of work much more than soaring speeches and sermonizing.*

• *Some influential families place members in one party and others in another party, ensuring a part of the family remains in the place of power regardless of which party wins.*

• *It is the great politician, politics and deceitful keepers of accounts that are the bourgeoisie and who can hide even their hatred if it is for their own benefit.*

• *Nations must never forget that the only condition for national greatness is to have an enduringly moral character.*

• *A nation can only survive if it possesses a conscience.*

V.I. Lenin.

He read Lenin's "Theses on Bourgeois Democracy and the Dictatorship of the Proletariat" in a collection of the communist revolutionary's writings and put it in his library. The Communist Organization of Turkey had published the collection in Baku, and it was banned in 1920.

He read materialist German philosopher Ludwig Büchner's *Force and Matter*. He marked the chapters concerning the brain, consciousness, memory, intelligence and thought.

He read Professor Avram Galanti's book from 1925, *Hamurabi Kanunu* (The Code of Hammurabi), and took notes.

He read John Stuart Mill's *On Liberty*, the Rubaiyat of Omar Khayyam, Shakespeare's *Romeo and Juliet* and Homer's *Iliad*.

He had surprising interests, as well. For example, he'd read Osman Nuri's *Fenn-i İnşaat* (The Science of Construction). He marked the chapters that dealt with brick production.

He would check out books from the Istanbul University library and sign a slip that said he would return them within 15 days, just as ordinary citizens did when checking out books from the state libraries.

He didn't permit privilege for himself.

He would send lists of book orders in official lettering to the Turkish Embassies in Paris, London, Rome and Vienna. He paid for them all out of his own pocket. He said he wouldn't dare have it any other way.

He would ask for the bills, as well. This way he would check to make sure a meddlesome diplomat hadn't used any state money instead of his own.

Münir Ertegün became the Turkish ambassador in Paris in 1930. He didn't know how sensitive Mustafa Kemal was to the issue of payments. He sent the bill for two history books he ordered for Mustafa Kemal to the Foreign Minister.

Three days later, a telegraph from the Çankaya Mansion came to the embassy in Paris: "The President of the Republic's private expenditures cannot be covered from the budget of the Foreign Ministry, and as such, you are to address and send the bills to him."

He didn't wait for the ambassador to write and his top aide asked for the bills from the Foreign Ministry. The money for the books—571 francs—was transferred through İş Bank to the embassy in Paris.

He scoured a wide array of topics. Among the topics from the list of books he sent to the embassy in Paris in 1935 were statistics, sociology, constitutional law, anthropology, history of religions, history of diplomacy, history of philosophy, history of the sciences, art history and modern literature.

Sometimes he ordered directly from foreign bookstores. For example, an order he sent to the French bookstore Sirey was four, full, typewritten pages. The delivery was sent in 24 packages.

He had works by Descartes and Kant translated into Turkish. He had come across Auguste Comte's ideas while he was still a student. He also read Durkheim.

DICTIONNAIRE, GRAMMAIRE ET CHRESTOMATHIE

LA LANGUE MAYA

ETUDE SUR LE SYSTÈME GRAPHIQUE

M. BRASSEUR DE BOURBOURG

PARIS

He gave great importance to dictionaries.

He never removed from his desk the four-volume comparative dictionary of Turkic languages by the pioneer of Turkology, Vasily Radloff.

He would often consult Eduard Karlovich Pekarskiy's *Dictionary of the Yakut Language.*

Those with a place of honor in his library included the following: Julius Pokorny's *Etymological Dictionary of Indo-European Languages*, Emile Boisacq's *Etymological Dictionary of the Greek Language*, Antoine Meillet's *Etymological Dictionary of the Latin Language*, Oscar Bloch's *Etymological Dictionary of the French Language*, Friedrich Kluge's *Etymological Dictionary of the German Language*,

Anatole Bailly's *Greek-French Dictionary* and Louis-Marie Quicherat's *French-Latin Dictionary*.

He had read Charles Étienne Brasseur de Bourbourg's *Troano Codex* on the Mayan language.

He also had dictionaries of Akkadian, Hebrew, Syriac, Arabic, Persian, Sanskrit, Mandarin, Japanese, Finnish, Hungarian and ancient Egyptian.

He would also look through Friedrich Delitzsch's *Sumerian Grammar*.

There was an L-shaped library in his study at the Çankaya Mansion. He would carry books with him every time he returned to Ankara from Istanbul. They wouldn't fit in his suitcase.

It was on one of those days when he found the librarian Nuri Ulusu brooding over something—he had prepared more than 50 books, but how was he going to get them to the train without damaging their covers?

Mustafa Kemal called his aide and had ammunition crates brought to the library.

"These crates are very important," he said. "We carried ammunition in them in the war, but now that war is over and our war for culture and art has begun. The ammunition for our new war is books."

He kept a red and blue pen with him when he read to write on the margins and underline passages.

xx meant it was significant.

xxx meant it was very significant.

If it was important, he wrote *müh.*, short for *mühim*, or important.

If it was very important, he wrote ç. müh., short for çok mühim, or very important.

D was for *dikkat*, or attention.

He would put a question mark next to ideas he found suspicious.

He used red to underline sentences with ideas he agreed and blue for those with ideas he didn't like.

He read history books with a map next to him. He sketched while he read books on war. There was only one exception—he never marked up books he borrowed from the Istanbul Library and would return them clean and in good condition.

Sometimes he would read for 48 hours straight. He would only take a break to bathe and then continued.

He had muslin cut into small pieces and would use the absorbent strips to wipe his eyes when they would tear up from reading.

He called reading a special art.

He even read on his deathbed. He went into a coma on October 15, 1938, but, the last thing he read before his eyes shut was the Turkish Historical Society's *Bulletin* magazine.

∞

He was a revolutionary.

No leader in history has ever achieved such a great transformation in such a short amount of time. It's not even close.

Famous British historian Arnold J. Toynbee spoke of it with amazement, respect and envy: "Think for a moment of the Renaissance, Reformation, the scientific and cultural revolution of the late 17th century, the French Revolution and the Industrial Revolution all squeezed into the lifespan of an individual and imposed by law."

Mustafa Kemal ran through the steps he'd taken every day without fail.

"Morning, evening, night—whenever you can," he said, "if for half an hour or a quarter hour—if you can set aside however much time—withdraw into yourselves, look over the work you did that day and weigh your thoughts. Look over yourselves once every day, what you've done and worked on. You wouldn't be able to imagine how useful the answers that come from your consciousness will be."

He was calm.

It would have been impossible for a man who could not control his nerves to risk his life from the age of 23 and survive through it all—the Druze Rebellion, the 31 March Incident, the Albanian Revolt, the Italo-Turkish War, the Second Balkan War, the Battle of Gallipoli, the fighting on the eastern front, clashes on the Syrian-Palestinian front and the War of Independence.

He didn't shy away from dangers.

The Bursa-Yalova highway had recently opened. Bandits cut off the road the day it opened and robbed the people passing by. Mustafa Kemal was in Istanbul when he heard of it.

"Prepare my car," he said. "I'm going to Bursa."

They told him it could be dangerous. He didn't answer them and just left, setting off on that same road to Bursa.

About the incident he said, "How can a citizen use a road I can't use? The president will use that road, and so, too, will the citizens without hesitation."

He was humble.

"It is necessary to defeat pride in success and resist desperation in disaster. A person should always seek success, but it is pointless to boast of doing this or that. The boastful are things of the past."

He believed in teamwork. To those who asked, he would say that a team was the secret to his success.

"A team is necessary," he said. "That is, an entire success cannot be attributed to a single person. It is necessary to organize so success can be achieved. Whatever I did, I was able to do with support from my friends and the people. It cannot be attributed to me alone."

He was a man of obligation. He had the opportunity to live otherwise, but he didn't. His sense of social responsibility always made him feel obliged.

His compatriot İsmet İnönü knew Mustafa Kemal very closely and described this feature of his: "He came forward against the cruelest and most unjust accusations we have come across in history. He claimed and declared that the Turkish people are without guilt and are righteous. After he won the great victory, he spent his life only proving the Turkish people's rights."

He spoke with an accent from Rumelia. There were some words he pronounced peculiarly. He would say *tabanca,* the word for pistol, as *tapanca,* and *kırbaç,* or whip, as *kırpaç*. For yogurt—*yogurt* in Turkish—he said *yuğurt.*

When he wanted to encourage someone, he would say, *hade de, hade de,* or *come on and say it,* instead of the Istanbul accent's *haydi de.*

To ask a question, he used the word *yani,* meaning—*that is to say*—quite often.

He would grow impatient when someone would go on at length explaining a request and ask them, *yani,* so they'd get to the point.

He referred to his attendants as kids. He didn't use terms like cook, waiter, butler or driver. He called all of them kids. It showed both his sincerity and respect for the employees.

He'd throw around the word animal when he was angry. The greatest insult he gave was to call someone a *hebenneka*. It was a common term in Ottoman Turkish for someone who thinks they are intelligent despite being an idiot.

He found amusing descriptions for those whose character he disliked. For example, he would say, "Leave that wooden man be."

It was thought until 2010 that his voice was high. As for the technology in the 1930s, film was cranked by hand to record. It was impossible to capture the actual full sound of the voice of a person speaking and instead rendered it high pitched. And this is what all extant recordings of Mustafa Kemal were like.

Film of Mustafa Kemal found at the Mimar Sinan University State Archive was restored in 2010 with modern technology. His true voice was revealed and published. His voice was much lower than had been known before.

He would prepare as if for a test before going on tours of the country. He wrote his speeches himself. He memorized them and didn't read from the paper.

If he was to give five speeches in five cities, the contents of the five speeches would be different. He never fell into repetition. No sentence of his resembled any of his others.

∞

He gave headlines to the press. He chose memorable words in the form of catch lines. This was because he had a journalistic aspect, as well.

The newspaper *Minber* (The Pulpit) came out in Istanbul in 1918. Mustafa Kemal wrote columns under the penname Hatib (preacher). It was forbidden for him to write under his real name due to his military credentials. He criticized the government.

In one column, he called Damad Ferid "ignorant, a calamity, impudent, arrogant, careless, ridiculous and in need of reading a book."

It was censored in a flash and copies of the newspaper were confiscated.

He didn't even have enough money to buy a train ticket when he was on his way back from Syria. His only things resembling material possessions were four mares he doted on. He sold them for 2,600 *kuruş*. He took the money he got from the mares and bought a share in the newspaper. He did it jointly with Ali Fethi Okyar and Doctor Rasim Ferid. Their funds, however, could only suffice for so long. They were able to put out 51 issues in seven weeks before they closed shop.

The İrade-i Milliye (National Will) newspaper was published during the Sivas Congress. It was the National Campaign's first media production. It published official reports on the congress and notices. Below its logo was written: "The want of the nation and defender of desire."

The papers were four pages and had a circulation of 5,000 copies.

The Hakimiyet-i Milliye (National Sovereignty) newspaper came out in Ankara. Mustafa Kemal wrote its first editorial. The paper published the work of the Ankara government. It was two pages. As for its size, it was printed as a tabloid due to the paper shortage. Since 1934, the paper has been published under the name *Ulus* (Nation).

There was a newspaper in Istanbul in 1937 called *Kurun* (The Times). It was the highest-selling newspaper with circulation of about 10,000. Mustafa Kemal wrote articles for the paper under the penname Asım Us.

The most important item on the agenda was the Hatay problem. He sent messages directed at France in his articles in a type of newspaper diplomacy. In one piece, for example, he wrote they would go to war: "It is Turkey that is right in the Hatay case, and much attention should be paid to what promises came from whose mouth. A Turk's word is his bond, and it should never be doubted that what those who show the courage to disobey him, repudiate him and disregard him will confront the consequences they haven't thought of."

Asım Us' pieces played a large role in wresting Hatay from Syria with ease, like plucking a hair from butter.

The only leader in the Middle East to win territory without firing a bullet has been Mustafa Kemal.

He saw journalism as one of the sacred professions. Once, he told Sabiha Gökçen: "I would have entered journalism if I hadn't been a soldier."

Ali Kemal.

Ali Kemal was the owner of the *Peyam-ı Sabah* (Morning News) newspaper. His actual name was Ali Rıza. He was a great fan of poet Namık Kemal and so wrote under the name Ali Kemal. He may have taken the name of this poet so important to the country, but he turned into the most renowned traitor in the history of the country and the press.

He was one of the founders of the British Friendship Society. He was an enemy of the National Campaign. In one piece he wrote, "Which Asian tribe has succeeded in overcoming Europe so that we can?"

He had a personal hatred for Mustafa Kemal. He also worked up an obsession with Mustafa Kemal. Of him he said, "Shaking hands with him is to reach out to a bandit."

He also called Mustafa Kemal a vagabond.

"They set up a ragtag army and they fight away," he said of the National Campaign. "They're nutty. They insist on full independence, but what do the Arabs say—power goes to the victor—that is all it is."

He wrote about the revolutionaries:

"We've shut them up, their morale is very low, most of them are barefoot, they lack equipment and, whereas they do have a few trucks, none of them can be used. The broken-down motors can't be fixed, they have no gasoline, they have no spare parts and they have oxen they can use to move them. Mustafa Kemal and his men are of no use for anything. Thank goodness they are few in number. They must be severed like a diseased limb and cast away."

"Mustafa Kemal is undertaking insanity in Anatolia in order to turn the civilized world against us."

"O Muslim brethren, don't be fooled by nationalist organizations. These men are vagrants with no country and a Bolshevik mindset."

"The National Forces are buffoonery. I wouldn't change my view even if they take Afyon, Eskişehir, Kütahya, Bursa and the others."

On the day the Grand National Assembly of Turkey opened, he wrote, "One wouldn't want to trample on a snakes head as much as the heads of these nationalist creatures. Enemies are better than them a thousandfold."

On the day the Great Offensive began, he wrote: "Until today, the National Forces have lost in everything they've done and have never won a thing. Ankara is constraining us from entering the right path. If I am wrong in these thoughts, I won't only break my pen, I will even resign my humanity. The events will show, however, that I am not mistaken."

Mustafa Kemal didn't only set the National Campaign against imperialist countries, but also against these types of collaborators.

Ali Kemal was lynched while he was taken to Ankara after his arrest to be tried at the Court of Independence.

The Turkish Journalists Association declared him a martyr of the press 78 years later in the year 2000.

Ali Kemal said of Mustafa Kemal and the National Forces that they were a diseased limb, vagabonds, murderers, a snake whose head must be crushed and a thousand times worse than enemies. Despite this, he was placed on the same list as Hasan Tahsin, who fired the first bullet at the Greek forces occupying Izmir.

Ali Kemal's first wife was Anglo-Swiss. Their marriage ceremony was held in a church. Their son's name was Wilfred and he grew up in England. He later became an officer and then a pilot and received the Conspicuous Gallantry Medal of the United Kingdom for the bravery and effectiveness he showed during World War II. He was married and had a son, who grew up, married and had a son named Boris—his full name is Alexander Boris de Pfeffel Johnson. He became a journalist like his grandfather Ali Kemal. Later he was a parliamentarian for the Conservatives, the mayor of London and then the British foreign secretary.

Ali Kemal's second wife was Turkish. He had another son—Zeki Kuneralp. He grew up in Switzerland and studied law. He said he would return to Turkey as he was finishing up university. The elders of the family objected, saying he wouldn't be allowed to sustain himself, but he didn't listen. He was a capable young man who knew English, German and French. He took the Foreign Ministry service exam and scored very high.

Mustafa Kemal had passed away and İsmet İnönü had become president. They brought the files of those who passed the foreign service exam, but one had a negative note on it that said, "Unsuitable for employment." It was prejudicial.

İsmet İnönü opened the file and read it. It was written in red pen that he was Ali Kemal's son. He crossed out the word negative and wrote positive, he crossed out the rest and wrote that he approved it and then signed it. "Grudges are unseemly for the state and the crimes of a father should not fall to his children," he said. "We established this republic with blood, but we will bring it up with people."

It was this that was the spirit of the National Forces.

Zeki Kuneralp was the Turkish ambassador in Paris, Berlin, London and Madrid, and was the undersecretary of foreign affairs. Just look at the game of fate. Spurred on by the Americans and British, Ali Kemal proposed selling the eastern cities to Armenians, and so was given the nickname Artin Kemal—Artin being an Armenian name. Ali Kemal's son lived through the Armenian Secret Army for the Liberation of Armenia (ASALA) terrorist attack in Madrid. He was just barely saved, but his wife, Necla Kuneralp, was killed. Ali Kemal was a stain on this, as he was everything.

Ali Kemal wasn't alone, either. For instance, Refi Cevad, a writer for the *Alemdar* (Standard Bearer) newspaper, was nearly begging the British, having written: "We are waiting for the British. The Turks cannot be men with their own forces. The British will take us by the hand and save us." Of Mustafa Kemal, he said that he's not crazy, but fully insane.

It had become fashionable among journalists defending British protection to insult Mustafa Kemal by calling him crazy. Refik Halid Karay wrote in the magazine *Aydede* (Man in the Moon): "There's a fracas in Anatolia, a racket, declarations of congresses and such as if they will be able to do something. What force do you have, what kind of dream is this my little lamb Mustafa Kemal? Are you crazy?"

Mustafa Kemal loved to visit high schools. He would enter the classrooms, sit in the rows of students and listen to the teachers.

He would also ask the students questions as if he were the superintendent.

He went to Galatasaray High School in 1930, by chance on the day when the middle and final year students were taking a history and geography exam. He entered the exam room, made the students stand up one by one and asked them questions:

• *How many men were in the first Arab army to cross from Africa to Spain in the time Attila was battling the Romans?*

How many Turks were in it?

In what direction did it go?

Which was the first city it seized?

• *Compare the Treaties of Sevres and Lausanne.*

• *What are the differences between the climates of the Aegean Sea and Archipelago Sea?*

• *What are statism and individualism?*

• *What does legislative power mean?*

• *How are laws made?*

• *What is railroad politics?*

• *Which railways were built in Turkey after 1914?*

• *What is the importance of western Anatolia?*

• *What does ancient civilization mean?*

• *Explain the battle between the Hittites and Egyptians.*

• *Which are the Turkish civilizations in Anatolia?*

• *Of the Hittite, Sumerian and Egyptian civilizations, which is the oldest?*

• *What are the differences between the election of the president in Turkey and in Germany?*

The middle school students in 1930 Turkey were well equipped enough to be able to answer these intense questions.

With Mustafa Kemal's vision, an illiterate country was raised to this height in merely seven years.

∞

He was a genius of foresight.

The chief of staff of the United States Army, General Douglas MacArthur, visited Istanbul in 1931, when Hitler was yet to take power. This is when Mustafa Kemal told him: "Hitler will come to power in Germany within two years and, having its pride destroyed in the Great War, it will gain ambition for payback for its crushed pride. War will break out in Europe by 1940 at the latest."

He spoke similarly in 1933 to Professor Rudolph Nissen, who was among the German Jewish scientists who had taken refuge in Turkey: "You know, professor, the history of the world is full of examples from all times of catastrophes humanity is driven into by supposedly the most talented and heroic commanders. Hitler is no different from these people. He will drive his society and the world into a great catastrophe, and that's how it will be remembered in history."

∞

He explained the most complex of issues in ways everyone could understand.

France's famous Maginot Line was a topic of discussion in 1933. It was said this gigantic fortification still under construction along the border could never be breached. Mustafa Kemal was in the company of foreign diplomats who asked him what he thought of it.

His answer was more of a narrative: "A typical example of this line had been set up in Anatolia. Don't you know of the tomb of Nasreddin Hodja? The façade is woven in with the wall and there's a huge lock on the door, but three of its sides are completely open."

And that's exactly what happened. German tanks in World War II entered France as easily as it is to go into Nasreddin Hodja's tomb.

He was humorous and clever.

Celal Sahir Erozan, a founding member of the Turkish Language Association and poet, was reciting his latest poem:

Empty, empty, empty—
Streets are empty,
Squares are empty,
Shops are empty,
Everything is empty,
The horizon is empty,
The earth is empty

Mustafa Kemal couldn't help himself.

"What's that, Sahir?" he said. "Did you write this poem on the day of the census when it was forbidden to step outside?" Then he broke out in laughter.

King Alexander of Yugoslavia had come to Istanbul. A dinner was given in his honor at Dolmabahçe Palace. The king was sincere in their conversation: "In fact, the British government wanted to set out to ask us for troops to land in İzmir before they went to the Greeks. I didn't agree to it."

Mustafa Kemal smiled and said, "Then I hope you and your people recover from it soon, Your Excellency."

His upbraidings were tinged with humor.

Ince, he sent word to Istanbul Police Chief Salih Kılıç, telling him to find Yahya Kemal at once. They searched and combed the city, but couldn't find him.

Then Mustafa Kemal laid into him: "If you're incapable of finding my friends, how will you find my enemies?"

He was quick at repartee.

A conversation around the dinner table once concerned the relationship between foreign language education and intelligence. There was a suggestion that intelligent people learn foreign languages more easily. He shot back with an example: "If you are looking for intelligence in those who know foreign languages, go to Beirut. Even the porters there know at least seven languages."

He was known for his furrowed brow and stiff facial expression, but he was actually an extremely cheerful person in his private life.

"People who have no joy are suspect in two ways," he said. "They are either sick or have a delusion they don't want to let others know of."

Wastefulness was one of his enemies. He never tolerated those who splurged using the nation's money.

(The War of Independence is the only war the world has seen that was won without inflation.

The black market was combated against in even the bloodiest days of the war.

Hoarders, opportunists and the costliness of life weren't left to pass unchallenged.

Prices didn't increase with the founding of the republic, but rather decreased.

In 1923, $1 was 1.67 liras.

In 1939, $1 was 1.28 liras.

The dollar fell while Turkey grew by 8 percent every year for 15 years and while deposit accounts grew 57 times over.)

He knew poverty and never forgot the days when he had no money.

In 1927, a 1 oka (1,283 grams) loaf of bread was 4 *kuruş*. The government was considering a rise in the price.

There were ministers around the table discussing this issue. Mustafa Kemal motioned over to İbrahim Ergüven, who had prepared the table, and said, "Let's ask İbrahim, as well. He's a man of the people."

Everyone turned to İbrahim.

İbrahim was very clear in what he said: "People bring three or four loaves of bread home, so a 1 *kuruş* raise in price means 3 or 4 *kuruş* more coming out of their pocket. If the price of bread is raised, then so, too, should be the price of products the wealthy eat like pastries and French bread."

Mustafa Kemal turned back to the members of government and settled it: "Now that's the truth. This discussion is over."

The price of a loaf of bread stayed at 4 *kuruş*.

He was at the Forest Farm one day, walking toward the Marmara Mansion. A hefty man burst out from the trees screaming, "My sultan, my sultan!" He was thought to be an assailant. It was a mess. They took hold of the man and marched him away.

Mustafa Kemal, however, was curious.

"Call him and let's see what he wanted," he said.

The man was brought to him. The poor fellow hadn't heard of the founding of the republic or anything. He worked as a laborer at the Forest Farm.

"They pay once a week," he said. "I'm hungry."

Mustafa Kemal listened with a worried expression. He turned to his aide and asked who was in charge of pay. They brought the forest engineer who paid the salaries.

Mustafa Kemal was angry. "Have you ever been hungry?" he asked the engineer. He didn't actually wait for an answer. "From now one you'll pay the daily wage every day," he ordered.

He didn't content himself with just that. He personally called the agriculture minister, Rahmi Köken, and asked him the same serious question: "Have you ever been hungry?"

The agriculture minister had to resign.

He wouldn't offend the poor even for stealing.

The construction of new buildings of the Çankaya Mansion was underway when he heard shouts and noise from outside. He looked out the window. They had placed the workers side by side on their knees and were searching them.

Mustafa Kemal asked why. As it turned out, one of the workers had gone into the mansion on the sly, swiped a pack of cigarettes from a table and was caught on his way out. They were all searched to see if any others had done the same.

"Leave them be at once," he yelled. "This is behavior that embarrasses us. No one in this country steals cigarettes, and at most they want to bring a souvenir from us to their families. Give each of them a pack of cigarettes."

He had limitless tolerance for the citizens of the country.

He saw while looking through the Anadolu Agency news bulletins that an investigation into a villager who had cursed him had been opened. He wondered what he had done to the man. He was told the man had used newsprint to roll a cigarette. It had all gone up in flames when he lit it and that's why he had sworn at him.

Mustafa Kemal smiled a bitter smile. "Have you ever smoked a cigarette rolled with newsprint?" he said. "I did when I was in Tripoli. It's quite wretched. That villager deserves to swear at me more. You ensure you indict him and that he smokes cigarettes like a human."

∞

He loved to host guests. At the end of the night, he would see everyone off from the door. Even if he had friends coming over every evening, he would without exception take care to greet them and send them off as if it were the first time they had come.

He had an interest in decorating. He would walk through each room when he was a guest at somebody's house. He would give his opinion about the furniture and give suggestions like moving a painting to another wall or putting flowers in a certain corner.

He didn't like clashing colors. He would look over the bathroom without fail. He asked questions about the plumbing. He would go into the kitchen and poke around with the drawers and cabinets. He would also comment if the drawers weren't installed correctly.

He also didn't like eating in cramped rooms. If the table was in the kitchen or dining room, he would ask the host and have it moved to the living room.

The Turkish ambassador in Berlin, Kemaleddin Sami Pasha, was married to Emine, the sister of Prince Abbas Halim Pasha of Egypt. They would come to Istanbul on vacation in summer and stay in the mansions on the Princes' Islands' Heybeliada.

Mustafa Kemal was very fond of Kemalleddin Sami Pasha, who was a hero of the National Campaign, and wanted to visit him. He went to Heybeliada on his yacht, the *Söğütlü*.

He hadn't sent prior word and him coming was a surprise. He sat down and drank some coffee. He wanted to tour the mansion, as was his habit.

Princess Emine began to give him a tour. They went through the guest room, dining room and then on into the bedrooms. She opened a door and said it was her bedroom. It was richly furnished, the curtains and side tables were elegant and there was a magnificent bed.

Then she opened the next door down and said it was Kemaleddin's room. The sofa had been contrived into a bed, the bedspread was crumpled and haphazard and the pillows were dirty.

Mustafa Kemal was startled. He was careful with his words. "I didn't sleep in such a room even when I was a young officer," he said.

The tour of the house ended half way through. He left, his face sad, without even looking at the princess, whose face was now red with embarrassment. He never again went to visit and neither did he extend invitations to the princess.

He loved to give gifts.

He didn't buy them—the gifts were rather his personal belongings. He would hand out his jackets, hats and shoes. He wanted the gifts to be souvenirs.

A package came to the Çankaya Mansion from Poland in 1936. They opened it. Inside was a tiny box and a letter. They opened the little box. In it was a piece of amber with an insect encased inside. Then they opened the letter:

This amber is an auspicious object in our family. I thought of giving you this gift with immaterial value because you are the greatest man of our century. I see its auspiciousness and fortune as worthy of you. Please accept it.

Mustafa Kemal was overcome with emotion. This sincere surprise from an ordinary European whom he had never met was perhaps the most precious gift given to him throughout his life.

It wouldn't do to put it on a counter or carry it in his pocket. He wanted it to somehow be a part of his life. He thought long about it and gave it to his adopted daughter Afet. The amber with an insect encased inside was placed in a gold casing and made into a necklace. Afet wore it around her neck throughout her life.

He used to give foreign statesmen gifts of stories.

In Iran, with which Turkey had experienced border disputes, the Qajar dynasty was deposed and replaced by the Pahlavi dynasty. Mustafa Kemal considered this change as an opportunity for convergence. He sent a special delegation to Reza Shah Pahlavi's coronation ceremony and gave him a gift of a bejeweled sword.

It was no ordinary sword. It was Sultan Mehmed V's sword he had sent to the emir of Afghanistan, Habibullah Khan, during World War I. Habibullah Khan had been assassinated before the Ottoman emissary carrying it was able to make it to Afghanistan. Rather than taking this sword of very high material and intangible value along with him, the emissary left it at the German Embassy in Tehran to be sent safely back to Istanbul.

In the meantime, Istanbul fell under occupation, the War of Independence began, the Ottoman Empire collapsed and the Republic of Turkey was established. The German Embassy in Tehran entrusted with the Ottoman sword delivered it to the Ministry of Finance of the Republic of Turkey.

It was this sword so full of adventure that Mustafa Kemal gave Reza Shah Pahlavi. With its gripping story, this sword became the most prized object in his collection of gifts.

Reza Shah Pahlavi came to Turkey in 1934. This time, Mustafa Kemal gave him a plane produced at the Kayseri Aircraft Factory.

The news spread around the world. The Republic of Turkey was born out of the victory of the War of Independence—won with an ox cart—and now, only 11 years later, was producing aircraft.

King Edward VIII of Britain came. Mustafa Kemal hadn't decided yet what he would give the king. He reckoned he would get to know the king's character and then give a gift accordingly.

He offered the king a cigarette during a chat. It was a Boğaziçi cigarette produced by Tekel. Edward liked it quite a bit.

"It's quite nice," he said, "although I'm afraid of getting accustomed to the flavor since I won't be able to find them in England, but I would ask if you could send some."

There it was—the gift.

Edward had come to Istanbul on his royal yacht, but was going to return through Vienna, so Mustafa Kemal provided his white train.

Edward's train car was loaded with two cases of Boğaziçi cigarettes. There was also a gold cigarette case left inside along with a signed photograph of Mustafa Kemal.

Sotheby's in New York sold Edward VIII's personal belongings at auction in 1998. Among the pieces at auction were the gold cigarette case Mustafa Kemal had given him and the signed photograph. Vehbi Koç's daughter Suna Kıraç bought the photograph for $39,100 and the Turkish Consulate in New York bought the gold cigarette case for $17,250.

The United States, which had always had a skewed view of the National Campaign and conducted its diplomatic relations halfheartedly from its embassy in Istanbul, finally appointed an ambassador to Ankara in 1927, four years after the declaration of the republic.

Mustafa Kemal preserved contact and distance with the U.S. Presidents Calvin Coolidge and Herbert Hoover when they were in office.

Franklin D. Roosevelt was elected president in 1933.

Mustafa Kemal made a move. He showed affinity with telegraphs and letters, and found the same affinity in return. Turkey's relations with the United States were repaired, as they had been with Britain.

Then it was time for a gift.

Roosevelt was a stamp enthusiast. And not just any ordinary one—he was one of the most important stamp collectors in the world.

Mustafa Kemal had a series of non-stick, Turkish postage stamps prepared and sent to the White House.

The 3 *kuruş* stamp was priceless.

Roosevelt wrote a thank you letter. In it he explained his delight as a collector to receive the surprise gift:

Dear Mr. President,

In my rare times of relaxation, I look at the Turkish Postage Stamp Collection that you were kind enough to send me and I hope to one day see the scenes depicted with my own eyes.

With sincere respect and good wishes,

Franklin D. Roosevelt

Mustafa Kemal's emotional intelligence was making the U.S. president—who had never before set foot in Turkey—visit the country.

(Roosevelt responded in kind. He considered Mustafa Kemal's personal interests instead of material value and sent a music box with an inlaid crescent and star. It's today on display at the Atatürk Museum in Şişli, Istanbul.)

∞

He was loyal.

He had close interest in his friends. And if they had any troubles, he would always spend time to find a way to manage them.

He paid for their children's' weddings himself. He provided financial support to those in need without offending them.

One morning, he was on his way to Ulus through Samanpazarı. He very much enjoyed stopping by Ali Efendi's bookstore. There was an amazingly beautiful rug hung on the shop's shutters. "What is such a precious rug doing here?" he asked. "How much is it—whose is it?"

Ali the bookseller didn't want to say who owned the rug: "The person who left it here for safekeeping asked I not give his name. He wants 40 liras for it."

Mustafa Kemal insisted and asked again whom it belonged to.

The bookseller was obliged to say, it belonged to Abdülhalim Çelebi Efendi

Abdülhalim Çelebi Efendi descended from Rumi. He was the sheikh of the Mevlevi Lodge in Konya. He was a hero of the National Campaign, a recipient of the Medal of Independence and a parliamentarian representing Konya. He was an honest, generous, straightforward and direct man.

He had found himself in such financial dire straights that he had to sell the rug from his house, but he didn't tell anyone, never closed his door to anybody and continued hosting those who came.

It saddened Mustafa Kemal. He turned to his aide and told him to leave the man 40 liras.

He spoke again while the bookseller was wrapping up the rug: "Send the rug to Abdülhalim Efendi and we'll pick it up there. Tell him we'd like to stop by in the late afternoon for a coffee." Then he got in his car and left.

He arrived at Abdülhalim Efendi's home before evening. He was greeted at the door to the courtyard. He took a look and saw the rug packed up and sitting next to the door.

They sat on cushions in the modest house and drank coffee. Abdülhalim Efendi couldn't restrain himself any longer and said, "Pasha, you bought my rug and came to my house; with your permission, let me put the rug in your car."

Mustafa Kemal put his hand up for the man to stop. "The rug is ours, but let's leave it in your care," he said. "When we come for coffee we can look at it." Then he gave the order and the rug was spread over the floor of the room.

Abdülhalim Efendi took this trust to heart. Upon his death, his heirs donated the rug to the Mevlana Museum.

In 1931, he attended the wedding of Field Marshal Fevzi Çakmak's daughter Muazzez. He gave 10,000 liras as a wedding present. And just how much was 10,000 liras at that time? Well, 1,000 liras could buy a brand-new car.

Nobody could make heads or tails out of why Mustafa Kemal, who always gave wedding presents with a keepsake quality, gave so much money this time.

Only Fevzi Çakmak understood its meaning.

Muazzez had a respiratory ailment and needed to go abroad for treatment. It was impossible for Fevzi Çakmak to cover the cost and it was also impossible for him to ask his son-in-law for monetary help.

Mustafa Kemal knew of this dilemma of such vital importance and provided the money for the treatment very gracefully, as if it were a piece of wedding jewelry. He knew Fevzi Çakmaz wouldn't accept it if he had tried to give it directly to him.

Fevzi Çakmak tearfully recalled his memory of it years later as, unfortunately, Muazzez couldn't be saved.

He wouldn't permit disloyalty even to those who were disloyal themselves.

Cahit Yalçın was a journalist and writer who was strongly opposed to the abolition of the sultanate and declaration of the republic. He was even mixed up with the assassination attempts on Mustafa Kemal. Because of all of this, he was sent into exile in Çorum. He fell into financial trouble and put his friends in Parliament in action, asking them to have the National Education Ministry buy his novels and books of stories.

Mustafa Kemal's eyes filled with tears when he heard of it. "We have no right to cause material suffering," he said. "If the ministry's funds aren't enough, then take it from my money at İş Bank and buy the books."

He was miserable whenever a friend of his fell ill and would fuss about until they regained their health, calling the doctor, having them operated on and following along.

One evening around the dinner table, his dearest friend Nuri Conker said without thinking that his stomach hurt. What a thing to say! Mustafa Kemal took him by the hand, trundled him into the car and brought him to the Şişli Health Center He laid him on the first gurney he found and caused quite the stir. "I think it's appendicitis. Hurry—take him into surgery immediately if need be," he bellowed.

The doctors calmed Mustafa Kemal down and said that with his permission, first let them do an examination, and they took Conker from the gurney.

Nuri Conker told the doctors: "God bless you and save me from Mustafa Kemal."

It wasn't appendicitis or anything. All he'd done was eat too much.

∞

He didn't attend the funerals of those he loved—he couldn't handle it.

His mother died and he didn't attend her funeral. His friend Nuri Conker—who was like a brother—died and he didn't attend the funeral. He didn't go to his adopted daughter's funeral.

It was a defense mechanism. He would act as if the death hadn't happened. He never spoke of their deaths.

Throughout his life, there was only one person for whom after their death he beat his chest and cried—*oh Necati, oh Necati.*

Falih Rıfkı Atay said he had seen Atatürk heaving sobs as if he was crying over his own child.

Mustafa Necati.

It was Mustafa Necati.

He was from Izmir, born and raised.

He had been a teacher at the Mekteb-i Sultanisi in Izmir—today, it is İzmir Atatürk High School. One day before the Greek occupation began, he had called the patriots in the city to a meeting at the school and organized a resistance. He organized a protest rally in Maşatlık, which thousands of people attended, while the occupation ships made their final preparations in the Gulf.

He stepped up to the podium and exclaimed: "Greece is annexing İzmir and the occupation is beginning. This evening is our last in beautiful İzmir, and it is historic.

We are standing. Guard your dignity and peacefulness. Prepare yourselves to join the army. We will not surrender!"

The next morning, Greek boots set foot in the country, Hasan Tahsin pulled the trigger, Mustafa Kemal boarded the *SS Bandırma* and Mustafa Necati had gone to the Aegean mountains to strike.

He was Mustafa Kemal's companion. He was the national education minister who realized the Alphabet Reform and the Law on the Unification of Education, who took control away from foreign schools and laid the foundation for the Village Institutes.

He once said, "I will leave not even one child in the country without access to a school."

He was a potential candidate for prime minister.

He passed away when he was only 35.

It was the first time Mustafa Kemal had sobbed in his life, crying out his friend's name.

∞

He was benevolent.

If he yelled at someone or broke their heart, even if he was in the right, he would find a way before the day was out and would always atone for it.

He never held a grudge.

Sometimes he would ignore what he saw.

"I forgive because I have a heart," he said. "To be civilized is to forgive."

He was always indulgent of those who showed regret.

∞

The child in his heart never grew up.

He would play on the swing he had installed on the deck of the *Ege* ferry for little Ülkü and play rings with his enjoyment shining on his face.

The photographs of Mustafa Kemal on a swing that Cemal Işıksel immortalized in 1930 and 1935 are possibly the one's that best describe him.

He was like a child around children.

Mary—the daughter of Julian Gillespie, who was the commercial attaché at the U.S. Consulate—50 years later in 1981 recounted what had happened in Florya when she was 7 years old:

"One day, Mustafa Kemal Atatürk came to us. My father and the Americans there welcomed respectfully. My father introduced my brother and me to Atatürk. We were small and so couldn't grasp his greatness. We wanted him to drink tea with our toy cups. We had made cakes out of sand. Atatürk took one our toy cups and acted like he was drinking tea and eating the sand cakes. He said it was wonderful. We were so happy. Atatürk would play ball with children and walk around with them on his shoulders. We would wave when we saw him when we were swimming in the sea and call him over to play with us. I was crying once and he came and he asked what was the matter. I said my doll was sick. He left and came back with a man carrying a black bag and said he'd brought a doctor. The doctor put his stethoscope to my doll's chest, listened and then gave peppermints as medicine. Now, when I think of this great man befriending us children and not breaking our hearts, I have unending respect and admiration for him."

∞

He was a night owl.

He didn't go to bed before 5 in the morning at the Çankaya Mansion. Most of the time he went to bed after dawn. He would sleep five to six hours, and very lightly at that.

He was so accustomed to being awake at night that he wouldn't even go to bed on the evenings when there were no guests and would instead shut himself in the library and read until morning.

He deplored the time he spent asleep. He dreamed of a pill so he wouldn't have to.

"Life is quite short," he said. "Childhood and school take a portion of it and half of what's left is taken up by sleep. Medicine has created wonderful pills that make people sleep. How nice it would be if tablets were invented that drove off sleep and gave the body the comfort sleep provides. One day there will be."

When he was at Dolmabahçe Palace, he would get in his motorboat, the *Sakarya*, after midnight, around 1:00

or 2:00, and go off to tour the Bosporus. He would motor around the islands and go to Kavaklar while all the rest of Istanbul was asleep.

He boarded the *Ertuğrul* yacht on his way back from Yalova at 3 in the morning so as not to lose time during the day. He usually traveled at night so he wouldn't lose time during the day.

He didn't know what tiredness was.

Halide Edip Adıvar made an interesting analogy: "Mustafa Kemal Pasha has unending power that feeds him like a perpetual motion machine."

Falih Rıfkı Atay gave examples of Mustafa Kemal's tempo: "One of his features that astounded us was his ability to work without tiring physically or mentally and without breaking his attention. We heard from his friends that he and his friends were out at a *gazino* [nightclub] until midnight the day before they had maneuvers. He sent them all off to bed and the next morning, was still at the battalion earlier than everyone, with a clean face and freshly shaven."

❈

In his civilian life, he would go to the toilet in the wee hours of the morning around 5 o'clock before going to bed.

It was a habit he had formed while on the front. In wartime it was uncertain what would happen throughout the day, where he would be and whether or not he would have a chance to go. And so he would go as soon as he woke up around 5 in the morning and get it out of the way.

This forced habit continued throughout his life. His body clock was set for 5 in the morning.

He had a buzzer he would ring when he woke up in the morning. His attendants would then bring him coffee and the newspapers.

When he was alone he would sit cross-legged on the couch and read. That's how he had his morning coffee. He read the newspapers for an hour.

∞

He would never be seen in pajamas.

He also changed his cloths every day.

He would bathe every morning, no matter what.

During the most critical days of battle in Tripoli, Gallipoli, Muş, Palestine and Sakarya, he would heat water in a tin basin and bathe in his tent.

They were at an oasis in Derna, Libya, and found some muddy water. They strained it through muslin cloths and filled their canteens. Even though they were supposedly keeping it for when they had no other water, Mustafa Kemal never stopped using it to wash his face every morning.

After he went to Ankara in 1920 and set himself up in the Steering Building, the first question he asked was how they would find a solution to the issue of the bath.

He had the railway workers fashion a bathtub out of sheet metal. It was placed in his bedroom. He used it for a year and a half until he moved to the Çankaya Mansion.

He spent the night in Çankırı while on the road from Kastamonu in 1925. He wanted to bathe, but there was no bath. He sent word and a tinsmith was found. He had the craftsman make a bathtub and had it put in his room. A samovar was also brought from a hospital. He filled a boiler with water and put it on top. For years he spoke about this samovar with a laugh.

After he became president, he would bathe twice a day—once in the morning and once evening—in Dolmabahçe, Florya and Yalova. If there was a function of some sort to attend like a ball, concert or wedding, he would never go without bathing again even if it was winter and snowy.

When he was nearing his deathbed in 1938, he even asked if he could bathe while 3 gallons of fluid were removed from his abdomen with a needle.

He cheered up and became enlivened from his exhaustion so much so while bathing that the doctors were amazed and said they doubted he was sick when he got in the bath.

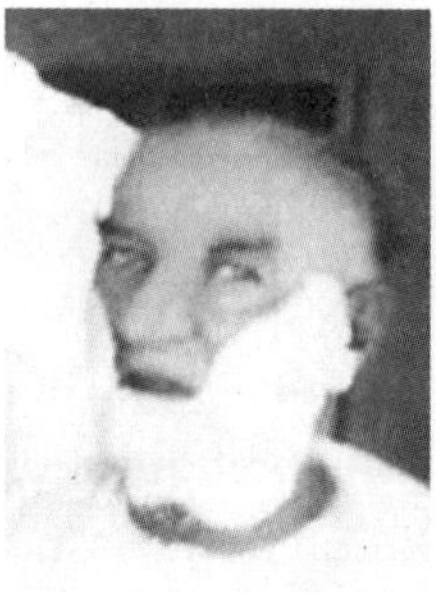

He was meticulous and clean.

He gave great importance to personal grooming.

He shaved every morning. He would have a weekly haircut. He never liked how long it took to get a haircut.

He spent his life trudging from front to front, slept on the ground much more than in a bed and would sleep in the trenches, but there isn't one photograph of him looking bedraggled.

The only time he had a beard in his life was when he was in Tripoli.

He had had a mustache since his student days. He shaved it off in 1925 and never grew another. People asked him why.

"Europeans view us as having handlebar mustaches, conical hats and daggers in our waistbands, and that's how they depict us in their works, so I shaved my mustache in order to change their misconceptions."

He didn't use perfumes. He only used eau de cologne. He preferred Hasan Şevki Cologne. He would have it bought for him from Karaköy, Istanbul. It was the republic's first national cologne manufacturer.

He loved to have his shoulders massaged. He would have Ferahşan Hanım massage him when he was in Yalova and Üflet Hanım when he was in Çankaya.

∞

He laid great importance on the rules of protocol. Although, he despised it when they were exaggerated and snobby.

For example, Safveti Ziya Bey was the director of protocol.

He wore a monocle, always gave examples from European countries and spoke with such delicate pronunciation as to be off-putting.

Mustafa Kemal would put Safveti Ziya on without hiding his displeasure.

At a crowded table, he had a fig put on Safveti Ziya's plate and very seriously asked, "Now please teach us, Safveti Ziya Bey, how should this fig be eaten in accordance with protocol?"

Then, with the same seriousness, Safveti Ziya showed how to eat a fig with a knife and fork and without touching it with the fingers.

Mustafa Kemal's friends around the table would have a hard time holding back their laughter when he would ask the rules of protocol for eating grapes or cherries, and having Safveti Ziya explain the etiquette for eating them all.

He would tire of affected and contrived ceremonies.

Before he would come from Ankara to Istanbul, he would always first send official notice from the Interior Ministry to the office of the governor that would say that he did not want a welcoming or leaving ceremony.

He went on his trips like this, asking for no ceremonies to be held and with nobody knowing. Sometimes he would do it for a surprise.

He went to Antalya in 1935 on the *Ege* ferry. Flags had been rigged up on the pier. The streets were decorated with wreathes and garlands.

"My God," he said, "who had word we were coming?"

They anchored off the coast and took a motorboat to shore. There was no one there to meet them.

He got into a taxi with his aide and went to a mansion That mansion is a museum today.

And what did he see there? The speaker of Parliament, Kazım Özalp, some parliamentarians and their wives had come to the city and were staying at Atatürk's mansion.

This was the reason for the flags and garlands along the pier. No one had gotten word from Mustafa Kemal or anyone else that he was coming. The speaker of Parliament had requested a flamboyant welcoming ceremony. All the pomp and fanfare had been for him.

Atatürk's mansion had basically been converted into a hotel. There were even people staying in Mustafa Kemal's bedroom.

They weren't at the mansion at the time, as they were touring the city altogether as a committee.

Mustafa Kemal had a fit. He went through the rooms with Nuri Conker and Kılıç Ali. There were suitcases and clothes everywhere. He opened the door to the bedroom. The bed there had even been moved. He moved back to its place. Then, he told them to throw everything there that wasn't his outside.

He went to the yard, asked for a coffee and lit a cigarette. Then he calmly waited as he sipped away at his coffee.

Kazım Özalp came running and pouring sweat. His wife was at his side. Right behind them in a line were the other parliamentarians.

The only thing Mustafa Kemal said was: "I didn't know you were coming to Antalya. What's the purpose of your trip?"

Kazım Özalp, embarrassed, hemmed and hawed as he stammered.

He was a relative of the governor of Antalya, and so went to his house. Local party members were made go-betweens. The parliamentarians were set up in houses as forced guests.

That evening, he invited Kazım Özalp and the lawmakers with him to dinner with their wives, as if none of it had ever happened. He chatted cheerfully without ever breeching the subject and was a great host, but Kazım Özalp was never again the speaker of Parliament.

∞

He would act like a normal citizen at every chance. He would use the municipal ferries to cross the Bosphorus and would expressly board the second-class area of the tram after paying for his ticket.

Without having planned it, he would stop his driver in Beyoğlu and sit at the Lebanon patisserie. Sometimes he would go to Vefa to drink *boza* and treat the other customers there to the same.

He was very happy when he saw people going to restaurants and nightclubs as families. He would speak with the families with children in these types of places to offer encouragement.

He would visit the Tokatlıyan Hotel without fail when he came to Beyoğlu. There he'd call for the headwaiter, Karabet Efendi, and ask him how he'd been doing. Karabet Efendi had been under his command during the National Campaign.

He wouldn't take security measures, saying that security creates unrest and frightens the people. He didn't want to have uniformed military police protection.

He didn't like being confined and so would sneak out.

One early morning in 1929, he put on his overcoat and hat and left Dolmabahçe Palace without telling anyone. He walked until he got to the tram and then walked around Sultanahmet.

He went to the Topkapı Palace museum. It wasn't yet 9 o'clock and the museum wasn't open. He didn't know the guard at the door.

He introduced himself. "I am the president," he said.

The guard shrugged his shoulders: "Nobody can go in, no matter who it is."

Mustafa Kemal told him he was right and waited.

The clock struck 9 and the museum director arrived. He started pouring sweat when he saw who was waiting at the door.

Mustafa Kemal walked through the museum. He left as he came, walking a bit before he got into a taxi. From there he went to Etfal in Şişli.

Sabiha Gökçen was feeling unwell and was staying at the hospital. He went there to visit her.

Meanwhile, there was panic back at Dolmabahçe Palace. Mustafa Kemal was missing. Everyone was up and about. Security had been given the alarm and a diving team was even called to search the Bosphorus.

Then, the director of the Topkapı Palace Museum called Dolmabahçe Palace and explained that Mustafa Kemal had come alone, left alone and that he hadn't been able to ask where he was going.

Then, off to the races, all police cars set on the taxis waiting around Topkapı, asking if anyone had seen

Mustafa Kemal. This time, fortunately, a phone call came to Dolmabahçe Palace from the hospital—the president was there.

He was standing at the foot of Sabiha's bed when his guards and aides rushed into the hospital in a flurry—there, father and daughter chatting happily.

Mustafa Kemal smiled and laughed whenever he related this story, as he had told the cabbie to wait for him because he'd be back, but like the guard at the museum, the taxi driver hadn't recognized him, either. The aides from Dolmabahçe Palace came running, and all the taxi driver could tell them was that he had brought someone to the hospital, but that he didn't know who it was.

Sometimes he would take a taxi and walk alone in Haramidere Grove. Sometimes they'd find him talking with the fisherman at Kireçburnu along the Sarıyer coast. At other times he would leave in the dead of night, go to the coffeehouses in Beşiktaş that were open for early risers and treat everyone there to tea and coffee.

Everybody calls Dolmabahçe a palace. Mustafa Kemal called it a cage.

He wanted to go to the Balkans. Not on an official visit, though. He wanted it to be as a normal tourist.

He explained it to Yunus Nadi: "What would you say if I take a couple friends with me and go to the Balkans without saying a peep—to Athena, Belgrade, three or five days in Bucharest and then on to Sofia to see my old friends, all without giving notice and without ceremonies and pageantry?"

He had unfulfilled desires.

∞

His chef was Mehmet Yücel.

He was from Mengen in Bolu. He had been a cook for the sleeping cars on the state railways. For 14 years, from 1924 to 1938, he worked in the kitchen at Çankaya Mansion. For the summer months he was in the kitchen at Dolmabahçe Palace.

He was competent at his work, clean, trustworthy and, as the one entrusted with every morsel that would pass down Mustafa Kemal's throat, more important than the rest. Mustafa Kemal trusted him with his life.

He didn't make even the smallest personal request after Mustafa Kemal died, and returned to his position as a cook on the state railway sleeping cars.

He had a team of six people in the kitchen since Mustafa Kemal would host 10 to 15 guests for dinner every evening. They wanted to have a night once when Mustafa Kemal was out of Ankara. They set up a small table with a few small dishes and drinks and tied one on. The trouble, though, was that Mustafa Kemal appeared.

He flew through the kitchen door. The team of cooks was caught. They thought they were going to be fired, but then he asked for a drink for himself. He sat down and ate a little.

He told them to keep on relaxing and left.

Mustafa Kemal was in Yalova one summer day. He was going to return in the late afternoon and a bunch of guests were due. Mehmet Yücel was plugging away in the Dolmabahçe kitchen in preparation. The oven exploded and a fire broke out.

Black smoke was rising from the palace.

Firefighters arrived and put out the fire, but Istanbul had gone astir, the people had assembled in front of the palace and exaggerations spread from person to person—there was a bombing, there'd been a bomb in the kitchen.

The cooks were trembling.

And what did Mustafa Kemal say and how angry did he get? He came and the only thing he said was: "You'll be fine, boys."

One of the cooks, Halit, was young and a bachelor. He had been exchanging letters with a young woman who was one of the servants.

There was a dishwasher named Nazif who was a gossip and mean spirited. He learned of their letters and went to Halit. "Gazi Pasha is really angry," he said. "He's having people look for you everywhere. Get out of here."

Halit was scared and ran away to his village.

Mustafa Kemal only got word of the matter much later. He fired Nazif. Then he sent word to Halit. "Have him come right away," he said. "I'll marry them off and they'll work as husband and wife at the Forest Farm."

He was gravely ill in 1938. Fluid had been removed from his abdomen. His doctors often put him on a diet. The chef, Mehmet Yücel, came into his bedroom holding a tray. He brought a small slice of buttered bread.

"What do you make of me, Mehmet?" he asked. "You think I'll live?"

What could Mehmet say? "For goodness sake, Pasha," he said. What kind of thing to say is that?"

He grabbed Mehmet by the arm as he was about to put the try down on the side table next to the bed and lowered his voice so no one would hear: "Make me some baked pasta. I've got a craving for it."

He gave Mehmet a warning as he was leaving: "Get it done without mixing the doctors in with it."

Mehmet cooked the pasta with tears running down his cheeks. It was the last meal Mustafa Kemal was able to eat with an appetite.

∞

İbrahim Ergüven had prepared a table.

He had worked with Mustafa Kemal from 1926 until his death. Mustafa Kemal had bestowed him with his surname, which means trustworthy man.

Among others, there was also a denture code, of sorts.

Some of Mustafa Kemal's teeth were prosthetics. When he ate fruit like figs or strawberries, little bits would get stuck under the false teeth and he would be forced to get them out and clean the dentures. And so, whenever Mustafa Kemal traveled around the country and was given figs or strawberries, Ergüven would immediately go and take them from the table. Since Mustafa Kemal never said anything about it, no one else could ask why he'd had them removed.

Mustafa Kemal paid fastidious attention to details such as the ironing of the tablecloth, the placement of the silverware and flowers for the table.

He couldn't stand crumbs.

Ergüven was very good with seeing to these details. He would surprise with messages in flowers on special days, such as October 29 and August 30.

When Atatürk died, it was Ergüven who took the plaster cast of his face and right hand under the supervision of professors.

∞

His driver was Sadık Kutlu.

He was always at the wheel from 1925 to 1938.

He was always ready and waiting in a suit and tie since it was never clear when and where to Mustafa Kemal would be going. He went to bed after Mustafa Kemal and rose before him. Of all the attendants, his shift was the longest. Whether Mustafa Kemal went somewhere by train or by ship, Sadık Kutlu was there beside him. He would use whichever car was given him.

There were other drivers at the Çankaya Mansion and Dolmabahçe Palace, but Kutlu's place was different—he was a man held in great trust.

When Mustafa Kemal sent his adopted daughter Sabiha to Eskişehir to train to be a pilot, he entrusted her to Sadık Kutlu: "Keep an eye on Sabiha even when she's in the air."

Sadık Kutlu was an older brother, driver and bodyguard for Sabiha until she received her pilot's credentials.

A blackboard had been set up in the yard of the Çankaya Mansion, like in a classroom. Mustafa Kemal was taught the employees who worked there how to read and write with the new alphabet. Kutlu had finished junior high school and so quickly grasped the new alphabet. He would do the teaching when Mustafa Kemal was busy.

There were two cars used in ceremonies. One was a 1934 Lincoln KB. Only 45 were made. It was black, had four doors and was a ragtop convertible. The seats were of brown leather. It had a V-12 engine and a three-speed manual transmission.

The other was a 1936 Cadillac Series 80. It was also black with four doors. The seats were leather, as well, but white. It also had a V-12 engine and a three-speed manual transmission.

He also had a motorcycle with a sidecar—a 1934 model from British maker Ariel.

Mustafa Kemal loved to drive tractors. Sometimes he'd go back to the Çankaya Mansion from the Forest Farm on the tractor he used there.

∞

Nazım Canca was his close bodyguard.

He was an energetic young man who had an adventurous life. He was born in Rize, moved in with his uncle in Batumi and stayed there until he finished high school. He got a job with a Russian circus and traveled around Europe. He worked for four years at the Turkish Embassy in London, and another year at the one in Paris. He knew Russian, English and French.

He returned to Turkey in 1934 to do his military service. He was assigned to the Çankaya Palace since he knew foreign languages. His Russian translations attracted Mustafa Kemal's attention. He knew judo and laid soldiers larger than him when sparring. He got in quite well with Mustafa Kemal.

With a request from Mustafa Kemal, he applied to be a police officer when he finished his military service and was accepted. He was Mustafa Kemal's bodyguard from 1935 on.

After Atatürk, he was also a bodyguard for İsmet İnönü and Celal Bayar. He was one of the pioneers of judo in Turkey, a founder of the Turkish Judo Federation and its deputy chairman. He trained champions and contributed to the establishment of the country's taekwondo and karate federations.

Another of his bodyguards was Bekir Çavuş, who was a veteran.

He was put under Mustafa Kemal's command at the Erzurum Congress, when he had been under Kazım Karabekir's command.

They never split. He was Mustafa Kemal's shadow and they were very close.

On the eve of the Battle of Sakarya, Mustafa Kemal had broken his ribs and so couldn't lift his arm. He sat on a chair in his underwear while Bekir Çavuş washed his body with a soaped-up sponge.

He had lain his life down for Mustafa Kemal. He was badly beaten and took three bullets the night Topal Osman attempted to raid the Çankaya Mansion. A bullet had lodged in his spine. Mustafa Kemal sent him to Vienna for treatment. He recovered, but the bullet couldn't be removed from his spine.

From making food to gardening, he was skilled at everything. He never took offence at whatever task he was given.

He took the surname Cingöz, which means crafty and cunning.

He was a very good driver.
His pistol was also always at his side.

Both Fikriye and Latife had trained him concerning clothing and dress, and he would tie Mustafa Kemal's bowties and neckties.
He retired from the police force.

∞

His librarian was Nuri Ulusu.

His father was Hacı Tevfik Bey, who was the steward on the *Bandırma* steamer and was among the crew that brought Mustafa Kemal to Samsun. Nuri Ulusu's father brought him aboard before they left on May 16, 1919, and he kissed Mustafa Kemal's hand before the most important journey in Turkey's history.

He was assigned to the Çankaya Mansion eight years later in 1927, when he came of age for his military service. He reminded Mustafa Kemal of who he was and became the librarian.
He was there until Mustafa Kemal died.

∞

His barbers were Mehmet and Rıdvan.
They were both from Salonika.

Mehmet was a reminder of Mustafa Kemal's father–a type of keepsake. His father had been friends with Ali Rıza Bey.

He personally gave them their surnames. To Mehmet, he gave the surname Tanrıkut Mete, which is associated with the legendary Oghuz Kaghan. To Rıdvan, he gave the surname Gürarı, or strong bee, since that's how he worked.

They were with him from 1925 until 1938.

Mustafa Kemal had no nurse. When he got sick, Mehmet would undertake seeing to all his needs.

Mustafa Kemal had three-day stubble when he died on November 10, 1938. A death mask was going to be taken. They thought it would be better if he were shaven. Mehmet couldn't do it. "This is what I've done my whole life, but my heart can't take it this time," he said.

Mustafa Kemal's death mask has his stubble.

İsmet İnönü asked him to stay on after Atatürk died, but Mehmet didn't accept.

"There's something to remind me of Mustafa Kemal Atatürk in every corner of the mansion," he said. "I can't live here without him."

He moved to Yalova.

Strands of Mustafa Kemal's hair and his dentures stayed with Mehmet. He donated them to the Celal Bayar Museum.

The shaving kit Atatürk last used is on display at Anıtkabir. It has eight razors—one with a white handle and the rest black—a ceramic plate, metal bowl, mustache clippers, hair clippers, beard brush, whetstone, silver hand mirror with the initials K.A. engraved on the back, a metal bottle of scented oil with a crescent and star on the cap, a glass vessel for cream with flower motifs and an emery board.

Cemal Granda was his butler.

He was a waiter on the state sea lines. He worked at the Çankaya Mansion for 11 years.

Mustafa Kemal's sense of belonging for him was very high. He was very connected to his employees. Every time he saw them, he wouldn't neglect to ask how they had been. He would ask them if there was anything they needed. When they were sick, he would mobilize his personal doctors. He'd also have teeth made for them.

One day, he asked Cemal how much he got paid. He made 50 liras per month.

"I'll leave the presidency one day," Mustafa Kemal said. "You might not make that kind of money then and might only get 5 liras a month. Let's not leave each other when that time comes."

Cemal was able to leave the presidency, but he couldn't bear the thought of being separated from the people he lived with.

∞

(Mustafa Kemal was sincerely committed to his employees, as seen with Cemal Granda.

But was this butler as attached to Mustafa Kemal?

Cemal Granda retired when Mustafa Kemal passed away. Rather than retreating to a corner, though, he sought out employment with the parliamentarians he knew. They helped out for the sake of the years past. They got him a job as a waiter at the Denizcilik Bank hotel. He worked there for a short time, but didn't like it and quit. Then they gave him a job as an official at the Etibank Ereğli Coal Operations. Again, he didn't stay.

His demands didn't end there. He said he needed a salary in order to get by. He started to make threats. He tried their patience and was taken into custody. He wasn't arrested, but he was kept a close watch on for a long time.

He disappeared for about 15 years. He reappeared in 1959. He sold his story about Atatürk to the Şehir Gazetesi (City Gazette).

It was published in instalments over three months. Subsequently, the book *Atatürk'*ün Uşağı İdim (I Was Atatürk's Butler) was published.

One might ask why this is so odd.

Pressed for money, Cemal Granda recounted his memories as a historical document in the corner of a card house in Nuruosmaniye.

The Democrat Party was in power at the time the *Şehir Gazetesi* published his account. The newspaper was overtly pro-Democrat Party and supported it with official announcements. The paper's editorial director, Con Kemal, who was known as Kemal Onan, was a journalist who always wrote for the benefit of the Democrat Party. He was famous for contrived stories. He also heavily criticized the CHP.

And unfortunately, there was information contrary to fact in his published accounts. He said incorrect things and exaggerated concerning drinking, women, and Mustafa Kemal's characteristics and personelity.

He even claimed Mustafa Kemal had "taken more than 10 women who were Şişli socialites to the Beylerbeyi Palace and had them swim naked in the pool."

Opponents of Mustafa Kemal have used these false claims from Cemal Granda in his accounts 21 years after Mustafa Kemal's death, and which no one else witnessed, as a tool for half a century to attack him as if they are proven evidence.

So, then the question becomes whether Cemal Granda fabricated his accounts since he was strapped for money, the Democrat Party manipulated him in its fight against the CHP or dishonest journalists were paid to blow the whistle and falsify it.

As a journalist myself, I see it as a duty to Mustafa Kemal Atatürk to blow the lid off these untruths.

I also invite historians to refute Cemal Granda's inaccurate accounts.)

∞

(Mustafa Kemal was called a Sabbatean. The source for this is also Cemal Granda's book.

In Granda's account he says:

One day I was sitting and talking with the barbers Mehmet and Rıdvan from Salonika in the foyer of the Çankaya Mansion. They considered themselves privileged since they were from the same city as Atatürk and they were speaking loftily. Even if it was a joke, I indulged their boasting and posturing, but I still tried to feign ignorance. Despite my full attention, the discussion didn't lack a thing. They said we wouldn't have been saved if they weren't from Salonika. I told them we saved ourselves and didn't need the Salonikans, and for whoever there is in Salonika, it's a whole bunch of Jews, anyway. We didn't see Atatürk slowly coming down the stairs. He inadvertently heard our conversation and that night at the table asked Nuri Conker, who's also from Salonika: "Nuri Bey, what are there a lot of in Salonika?"

My head was tingling when I heard it. What I was afraid of had happened. Atatürk had heard everything we'd said in the foyer.

Since Nuri Conker was an old childhood friend of Atatürk who put up with his whims and humor, he didn't hesitate to say what was running through his mind. It was like Nuri Conker knew everything we'd said, too. It seemed like he'd decided to defend me when he said there're a bunch of Jews there.

In response, Atatürk spoke to all the gossip he had heard before with a sardonic smile. He said some people want to say he's Jewish because he's from Salonika, but that one shouldn't forget that Napoleon was an Italian from Corsica who died a Frenchman and is written in history as being French. He said people need to see to their own communities.

I don't remember any time in my 12 years of service when I was humiliated in front of Atatürk. Maybe the biggest embarrassment in my entire life was this. I never said the word Salonika again after that.

This account from Cemal Granda was taken as a reference and bent and twisted around. He claimed Mustafa Kemal was Jewish and it was written that he was a Sabbatean.

However, this dialogue won't be encountered if one reads every memoir published concerning Mustafa Kemal.

Nobody else seems to have heard this conversation other than Cemal Granda.

It's not in Conker's accounts. Neither did any of the people who were around the table remember it. The barbers had no memory of it. Only Cemal Granda had heard it.

There's also no other employee who heard this account from Cemal Granda before 1959. The driver didn't know of it and neither did the librarian or the chef.

Unfortunately, though, there are hundreds of historians who in their books accept Cemal Granda's account as fact.

It was even claimed based on Cemal Granda's accounts that Mustafa Kemal was descended from Sabbatai Zevi.)

∞

The waiters at Dolmabahçe Palace and the Çankaya Mansion wore tuxedos and patent leather shoes.

There was a shop called Trink in Galatasaray that sold quality goods where they would do their clothes shopping.

The other men on staff wore suits.

The ladies Ülfet, Fatma and Pakize were at the Çankaya Mansion. Binbir Hanım was at Dolmabahçe Palace. Her name was actually Binnaz. Mustafa Kemal called her Binbir, though. They were in charge of the laundry, ironing, cleaning and other housework. Ferahşan Hanım was in charge of the same work in Yalova.

Ferahşan Hanım was a black woman from Tripoli. She worked with Mustafa Kemal for 10 years.

Of him she said, "I had the opportunity to know Atatürk as a person. The most precious things I've gotten in my entire life are my memories of him. He was a very noble and fine person. He always thought of those around him more than himself. Once when we were on a trip, he personally saw to where we would all sleep, what we would eat and if we were comfortable. On the nights he would sit in contemplation for hours in his office, nobody was willing to go in and disturb him. Sometimes, when he'd get hungry late at night, he'd go to the kitchen by his private apartment, heat up some food himself and eat alone there in the kitchen."

∞

Nesip Efendi had a totally different place. He was also black, but from Sudan. He was in his 60s.

He had been taken to the palace as a stable boy during the reign of Sultan Abdülhamid II. He had been a cleaner at the Ottoman Chamber of Deputies. He was taken as a doorman for the Çankaya Mansion on recommendations from the parliamentarians coming from the Chamber of Deputies to Ankara when the Grand National Assembly of Turkey was being established.

His broken Turkish made him extremely likable. He didn't gossip about anyone, did his job earnestly, could keep a secret, was trustworthy with money and was an honorable man. He quickly became Mustafa Kemal's favorite employee and he took him home.

Only Nesip Efendi could enter Mustafa Kemal's bedroom without asking permission from anyone. He tidied all the drawers, including Mustafa Kemal's underwear, and prepared the clothes he would wear, as well as his suitcases when he was going on trips.

Mustafa Kemal entrusted his adopted daughters to him.

Nesip Efendi would drink in the evenings. He was the only one among the employees as the mansion who had the freedom to drink *rakı*. He would get some small mezes from the kitchen when night fell and go to the guard shack in the yard to drink. Mustafa Kemal looked past it, so the aides couldn't say anything otherwise.

He drank too much one night and passed out. His cigarette fell from the ashtray and caught the shack on fire. The police at the mansion's door got buckets and labored to put out the flames. When they finally did, they saved Nesip Efendi, who was burning alive and still asleep. The top aide, Rüsuhi Bey couldn't hold himself back when he saw him and said, "Damn him, get him out of my sight. He's lost it—the mansion would have burned if it went just a little longer," and chased Nesip Efendi away.

He wasn't there the next day—or the next. Mustafa Kemal was worried and asked where he was.

They explained what had happened. Mustafa Kemal was enraged. "When you chased this man away, did you think of where he would go at his age," he yelled. "He has no children or anyone else to look after him. Where will he sleep; where will he stay? Go and find him and bring him back.

They hemmed and hawed and said he was going to burn down the mansion.

This only angered him further: "We didn't burn, brother. We'll think about it when we do."

They found Nesip Efendi and brought him back. And without batting an eye, he kept on with his evening drinks. Now, though, they would come and check on him periodically in order to avoid another emergency.

All the employees would line up and kiss Mustafa Kemal's hand on holidays, but he wouldn't make Nesip Efendi do so. Mustafa Kemal would hug him and kiss him on the cheeks. He didn't respect him only because of his age, but because he didn't care about what people said or who they were.

Unfortunately, he wasn't taken care of after November 10, 1938. He was let go at the Çankaya Mansion. He had no house and no family. He was given a small room in the basement of the Central Bank and that's where he died.

∞

Cemal Işıksel took all of the photographs with documentary value after Mustafa Kemal declared the republic. He was known as Mustafa Kemal's private photographer.

He was born in Istanbul. He began to work as a journalist while he was studying law at Ankara University. He was Turkey's first photojournalist and worked for both the *Ulus* and *Cumhuriyet* newspapers.

His father, Hasan Fehmi Efendi, was a cleric. The Ankara Fatwa in defense of Mustafa Kemal was published when Sultan Mehmed VI issued the fatwa for his execution, and he was one of its 153 clerical signatories.

He first photographed Mustafa Kemal in 1924, at the Ankara Train Station. He followed Mustafa Kemal on all his tours of the country. The richest photograph archive from the first 15 years of the republic is all his shots.

He had a German-made, Goerz bellows camera. He used a German-made Leica from 1932 onward.

The photographs of Mustafa Kemal he immortalized with his lens were printed on money and stamps. For example, he had taken the portrait used for the 200-lira bills put into circulation in 2009, at the Çankaya Mansion in 1934.

The De La Rue company in the U.K. printed Turkey's first banknotes in 1927, with a portrait of Mustafa Kemal. In addition to Mustafa Kemal, the notes also had depictions of a wooden plow, a grey wolf, a village, the Ankara Castle, the Parliament building, the Akköprü bridge in Ankara, the Sivas Gök Madrasa, and the Afyonkarahısar and Sakarya railways.

The first stamp with a depiction of Mustafa Kemal was form a series relating to the Treaty of Lausanne. The Düyun-u Umumiye printing house in Istanbul printed it in 1924.

The first postage stamps with Mustafa Kemal's likeness were printed in London, and put into circulation in 1926. After the Alphabet Reform, the first stamps printed with a picture of Atatürk and Turkish in the Latin alphabet were also produced in London, in 1929.

Seven hundred of the roughly 3,000 postage stamps issued in Turkey had the portraits, photographs and statues of Atatürk used for their composition.

The stamps have been printed in 13 countries: Pakistan, Tunisia, Argentina, Macedonia, Bangladesh, Mauritania, Iran, Afghanistan, India, the Marshal Islands, Egypt, Guinea and Nicaragua.

∞

Mustafa Kemal's view on the concept of money was the same as Abu Bakr's.

One of the writers Mustafa Kemal followed closest while he was a student at the military high school was Şehbenderzade Ahmet Hilmi, who was the most widely read journalist of the Constitutional Period and had ideas focusing on freedom.

He read Ahmet Hilmi's İslam Tarihi (History of Islam) when he was 17. He kept it carefully for many years and put it in his private library at the Çankaya Mansion.

He underlined the passages in the book about Abu Bakr with a red pen and wrote, *very important*, in the margin.

The passage he marked as very important said: "Abu Bakr lived on the subsistence allowance provided by the treasury of the Islamic state. He had no money when he died. He was given a camel and a slave from the goods of the Islamic state and returned them in his will."

Mustafa Kemal underlined this passage when he was 17. He lived in accordance with it and died in accordance with it, returning all the property and money allocated to him to the nation.

He didn't use his power to enrich himself. He didn't make a personal fortune. "A person should only have money as a means of liberty," he said, "not to be enslaved to money."

He received a salary of 5,000 liras as president. It was lowered from 7,000 liras in 1927. He had no other burden on the state—not a single *kuruş*.

He personally paid the salaries of the chef, driver, barber, waiter, gardener and all the other employees at the Çankaya Mansion himself—their food, drink and housing costs—along with the expenses for repairs to the mansion.

He never took a travel allowance when he went on trips.

He always avoided extravagances and luxury. He didn't fill his own pocket. He filled the state treasury.

∞

He was appointed to the 7th Army Command in 1917. He was about to depart Istanbul for Aleppo. A German officer came with seven chests to his house in Şişli. They were full of sparkling gold.

Mustafa Kemal asked what it was. The German officer explained, "The Thunderbolt Army Group commander,

Field Marshal Falkenhayn has sent to the person of Mustafa Kemal."

There was no document or record. The German field marshal was accustomed to buying Ottoman officers for money. He sent a bribe out in the open not for his state, but to serve the interests of the German Empire. Mustafa Kemal did not accept it. He had a report prepared. He had the German officer and witnesses sign it. He sent the gold that came for him to the storehouses of the 7th Army and the report to Falkenhayn.

"It's easy to guess the possibility that Field Marshal Falkenhayn has sent these chests to many more people than me to seduce them," he said of it.

The British also tried the same road of seduction. The British government sent intermediaries throughout the National Campaign who offered Mustafa Kemal money and a villa in Italy for him to give up the Anatolian resistance.

The command of the British occupation forces in Istanbul was well aware in 1921 that the offer of money and a villa was pointless. The command sent a note to the British War Office, which was insisting on the offer, that said: "Mustafa Kemal is the only one of the unionist [Committee of Union and Progress] leaders who has never accepted a bribe."

The republic had still yet to be declared in February 1923. Opposition parliamentarians filed a motion with the speaker. Their offer was, providing Mustafa Kemal gave up his governance of the country and withdrew, he would be given a private palace and a monthly salary of 10,000 liras.

He smiled painfully when he heard this strange proposition. They put a price on Mustafa Kemal's ideals of country and nation. On top of that, the offer from the parliamentary opposition was in line with the one from the British government two years earlier.

❈

Opposition lawmakers in the same Parliament made the offer again while negotiations in Lausanne were ongoing. According to the proposed law, "those who have lived outside the borders of the country and migrants who have not lived continuously for five years in the city in which they have settled are ineligible to be elected as representatives."

It was quite clear. Salonika was now outside the borders of the country. Throughout the War of Independence, Mustafa Kemal was unable to stay in any city for five years on end while he ran from front to front.

They didn't want Mustafa Kemal to be a parliamentarian.

They wanted to throw him out of the Parliament he had established. This wanton proposal was rejected, but all the revolutionaries, Mustafa Kemal foremost among them, knew the British mentality was in Parliament.

❈

Sultan Mehmed VI had fled abroad on a British warship upon the abolition of the sultanate and was living in San Remo in 1926. Look at the twist of fate—Mehmed VI was living in the villa the British had earlier offered to Mustafa Kemal.

A letter arrived for Mustafa Kemal from Ottoman general Keçeçizade İzzet Fuat, who had settled in Egypt after the founding of the republic. They had known each other since their time in Aleppo. He wrote trusting in the memories of those days.

He wrote in the beginning of the letter that he had gone to San Remo to visit Mehmed VI, who sung Mustafa Kemal's praises. Then he came to the point: "I saw from Vahdeddin's [Mehmed VI] state and demeanor that he is in financial distress. I sensed he needed help and I ask for your favor."

Mustafa Kemal looked sadly at Hasan Rıza Soya, who had brought the letter, and said, "You see the state of the world, boy? Where there's that greatness and where there's that sultanate, they all vanish. Nothing in this world is trustworthy and a man must always be measured in life.

"How can he be helped? I have no personal fortune, the state treasury is lean, and even if it weren't, we have no right to provide aid from the state. The mistakes made by the person mentioned in this letter devastated this country. It's best to leave this topic here, but keep the letter as documentation."

And that's what was done. It was preserved on order and recorded. A private secretary was delivered to the presidency.

∞

(The year 2004 saw a first in the republic. Ertuğrul Osman was a guest on an ATV live news program. He was a grandson of Sultan Abdülhamid II.

Ertuğrul Osman.

He was the last Ottoman prince born in a palace. If the sultanate had continued, he would have been known as Sultan Osman IV or Sultan Ertuğrul.

It was the first time the head of the Ottoman dynasty had addressed the Turkish public. What he said created worldwide interest.

"It was very bad for our family, but Turkey won," he said. "I was born a Turk and I'll die a Turk. Atatürk was a magnificent leader for the Turkish people. Without Mustafa Kemal, there would have been no Istanbul. The only way to save the country was to establish the republic."

He was neither angry nor held any grudges. He only showed gratitude.

He later gave an interview to CNN Türk. In that interview, he was also well composed.

"All Turks, including myself, are indebted to Mustafa Kemal Atatürk," he said. "He saved the country. He did very well to establish the republic. God knows what would have been if there hadn't been Mustafa Kemal Atatürk. Everything would have been left behind—the sultanate, monarchy, the caliphate, the Sharia. May the young people stake their claim for secularism and the integrity of the homeland."

He spoke to the *Hürriyet* and *Milliyet* newspapers.

He always emphasized the same sensitivity: "Let it not be forgotten that without Mustafa Kemal, none of us would have been able to exist. You, me, all of us owe our existence to him. True, his revolution was bad for our dynasty, but Turkey and the Turkish people are here thanks to Mustafa Kemal Atatürk.")

∞

Mustafa Kemal came to Ankara municipal nursery garden in the winter of 1927. He went into the greenhouse and started looking over the flowers. He liked the house plants and picked out eight pots. Then he instructed the director of the municipal garden: "Send these to the mansion tomorrow. You come, too, and plant them where is best for them and teach our gardeners how to care for them."

The pots came the next day and were placed in corners that would be good for them. Mustafa Kemal got word, came and looked them over. "They're very beautiful. How much do we owe you?" he asked.

They knew if they said they were a gift that he would get angry and ask on what authority they give gifts of the nation's property. The director of the gardens, Salih Bitici, was prepared. He held out a piece of paper with the plants and their prices on it. Mustafa Kemal took the paper and told his aide to pay. Rüsuhi Bey went to the office, came back out with an envelope of money and asked them to send the bill the next day.

President Mustafa Kemal paid out of his own pocket even for flowers from a state-owned nursery for a state-owned mansion. It was intentionally documented so no one could say later on that he had gotten the flowers for free or that the state had paid for them.

In 1928, he was at the mansion looking out a window and saw his adopted daughter Nebile get in a car and leave. He called his aide and told him to go immediately after her and bring her back. They did as instructed.

He confronted her: "You are my daughter, but these cars aren't your father's property. They belong to the nation and can't be taken on a whim."

He spoke roughly to those who misused state property. He would also get angry with those who had forgotten where they'd come from.

He had great respect for oxcarts, for example. He saw them as a symbol of the War of Independence.

Those creaking oxcarts were the sound of the clenched teeth of the Turkish nation through its suffering.

He never forgot how those primitive, two-wheeled oxcarts driven by women had won an epic victory over railways and motor vehicles. In all military history, only in Turkey there is the feeling of loyalty to the oxcart command, which was born out of need and desperation.

He had great respect for the wooden plow.

"Those who conquer with the sword are doomed to defeat by those who conquer with the plow," he said.

He made the oxcart and plow national emblems.

He had a plow placed on the 1-lira banknote put into circulation in 1927—the republics first paper money.

He had hung Namık İsmail Bey's painting, *Harman* (The Harvest), in his study opposite his desk.

There were also ivory oxcart trinkets in the library.

An official parade was held on the 10th anniversary of the republic in 1933. Next to the regiments of soldiers, students and civil servants were oxcarts, which were specially included in this historic procession.

He never made one faulty economic decision throughout his life. One hundred percent of the state-owned companies he founded have succeeded.

İş Bank Turkey was founded in 1924.

And now, nearly a century later, it is still the leader of the Turkish banking industry.

Thousands of books have been written on his political and military genius, but none have been written that say he is Turkey's most visionary and unerring entrepreneur ever.

One piece of evidence of his economic genius is the Sümerbank Cloth Printing Factory in Nazilli, which is accepted as the foundation of Turkish textiles.

He hired Russians to build it. Russian gave the loan. Russians brought the machinery Russian engineers set it up. The Russian engineers also trained and taught the Turkish workers.

Mustafa Kemal personally opened it in 1937. It employed 2,500 people. Balls were held for the workers with women and men together. There was a cinema that sat 700 people and ran film six days a week. There was a theater and workers' theater club. There was a music group and a choir. The factory also had its own radio station. It had a piano. There were painting and sculpture exhibitions, and a pool in the yard with bronze sculptures of women.

It had a sports club—Sümerspor. Turkey's first soccer field over compressed soot was there. There was a basketball and volleyball court, wrestling mats, a boxing ring, tennis court, skating rink and bicycle track.

There was a 40-bed hospital with an operating room and laboratory. There was also a pharmacy.

There was a primary school and kindergarten for the children of the women who worked there.

This isn't 2018. This was in 1937.

There was a garment cooperative. It had a bakery. There was a small train called the *Gıdı Gıdı* to transport the workers between the city and the factory.

It produced its own energy and had a transfer station. It also provided electricity to Nazilli.

Free courses were held at the factory for the people of Nazilli, and especially for young women, so they could acquire a profession. There were reading and writing courses. Health workers were sent to the surrounding villages where they treated the sick and distributed free medicine. The factory's medical team also squashed the malaria epidemic in the region.

The lodging for the workers had 264 apartments with 1,000 people living there.

There was a bathhouse for the workers, which was also open to the public.

Free printed cloth was distributed to the local people every six months.

It had an ironworks, carpentry shop and foundry. It also produced material for other factories.

It had a research and development department. The cotton derivative that would be used at the factory was developed before it even opened. Their innovations resulted in the patenting of 28 cotton varieties. Cotton production in the whole of the Aegean region increased with these cotton derivatives.

Two hundred mechanical sowers were brought from Russia. Modern agricultural equipment was brought in, again from Russia, and was distributed to farmers for use in the cotton fields.

Tens of thousands of trees were planted in the surroundings. It wasn't that the factory contributed to the city—the factory was the center of the city's socio-cultural life.

And Mustafa Kemal did all of this without paying one single *kuruş*. Rather, he repaid the Russians with citrus.

Turkey's most modern and largest factory was paid for with oranges, tangerines and grapefruits. It wasn't established with money, but with intelligence and reason.

∞

He convened the İzmir Economic Conference in February 1923, before the Treaty of Lausanne was signed and before the declaration of the republic.

He knew that without an economy, there wouldn't be a republic or anything else.

One thousand one hundred thirty-five delegates of merchants, industrialists, farmers, workers and educators attended.

The decisions made there were as follows:

• *A state-owned bank should be established to lend credit to private enterprises.*

• *Handicrafts should be mass produced at factories.*

• *Foreign monopolies should be avoided.*

• *Whereas Turkey isn't opposed to foreign capital, it should not be established contrary to the country's laws.*

• *Those competent should be called workers instead of unskilled laborers.*

• *The rights of unions must be recognized.*

• *The Turkish people must produce the goods they use.*

• *Wasting money on imports should be avoided.*

• *The forests should be loved like a child and cultivated as such.*

• *The treasure we have should not be forgotten.*

• *Our mines should be operational.*

• *Our greatest enemies are theft, lying, hypocrisy and laziness.*

• *We should readily embrace innovations.*

• *The maritime legacy of our forbearers should be expanded.*

• *Like people, animals should be paid attention to and increased.*

• *Professional and community associations should be established collaboratively.*

• *Turkish women should raise their children in line with the national economy.*

Mustafa Kemal gave the opening speech:

"There is a truth remaining from the filter of history and experience. If one examines Turkish history, one sees that the reasons for decline and collapse are tied to economic problems.

"There are these rules for full independence: National sovereignty should be supported along with fiscal sovereignty. The only force that will lead us to these goals is the economy. No matter how great political and military triumphs are, they will not endure without being crowned with economic victories."

∞

He only ever bought one toy, so to say, in his entire life—the *MV Savarona*.

The market price was $10.4 million.

An American woman had had it built in Germany, but couldn't bring it to the U.S. due to the tariff wall. He meticulously followed the developments and aspired to buy it. It was second hand, but had never been used and hadn't sailed an inch. He bought for $1.2 million dollars—one-eighth of the price. Nearly a century has passed since then and now its price is $45 million.

It is, of course, priceless, but its material value has increased over the years rather than decrease, as it was a visionary investment.

The *MV Savarona* had a table with 12 chairs that had belonged to King Louis XV. There was a Venetian commode opposite the fireplace. Its library had 1,500 books. The ventilation in the kitchen was extraordinary and it was impossible for the smell of food to enter the cabins. There were separate refrigerators for meat, vegetables and fruit. There was a small bread oven. Mustafa Kemal was only able to spend 56 days on this yacht.

∞

The *SS Bandırma* and the *MV Savarona* were the ships that played the most important role in his life, but the one he regarded highest was the *Karadeniz* steamer.

It was his personal project. It was a floating fair. This was a world first.

On exhibition were carpets from Hekere, Kütahya tiles, *lokum* from the Hacıbekir confectionery, soaps from Edirne, embroidery, çeşm-i bülbül blown glass, copper trays, tobacco, wool, silkworm cocoons, hazelnuts, figs, grapes and opium poppies—all Turkish production. There were ancient artifacts in glass cases that were selected from the Museum of Anatolian Civilizations.

He had a vision to not wait for the world to come to Turkey. It was this ship that was young Turkey's relations with the international public.

It was purchased from the Netherlands in 1924. It was 426-feet long, 52-feet wide and black. It was towed to the Golden Horn and painted a gleaming white like a swan.

It was ready in 1926, only three years after the declaration of the republic.

Mustafa Kemal boarded it at Mudanya. He did the final inspection himself. He went over the deck and through the salons, stands, cabins and kitchen one by one. He looked over the products and met each staff member one by one.

In the ship's logbook he wrote, "This is an undertaking that has thrived and has given me a very good impression. The presentation style is very good. I extend my appreciation and congratulations." He took the *Karadeniz* steamer to the Bandırma and bade farewell from the pier.

It went on an 86-day cruise, stopping off in Barcelona, Le Havre, London, Amsterdam, Hamburg, Stockholm, Helsinki, Leningrad, Gdansk, Copenhagen, Antwerp, Marseille, Genoa and Naples.

There were 180 passengers and a crew of 105. The passengers were Turkey's intellectuals. There was Vâlâ Nureddin; Mahmut Baler; Kemalettin Kamu; Celal Esat Arseven; one of the first woman in Parliament, Mebrure Gönenç; one of the first woman to work as a journalist, Bedia Celal; one of the first female sculptors, Nermin Faruki; and singers and actors. They took on the duty of hosting the foreign visitors who boarded at the ports.

The Presidential Symphony Orchestra was on board with 47 musicians under the direction of Zeki Üngör, the composer of the *İstiklal Marşı* (National Anthem). They played the country's national anthem at the ports they docked at and gave concerts.

The exhibition halls were decorated with sculptures, paintings and curios made by student at the Sanâyi-i Nefîse Mektebi—the fine arts academy. There were paintings by Turkish artists such as İbrahim Çallı.

Lütfü Bey captained the ship—the legendary captain of the *Gülcemal* steamer, Turkey's first passenger ship to cross the Atlantic. The general director of port operations, Rauf Manyas, was the director of exhibitions. Samiha Hanım knew seven languages and was the director of protocol. Architect Naci Bey did the decorating. Mustafa Kemal had chosen them for the staff.

A custom logo was prepared for the steamer. Hermes, the messenger of the gods, led the *Karadeniz* steamer. Instead of his scepter, he carried the emblem of the Maritime Lines.

Brochures were distributed in English, French, German and Russian. The labels for the goods on the ship were also in these four languages. There were stands to establish Turkish export relations with foreign merchants. There was even an İş Bank branch on board.

Balls were held on deck and people danced. Notables of the cities were hosted for evenings with dinner.

More than 100,000 people visited it. Twenty-five thousand people toured it in London alone. In Barcelona,

15,000 toured the ship. There were throngs waiting in an hours-long line. Everyone who boarded was given candies from the Hacıbekir confectionary.

British, French and German newspapers ran headlines about "Kemal Pasha's shorthaired girls". More than half the crew were women selected from the country's prep schools who spoke English and French. Their hair was uncovered and they wore colorful dresses. They were European and, in an instant, destroyed the image of the country of men in fezzes. Europe was astonished and got acquainted with Turkey's modern face.

The Presidential Symphony Orchestra gave concerts in city parks. There was almost a stampede for a concert in Amsterdam, which had an audience of about 10,000 people.

Bedia Celel, who spoke fluent English, led the mayor of Amsterdam through the *Karadeniz* steamer. Of her, the mayor said, "I never thought I'd meet such a Turkish woman."

The male crew wore navy blue jackets and trousers with crisp, white shirts and elegant neckties.

Those who thought this steamship came from the Orient and would bring with it an oriental air were sorely mistaken. On board they met smiling, modern Turks.

It was a reflection of Mustafa Kemal's acumen.

This floating fair, which was for the socio-economic promotion of Turkey, was a signal flare for the İzmir International Fair.

The republic had turned 10 and a contest was held for the *Onuncu Yıl Marşı* (10th Anniversary March). Faruk Nafiz Çamlıbel and Behçet Kemal Çağlar's lyrics were choses and Cemal Reşit Rey was going to compose the music.

Mustafa Kemal wanted to see the lyrics.
They brought them to him.

We emerged successful from every war over 10 years,
We created 15 million young people of all ages,
At the head is the commander-in-chief respected the world over,
A chimney rises continually over the hillsides.

He read over them and crossed out the final line.

In its place he wrote, *We knitted together the motherland with an iron web.*

Then he turned to Behiç Erkin, who had been a friend since his time in Gallipoli, was a hero of the National Campaign who had received the Medal of Independence and who founded the state railways and was its first general director. "It didn't describe your 10 years of labor," he said, "so I changed that verse."

Mustafa Kemal put his signature on the Republic of Turkey's miraculous, 10-year move for development. He also put his mark on the *Onuncu Yıl Marşı* like a railroad spike with his metaphor of an iron web.

∞

He never carried money in his pocket.

He didn't have a wallet. His salary was delivered to his aide and it was his aides who made his payments.

He had eked out a living from his student days to when he was a general.

He wrote in his notebook in 1904 when he was 23: "I looked over me entire account of my budget today. I found my costs to be much higher than my income. I haven't even thought about calculating how much money I put in my bag until now. I've been crushed spiritually and materially under this quite great impending misery as the bad result of this lack of accounting."

His wealth was in his heart, though. The tips he gave were much higher than needed.

He and his compatriots were heading to the Erzurum Congress in 1919. Their money was on a shoestring. He asked if it would be enough to get to Ankara.

"Maybe it'll be enough if we don't waste it along the way," Mazhar Müfit Kansu said.

This wasn't the answer Mustafa Kemal had been expecting. Mazhar Müfit had been holding himself back until then and exploded: "It means not giving a 5-lira tip for this and a 10-lira tip for that. Let's tip the workers at the places we stay, but leave the amount for it to me. Don't give 10 liras for a place that costs 2 liras. You tell me who to give it to and I'll determine how much to give."

Mustafa Kemal reluctantly agreed like a naughty child who'd been caught while up to no good.

He retired from the military in 1927 at the rank of marshal. He was given a monthly pension of 150 liras.

His length of service was 41 years, three months and 29 days. It was actually 28 years, three months and 29 days from when he entered the Military Academy until he retired. He was given an additional two years for the Italo-Turkish War, one year for the Balkan War and an additional five years for the War of Independence. With this, it came to 41 years, three months and 29 days.

He was the sharpest dressed leader the world had ever seen and was charisma in the flesh.

Examine the photographs of him in crowds all together. It's as if there is a floodlight on him alone and only his face is illuminated.

He always occasion light-colored shirts—mostly white. They had round collars, wingtip collars and embroidered collars. The cuffs were embroidered with either the initials *K.A.* or *G.M.K.* He liked cufflinks and used collar pins. He wore short-sleeved linen shirts at his summerhouse and while aboard the *MV Savarona*.

He didn't like navy blue or double-breasted jackets. Generally, he would black, three-piece suits made.

He always showed great care that everything was ironed. He couldn't ever abide wrinkles, crumpling or droopy clothes.

He wore ties in contrast to his crosshatched and patterned suits. His favorite tiepin had the emblem of the state railways with a twisted housing made of gold.

His handkerchiefs were silk and embroidered with K.A. There was also a zigzag motif around the edges.

While traveling he usually preferred tweed suits and chamois jackets. He would also wear a riding coat and jodhpurs.

Flat belts bored him and so he would have braided belts with buckles made.

He would wear a white bow tie with a tail coat. He wore a cape better than good actors. The scarves over his shoulders were sometimes blue, but never ever black.

He liked black, laced, patent leather shoes. They were lined in red velvet. He also wore striped, black socks.

According to place, he would wear gaiters if need be. He wore boots in his city life, and not only in the field.

His shoehorn was of ivory.

He would wear white or dark blue and white shoes with his summer attire, and without socks. Sometimes he would wear beige sandals.

He found overcoats to be bulky and would try not to wear one as much as possible. If he had to wear one, he chose greys or browns over dark colors.

Patterned scarves were a must for wintertime. He wore Sulka & Company scarves from the U.S. that he found in shops in London and Paris.

He had gloves in almost every color. He loved gloves lined with wolf fur and around the wrists.

He would wear an off-white, shawl-collard smoking jacket with blue and dark blue stripes over his pajamas in the evenings. His pajamas were silk, tops and bottoms, with a tasseled belt. His pajamas' collars, cuffs and pocket flaps were banded in different colors. He didn't sleep in pajamas, though, and rather laid down in a loose robe.

❉

No one has ever been as handsome as he in a kalpak, top hat, Panama hat, boater, Clark hat, bowler, fedora or newsboy cap. He wore them all.

The kalpak was a symbol of the National Forces. It was a trademark of the War of Independence.

The toadies of the time immediately started to wear kalpaks to show how patriotic they were. Even foreign merchants on government business would have kalpaks on their heads when they came to Ankara.

They were made from lamb, beaver or marten pelts brought from Europe and the Caucasus. An astrakhan kalpak from Europe was at most 5 liras whereas one from the Caucasus could be as much as 100 liras. There were two types—one that covered the forehead and one that didn't. Mustafa Kemal preferred the former. And as such, that type was called the Kemal kalpak.

He had the Strongilos Brothers in Beyoğlu make his shirts before he went to Anatolia for the National Campaign in 1920. This tailor also made shirts for the palace. The head tailor there, Yani Delagramatika, was always the one who took the measurements.

Mustafa Kemal didn't change his habits after the beginning of the War of Independence and still wanted the Strongilos Brothers to make his shirts. That's what he wanted, but the country was at war with the Greeks. The local Greeks were banned from going to Anatolia.

The Strongilos Brothers didn't want to offend Mustafa Kemal while the country and Greece were at each other's throats, and so sent Yani Delagramatika to Ankara.

He passed through Anatolia on adventure-filled smuggling routes, took the measurements and returned to Istanbul on the same smuggling routes. The shirts were made and packaged up and then he set out to again to deliver them to Ankara by hand.

It really is saddening that this magnificent relationship hasn't been turned into a film, made into a documentary or had any books written about it, and has been nearly been completely ignored.

Yani Delagramatika was from the local Greek population, and he never left the city of his birth, where he had also grown up. He continued to live in Istanbul after the founding of the republic.

He opened his own shop and changed his name to Kemalât, which means moral character, with inspiration from Mustafa Kemal.

The Strongilos Brothers were Konstantinos and Theoklis. They had inherited the profession from their father and their shop had been in Beyoğlu since 1880. They migrated to Greece in 1925, and opened a shop with the same name in Athens. They handed the shop to their cousins, who continued with their names. They made shirts for the Greek royal family and politicians, including

Georgios Papandreou and Konstantinos Karamanlis. They fell victim to the Greek economic crisis of 2013 and shut their 133-year-old label.

❉

The initials *G.M.K.* were embroidered on Mustafa Kemal's shirts, handkerchiefs and gloves as standard, as if it were the maker.

İsmail Hakkı Altunbezer, who was the greatest calligrapher of the time, designed it upon personal request from Mustafa Kemal. The *G.M.K.* monogram that Altunbezer designed at the Academy of Fine Arts was used for Mustafa Kemal's personal items such as luggage, watches, cigarette holders, plates and drinking glasses.

❉

He had his shoes, boots and slippers made for nearly 40 years at Altın Çizme (The Golden Boot) in Sirkeci, Istanbul.

He wore size 42.

The owner of Altın Çizme was Onufri Karkilidis. He had done his military service in Damascus under Mustafa Kemal's command. He was also one of his poker buddies. If there weren't enough people to fill the table, he would call Karkilidis.

❋

He sent students with sparkling hope to Europe to study engineering, archaeology, the arts and law after the proclamation of the republic. He also sent six promising head tailors to Paris.

One of them was Levon Kordonciyan. He opened a workshop in Sultanahmet upon his return to the country. Mustafa Kemal had him make his tuxedos, tails and morning coats.

The finance minister, Celal Bayar, went to London for an international monetary conference in 1932. He stopped by the Çankaya Mansion before he left and asked if they wanted anything.

Mustafa Kemal said, "Buy some Burberry fabric, get some for yourself, too, have it sewn up and we'll wear it." Then he remonstrated a bit: "You can't make fabric at that standard, but we must."

Celal Bayar said *aye aye* and left. He didn't by any Burberry. As soon as he returned to the country, he called the director of the Hereke Factory, who had taken extensive steps concerning quality, and asked him to prepare fabric for two suits. Then he went to the Çankaya Mansion.

Mustafa Kemal examined it in his hand and said, "Now look, Celal Bey. When will you make fabric at this standard in my country?"

Celal Bayar spoke with the pride of the risk he'd assumed: "They were made in our country, Gazi your grace—these are Hereke."

That day was a milestone. From that day onward, he never used imported fabric for his suits.

❈

His canes were not to be underrated. They were a hobby.

Some were ivory and some were meerschaum. There was one cane with a bayonet that pulled out. A sword came out of another. There was another with a snakeskin handle.

The one with a trigger that could fire a single bullet is the most famous, but he actually most liked his wooden cane with a metal tip and a figure on the handle of a lion with a caught hare.

❈

He wore a watch and chain. It was a platinum Zenith.

❈

He carried *tespihs* (rosary beads) as an accessory. Some were amber and some had silver tassels. He had *tespihs* made of Indian sandalwood and meerschaum. He would take whichever one matched his outfit.

He was swinging a black cane at the Sivas Congress. He had a coral rosary in his hand on September 9, when he entered Izmir.

He loved the one of pressed amber.

At the same time, he said he used them for his health, in a way: "They call it yellow amber around Baghdad, but our experts call it pressed amber. It's amber dust hand pressed into a stone. It's very precious. I read an article in a foreign magazine by a doctor from Munich who said amber is beneficial for the health, you can smell its scent on your hand and it guards against microbes."

He would stop by the expert *tespih* makers in every city he traveled to. He wouldn't return from Erzurum and Adana without buying a jet stone *tespih*. His *tespihs* had 33 beads. He also had a *tespih* with a silver tassel and 99 coral beads.

He had two charms on tiny chains that he wore beneath his undershirt.

He wore Ray-Ban sunglasses in his final years.

His suitcases were from the United States, made by Innovation.

He had a special suitcase for his hats. He also had a wicker suitcase with plates and cutlery for picnics.

He encouraged those around him to dress stylishly. He'd do so by giving them his own clothing, ties, shirts and belts. According to Sabiha Gökçen's account, there were days when he would give out his entire wardrobe and was left with only one shirt.

He followed global fashion. He would draw models like a designer. He would design models to be made for himself, as well as for his adopted daughters, Afet, Sabiha, Rukiye and Nebile.

Coco Chanel.

He hired French fashion icon Coco Chanel to design the general uniforms for the Turkish Armed Forces.

Chanel is the only fashion designer who's succeeded in making onto *Time* magazine's list of the 100 most important people of the 20th century. She was an extraordinary trailblazer who had women wear trousers for the first time and made black, which until then had been accepted as the color of mourning, an indispensable color for women.

This vision of Mustafa Kemal's was a first in the world.

Years after the Republic of Turkey worked with Chanel, Hugo Boss designed the uniforms for the German military in 1938.

The renowned American sunglass-maker Ray-Ban produced sunglasses with green lenses for U.S. Air Force pilots in 1937.

The English classic Burberry produced gabardine trench coats as an alternative to heavy overcoats for the British military during World War II.

Mustafa Kemal was in the lead.

He became an example of the concept of fashion for militaries of the world.

The documents Mustafa Kemal gave Coco Chanel with his orders in 1930 are at the National Library of France. The Turkish Armed Forces used the uniforms Chanel designed until 1985.

∞

He wasn't a picky eater. He made no special requests to the chefs. He ate whatever was cooked.

He loved white bean stew. He said he'd gotten used to it in school and never grew tired of it. He also liked okra and eggplant. He particularly loved eggplant filled with ground meat and would eat it mixed with pilaf.

It was rare for the meals at the Çankaya Mansion to have red meat. There's not even any mention of steaks or chops in any memoir. In 40 years, he ate one whole chicken and one whole turkey.

He usually ate fish when in Istanbul. He didn't search it out, though.

According to Latife's sister Vecihe, "They would make grilled sea bream when he came to İzmir. He liked flathead mullet and his father-in-law Muamer Bey would send sea bream to Çankaya from İzmir."

He abstained from eating bread.

It wasn't that he disliked eating—he just ate lightly. He considered eating a lot to be bad for his health and wasteful and considered it shameful, mentioning where in the country it came from.

"Banquet tables won't be full of many dishes," he said. "They'll be full of plenty of conversation and a variety of topics."

He wouldn't eat breakfast in the mornings unless he was on a trip. He would pass through the afternoons with a slice of bread and a glass of *ayran*. He would take bits of bread and dip them in his *ayran*. Sometimes he would have lemonade instead of *ayran*.

His favorite fruits were melon and grapes. He didn't care for dessert. He only wouldn't say no to rose jam. He would have Noah's pudding made since Nuri Conker liked it and he would take a taste. He also drank cold water in summer and winter.

He was crazy for ice cream. He ate it like a child with a big smile across his face. He'd ask for it two or three times a day in summer.

He had an incredible craving for ice cream when he and his mates were on their way to Tripoli in 1911. Nuri Conker somehow managed to find some. He often recounted it with a laugh: "I fed him ice cream in a desert where there wasn't even any water to be found. I still couldn't curry his favor."

He would have an omelet made if he got hungry in the middle of the night. He would ask for it without feta since it would make his stomach acidic. He usually would eat mild *kaşar* cheese or İzmir *tulum*.

There were never more odoriferous foods like onion, garlic, *pastırma* or dry sausage since Mustafa Kemal was very sensitive to ensure he didn't have body odor or bad breath.

For mezes, he loved fava. He also liked broad beans in olive oil. He ate a lot of fresh greens like lettuce and arugula.

Roasted chickpeas were a must.

Villagers held a market on Tuesdays in Ankara. Sometimes he'd get on his horse and ride there. He'd both chat with the villagers and shop.

He would pay his bill at restaurants without fail. He never ate for free. He'd also pay the tabs for those in his retinue.

He was on a train going to Eskişehir with about 20 people in 1927. They set off from Ankara in the early morning hours and ate breakfast in the wagon. State Railway waiters and chefs served them lunch, as well.

They were sipping their coffees when they heard Mustafa Kemal's top aide, Rüsuhi Bey, quite angrily say, "What is this, brother—was it gold we ate?"

Mustafa Kemal was curious and asked him why he got angry.

Apparently, since he was the one who paid for Mustafa Kemal, Rüsuhi Bey had asked the waiter for the bill, which was 75 liras. Normally, that kind of breakfast and lunch at a restaurant wouldn't cost more than 2 liras, so for 20 people the bill should've been 40 liras at the very most. The State Railways were ripping off the president.

Mustafa Kemal took Rüsuhi by the arm and said, "I don't steer clear of anything, but I do of waiters. They'll spread it around that we didn't pay and shame us all. It would be best if you paid the 75 liras, put another 5 liras on top for a tip and be done with it."

He didn't like luxury at the dining table. His first order of business when he first got to Dolmabahçe Palace was to get rid of the sultans' solid gold cutlery that had been used there.

∞

The dining table was a school of sorts.

There was a blackboard and chalk in the dining room. This blackboard is now at the head offices of the Turkish Historical Society in Ankara.

A notebook was put next to each place setting. Guests ate, drank and took notes.

A list of names was put together based on which topics would be discussed on a certain evening. There were evenings with historians and others with lawyers, artists or diplomats.

Dinner would be served around 8 o'clock in the evening. Nobody would leave the table until 3 or 4 in the morning. Food was just the pretext. They would talk freely for five or six hours around the table.

The table was democratic.

The topic was education one autumn night in 1931. Reşit Galip, who was a lawmaker from Aydın, didn't mince his words and was a revolutionary on the offensive. He was laying into the national education minister, Esat Sagay, who had been one of Mustafa Kemal's instructors at the Military Academy, accusing him of being reactionary.

Mustafa couldn't contain himself and said, "I can't allow you to speak like that about my teacher when he's not here."

Reşit Galip challenged him: "We're working with torn shirts without expecting anything in return and here you scold us."

It got tense.

Mustafa Kemal responded in a fatherly way: "You're tired—go and rest." It was his way of politely asking him to leave the table.

Reşit Galip didn't step back, though, and doubled down: "This table isn't yours—it's the nation's, and we're discussing the nation's business. I have as much of a right to sit here as you."

The atmosphere had gone thoroughly icy.

Mustafa Kemal—the country's most powerful man—conducted himself in a way that will pass into the history of democracy when he said, "In that case, let me leave." He rose to his feet and left the room.

The incident spread by word of mouth. Reşit Galip was embarrassed to the point where he couldn't show his face. Again, it was Mustafa Kemal who put an end to this unpleasantness.

He invited Reşit Galip back a week later and talked as if nothing had happened. And more than that, he made this hotheaded revolutionary who didn't hesitate to challenge him in order to defend a position the minister of national education.

Faruk Nafiz Çamlıbel described it more poetically:

"The Gazi's table was open to countless guests and topics like a soup kitchen throughout his professional and political career, from his time at the Military Academy until his passing.

"On the table, of course, were delicious drinks and fabulous dishes, but those fortunate to be at the Gazi's table ate such a tasty *subböreği* [steamed phyllo with feta] and then over that date dessert that ordinary words can't describe.

"There's no doubt that there was an elixir at that table that was totally separate and defeated the excellent drinks and tasty food. What was left in the minds of those who left his table wasn't the well-cooked food, but the exciting conversation. Those around the table weren't privy to a feast for the stomach, but a feast for the mind.

"He prepared the table for advocacy for the country. He prepared the table on the basis of national sovereignty and its most obvious incarnation in the form in the republic.

"The defects of a one-party, authoritarian, unchecked administration were disputed at that table. Scholars were invited to the table in order to lend a national identity to our history and language. The table was a battlefield for everything—revolution, reform, agriculture, industry, science and the arts. Every topic was open for discussion at the table."

Yakup Kadri Karaosmanoğlu said of it: "So many very deep, sweet and exemplary memories concerning life and humanity and valuable lessons have remained in all our spirits and minds from that table."

Édouard Herriot, who had served three times as the French prime minister and three times each as the president of the Chamber of Deputies and president of the National Assembly, and who was awarded the

International Peace Prize, gave a quite sincere statement to the French press after arriving in Ankara in 1933: "I can say without hesitation that I would like to be a secretary to Mustafa Kemal. I would want to be a secretary and sit at his table every evening to feed his thoughts. I'd finish university a second time around Mustafa Kemal's table."

He was always fit.

Whereas the idea that sports are good for a healthy life and the awareness of exercise only became widespread in Turkey in the 1970s, Mustafa Kemal had used a rowing machine since 1925.

He read Distinguished Professor Osman Cevdet's book from 1933, *Masaj and Hareket Tedavisi* (Massage and Movement Therapy). He researched the massage methods in Germany, Austria, Sweden and Italy. He looked into the root of the word massage, water massage and sun massage.

One of the books in his library was Victor Pauchet's work form 1928, *Restez jeunes* (Stay Young).

He underlined the following passage in this book of suggestions for healthy living: "Be as orderly and neat as your posture, gait and dress. Always walk upright and erect to show that you are strong. Pay attention to your washing, your hair, your face and your hands. Take good care of your clothing, posture and laundry. Is digestion easy? When it is, you will feel cheerful and agile. Does digestion take more effort? Then you feel heavy and lazy. If you have regular bowel movements, then your mind and spirit are alert. If you breathe deeply into your lungs, then you bring in life. If your breathing is poor and insufficient, then your vitality languishes. Like meal times, sleep time should also be regular. Establish a time to wake up in the morning. No matter how tired you might be, wake up at that hour. If you think I'm starting to get old by now, then take that thought from your mind straight away. The result would be catastrophic if you allow it to settle in your sly brain and you'll return to your old behavior. Every day, repeat the phrase: I am forever youthful, and accept new and fresh ideas.

He was 5 foot 8 inches and 163 pounds. That's how it was recorded on November 21, 1925 at the Office of the Chief of Staff Department of Personnel

The average height of Turkish men in the 1920s was around 5 foot 5 inches, so Mustafa Kemal was considered tall.

Considering the average height of Turkish men in 2018 was 5 foot 7 inches, he'd even be taller than average today.

His favorite sport was wrestling. He loved to wrestle as well as to watch it. There was a wrestling mat made out of white tent cloth at the Çankaya Mansion.

He didn't grow up along a coast and he spent his life on the front, so he didn't know how to swim. He read about the theories of swimming in a French book when he was 50. He managed to implement them in the sea off Florya, where he taught himself to float and swim crawl stroke.

He particularly wanted photographs taken of him in his bathing suit. He particularly wanted photographs of him swimming with young men and women and sunbathing on the beach to be published in the newspapers. Even though he only stayed there three or five days a year, there are about three times more photographs of him in Florya than at Dolmabahçe Palace. He used himself as a personal example in order to guide the citizenry to the countryside and encourage them to the beaches, as they were inhibited by the bigotry in society.

He would even swim in the Bosphorus.

He had a sea bath of sorts he had made at the maritime factory. It was a mobile pier that was closed on all four sides and floated on pontoons. He would have a boat tow it in and have it tied to the Dolmabahçe wharf on the hot summer days when he couldn't go to Florya.

He had learned how to ice skate during his time in Sofia.

He also used golf as a tool for diplomacy. He played golf with foreign diplomats at the Istanbul Golf Club's 18-hole course in Maslak.

He learned the fundamental rules and concepts of soccer from Turkish soccer legend Gündüz Kılıç, whom he asked to draw them out with pen and paper. Afterward, he said, "Well, what do you say. This thing called soccer is like our war games—there's defense, offence, and it requires strategy and the mind of a staff officer."

He used soccer in war games.

Anadolu Agency announced on July 28, 1922, that the army units under Mustafa Kemal were going to play a soccer match in Akşehir. Around the pitch was packed. Mustafa Kemal Pasha, İsmet Pasha, Fevzi Pasha, Nurettin Pasha and Yakup Şevki Pasha were all among the crowd.

British and Greek intelligence, which were following developments by the hour, reckoned it was a match to boost morale. It was understood that since all of the Turkish commander were there, it would be awhile longer before they went on the offensive.

The match was a smokescreen, though. Knowing that the occupation intelligence was following their every step, Mustafa Kemal brought together the commanders from the different fronts as if they were coming to watch the match. He explained to them in a tent set up to the side of the field his plans for the Great Offensive.

The match ended 2-2.

The Great Offensive began a month later. The occupation forces had no idea where it came from.

He was also aware of the propaganda power sports has. He proclaimed the republic in 1923, and ensured the country's participation in the 1924 Paris Olympics.

He whipped out Turkish soccer, wrestling, track and field, weightlifting, fencing and cycling onto the world stage while it was still unclear whether or not the young Republic of Turkey would be recognized diplomatically.

I'm sure you won't believe it when you read it, but he had an official application submitted to the International Olympic Committee in 1921, while the War of Independence was still ongoing.

The first Olympic gold a Turkish athlete won was in Greco-Roman wrestling at the 1936 Berlin Olympics—it was Yaşar Erkan, a wrestler at 61 kilograms.

Mustafa Kemal sent a congratulatory telegram to Berlin: "You're small, but you've done great work for the country and your name has passed into Turkish sporting history. Long live Yaşar!"

This gold medal-winning wrestler's name was actually Yaşar Naçar. Mustafa Kemal got rid of his surname Naçar, which means helpless, and changed it to Erkan—important man.

He started the Gazi Races to promote horse breeding. The first of the Gazi Races was run in Ankara in 1927. Mustafa Kemal was in the stand and watch excitedly. Ali Muhittin Hacıbekir's horse Neriman was the winner.

In 1929, it was Celal Bayar's horse Cap Gris Nez. In 1930, İsmet İnönü's horse came in first.

Mustafa Kemal had a competition held for the building of a racetrack. Italian architect Paola Vietti Violi was chosen. The foundation stone was laid in 1936, and it opened in 1938. Mustafa Kemal said, "Horse races are a necessity for modern societies."

The historical field for Kırkpınar oil wrestling was under Greek occupation, and so the Kırkpınar tournament couldn't be held from 1919 until after 1922. Oil wrestling was also saved when the War of Independence was won.

Turkey's sports history has never been given the space. Turks owe it to Mustafa Kemal that the tradition of Kırkpınar oil wrestling still continues today after surviving 700 years.

He was the first statesman in the world to make physical education compulsory. He was also the first statesman to declare a sports holiday.

∞

He was an environmentalist and a lover of nature.

"Before nature, people are nothing," he said.

He planted his first tree at age 6.

He had moved in with his uncle in Langadas when his father passed away. He had found a wounded crow he called Hacı that he took care of. Hacı had gotten his name from a farmworker named Muharrem. Muharrem was illiterate and hadn't gone on the hajj (pilgrimage), but everyone called him a hajji (pilgrim). He was a very beloved man. Mustafa was inspired by this hajji and so named his crow Hacı.

Sadly, the farm dog killed it.

Mustafa was distraught. He and his uncle buried it next to a haystack and planted a mulberry sapling over it. The tree has always been called the hajji mulberry.

During the bloodbath of the War of Independence, when the end result for the country was still uncertain and even when the republic had yet to exist, Mustafa Kemal was talking about the importance of forests.

He emphasized forests in his opening speech when bringing the Grand National Assembly of Turkey to life in

1922: "It is one of our most important bases that the forests be renewed with modern measures and increased, as forests are important for the vitality and health of the country."

He established a farm called the Forest in the middle of the Anatolian steppe. There was unending grass and he called it a forest.

The Forest Farm was the name of his vision.

He had a mud brick hut built in Söğütözü. It was a 9-foot by 6-foot hole in the wall. With his accent, he called it a *koliba* instead of *kulübe,* the word for hut. There was a mattress, two wicker chairs and a very small side table. He also put in a kerosene lamp. He would stay there some nights.

"I find peace in nature," he'd say.

He would sleep in a tent, under the starts, when he went to Kızılcahamam.

His favorite flower was the red carnation.

An American landscape architect sent a letter to the Çankaya Mansion and asked him which flower was his favorite.

He sent back a reply—red carnations.

When it came to roses, though, there were only pink roses grown for oil in the Isparta, Burdur and Denizli regions. He established a rose nursery at the Forest Farm. A train car full of colorful rose stalks from Germany and the Netherland were shipped in and cloned. The roses were planted in the capital's parks, sold to embassies and distributed to residents with gardens.

It was a milestone in the field. Before Mustafa Kemal, there hadn't even been any red roses in the country.

The Battle of Sakarya was won in 1922, and belief in victory strengthened. Everyone was a little more relieved. Mustafa Kemal had yet to move to Çankaya and was still at the Steering Building.

One evening, he sat down to dinner and asked if there weren't any flowers, since he wanted some for the table. Those who had prepared the table were embarrassed and hung their heads.

He called an orderly. "Find me some empty gas cans," he said. He had them washed out, cleaned and filled with soil.

There was an apricot tree at the entrance to the Çankaya Mansion. It prevented cars exiting the garage from pulling by the door. There was just an inch of space to move in. They were thinking of cutting it down when Mustafa Kemal got word.

"I won't stand for this tree whose fruits I've eaten to be cut down," he said, "or even its branches to be broken."

One of his biggest dreams was to transform Istanbul into a city in the forest. He was going along the Bosphorus by motorboat in 1928. As they were passing Salacak, he turned to Istanbul Mayor Muhittin Üstündağ and said, "I'd like to be mayor of Istanbul so I could beautify the city even more with trees."

There were no flower shops in the capital in 1929.

There was Sabuncakis in Istanbul, which was owned by Yorgaki Sabuncakis. Mustafa Kemal called him to Çankaya. He didn't have a flower order, but an order for a shop. "You open a shop in Ankara," he said. "Go with the governor to Ulus Square, chose the shop yourself and open it wherever you like."

It wasn't difficult for Sabuncakis to open a shop. Who was he going to sell flowers to, though? There wasn't even a green grocer in Ankara at the time. He openly voiced his concern. Mustafa Kemal smiled and said, "Who will you sell to? To me of course. And if nobody buys anything, I'll buy them all."

The capital's first florist opened across from the Ankara Palas Hotel.

The gardener at Dolmabahçe Palace was a local Greek man named Pandeli Roketos.

He was brought to the Yalova farm. Mustafa Kemal had drawn up the garden plans himself, showed where to plant which tree and handed it over to Pandeli Roketos.

In 1929, he had sequoia, Paulownia, Arizona cypress, Blue Atlas cedar, lilac and Japanese maple saplings brought to Yalova from a variety of countries. There he established Turkey first arboretum.

In 1930, they cut branches off a plane tree right next to the wooden pavilion at the Yalova farm.

Mustafa Kemal intervened as soon as he saw. "Don't cut down the tree," he said. "Move the building."

The chief municipal engineer of Istanbul, Ali Alnar, and a team were brought out. The ground was excavated around the building down to its foundation. They brought in train tracks and inch by inch slid them beneath the foundation until the entire building was sitting on them. In four days, they moved the two-story, wooden building 15 feet.

He had a chair brought to the site and watched the work continuously. The workers were staying in a tent. A tent was also set up for Mustafa Kemal and that's where he slept.

Cumhuriyet ran an article about this "walking" pavilion on August 10, 1930.

It became the subject of serious criticism—didn't the state have more important business? And was a branch that precious? The criticism was quite normal considering that environmental consciousness only developed in the 1970s.

Mustafa Kemal welcomed the criticism. To those who asked if the state didn't have any more important work to do, he replied, "That plane tree is the state!"

He entrusted the flowers at the Çankaya Mansion to Sabiha Gökçen in 1937. He told her as if he were bequeathing them to her: "Sabiha, my daughter—look, when I'm alive, I tend to my flowers with my own hands, look after them and have them looked after. Without us, they have no language to ask for water, say which fertilizer to use or how they like sun or shade. Fate will come knocking one day, though, and invite me to the other world, and then looking after these flowers and bringing flowers to my grave will fall to you. A few roses are enough—they'll get bigger. But have them be alive and full of vitality."

Anıtkabir sits within a forest.

Only Mustafa Kemal's body wasn't yet interred at Anıtkabir while it was designed. At the same time, he was planting the seeds of ideas. Inspired by his love of trees and vision of *peace at home, peace in the world,* the International Peace Park was created to surround Anıtkabir.

Anıtkabir is spread over 185 acres. The mausoleum block sits on 30 acres. The remaining 155 acres are the Peace Park.

Tens of thousands of trees representing peace in the country were brought to nurseries in Ankara, Istanbul, Eskişehir and Samsun.

Twenty-four countries were invited to be representative of peace in the world:

- The United States sent spruce, cypress and cedar saplings.
- Germany sent oak, birch, linden, Atlas cedar, cypress, pine, plum, juniper and rose bushes.
- Belgium sent cotoneaster, boxwood, thuja, juniper, cedar, maple, yew, fir and yellow pine.

- Austria sent mountain pine.
- Denmark sent beech.
- Finland sent birch.
- Afghanistan sent white poplar and hackberry.
- France sent alder, yellow pine, cluster pine, nut pine, European hybrid fir, beech and spruce.
- China sent fir seeds.
- India sent cluster pine.
- Iraq sent Mosul pistachio.
- Israel sent cluster pine.
- Sweden sent birch.
- The United Kingdom sent cherry trees, yew, larch and oak.
- Japan sent cherry trees.
- Canada sent alder.
- Spain sent elm, cypress, cluster pine, ash, chestnut, juniper, walnut and oak.
- Cyprus sent pine.
- Norway sent hornbeam.
- Italy sent cherry laurel, cypress, nut pine, blue cypress, larch and cedar.
- Portugal sent cypress and cluster pine.
- Egypt sent catalpa, honey locust and acacia.
- Yugoslavia sent linden, Japanese pagoda, chestnut, Judas tree, plane, poplar, catalpa, hazelnut, Osage orange, hackberry, oak, Polyntha rose, thuja, cypress, juniper, larch, birch, hawthorn, common laurel, barberry, blue cedar, dwarf juniper, lilac, cherry laurel, Mahonia, yew and willow.
- Greece sent beech, fir, yew, holly and larch.

One of Mustafa Kemal's greatest pleasures was to sit on the terrace of the Çankaya Mansion and listen to the rustling of the trees.

If you go to Anıtkabir, please close your eyes and listen to the sound of the wind. I'm sure you'll hear the rustling of the Peace Forest that surrounds Mustafa Kemal.

∞

He was an animal lover.

His uncle had two puppies on his farm when Mustafa Kemal was a child. Their names were Cin and Alev.

He acquired a puppy he named Alp while he was a military attaché in Sofia. It was a hunting dog—an English setter, white with black spots. He was at his side during the Battle of Gallipoli. He was with him at the eastern front. He was with him in Syria.

They came under fire on the way to Nablus in 1918. Alp disappeared in the bloodbath. There was no trace of him.

He got a dog during the War of Independence that had escaped from the car a Greek officer had left it in.

It was a pale-yellow hunting dog. He named it Alber. He was at Mustafa Kemal's side at the proclamation of the republic. He was sick to his heart when Alber died.

Foks held a separate place. He was a brown German pointer—also a hunting dog. He was owned by Hasan

Efendi, who was a photographer at the hot springs in Yalova. He gave him the name of a photographer when he was a puppy. Mustafa Kemal saw him on a morning stroll, bent down and gave him a pat. Hasan Efendi wanted to give the dog to him, but Mustafa Kemal told his aide to pay the man 50 liras. Then he picked the dog up and walked off. His aides gave the photographer 50 liras, which was quite a sum at the time.

Having spent his life on the streets until then, Foks found a home at the Çankaya Mansion.

Like Alp and Alber, Foks also slept in Mustafa Kemal's bedroom. There was a special cushion on the floor at the foot of the bed.

He would curl up under the dining room table and keep the conversation around it company until morning. He wouldn't sack out until Mustafa Kemal did.

He was famous for biting the guests he didn't like and gnawing on shoes.

Mustafa Kemal was quite devoted to Foks.

He had a type of immunity to him. Foks would jump on the table when they were playing billiards and mess up the balls. Mustafa Kemal would smile and laugh at his mischief.

It would be loud, but Foks was very smart. He would enter the study, be well behaved and sit down and not make a sound.

He was always in the protocol at ceremonies and balls. The place of honor was his in Mustafa Kemal's car. He had a place in the accounts of every foreign diplomat. He was always at diplomatic negotiations. He would always accompany Mustafa Kemal to the Grand National

Assembly. He always boarded the steamer first when it was time to go for some enjoyment on the sea.

Mustafa Kemal would take him on the train wherever he went. If one looks at the photographs from Istanbul, Erzurum, Konya, Trabzon, Gaziantep, Mersin, Tokat and Kırklareli, Foks is always there.

He went missing all of a sudden while they were visiting Babaesi in Kırklareli. They search and combed everywhere, but he was nowhere to be found and everyone was worried. Mustafa Kemal calmed them down: "Don't worry. He got lost like this in Erzurum, and Kılıç Ali found him. He'll find him again."

And, indeed, that's what happened. Kılıç Ali found Foks and brought him back. Other than Mustafa Kemal, Foks only loved Kılıç Ali.

Foks was uncharacteristically quiet when they were on a trip in Gaziantep. He didn't touch the food put in front of him for dinner. Mustafa Kemal rubbed his head and, knowing his character well, said that someone must have said something and Foks must be cross.

It wasn't known what had happened until the cook at the governor's mansion explained in an interview years later. Foks had gone in the kitchen and sniffed around. The cook had gotten angry since he was getting too close to the food and had hit him with a ladle.

Foks died in 1933. He was then taxidermied without Mustafa Kemal's knowledge and placed in a showcase at the Forest Farm.

It was quite a shock when he was showed it, and not a very pleasant surprise, either.

Mustafa Kemal was taken aback at what he saw and his emotions welled up. He pulled out a chair, sat down and looked at it for a long time. Then he said, "I loved him so much. I won't see him this way. Bury him someplace proper on the farm."

The request was never fulfilled and Foks was never buried. Gazi Institute for Education instructor Necdet Pençe, who had founded the zoo at the Forest Farm, carefully secreted it away. Nobody knew for 35 years. Then, in 1969, Necdet Pençe's wife İrfan Hanım donated it to Anıtkabir.

It is on display at the War of Independence Museum at Anıtkabir.

❈

He was passionately bound to his horses.

He had good horsemanship. He would go on trips to the countryside with Latife and his adopted daughters, telling them to ride strategically. As if he were in battle, it had the meaning to ride without stopping, come what may—rivers, hills, ditches or pits.

His favorite horse was Sakarya. He had given it to Latife as a present.

She had started riding with a horse she named Çankaya.

He did a symbolic run of the course for an equestrian jumping competition and finished without knocking over any gates. This talented horse was given to Saim Polatkan, a legendary equestrian who represented Turkey at the 1936 Berlin Olympics.

There was a mare Russia had sent Mustafa Kemal. He named it Karadeniz. Verite was the name he gave the horse France had given him. He also had three black horses—Akın, İnci and Yıldız.

Sabiha Gökçen once said of her adoptive father's love for horses: "He loved all animals, but he had a totally different weakness for horses. I must have seen his hands shake and eyes shine with love many times when he stroked their manes, backs and tails. I've never seen anyone ride a horse so beautifully. He often went horseback riding, throw his exhaustion onto its back and rest while talking to them. Gazi Pasha's voice would immediately calm the animals acting up or disobeying the stable keepers. The horses would calm down and resign themselves to their riders. Watching him on horseback was a real pleasure."

There was a foal he loved that had been born on the stock farm at Çankaya. It contracted glanders. The veterinarians forbid going close to it and they were forced to put it down.

Mustafa Kemal couldn't stop himself from putting on gloves and going to stroke the foal. "There was reason and incident when I had no children," he said. "If I were to suffer the disaster of losing a child, my heart wouldn't be able to stand the pain and grief."

He got a Saint Etienne hunting rifle as a gift. He went hunting at the Forest Farm to give it a go. He shot a turtledove. They got the bird and brought it to him, but he immediately regretted what he'd done when he saw the state it was in. "Give this gun to someone else," he said.

It was the first and last time he went hunting.

He had two white canaries. He would open their cages and watch them fly around. They were used to it, would fly about the living room and then return to their cages.

On one such day, one of the canaries went into a Chinese vase the size of a person. There was the sound of frantically flapping wings and it was hitting back and forth. It was stuck.

The gigantic vase had been a gift from Chiang Kai-shek. At a time when the price of a quarter gold piece was 90 *kuruş*, this vase was 45,000 liras.

Mustafa Kemal was alarmed and yelled for them to break the vase. They said it would be a shame to break it, but it was in vain.

He shouted for them to break it open.

Three or four people laid the vase on the floor. The canary was rolling back and forth and came out with a flutter. Mustafa Kemal took a deep sigh of relief. He caught the canary, which was going back to its cage, and gave it a kiss.

That canary would always come to his mind. "The vase had a price however high," he said, "but all animals are invaluable."

He raised pigeons in the mansion's back yard. There was a Bokhara trumpeter, Reverse-wing Pouter, tiger swallow, wood pigeon from Thessaly, black and colorful peafowl, Seljuk fantail and Chinese Flying pigeons. There was also a pigeon keeper named Nuri to look after them.

There was a gazelle calf in the inner garden of Dolmabahçe Palace that the Ottoman royal family had received as a gift. Mustafa Kemal would sometimes go to the garden, feed it by hand, pet it and have his photograph taken with it. When it got bigger, it was sent to the zoo so it wouldn't be alone.

Once when driving through Istanbul with little Ülkü, they met up against a flock of sheep. Ülkü saw the lambs and grabbed one. She asked to keep it.

They took it with them to Dolmabahçe.

It was nothing but trouble. Ülkü didn't leave her lamb for a second. She came down to eat with it, went to bed in her room with it; it was in the study, the library and even the official cars.

Mustafa Kemal needed to find a solution without breaking his little daughter's heart. He called for the interior minister, Şükrü Kaya, and whispered something in his ear. The next morning, he told Ülkü they were going to Yalova. He got Ülkü and the lamb and they boarded the *Ege* steamer.

Everybody was stunned. It was January, the winter had been quite harsh and the sea was seriously choppy—it wasn't the season to go to Yalova.

They got to Yalova and went straight to the farm. Şükrü Kaya greeted them there. He had a little lamb in his lap.

Mustafa Kemal acted like he had no idea. Playing along, Şükrü Kaya said, "We're collecting little lambs like Ülkü's here where they play with their friends and grow up happily with them. They die if they stay alone. If you want, you can also leave Ülkü's lamb here."

And again, as if he were surprised, Mustafa Kemal said, "No, no, that can't be. My daughter won't leave her lamb. We can't give it up."

Ülkü had been listening intently and interrupted with the excitement of a child to intervene. "Let's leave it; don't let my lamb die," she cried.

The operation was complete. They left Ülkü's lamb behind. They ate lunch, got back on the steamer and went back to Istanbul.

This is just a brief vignette of Mustafa Kemal's love for children and animals—leaving his work on a bitterly cold winter day and managing the matter without breaking Ülkü's heart while also returning the lamb to a natural environment.

He wouldn't allow animal sacrifices at welcoming or farewell ceremonies. He would react very sternly to those who insisted.

He was even against sacrificing for *Eid al-Adha* (Festival of the Sacrifice). He asked Religious Affairs Minister Rıfat Börekçi if it was right or not from an Islamic perspective to donate to charity instead of making a sacrifice.

He was the first and only statesman to conduct diplomacy with cats.

Greek Prime Minister Eleftherios Venizelos came to Ankara in 1930, and attended Republic Day ceremonies. He had brought a case of Athenian wine to toast the two countries. Mustafa Kemal gave him a white Angora cat as a symbol of friendship.

❉

He had preparations made for his Ideal Village of the Republic project.

The ideal village project had a circular layout and included a school, library, health center, residences for teaching doctors and midwives, a factory, hotel, telephone exchange, fire station, veterinarian, conference hall, children's park, fairground, nightclub, public bath, mosque, sports field, youth club, public office, agriculture museum, cooperative building, dairy, coppice forest, barn, stockyard, slaughterhouse, tile works, public toilet, village square and cemetery. There was even a cemetery for animals.

This was a time in Turkey when there was no concept of having house pets. It was also a time when people didn't know about the concept of hygiene. Turks had abandoned animals' health, and it was a time when even human life carried little importance.

It was an unprecedented vision the world around at that time to design a cemetery for animals for all the country's villages.

It is just more evidence of the extraordinary value Mustafa Kemal placed on animals.

∞

He loved music.

He wasn't only interested in the physical and mental aspects of the culture of music, but also its social aspects.

He had just started his mission in Sofia in 1914. He went to the opera with his friends Şakir Zümre and Fethi Okyar. They watched *Carmen*. He liked it very much, but he was very sad. "We know Bulgarians as a nation of shepherds," he said, "but they have opera houses, stage actors, musicians and set designers, so I can see better now why we were defeated in the Balkan War."

He loved to listen to music. He loved to sing. He knew how to read notation even though he had never been taught. He also knew the Turkish *makam* system.

He would say that life is music and that "creatures with no interest in music are not human."

He particularly loved folksongs from Rumelia. He never tired of listening to *Vardar Ovası* (The Vardar Lowlands).

Falih Rıfkı Atay once spoke of Mustafa Kemal's love of these songs: "There was a deep and incurable homesickness and yearning for his home in his eyes when he listened to Rumelian folksongs in particular. It was like he smelled the fields of Rumelia and Macedonia and heard the streams and bells of his childhood. His eyes would fog over in a far-off stare. He would descend into memories of which we didn't have in us."

Mualla Gökçay, a shining talent of the time who had sung before Mustafa Kemal, once described him: "He liked Turkish music in general, but he preferred Rumelian folksongs to everything else. He practiced Rumelian folksongs himself. He would warn us to articulate. He knew the music well and would pick up on the slightest mistake immediately."

Aliş'imin Kaşları Kare (My Dear Ali's Black Eyebrows), *Ayağına Giymiş Sedef Nalini* (She Wears Mother of Pearl Shoes) and *Bülbülüm Altın Kafeste* (My Nightingale Is in a Gold Cage)—he had them sung over and over.

He loved the lyrics written by Fuzuli and Nedim. Nihavend, Rast and Segâh were his favorite *makam*s.

He didn't care for singers who shouted when they sang.

He found Bektashi singing to be very impressive. He made people recite ghazals. He also loved *fasıl* music.

He would call for a small ensemble of strings and percussion (*incesaz*) when his close friends and guests he liked came. He would write song requests out in front of them. According to the leader of the *fasıl* ensemble, Yaşar Okur, there was just such an enjoyable night on November 24, 1926, and Mustafa Kemal gave this list:

1. *Meyhane mi bu, bezm-i tarabhane-i cem mi* (Is This a Meyhane or a Gathering Bacchanalia of a House of Pleasure?)
2. *Ruhum, emelim, kalb-i nizarım zedelendi* (My Soul, My Desire, My Weak Heart Have Been Damaged)
3. *Cânâ rakibi handân edersin* (My Love, You Beguile My Rivals)
4. *Yeter artık çeker oldum şu cihanın gamını* (Enough Already, I have Left this World of Grief)
5. *Bade-i vuslat içilsin, kase-i fağfurdan* (May the Wine of Union be Drunk from the Porcelain Cup)
6. *Mani oluyor halimi takrire hicâbım* (My Shame Prevents Me from Explaining My Situation)
7. *Atladım bahçene girdim* (I Leapt into Your Garden)
8. *Şahane gözler, şahane* (Magnificent Eyes, Magnificent)

When would have the song *Makber* sung, with its lines, *Everywhere is dark, that place full of light,* he had the lights turned off and had it sung in darkness.

He would invite the artists he wanted to hear to the Çankaya Mansion and Dolmabahçe Palace. He only went to one concert after becoming president—one by Radio Ankara artist Melek Tokgöz at the Yeni Sinema. He also sent her a bouquet.

The capital was awash with gossip. The reason for it, though, was entirely different.

Ottoman art music had been banned for a while in order to make folk music and Western music more popular. Mustafa Kemal having gone to this art music concert was the official announcement that the ban had ended.

An 18-year-old student of Sadettin Kaynak, Selahattın Pınar and Nubar Tekyay caused a storm on the radio in 1936.

Mustafa Kemal wanted to have a listen and so extended an invitation.

They brought the singer to Dolmabahçe Palace. The young woman's legs were shaking with excitement, she couldn't tell if she'd walked or flown, but she found herself in a hall.

Müzeyyen Senar.

He told her to come to him and sat her down in a chair next to his. The young woman was holding a chapbook. He took it, looked through the pages and marked three of the around 600 songs in the book. Then he instructed her to sing those songs. One of the songs he had marked was by Tatyos Efendi—*Mâni oluyor halimi takrire hicâbım*.

This young woman who won Mustafa Kemal's great admiration with her voice as well as her stance on life was none other than Müzeyyen Senar—later known as the diva of the republic.

Safiye Ayla.

He called Safiye Ayla universal.

He couldn't get enough of listening to her sing *Yanık Ömer* (Weather-Beaten Ömer).

Tears would fall down his cheeks when he listened to *Yemen Türküsü* (Song of Yemen).

He said to her once, "You always come to us as a guest. Let's go to your house one evening as well and listen to your songs in your own house."

Safiye Ayla was on cloud nine, but was also thinking darker thoughts, as she was an orphan who had grown up at the Dârüleytâm orphanage and become a teacher. Her salary was low, she was poor and there was no furniture to speak of in her house. How could she host a guest of honor?

Mustafa Kemal, however, knew her situation quite well already. And it was because of that for which he had invited himself.

Two trucks stopped in front of Safiye Ayla's house the next day. Beautiful housewares were unloaded from the trucks for the kitchen and living room and everything in between. It was a surprise gift from Mustafa Kemal.

Münir Nurettin Selçuk.

One day, he was sipping his coffee on a train while on a trip. His librarian, Nuri Ulusu, was with him. He told him to put a record on the gramophone. Nuri selected a record without looking. By coincidence, it was Münir Nurettin Selçuk. Mustafa Kemal leapt from his seat as soon as he heard it.

"Take it off now and put on another," he shouted.

Nuri Ulusu was surprised and didn't know where this reaction had come from. He whipped the Münir Nurettin record off the player and put on Safiye Ayla.

"Alright, now that's better," Mustafa Kemal said. "Pick out all the Münir Nurettin records and give them to me."

Nuri Ulusu looked through the pile of records—there were four by Münir Nurettin.

Mustafa Kemal told him to open the window. Then he threw the Münir Nurettin records outside and continued to sip his coffee, although angry now.

The trip finished and they went back to Ankara.

Nuri Ulusu explained what had happened to the employees at the mansion. The barber, driver, gardener—everyone was talking about it. The waiter, İbrahim, couldn't help himself and brought it up at the right time when Mustafa Kemal was in high spirits.

"Pasha, we're dying of curiosity. Why did you throw out the records?" he asked.

Mustafa Kemal smiled and laughed at what he'd done. Then he explained: "You'll remember when Münir Nurettin Bey came to Dolmabahçe. We were at the table and he was pleasantly singing a song. I was quite happy and was singing along. After a time, he stopped singing, leaning over to me and whispered in my ear so no one would hear: 'Please don't sing with me, you're messing up the song and I can't sing comfortably.' Maybe no one noticed, but I shut up, didn't answer and didn't sing along anymore. Music isn't our job, but we have fun, we sing, and it made the gentleman uncomfortable. I was offended, of course. That's what it was."

That's how he liked to sing, though.

It was a childish grudge to hold. And, of course, he regretted it. He invited Münir Nurettin back to Dolmabahçe Palace. He only listed this time and didn't join in. He went on collecting Münir Nurettin records.

He established Ankara's first symphony orchestra.

Zeki Üngör had been in the *Mızıka-yı Hümâyun* (Imperial Ensemble), and in 1923 was first violin with the *Makam-ı Hilafet Mızıkası* (Ensemble of the Office of the Caliphate).

The caliphate was abolished.

Mustafa Kemal wrote him a letter calling him to Ankara. "Let's work together, already," he said.

Zeki Üngör put together a list and had pianist Sadir, violinists Halim and Nedim, and flutist Kadri brought to Ankara. The capital's first orchestra gave a concert for Mustafa Kemal at the Çankaya Mansion.

This was just a taste. Then he had the Palace Orchestra in Istanbul moved to Ankara. The entire orchestra of 85 people was brought to Ankara. They were set up at the Ottoman Bank warehouse at the train station and prepared a symphonic concert for the people.

They were the core of what became the Presidential Symphony Orchestra.

Ulvi Cemal Erkin gave a recital at Çankaya in 1930, upon finishing his studies in Paris and returning home. Mustafa Kemal was so proud of the young man he gave him the piano at the mansion.

A few days passed. The piano was still where it had been at the Çankaya Mansion. He asked why it hadn't been sent off. He was told Ulvi Cemal Erkin could barely rent his very small house on his teacher's salary, there was no room for a piano and it wouldn't even fit in the room.

"In that case, rent a house that can hold a piano," he said.

He studied music books. He read French music scholar Albert Lavignac's *Music and Musicians* in the original French and wrote notes in the margins.

He was interested in baroque music. He also researched the historical development of instruments.

They counted his records after he died. There were 464 records at the Çankaya Mansion.

He had bought the albums of the Vienna Philharmonic and Philadelphia Orchestra's performances of Beethoven.

He also listened to jazz.

Paul Whiteman.

Jan Garber.

Jack Hylton.

Harry Roy.

His music archive included Paul Whiteman's *Last Night*, Jan Garber's *Sweet Georgia Brown*, Jack Hylton's *Nothing Else To Do* and Harry Roy's *Cheek to Cheek*.

He listened to rebetiko. He loved Roza Eskinazi's version of *Mourmouraki*. He also had tango, waltz and foxtrot records.

Of course, the most abundant on the list was Ottoman Turkish music.

He loved listening to Hafız Kemal Bey's ghazals and the *taksims* by clarinetist Hafız Osman Efendi, Udi Nevres Bey, Tamburi Cemil Bey and Kanuni Hüseyin Sadettin.

He had around 20 records by Deniz Kızı (The Mermaid) Eftalya.

He had Münir Nurettin's *Etme Beyhude Figân Vazceç Gönül* (O My Heart, Give Up and Do Not Moan Needlessly) and *Yüzüm Şen Hatıram Şen* (My Face Is Merry, My Memory Is Merry), Hikmet Rıza Hanım's *Kirpiklerinin Her Teli* (Every One of Your Eyelashes) and *Son Hatıra* (The Last Memory), Belkıs Hanım's *Aşkıma Uzaktan Bakan Sevgili* (The Lover Who Looks at My Darling from Afar) and *Öpüşürken* (As We Kiss), Afitap Hanım's *Benim Tatlı Esmerim* (My Sweet Brunette), *Bahçenizde Bir Gül Olsam* (If I Were a Rose in Your Garden) and Nezahat Hanım's *Seni Sevdim* (I Loved You)

There were gramophones everywhere, at the Çankaya Mansion, Dolmabahçe Palace, Yalova, Savarona and on his train. Sometimes he would listen to a symphony and gaze out at the forest and others he would listen to folksongs as he swam in the calm sea.

One day, he was talking with Ruşen Eşref. "I can't be without sound," he said. "I can't stand silence, and so this gramophone plays at my door 24 hours a day."

∞

He was a marvelous dancer.

He had been interested in dancing since he was a child.

Asaf Ilbay, who had been his friend from the neighborhood in Salonika, recounted: "We were in junior high. Mustafa Kemal went with a few of his friends who were making the most of the liberal life of non-Muslims and were going to the house of one of them. He played parlor games and danced to the music that was popular and whose names we didn't even know at the time like polka, mazurka, quadrille and waltz."

He went with another friend from the neighborhood, Fuat Bulca, to Halil Efendi's—Salonika's first dance school. They learned the waltz and polka there.

In 1935, legendary composer Dmitri Shostakovich came at the head of a group of the Soviet Union's most famous opera singers, musicians and ballet dancers. They stayed for five weeks and gave 23 concerts in Istanbul, Ankara and İzmir.

Mustafa Kemal put such great importance on the tour that Turkish ministers' official cars were given to the Soviet artists.

The artists included, Lev Oborin, Nikita Magarof, David Oistrakh, Lev Steinberg, Valeriya Barsova, Maria Maksakova, Aleksander Pirogov, Ivan Zhadan, Panteleimon Nortsov, Natalia Dudinskaya and Asaf Messerer. A ball was held in honor of the guest artists in Ankara after the tour ended.

Mustafa Kemal asked Bolshoi soprano Maria Maksakova to dance and they waltzed. The ball started at 10 in the evening and ended at 7 in the morning.

The Soviet artists who wrote about their visit to Turkey all mentioned that Mustafa Kemal was a very impressive dancer.

(Mustafa Kemal loved the voice of young tenor Ivan Zhadan. He invited the young man to assume Turkish citizenship in order to contribute to the country's cultural revolution and said he would take him as his own son so he would feel secure.

Zhadan didn't accept the offer and said he didn't want to leave his country. Unfortunately, the Nazis captured him during World War II. He performed for them for fear of his life. He became persona non grata after the war due to this and he was forced to immigrate to the United States. He continued his career there and became one of the most famous tenors around the world.

Mustafa Kemal gave the Soviet guests gold-plated cigarette cases. One of the artists, David Oistrakh, had his house robbed in 1968, and among what was stolen were a Stradivarius violin and the gold-plated cigarette case. This robbery has been made into a novel and a television series in Russia.)

❉

He was particularly talented at dancing the *zeybek*—a dance from the Aegean region. He wanted it to be the national dance. In line with that, he told Selim Sırrı Tarcan: "The *zeybek* should be danced between men and women in every social hall."

When he came upon village weddings, he would throw off his jacket and join in dancing the *halay* with spontaneous joy.

He was a patron of the theater.

He became acquainted with this art during his time in Sofia, Vienna and Carlsbad. He admired theater's power to describe people with people and he had great respect for thespians.

In the first years of the republic, he came to Ankara for a Darülbedayi theater tour headed by Muhsin Ertuğrul. They were going to perform Nedim Tör's play *Kör* (Blind) and Mustafa Kemal was going to attend.

Beforehand, the interior minister, Şükrü Kaya warned Muhsin Ertuğrul: "The pasha is very busy and he might be a little late, so don't lift the curtain before he arrives."

Muhsin Ertuğrul was a man of principles, and responded, "We will raise the curtain at 9 o'clock and start the play, as is our tradition."

They protested, but in vain. Muhsin Ertuğrul was determined. More than that, he knew Mustafa Kemal very well. "The president I know would drop everything to get to the theater on time," he said.

On the evening of the play, the first bell rang and Mustafa Kemal wasn't there. The second bell rang and he still wasn't there. The third bell rang and the curtain raised. Muhsin Ertuğrul was removing his jacket in preparation for his role as the curtain raised and looked out the corner of his eye. And yes, there was Mustafa Kemal in his box.

He received the actors in his box after the play and congratulated them one by one. He smiled and winked at Muhsin Ertuğrul. "How's that Muhsin Bey," he said. "I came right on time again, didn't I?"

He had gotten word of the exchange between Şükrü Kaya and Muhsin Ertuğrul, and instead of taking privilege for himself, he placed it on art.

He went one evening to see Galip Arcan's play *Sırat Köprüsü* (The Straight Path). He was happy at the beginning and had sat down happily. As the minutes passed, though, his face drew long and it was clear he was angry. The play ended and he called for Galip Arcan. They brought him.

"Did you write this?" Mustafa Kemal asked him.

"Yes, Pasha," he answered.

Mustafa Kemal got even angrier and exploded:
"No, you couldn't have written it. This is a near direct translation from the vaudeville *Fleur d'Orange*. Why didn't you mention that?"

This is how well he knew theater.

❈

Hazım Körmükçü was the stage actor whose friendship he most enjoyed. The man was also a master shadow puppeteer and would perform Karagöz and Hacivat shadow plays in Beşiktaş every evening.

He wrote the play *Karagöz Learns To Read and Write* upon request from Mustafa Kemal during the alphabet reform. The audience laughed during the performances and the people were also getting used to the new Turkish Latin alphabet.

He made efforts to keep puppet shows alive. He was encouraging.

The most famous puppeteer of the time was Hadi Poyrazoğlu. He would put on performances in the evening for 5 liras a ticket. He performed in front of Mustafa Kemal. He did what he did every night. One puppet played a zurna with its butt. The play ended and he went backstage. They nearly set on him in an attack. They yelled at him about what he thought he was doing and that it wasn't right to have butt jokes in front of Mustafa Kemal.

The puppeteer started to shake.

They told him Mustafa Kemal was calling for him and he nearly fainted from fear. But then—Mustafa Kemal had doubled over laughing from the puppet playing a zurna with its butt. He shook the puppeteer's hand and thanked him. He asked Hadi Poyrazoğlu to continue his plays as he had been. Then he gave him an envelope holding 50 liras.

He referred to shadow puppetry as live Turkish cinema.

∞

He looked at the movie screen and saw its power for global propaganda.

When it was still 1920, he said, "Cinema is such a discovery that one day it will be seen to change the aspect of the world's civilization more so than gunpowder, electricity and the discovery of the continents. Cinema will ensure that people living in the farthest reaches of the world get to know and love one another. Cinema will erase the different views and looks between people. He must lay the importance on cinema that it deserves."

He would go to the cinema when he had the chance while at Çankaya or Dolmabahçe in order to be an example for society and increase interest in it. He would even go on foot so everyone would see him.

There used to be the Opera Cinema in Beyoğlu. It opened in 1924. Its floor was covered with wall-to-wall, red carpet. The ushers wore frock coats and white gloves. It was here where he would usually go to watch films when he was in Istanbul.

In Ankara, he went to the Yeni Sinema. The Yeni Sinema in Ulus had a balcony and boxes with blue, velvet seats for six people. The middle one was reserved for Mustafa Kemal.

He loved the Ankara Cinema in İkiçeşmelik, İzmir and the Sinema Palas in Kordon.

We know he watched *Ateşten Gömlek* (*The Daughter of Izmir* or *The Shirt of Flame*), *All Quiet on the Western Front* about the horrors of World War I, a French film set in the Middle Ages and a musical love story set in Vienna—*Der Kongreß Tanzt* (Congress Dances).

He would laugh and enjoy himself while watching Charlie Chaplain as the Tramp.

He used movies to spread the new alphabet.

The subtitles for silent films were in the Ottoman Arabic alphabet. Studios such as Metro-Goldwyn-Mayer, Paramount, Kemal Film, Majik Film, Opera Film and İris were contacted. The cost was met by the Ministry of National Education and the subtitles were switched into the Turkish Latin alphabet.

He watched what is accepted to be the first Turkish talking picture in 1931, at the Elhamra Cinema on İstiklal Caddesi.

Muhsin Ertuğrul had directed it. It was a Turkish, Egyptian and Greek coproduction starring Turkish actors Semiha Berksoy, Hazım Körmükçü, Talat Artamel and İsmail Galip Arcan along with Aziza Amir of Egypt and Greek Periklis Gavrilidis. In the film, two brothers fall in love with the same woman and it depicts how their lives are ruined. Mustafa Kemal was both happy with the actors and the point to which Turkish cinema had come.

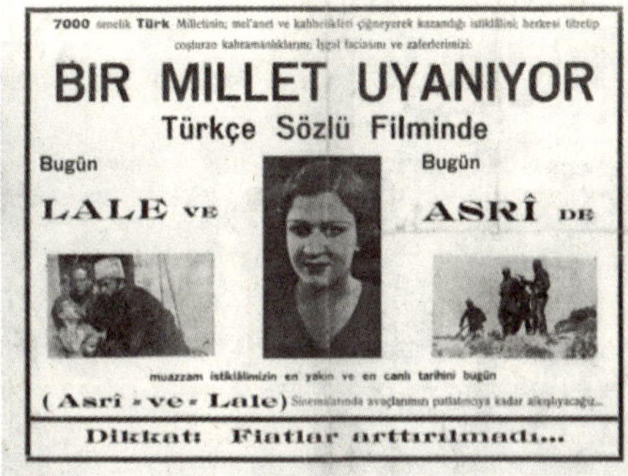

He personally contributed to the screen play for Muhsin Ertuğrul's 1932 film *Bir Millet Uyanıyor* (A Nation Is Awakening), which he also watched at the Elhamra Cinema.

Münir Hayri Egeli wrote the screenplay for *Ben Bir İnkılap Çocuğuyum* (I Am a Child of Revolution) with him in 1937. It was Mustafa Kemal's life from Mustafa Kemal's mouth. The film was to be presented as a documentary.

Unfortunately, his health failed and the movie wasn't filmed. He wrote by hand the instructions for the film:

Münir Hayri will be personally involved in the cinematography. He will go straight to Germany and refine our script. Hasan Rıza will acquire from me the necessary funds to cover the costs.

Mustafa Kemal

The screenplay for *Ben Bir İnkılap Çocuğuyum* runs 137 pages and the original is at the National Library.

∞

He established the Grand National Assembly of Turkey.

Then, only 16 days later, he gave instructions for the formation of the Directorate of Antiquities.

He wanted the Department of Cultural Assets to begin an inventory, determine the areas with ruins and protect them at a time when the future of the country was still uncertain.

Topkapı Palace was turned into a museum. Then so were the areas around Topkapı from 1921 to 1936.

He ensured the opening of the ancient cities of Ephesus and Pergamum, the Ankara Archaeology Museum, the Ankara Ethnographic Museum and the Konya Mevlânâ Museum along with museums in İzmir, Diyarbakır, Antalya, Sivas, Adana, Edirne, Kayseri, Tokat, Kütahya, Samsun, Van, Alanya, İznik, Silifke, Manisa, Amasya, Bursa, Afyon, Denizli, Isparta, Niğde, Kırşehir, Sinop and Çanakkale. He had 30 museums open over the course of 15 years.

He gave instructions for the establishment of a Hittite museum amid the bloodbath that was the Armageddon of the Battle of Sakarya, while occupation forces were closing in on Ankara, when the sound of artillery could be heard in the city, with the prospect of moving Parliament to Kayseri, and when the outcome for the country was as yet unknown.

He wanted to build the country on culture. He believed that if there was no culture and if culture wasn't ingrained, then it would be impossible to survive even if the war was won. His idea for a Hittite museum came to life as the Museum of Anatolian Civilizations.

He was the sponsor for the Hittite and Asiatic Research Association's journal, *Hittite*, published in France. The journal was prepared by French history and archaeology professors and on the copyright page it said, *Published with the patronage of Gazi Mustafa Kemal.*

The Hagia Sophia was in a dilapidated state as a mosque with its courtyard turned into a coffeehouse. Mustafa Kemal ensured it was turned into a museum.

He initiated archaeological excavations.

Upon his instruction, Alacahöyük became the country's first national archaeological dig. He visited the site several times, roamed around the excavation area and examined the finds.

The Hittite sun disk, which is the symbol of Ankara, was found there in 1935. He immediately went to Alacahöyük as soon as he heard, his excitement and happiness visible in his eyes.

He went to Izmir in 1924, purely for the archaeological work and toured Ephesus. He toured the ancient city of Pergamum. While he was there, he related the sorrow he had felt when he saw the Altar of Zeus while in Germany with Mehmed Vahdettin.

He went to Antalya in 1930, and toured Aspendos.

The surface survey of Hasankeyif began in 1932, upon instructions from Mustafa Kemal. He meticulously followed the excavations of Troy and their findings since they began in 1933.

Artifacts from the ancient city of Sardes were stolen on September 9, 1922, while the occupiers were being driven to the sea and Izmir was ablaze.

Americans had been excavating Sardes—in Salihli, Manisa—in the Ottoman period. The artifacts were taken to Izmir and stored at the warehouse of what is now the city's Atatürk High School.

Thinking this was their opportunity while the city was on fire, the U.S. Consulate packed up the artifacts from Sardes in 56 crates and sent them to the Metropolitan Museum of Art in New York.

They literally tried to hide it from everybody under cover of fire.

Mustafa Kemal never forgot this. He launched extremely harsh diplomatic exchanges as soon as the republic was declared. Fifty-three crates of artifacts were sent back in 1924. They said they couldn't find three of the crates, but the rest were retrieved, if nothing else.

The University Law was being prepared in 1933. He wasn't involved in its drafting, but he had it include the Institute of Archaeological.

"Every day entering deeper into the breast of nature full of secrets," he said, "human intelligence has found the sciences that illuminate the history of humanity in order to retrieve reality. It is archaeology that is at the head of these sciences. History is fundamental so long as it is supported by the documents these sciences find. Every piece of the historical documents from our soil is a reflection of our culture."

He coined the conceptual saying: *How happy is one who says I am a Turk.* This means that anyone who has ever existed in what is now Turkey irrespective of race, religion, language and even time is a Turk.

His welcoming with open arms the Jewish scientists fleeing Nazi persecution ensured the teaching of the study of cuneiform and the presentation of Sumerian tablets that had been left untouched for millennia to the scientific world.

He ensured the opening of Sumerian studies departments at universities. Until then, it had been called Sumerian studies, but Mustafa Kemal coined the term "Sumerology".

He had Turkey's first fine arts museum established in the Crown Prince Pavilion of Dolmabahçe Palace in 1937, and personally did the opening.

Exhibitions there included pieces by Osman Hamdi Bey, Şeker Ahmet Pasha, Hüseyin Avni Lifij, İbrahim Çallı, Nazmi Ziya, Hikmet Onat, Ivan Aivazovsky, Pierre Bonnard and Maurice Utrillo.

"One must admit," he said, "that a nation that does not paint and does not sculpt is a nation with no place on the road to progress."

Mihri Müşfik Hanım, Turkey's first female painter, painted a portrait of Mustafa Kemal in his field marshal's uniform in 1928. He didn't want to mention money when he was presented with the painting, and instead asked how he could repay her favor.

Mihri Müşfik Hanım responded, "Grant a strand of your hair and that's enough."

He rose from his armchair, bowed opposite her and said, "Here you are. As much as you want is yours."

It wasn't enough to honor the artists, he asked all state institutions to allocate a budget for their financial support.

Şevket Dağ—who was a student of Osman Hamdi Bey and teacher to Fikret Mualla—held an exhibition in 1935. Mustafa Kemal came on its final day. He asked which ones had sold. Unfortunately, none had found buyers.

"Didn't the minister of national education, minister of national defense and prime minister come to see your exhibition," he asked. They all had.

He turned to his secretary, Hasan Rıza, and said, "Since there were none who saw fit among this many ministers, let's take these masterpieces to Çankaya and take a closer look at them."

He wanted to prevent the disappearance of Turkey's traditional arts like calligraphy, illumination, miniatures and marbling with the help of the aging masters. For this, he ensured they were taught at girls' institutes and boys' art schools, bringing them from the past into the future.

He wanted examples used particularly of tiles, stained glass and stone decoration for the new public buildings being built in the capital.

He lived his life to the fullest without delay. He loved nightlife.

He was staying at the Splendide Hotel in Sofia in 1914. There was a nightclub on the ground floor and he'd stop by every evening. It was a favorite spot for Bulgarian high society and the top generals. The owner was a Bulgarian named Panayot Karagyozov who he'd befriended. It was killing two birds with one stone—he could both have a little fun each evening and get intelligence by getting Karagyoz to talk.

He would say that entertainment is just as important as work, and those who are able to successfully manage the two together are the civilized people.

"We know how to work and we know how to live," he said. "We are on the path of civilized people. Our ancestors gave us a saying: For blessings, there must be pains. Within blessing is pain; so, let's work, let's live."

He often went to Çemberlitaş with his friends and stop by Yorgo's Meyhane in the Chicken Market when he was a student at the Military Academy. They were all regulars and had running tabs. They would close them out at the beginning of each month when they received their stipends.

He was thinking about his younger days one beautiful summer evening in 1932, as he sat with Nuri Conker and Salih Bozok on the pier at Dolmabahçe.

"How about we go to Yorgo's," he said. They got up and left without giving word, as if they were on a raid. They burst in yelling out for Yorgo that they'd come and sat down.

In his white apron, old Yorgo's eyes filled with tears. He set the table just like the old days. The mezes were just as wonderful as they always had been.

Mustafa Kemal turned to the people at another table and said, "Forget who I am and don't be uncomfortable. I'd like to be among you as one of you, so enjoy yourselves."

They ate and drank for two hours. They delightedly sipped their coffees. They got up and walked to the door without asking for the bill or anything. As he did when he was a student, Mustafa Kemal said, "Write out the bill, Yorgo. I'll pay it at the beginning of the month."

And just as in those years, Yorgo gave a warm response: "Goodbye, Mustafa Kemal. Come again."

Of course, many times over the amount to cover the bill was sent the next day.

He had nothing hidden and no secrets.

"Stand up to evil-spirited people who gossip about me," he said. "And if they say Mustafa Kemal drank and danced last night, say yes, he did drink, and yes, he did dance. Everything—both sins and good deeds—must be made clear. Whatever we do, we will do before the eyes of the nation."

He didn't retreat from people after he became president. He would go to Tokatlıyan, Pera Palas, Garden Bar and Rose Noir. His favorite was the Anadolu Club on Büyükada in summer. During winter, he loved dining at the Park Hotel.

He was eating at the Park Hotel again one night. At the next table was a young officer dining with his wife and an 8 or 9-year-old son. He was very pleased that the country's people were having evenings out as families and were having fun as families. He waved his hand and called the young boy over. He pulled out his platinum watch from his vest pocket. "Take this," he said. "Let it be a gift from me. You'll use it when you are older."

The Turkish people attained the freedom to enjoy themselves together with the founding of the republic. The nightlife in Istanbul, İzmir and Ankara in the 1930s was very lively. There was an explosion of restaurants, clubs and music venues with variety shows and bars that people went to as families. Turkey had become an international stage for the musicians and artists who earned their livelihoods from these entertainment venues. Sounds of the Charleston, the shimmy and the foxtrot rose from the shops along İstiklal Caddesi. The *Reflector* magazine, which was in English, French and German, published nightlife programs that the people followed. A son of American slaves who had become a citizen of tsarist Russia, Frederick Bruce Thomas, owned and operated a nightclub called Maxim, which was the most popular spot in Beyoğlu. Tepebaşı Garden, Londra Restaurant, Pera Ambassadeur, Taksim Floria, the Park Hotel and Tokatlıyan Hotel were also popular spots. People would make reservations days in advance in order to see the Janko Orchestra, the Hungarian Women's Orchestra and Mezzy Ballet.

Mustafa Kemal needed a plan of operation in order to escape from Dolmabahçe to go off alone to an entertainment venue. This was because he had no money on him ever. He always gave his salary to his aides and they took care of his bills.

It was another day when he had grown quite bored. He called his head aide Rüsuhi, but couldn't find him. He found his aide Celal Üner. He didn't say he needed cash. He said, "Leave some change on the table, I'd like to please the wait staff."

It was a ruse for pocket money, though.

His aide Celal didn't get what was going on. He actually came back with a handful of change and left 1 lira and 2.50 liras in change on the table.

Mustafa Kemal waited for night to fall. He filled his pocket with the coins, put on a jacket and left through the outer door as if he were going for a walk. He got in the first taxi he saw and disappeared.

He told the driver to go to Tepebaşı.

There was a restaurant-bar there called Mazarik. He'd known it since he was a student at the Military Academy. He paid the cabbie and told him not to tell anyone. He went into Mazarik and order a double *rakı* and some roasted chickpeas.

He never sought out comfortable hangouts. Some nights he'd go to the local Greek restaurants in Kireçburnu and joyfully dance the *hasapiko* shoulder to shoulder with the other patrons.

He would also go to the coffee shops open in Beşiktaş for night drinkers.

He was a regular at the Karpiç restaurant in Ulus, Ankara. It was run by a Georgian who had fled the Bolshevik revolution by the name of Juri Karpovich, who was known as Karpiç Baba. The restaurant's name was actually the Şehir Lokantası (City Restaurant), but everybody called it Karpiç.

It didn't accept guests who weren't wearing ties. There was live music and a dance floor. The tables always had gleaming white tablecloths. It served both Russian and French cuisine and would serve complimentary caviar to its respected guests. The waiters wore tuxedos and the place was a center for social life.

One evening at Karpiç there were Romanian musicians playing jazz. Mustafa Kemal called for the director of the group. He asked the man if they would be able to play Turkish songs by sussing out the notes if he were to sing it.

He said they could.

He sang *Mani oluyor halimi takdire hicâbım* carefully and slowly without making a mistake. The Romanian director wrote down the notes and asked him to sing it again.

After Mustafa Kemal sang it again, the director turned back to the ensemble, talked a bit and played a few run-throughs.

Then they played the song magnificently. Mustafa Kemal rose to his feet and applauded. "You should include this song in your jazz repertoire," he said.

He never left a running tab anywhere, not even 1 *kuruş*. Since he knew that no one would ask him to pay, he would check before getting up to see if the nightclub owner had been paid. He wouldn't get up without getting an answer or if it were uncertain.

∞

There were three integral things for him at the table—coffee, cigarettes and *rakı*.

He never sought out tea.

He was a coffee man. He'd drink around 30 cups of Turkish coffee a day, one after another while he worked. He liked it to be foamy on top.

He drank his coffee without sugar. Sugar was very valuable throughout the years of the war, and it was even quite difficult to find on the black market. Like past generations who had lived through war, Mustafa Kemal had been forced to grow accustomed to drinking his coffee without sugar.

His librarian, Nuri, and waiter, İbrahim, who accompanied him on his domestic trips, would always bring along unroasted coffee beans, finely ground coffee and a *cezve* coffee boiler just in case they couldn't find it where they were going.

He drank his last coffee on the morning of September 7, 1938.

He was ailing and irritated. Professor Fiessinger, who had performed his exam, had given him a serious warning: "I see you don't pay much regard to my suggestions. It's good that you've cut back on cigarettes, but please don't drink coffee. Right now, a cup of coffee is more dangerous for you than alcohol. So please, give up your coffee habit."

Mustafa Kemal politely acquiesced, but said, "Then I propose we drink my last coffee together."

The coffees came. He drank it very slowly, as if he were bidding it adieu.

Sabiha Gökçen came in after the professor had left the palace. Mustafa Kemal told her to come over. His voice was sad. "I'm going to tell you a secret," he said. "I've been strictly forbidden from drinking coffee. You see this cup? It was my last one."

Sabiha took the cup. She acted as though she were bringing it to the kitchen to be washed. In reality, though, she hid it with the grounds still in it.

He smoked around two packs of cigarettes per day. It wasn't a secret that he would pull out a third packet if he was working longer hours.

(It's difficult to understand and consider reasonable from today's perspective of healthy living, but the adverse health effects from smoking unfortunately weren't known of until the 1950s. Smoking was even considered prestigious. There were even campaigns to bring cigarettes to the fronts during World War I. Having lived through the tragedy of the war years, Turks, like all of Europe, became addicted to nicotine. There was no age restriction for smoking, and so there was nothing abnormal for children of 9 or 10 to be seen with cigarettes.)

Tekel produced cigarettes specially for Mustafa Kemal with *G.M.K.* printed on them and with gilded tips. He also smoked Gazi brand cigarettes that came in a tin. His preferred brands, however, were Boğaziçi and Bozkurt. Sometimes he also smoked Bafra Maden cigarettes.

None had filters. He also rarely used a cigarette holder.

He never carried the actual pack in his pocket. Instead, he would empty a pack into a cigarette case. He had 20 cigarette cases at least—gold, silver, filigreed, wood and mother of pearl.

Latife took hold of the whole thing once they got married. Every morning, she would put 10 cigarettes in his case. She wanted those 10 cigarettes to last until the next morning. She thought she could make him smoke less by doing this. Mustafa Kemal, though, was like an unruly child. He had instructed his waiters to hide packs of cigarettes all around the Çankaya Mansion.

One day, Hasan Rıza Soyak caught him taking out one of his squirrelled away packs of cigarettes. He was embarrassed. He hurriedly tossed the pack back in the drawer. Then with a half-smile he said he had gotten them to hand out to guests.

He didn't sacrifice cigarettes like he did coffee. When Professor Fiessinger asked him how many packs he smoked a day, he said eight. Fiessinger was shocked and said he needed to cut down to two packs per day at the very least.

Mustafa Kemal smiled as the professor admonished him. Then he said, "I smoke two packs already, and now I'll have your official permission to do so."

He would think with a cigarette. If he looked off pensively without talking with anyone and puffed away wisps of smoke, it was understood he was on the verge of a critical decision.

He'd be cross with people whose fingers were yellowed from smoking. He'd get very angry when there were piles of butts in the ashtray and would have it cleaned or changed after nearly every cigarette he stubbed out.

∞

He drank *rakı*. It was his medicine to relax his mind. He had first tasted it on Büyükada, when he was a student at the Military Academy. According to his friend Ali Fuat's recollections, after he took his first sip, he said, "What a great drink. It brings out the potential poet in a person."

He drank measuredly and responsibly. He was never seen drunk. He was never seen to slur his speech.

He didn't drink during the day.

One would think a glass never left his hand, the way some people explain it, but there's not even one photograph of Mustafa Kemal with a glass of *rakı* in his hand.

It didn't pass his lips during the wars.

Halide Edip Adıvar put this sensibility of Mustafa Kemal in her novel, *Türk'ün Ateşle İmtihanı* (The Turkish Ordeal):

"We lived at the headquarters in the asceticism of monastic life, as it were. I controlled his desires while drinking. And while his fondness for drink has been rumored, he never brought one drop of alcohol to his mouth."

Three days later would be September 9, 1922—the Great Fire of Izmir.

Mustafa Kemal was at the Kramer Palas Hotel in Kordon. He sat at a bay window. He was watching the pale orange sun set beyond the Gulf of Izmir. The view was spectacular.

He called out for the local Greek waiter.

– Come here, boy!

The waiter was shaking with fear; he couldn't pronounce the "sh" sound and in broken Turkish said, "At your service, Pasa."

"Did your Kosti come here?" he asked, referring to Greek King Constantine I who had come swaggering to Izmir during the occupation.

– He did, Pasa.

– Did he sit at this table?

– He did, Pasa.

– Did he drink *rakı* as the sun set?

– He didn't, Pasa.

– And so, boy, did you ask him why he tried to take İzmir?

The Kramer Palas Hotel was reduced to ashes in the Great Fire of Izmir. When Mustafa Kemal would go to İzmir in the summer, he would go to Ilıca in Çeşme, to make use of the hot springs and stay in a villa owned by the Kramer family, who were the owners of the hotel. It would have been just opposite of where the breakwater in Yıldızburnu is today.

He drank from a glass nicknamed a *leylekboynu*, or stork neck. They were a little larger than a tea glass, half the size of modern *rakı* glasses and narrower at the base than at the mouth. *Rakı* glasses still hadn't been derived from lemonade glasses. Traditional *rakı* glasses were the *leylekboynu* and thimbles as big as modern shot glasses. Rakı was a single shot drunk without water, but Mustafa Kemal preferred the *leylekboynu* glasses since he drank doubles with water added.

His glasses were monogramed with *G.M.K.* and gilded around the rims.

He loved Dimitrakopulo and Bilecik *rakı*.

Dimitrakopulo *rakı* had been a private business in Istanbul run by the Dimitrakopulo brothers since 1883. It was a liquor that won a gold medal in Paris, in 1928. A law was enacted and private *rakı* distilleries were shut down when Tekel (Monopoly) started production in 1936. The Dimitrakopulo label continued on as a winemaker.

Bilecik *rakı* was produced in Galata, Istanbul, by İstepan Berberyan. It was a bit more expensive and had a higher proof. The Berberyan family was from Bilecik, hence the name of the *rakı*.

(For years there was conjecture that man sporting a bowtie on the Kulüp *rakı* label was Mustafa Kemal. He was likened to Mustafa Kemal and İsmet. It had been drawn, however, by İhap Hulusi, who was a pioneer in Turkey's graphic arts and used his close friend, poet Fazıl Ahmet Aykaç, as the model.)

When people who prayed five times a day, like Fevzi Çakmak, came to visit, he wouldn't drink or have drink service at the table.

Neyzen Tevfik was among the guests one evening. He asked for bread so he could prove how much he could drink and his durability. He put it on the empty plate in front of him, poured *rakı* into it and started to drink it with a spoon as if it were soup.

Mustafa Kemal lost all his cheer. "You're not to blame," he said. "It's on who called you to come drink."

Mustafa Kemal never put ice in his *rakı*. He would ask for ice-cold water.

He wouldn't get mezzes, either. Roasted yellow chickpeas were a must, though.

He never drank while he ate. First, he'd have *rakı*, then he'd eat on top of that. He would sit at the table for six or seven hours. At most, out of that, he would sit with his *rakı* for an hour or two.

It was rare that he would drink whiskey. He didn't care for sweet drinks or cocktails. He preferred wine and champagne during formal entertainment. He would come to the tables of foreign guests and treat them to it.

He'd occasionally have a cold beer on hot summer evenings.

(On a related note, Mustafa Kemal received unbelievable slander because of beer. There were aspersions that he'd set up a brewery in the Forest Farm, gave children bottles of beer—Ülkü foremost—and had the children drink.

In reality, though, a malt house had been set up next to the brewery. The factory produced malt extract that was beneficial to children's health and is, of course, alcohol free. It is a food supplement used for children around the world. Produced under the name *Şark Malt Hülasası* (Eastern Malt Extract), this nutritious drink was sold in pharmacies so it would be available to everyone.

Its health benefits were explained on the label:

This is a fare with great benefits for those with general infirmness. It helps children's teeth erupt easily, strengthens bones and increasing nursing mothers' milk production. One or two tablespoons before meals for children and one tablespoon before meals for adults.)

(As such, far from children drinking beer or any other alcohol, Mustafa Kemal gave the status of an association for public good to the Yeşilay (Green Crescent), which was campaigning to protect children and teenagers from alcohol.)

❋

Mustafa Kemal had a high tolerance for alcohol.

Mikhail Vasilyevich Frunze, one of the leaders of the October Revolution, came to Ankara in 1922. There was a dinner at the Soviet Embassy in honor of Mustafa Kemal. There were 120 guests and a gigantic table had been set up. Discussions covered Turgenev, Tolstoy and Dostoyevsky as the vodka flowed like water.

Frunze would rise to his feet from time to time, say *za zdarovye* and down three glasses of cognac one after another. It was both tradition and a show of how hard the Russians could drink.

In response, Mustafa Kemal would stand up, say *za zdarovye, tovarish—to health, comrade*—down five glasses from the same cognac in succession and then continue the conversation where he had left off.

There was a well-known story in those days. At a Green Crescent Association meeting, journalist and writer Ahmet Rasim asked, "If you put a bucket of water and a bucket of *rakı* in front of a donkey, which one would it drink?"

An answer came—of course it would drink the water. Rasim asked why. Then a humorous call came from the hall: "Of course, because it's a donkey, it's stupid."

Mustafa Kemal was wild about it and told the anecdote at every opportunity.

One evening, a worker was watching them as they sat at a table at the Forest Farm. He called the man over. The conversation came to *rakı* and Mustafa Kemal asked the worker Ahmet Rasim's question.

The worker said *rakı*.

Mustafa Kemal burst out laughing with this unexpected answer and said, "Mercy, let's not ask why!"

There was a cellar in the basement of the Çankaya Mansion.

After Mustafa Kemal passed away, according to the inventory of his estate, what remained was:

38 bottles of plum *rakı*, home made
50 bottles of Hungarian wine, red
25 bottles of Ren wine, white
3 bottles of Château Margaux, red

2 bottles of Médoc, red
2 bottles of Grand Pommard, red
1 bottle of Château Guiraud, red
1 bottle of Chambertin Grand, red
2 bottles of Gonzáles Byass, red
1 bottle of Chablis Premier, red
1 bottle of Royal Claret, red
17 bottles of Saint Reims champagne
1 bottle of Continental champagne
1 bottle of Anisado Refinado pastis
1 bottle of Nuyens cherry brandy
1 bottle of Black & White scotch
1 bottle of Insuperable brandy
1 bottle of Nuyens gin
2 bottles of Fine Champagne cognac
2 bottles of Lebron cognac
2 bottles of Martinique rum
3 bottles of Cinzano vermouth

"My friends," he said, "the sultans formerly drank this *rakı*, as well, but the difference between them and me is that while they drank secretly and two-faced, enclosed by the walls of the palace, I do so before my glorious nation. I drink with my honor."

∞

He was a master poker player.

He'd play especially for money. He would test his colleagues' ambitions, avarices and weaknesses at the poker table.

He returned his take when he won. If he lost, he'd pay his due.

Nuri Conker was the exception. He would always lose his mind when he lost his money.

They sat down opposite each other during a train trip. Conker was determined to win this time. He had coordinated with Salih Bozok, who was to sit behind Mustafa Kemal during the game, look at the cards in his hand and give signs with his eyes and brows that they had determined earlier. Conker would win and then they'd rib Mustafa Kemal. That was the plan.

They dealt the cards.

It was going well at first. Conker kept on winning hands. After half an hour, Mustafa Kemal all of a sudden went all in. Bozok had seen two kings and so gave Conker the sign for two kings. Conker met the bet.

They showed their hands. Mustafa Kemal had quad kings. He had been aware of the ruse from the beginning and knew that Bozok was giving signals. He acted as if he showed his cards, but had kept two kings hidden.

Mustafa Kemal had a delighted smile while Conker yelled angrily as he always did: "Bravo Salih, so you saw it all, huh, brother!"

He used poker as a vehicle for diplomacy and played with the British and French ambassadors.

He sat down for a game with U.S. Ambassador Mark Bristol, Nuri Conker and Falih Rıfkı Atay in 1926. Bristol was quite lucky at the beginning while the others couldn't even make a pair. Bristol was raining down full houses and fours of a kind and was in high spirits.

Ahmet Ağaoğlu was among those watching. "Money begets money," he said. Bristol's spirits were raised even more and he laughed as he won.

His luck took a quick turn after an hour or so. He had nothing while Mustafa Kemal and Conker were throwing down fours of a kind and flushes. He was getting angry and losing more and more. His wife Helen was also watching the game. Her face was drawn and hanging and she couldn't take anymore. She got up and said, "I don't feel well. Please, let's go," in an attempt to prevent her husband from losing any more money.

The ambassador, though, couldn't see anything but the table and was thinking that if he went on then his luck would turn again. He told his wife to go and that he would come after the game was over. Then he sent her off alone.

They kept playing until 4 in the morning. They counted their chips. Bristol had lost 10,000 liras—a small fortune.

Of course, it would be inconceivable to have that much money on him. He was beet red, embarrassed and angry, and asked for 24 hours to pay his debt.

Instead of answering him, Mustafa Kemal called for champagne. It came to the table.

"Can I ask you for a glass of champagne?" he asked.

Bristol popped the cork and filled a glass.

Mustafa Kemal lifted it up and said, "Drinking a glass of champagne from Mr. Bristol's hand is worth much, much more than 10,000 liras."

I don't know if the United States had ever been in such a position in its entire history, but Mustafa Kemal both squeezed the ambassador who had been a great admiral and saved the man's money.

The U.S. ambassador to Ankara following Bristol, Joseph Grew, wrote an entry in his diary in 1928:

"We were having a conversation with the British ambassador, Sir George Clerk, and Collins, a correspondent for the London Times. There was music and dancing and the buffet was richly laid out. Rushen Eshref Bey came to me and said Mustafa Kemal wanted to play poker with me.

"Two Turkish ladies, me, National Education Minister Mustafa Nedjati Bey and Mustafa Kemal sat at the gaming table. My luck was dreadful. I pulled out a four of a kind against the Gazi's full house. He pushed the chips to me and gave me a friendly rub on the cheek. But when the game finished in the morning, Mustafa Nedjati Bey had lost 4,000 liras and I'd lost 900. Only Mustafa Kemal had won. Rushen Eshref had been keeping the books. He took the stack of money and very gently gave us all back the money we'd lost.

"There was a winner and no losers. It was an unparalleled poker night."

He was dominant with card games—bridge, pinochle and canasta.

⁂

He started playing backgammon when he was at the Monastir Military High School. He and his friends would go to a coffeehouse in Kavaklaraltı on their Fridays off.

When he was at the Military Academy, they'd go to Stafan's Kiraathane in Babıâli, the Meseret Kiraathane and Yani's Kiraathane in Sirkeci—all gentlemen's coffeehouses.

He played billiards.

He had learned how to play at the Luxemburg kiraathane in Beyoğlu. It wasn't just a cafe game back then, it was a game for the rich, and educated families had billiard tables in their houses. It was a sign of privilege.

There were six billiard tables at the Luxemburg, and French was spoken there. The clientele were Levantine businessmen, diplomats, the children of pashas and students from the Military Academy. Anywhere from 300 to 400 people watched the tournaments played for prize money. Mustafa Kemal called the Luxemburg's owner, Niko Cankopulos, *professor billiards*.

There was a billiard table at the Çankaya Mansion, as well. It had been brought over from Paris. He would shoot pool with guests before sitting down to dinner.

He also used billiards as a vehicle for diplomacy. When he wanted to play billiards with visiting statesmen and ambassadors at Dolmabahçe Palace, he'd have tables brought from the Luxemburg.

If he was playing by himself, it meant he was thinking. He'd occasionally set aside the cue and write down notes.

He was respectful of religion and religious people and never tolerated bigotry against Muslim merchants.

"Religion is the bond between God and his servant," he said. "The class of religious fanatics should not be allowed in the brokerage of religion and those who procure material benefits from religion are abominable."

Some members of Parliament proposed Mustafa Kemal be caliph while meetings were being held concerning the abolishment of the sultanate. Some Muslims in Egypt and India were said to hold the same view.

He smiled bitterly through his anger. "They want to make me an otherworldly man," he said, "with a green turban on my head, a long beard on my face, wearing an ample robe and with a *tespih* in my hand. It's astonishing. These people with their thick heads don't understand me."

He would fast on *Laylat al-Qadr*. He would take breaks during Ramadan for gatherings with music and song. That's how *Laylat al-Qadr* was. He wouldn't drink. He would sit down for *iftar*—the evening fast breaking meal. He would call for Yaşar Okur to recite the Quran.

Yaşar Okur.

Yaşar Okur was a special hafiz—one who has memorized the Quran.

He grew up at a Sufi lodge and was educated in music. He would go to the palace and was the singer for Sultans Mehmed V and Mehmed VI and Caliph Abdülmecid II, as well as being the head muezzin. He went to Ankara with the declaration of the republic and became the head of the Presidential Fasıl Ensemble.

He retired from his position in 1930, but didn't retire form the Çankaya Mansion.

Mustafa Kemal never had anyone work for free. He paid Okur, who was volunteering, 100 liras a month from his own pocket from 1930 until he died. The retired hafiz received a double salary.

During the month of Ramadan, he would have the Quran read from beginning to end at the Hacı Bayram Veli Mosque and Zincirlikuyu Mosque for the soldiers who had fallen in battle.

Sadettin Kaynak recalled a remarkable incident from 1932: "It was Ramadan, and the hafizes had gathered in a large celebration hall at Dolmabahçe. The Gazi was holding Cemil Said's Turkish translation of the Quran. He first gave it to Hafiz Kemal and had him recite it, but he didn't like it. He said give it to him and he'd recite it. And he actually did. I can still see it as if it were in front of me—reciting with tone and comportment like a military commander, as if giving orders."

One of the works he took as reference was *Annali dell'Islam* (The History of Islam) by Leone Caetani, one of the most famous orientalists of the time. He underlined the passages on the Prophet Muhammad's leadership and battles with the note, *important*. The other passages he underlined where on fasting and the occurrence of *Eid al-Fitr*.

He studied the Battle of Badr from a military perspective and drew out his own map.

"Those who doubt that his holiness Muhammad was a prophet should look at this map and read the epic of Badr," he said. "The great victory won with a handful of people against the army of the wealthy Quraysh is not the work of mortal man and is the strongest proof of his holiness Muhammad being a prophet."

He knew the Quran and all its subtleties.

He read it in the original Arabic many times, as well its translations in Turkish and French scores of times and wrote commentary.

The difference between Mustafa Kemal and all other revolutionaries throughout history was religion. He meditated on Islam and faith on an intellectual level.

With Parliament having allocated a special budget, he had the Quran translated into Turkish, had commentary made and distributed tens of thousands of copies for free to the people, ensuring it would be clear in the language of the country.

He had the first scientific study of the hadith done. He had Buhârî's hadith, which is accepted as the fundamental hadith, translated into Turkish and again distributed tens of thousands of copies free of charge.

He worked so people could go to the mosques and understand and feel what happened there in their own language. He made the Quran read in Turkish, sermons in Turkish and the call to prayer in Turkish.

❃

It was the 15th day of Ramadan, 1931. Following the Friday prayer at Yerebatan Mosque, Yaşar Okur recited the Quran in Turkish for the very first time in history, starting with the names of God, the Compassionate and the Merciful.

Then, Hafiz Burhan, Hafiz Kemal, Hafiz Zeki, Hafiz Nuri, Hafiz Rıza, Hafiz Fahri and Hafiz Rifat recited the Quran in Turkish at Sultanahmet Mosque.

The most important part of the congregation was the women.

Hafiz Rifat Bey recited the call to prayer in Turkish at Fatih Mosque for the first time in history.

The first sermon read in Turkish was at Süleymaniye Mosque.

Thirty hafizes recited the Quran in Turkish at the Hagia Sophia on *Laylat al-Qadr*. Close to 1,000 people came to the Hagia Sophia. It was also broadcast over the radio.

"Nobody in the social life of Muslims has the right to preserve their existence as a special class," he said. "Those who see such a right do not act according to religious [Islamic] provisions. We do not have a clergy. We are all equal. We are compelled to learn the commands of our religion."

❈

He was on his way to Samsun on the *SS İzmir* one beautiful summer day in 1928. He stopped by Sinop where they sat in the shade of Sinop Fortress and chatted with city dignitaries.

He asked if there was anything to drink. Those traveling with him said there was cold beer on board the ship. He told them to bring it, and then afterward, gave it out to everyone.

Everybody thanked him as they took their beer. He saw, though, that one person hadn't taken one and it drew his attention.

He asked why the man why he didn't take a beer. The man was an imam—so he hadn't taken one.

"Don't let this dear man sit in this heat like that," he said. "Bring the hodja something cold."

They brought *ayran*. He suddenly turned to the imam as the conversation continued. "Hodja, should cold beer not be drunk in this kind of heat?" he asked.

"It's haram, sir," the imam replied.

"But why is it haram?" Mustafa Kemal insisted.

The imam couldn't answer.

"Is there no Quranic verse or hadith about this?" Mustafa Kemal asked.

Again, the imam couldn't give an answer and confessed sincerely: "Pasha, let me tell you the truth. I came her as a migrant. I looked for work, but couldn't find any. I do the work of an imam the best I can, but I don't know its depths to answer your questions."

Mustafa Kemal gave a sincere reply to the imam's sincerity. "Well done," he said. "Turks and Muslims don't lie. I pardon you for not lying. But look—this place is on the coast. If a foreigner comes here and asks about Islam, you are uninformed. You will go to the mufti and take lessons. Then I'll come and test you. You find yourself in the greatest position. You'll be knowledgeable and clean both inside and out."

He turned to the governor and said, "Have two suits made for the hodja on me."

Then he looked back at the group. He read out the verse from the Quran concerning drinking alcohol and explained its meaning. Everyone was astonished.

"Even a drop of what God has forbidden is haram," he said. "But God is great and a forgiver. May God forgive us."

He finished his beer and got up.

He also read the Torah and the Bible. He had an Old Testament and New Testament in his library. They were translations from Hebrew, Chaldean and Greek, and had first been published in 1886 at the Agop Boyancıyan printing house.

Angelo Giuseppe Roncalli.

Angelo Giuseppe Roncalli was a bishop. He was the papal representative in Istanbul. When the law stating that clergy could only wear vestments at houses of worship was enacted, he showed unwavering support and respect for the reform laws, asked for no institutional concession and became the first clergyman in Turkey to walk the streets in civilian attire.

Because of his deference, Mustafa Kemal gave Bishop Roncalli a gift of two suits, an overcoat and a fedora.

The bishop was a friend to Turks. He took lessons and learned to speak fluent Turkish. He kept a diary and, according to his recollections that were turned into a book years later, he followed Mustafa Kemal's reforms with admiration.

"There is a whole new world here," he said.

He lived in extreme comfort in the Republic of Turkey and was at ease, and even though he was a Christian clergyman, he explained that the main problem was that he had difficulty living in and entering Greece. He wrote again and again in his diary that he loved the Turks.

He became the pope in 1953.

Due to his love of Turkey, he was called the Turkish pope.

"The most beautiful 10 years of my life I spent in Turkey," he said. "They were peaceful and calm. And no one broke that for a single day. I only saw warm relations, friendship, sincerity and understanding."

Due to the friendly relationship Mustafa Kemal had established at the time and the "Turkish pope" to whom he gave those two suits, Turkey established diplomatic relations with the Vatican for the first time in history.

❋

Charles Sherrill, who was the U.S. ambassador in Ankara in 1932 and 1933, in his 1934 biography of Atatürk, wrote: "It has been said that Mustafa Kemal didn't care for religious discussions. However, he spoke with me on this subject freely and at great length. He Turkified and opened wide the doors of a great book like the Quran so Turks would be able to read and understand it in their own language.

"As the Battle of Sakarya raged for 22 days and 22 nights, Fevzi Pasha did not neglect his prayers even once and continued to pray to God. This dignified and brave commander went from position to position and read portions of the Quran to his soldiers to raise their morale. Ismet Pasha, who had the same calmness and never lost his courage and determination for a moment in battle, like Fevzi Pasha, is a Muslim devoted to his religion. These two religious commanders were Mustafa Kemal's closest generals."

Mustafa Kemal worked with a map in his tent during the bloodiest days of the Battle of Sakarya.

He ordered his aide to call for Fevzi Pasha at once. Aide-de-Camp Muzaffer Kılıç mounted a horse and galloped to Fevzi Çakmak's tent. When he entered the tent, he found the pasha loudly reading the Quran with his back turned to the door. He couldn't decide what to do, and so turned back without a sound and explained the situation.

Mustafa Kemal told him not to do anything: "Let's not disturb him when he's reading the Quran."

He had the hafizes recite the Quran and he listened with the pashas under his command throughout the War of Independence. There were notes for every day in his diary:

"Thursday, March 9. İsmet Pasha came. First, we ate, then the actions for the next day were agreed upon. After that, I had the hafiz recite the Quran."

"Friday, March 10. İsmet Pasha, Yakup Şevki Pasha and Selahaddin Pasha came. We ate together and I had the hafiz recite the Quran."

"Friday, March 17. We returned to headquarters. I was alone until 8 o'clock. Mustafa Abdülhalik Bey came and I had the hafiz recite the Quran."

"Monday, March 20. I came with İsmet Pasha. I invited Fahreddin Pasha and the staff to dinner and had the hafiz recite the Quran."

He was interested in Mevlevi philosophy.

When he took leave and went to Salonika when he was a student at the Military Academy, he would without fail go to the Mevlevi lodge and watch the *Sema* ceremony. He saw the turning to draw close to God in the *Sema* as an expression of Turkish genius.

He visited the Mevlevi lodge in Konya in 1923. In the guest book he wrote, "One of the principle sources of Turkish civilization."

He described Rumi as a great reformer. However, he considered Rumi's son, Sultan Valad, to be superior to his father because he wrote his works in Anatolian Turkish rather than Persian.

He stopped for the night in Hacıbektaş—a center of Alevism—while on his way to Ankara after the Sivas Congress in 1919, and designated a headquarters. In so doing, he didn't ignore the centuries of Ottoman persecution of the Alevis and buried in history the politics of their oppression and slaughter.

He was hosted by Cemaleddin Çelebi and watched the *Cem* ceremony. He also visited Dedebaba Salih Niyazi Baba—the head of the religious community.

Kılıç Ali was one of his closest friends. His real name was Asaf. When Mustafa Kemal was looking over his resume when they first met, he crossed out the name Asaf and underlined the Kılıçali neighborhood in Beşiktaş, which was his place of registry.

"There's no longer Asraf or anything else," he said. "There's only Kılıç Ali. Everyone knows his holiness Ali's other name was Kılıç [Sword], and the honed sword of God at that. If there's such a union, how would a man carry any other name?"

A Pan-Islamic Congress was to be held in Mecca in 1926, and the Republic of Turkey had also been invited. There were those around the world who were wondering whether or not Ankara would send a delegation.

Without wavering, Mustafa Kemal said of course Turkey would attend.

He called for Member of Parliament for Istanbul Edip Servet Tör. "You're going to go to Mecca and represent us, he told him. "You're Turkish and you're Muslim.

Turkishness is the pioneer and guide of being Muslim. You will enter Mecca wearing a hat so as to break down the superstitious beliefs that prevent Muslim nations from becoming civilized. If bigotry and fanaticism rise up to tear you apart, you will give your head, but you will not bend."

The issue, of course, was not about a hat. He was striking an attitude against the impositions of bigotry and against the acceptance of subjects with no relation to Islam as if they were religious law.

Walking around Mecca wearing a hat was forbidden—it was unimaginable to do so. This decision from the Republic of Turkey made news around the world, and Edip Servet Tör entered Mecca with a hat on his head.

He didn't experience any problems, and rather became the most respected delegate of the world's Muslim countries.

Mustafa Kemal would make his adopted daughter Nebile recite the *Ya-Sin Surah*.

He loved listening to the call to prayer.

An entry from 1928 in Mithat Cemal Kuntay's diary says: "An exceptional thing happened as the sun was rising in the morning after a long night. The Gazi made a request of his adopted daughter and Nebile Hanım climbed on a chair and started reciting the morning call to prayer. His tears fell to the sound of Nebile Hanım's voice. The Gazi was crying."

After his death, two boxes of his valuables that weren't mentioned in his will were handed over to Ziraat Bank and weren't opened until 1953, right before Anıtkabir was about to open. In addition to a gem-encrusted cigarette holder, cigarette cases, cufflinks and watches, there was also a piece of brass with the *Ayat al-Kursi* written on it.

One of the gravest lies about Atatürk was that he was an atheist, an enemy of religion and oppressed religious people.

The source of this lie repeated from generation to generation and still a continuous topic of discussion today is the imperialism that was unable to twist Mustafa Kemal's arm.

This perception project, which has had the aim to lessen him in the eyes and hearts of the public by presenting him as an enemy of religion didn't start after his death—it was initiated while Mustafa Kemal was still alive. It was put into action as soon as the Treaty of Lausanne was signed.

Expert on the Middle East and Nazi German diplomat Kurt Ziemke explained the British project in his 1930 book *Die neue Türkei*, (The New Turkey):

"Germany and Turkey were in ruins at the end of the Great War and both countries were forced to surrender. They are in a very different situation from each other now. The basic system of the state was destroyed in Germany, whereas in Turkey, the Turkish national state was created with the fundamental principles of Kemalism after the National Campaign.

"In order to achieve their goals in Mosul, the British both supported the separatist movements in Turkey and took measures to hobble the spread of Kemalism. What needed to be done was to suggest the theme that the Kemalist Republic was an enemy to religion and enemy to the Kurds."

The perception project targeting Mustafa Kemal had two objectives. Independent Turkey's own allies saw that the economy was growing in leaps and bounds and the population's level of education was quickly on the rise, and they were working to prevent Turkey from being a factor in Europe.

They also saw Muslim countries like Libya, Tunisia, Iran, Afghanistan, Algeria and Egypt taking the Republic of Turkey as an example and they tried to prevent the spread of Mustafa Kemal's reforms.

They used religious orders, congregations and factious tribes like pincers. Those who came from the outside and couldn't prevail now tried to solve it from the inside.

A British intelligence officer wrote the first biography of Atatürk—published in the United Kingdom—in 1932.

Harold Courtenay Armstrong had been a captain. Ottoman units captured him in Kut al-Amara during World War I and he was held in solitary confinement. It's because of this that he held a personal hatred. He was able to escape the prison camp with a bribe and took up service in occupied Istanbul and enjoyed having the captured revolutionaries executed by firing squad.

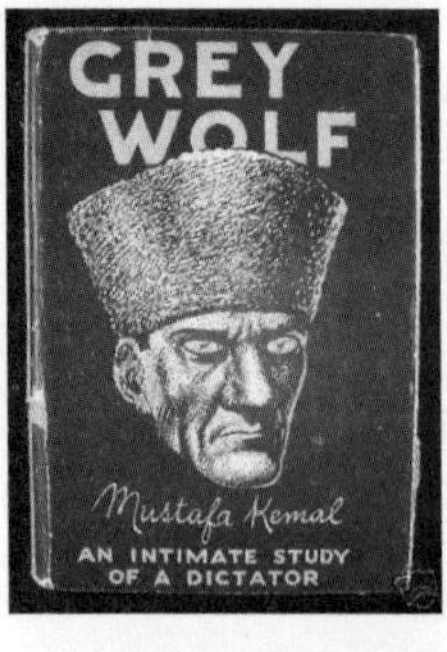

His book is known as *Grey Wolf* for short, but its full title is *Grey Wolf, Mustafa Kemal: An Intimate Study of a Dictator*.

As the title suggests, the book takes aim at Mustafa Kemal's private life as opposed to the historic process experienced in the National Campaign.

He calls Mustafa Kemal a dictator. In fact, he calls him "the most brutal of dictators throughout history." His style is aggressive. He describes Mustafa Kemal as one with an "unruly, ruthless and repugnant personality." He says "he was one to not value friendship."

There are no documents or witnesses to the claims.

As if related to Mustafa Kemal's views concerning Islam, Armstrong assembles allegations with no substantive foundation.

His sources gave ambiguous information that is the product of imagination.

Even what he explains concerning Mustafa Kemal's parents and the house where he was born have no basis in reality. There are clear errors in what he writes about Mustafa Kemal's time as a student, his relationships with his friends and his marriage to Latife.

There is intentional defamation on the topics of alcohol and women.

There are also fabricated dialogues.

The book is printed today with different cover photos. The original illustration of Mustafa Kemal on the cover was appalling and creepy.

Armstrong wrote the book as if he were closely acquainted with Mustafa Kemal, but that, too, is a lie. He didn't even know Mustafa Kemal's circle.

He wrote a letter to Latife and requested an interview, but he didn't even receive a reply. Despite having never met Latife, there are passages in the book that read as if he had heard them from her mouth.

Armstrong's book—full of distortions and misdirection—became the main reference source for Mustafa Kemal's opponents.

All of the unsubstantiated allegations, suspicions and prejudices in the book were scrutinized against documents and eye witnesses accounts.

Mustafa Kemal actually had the book brought to him, he read it and made corrections to the lies and slander. He then explained it to journalist Necmettin Sadak and it was serialized in the *Akşam* newspaper in 1932.

Despite all of this, defamatory books written by those hostile to Mustafa Kemal always reference *Grey Wolf*.

When asked what the proof for one's assertions were, *Grey Wolf* was always presented and the citations always came from there.

Some journalists in the Turkish press who wear the mask of Atatürkism have said that we mustn't fetishize Atatürk and should rather see his human side and human flaws. A documentary was even filmed with a focus on Armstrong's book.

❈

Rıza Nur.

This book with perverted accusations and the most severe slander ever against Mustafa Kemal was republished in Britain in 1968.

Rıza Nur was a doctor and member of Parliament. He was part of the delegation at the Lausanne Conference.

He hurriedly went abroad after the unsuccessful assassination attempt on Mustafa Kemal in Izmir, and lived in Egypt for 12 years.

Mustafa Kemal mentioned him in his *Nutuk* and openly incriminated him. It came to light that he had betrayed the country in the Balkan War, incited Albanians against Turks and conducted clandestine activities for the Albanian rebellion.

He had deep animosity for Mustafa Kemal when his actions were brought to light in the *Nutuk* a year after he fled abroad. His hatred bordered on madness.

He sat down to write a book in 1928. He titled it *Hayat ve Hatıram* (My Life and Memories). It was 2,000 pages of his professed memories.

In this book of preposterous delusions in which one lie refutes another, he calls Mustafa Kemal both a homosexual and a womanizer. On one page he says Mustafa Kemal raped a girl and on another that he lasciviously kissed men under a tree.

He claimed Mustafa Kemal "turned the Çankaya Mansion into a brothel and bedded down 30 women all together." He says Mustafa Kemal and his friends secretly rented houses and prostituted women at them, that members of Parliament were pimping women and that the police had raided the brothels and locked and sealed them up.

He says some members of Parliament gave their daughters to Mustafa Kemal so they could become ministers. He also says that Mustafa Kemal prostituted the female teachers he fancied and that he would traipse through girls' schools, and when he set his sights on a student, "would throw her over his shoulder like a bandit and carry her away."

He says Mustafa Kemal was a drunkard, roaming around three sheets to the wind morning and night.

He says Mustafa Kemal was a miser who made a personal fortune.

He says Zübeyde Hanım was a prostitute who had worked at a brothel in Salonika.

He says there was no such man as Mustafa Kemal's father, Ali Rıza Bey, and that his father was someone named Abdoş who was Serbian or Bulgarian.

He says Zübeyde wasn't Abdoş's wife, but his mistress, and that Mustafa Kemal was a bastard child, which is why he couldn't get his share of the inheritance.

He was so obsessed, he said Mustafa Kemal's "wife was an unvirtuous woman who would strip the girls at the house naked and make them dance. She would also sleep with other men ... and this cuckolding was Mustafa Kemal's doing."

Elsewhere in the book he admits that he himself was homosexual, that he found himself thinking about a cadet at the Military Academy who never left his mind. He says he fell in love with the boy and it resulted in sodomy.

I'm certain you can't believe what you're reading, but that is what he wrote.

He prepared a party program as he saw it: "The caliphate will be re-established, a Ministry of Race will be established, non-Turks will be removed from the civil service, those with hereditary diseases will be sterilized, men and women will not be equal, dancing will be banned and copies of the *Nutuk* will be collected and destroyed."

These ideas are enough to summarize the state of his mental health.

The book wasn't published.

One might ask what he did with it, then. He handed it over to the British Museum in 1935. He did so upon the condition that it not be published until 1960.

Why would he set such a condition, though? Well, he thought all the witnesses would be dead by 1960, and there would be no one left to refute his lies. If they were alive, they'd be out of the country.

He could have had it published at any publishing house whenever he wanted. He wanted to leave his hatred and malice for generations to come.

He died in 1942.

Kadir Mısıroğlu published this book, full of perverted slander, in Turkey, in 1968, at a publishing house supposedly called Altındağ Yayınevi. But such a publishing house didn't exist—it was a fabrication.

Mısıroğlu said, "I acquired the microfilm of the memoir Rıza Nur left to the British Museum and published it."

Was this book written by Rıza Nur, though? How much of it did he write? How much was set up? Who brought it to Turkey? This all remains an enigma.

There's only one thing that's known. Like the Nazi German diplomat Kurt Ziemke's writings from 1930, and British intelligence officer Armstrong's *Grey Wolf*, Rıza Nur's book of preposterous slander against Mustafa Kemal was published in the United Kingdom.

∞

Mustafa Kemal spent his childhood and youth in boarding schools. He was at various fronts and battles throughout his life. He always experienced difficult physical conditions. For this reason, he struggled with health problems throughout his life.

He contracted malaria when he was 15 at the Monastir Military High School. He was in no state to go home alone. His mother came and brought him back to Salonika.

He received a doctor's report for three months. He had a fever for two months and was in bed unconscious. This was his first return from the brink of death.

It's known he was hospitalized at the Gülhane Hospital in 1909, but the reason for it isn't.

The only thing he wrote in his notebook was: "I was hospitalized at the Gülhane Hospital on May 15, and left on May 18."

It's clear that he had an illness that required medication under the observation of a doctor.

He was injured by a horse kick when he was making the final preparations to set out for Tripoli in 1911, and was hospitalized in Alexandria. He was treated for 15 days by the renowned Greek doctor of the day Tsitsani. In the letter he wrote to Salih Bozok back in Istanbul, he said he'd "been hit by an animal."

His teeth were bothering him when he was in Derna, Libya, in 1912. He had cavities that had abscessed. There was no dentist there.

Mim Kemal was a surgeon who, like Mustafa Kemal, was in the Red Crescent convoy absconding to Tripoli, and he treated Mustafa Kemal for his teeth.

A piece of limestone flew into his left eye in the firefight to take the Qasr ruins in Derna. It filled with blood and the area around it turned purple. He tied a kerchief around it. He didn't want to leave the battle to go to the hospital.

Medical Lieutenant Colonel İbrahim Tali Bey went to his tent to examine him. Mustafa Kemal was sitting on a cot and putting on a good face, but his pain was clear. His left eye had started to turn purple and he couldn't open it. On top of that, he was also getting a fever.

İbrahim Tali Bey convinced him he would could lose the eye if left untreated. He was admitted to the Red Crescent field hospital where he was treated by ophthalmologist Ahmet Münir. He was able to leave after a month.

The severe pain in his left eye relapsed three months later. He couldn't even look at the light of day. He tied a kerchief around it again. The doctors advised him to go to Egypt, but it was no use—he wouldn't go. He said it would pass if he got some rest.

Eşref Sencer Kuşçubaşı wrote his recollections: "Mustafa Kemal Bey grew ill with the piece of lime that entered his eye. The treatment with boric acid from the medicine chest Prince of Egypt Omar Tosun Pasha had sent didn't work. He could neither sit nor lay down when the pain set in. The doctors agreed he should be examined by an authorized eye specialist immediately and they requested that he go to Austrian Professor Fuchs. Mustafa Kemal was opposed to it and said how he could go and leave them alone in that vital period. How many people are we anyway?"

He was in this state when he was shot.

Mustafa Kemal explains getting shot in his book *Reflections upon the Officer and Commander*: "I took seven mujahideen of the Mansur and Sellavi families under the command of Lieutenant Kasım and attacked the enemy, which wanted to occupy a critical point and cut off our line of withdrawal. We clashed with two enemy battalions at half past 10, and they were forced to retreat. I attacked the enemy's Eritrean battalion with about 100 mujahideen and military guards. They opened fire on us from the trenches. A bullet hit my right arm. I wasn't going to leave the line of battle so as to maintain the soldiers' morale even though I was losing a lot of blood. If I died, Remzi Efendi would take over my command."

He left Tripoli in November of 1912, and traveled through Egypt to Vienna. The most famous ophthalmologist of the time, Professor Ernst Fuchs, operated on his left eye. He stayed in Vienna for 10 days before heading back to Istanbul.

He launched a bayonet charge against heavy artillery fire in August 1915 to clear out Conkbayır. He felt something strike his chest. His uniform was torn and blood was spreading across the fabric—a piece of shrapnel had hit the watch in his right pocket. His dear friend Nuri Conker was with him. A chill ran down his neck, and he whispered to Mustafa Kemal: "You've been shot." Mustafa Kemal covered Conker's mouth and told him to be quiet.

He was in Gallipoli in September 1915. They had been in the rain for many days and nights. He had gotten very chilled and developed a high fever. He was shaking and was nearly tearing his lungs to bits from coughing.

Lieutenant Colonel İbrahim Tali Bey, who had performed his first eye exam in Derna, was now in Gallipoli. He later wrote: "I found him in grave shape. His chest was bothering him greatly. I felt sorry for him. We insisted that he go to Istanbul for treatment, but he refused."

General Otto Liman von Sanders got word of it and visited Mustafa Kemal's tent. Mustafa Kemal was lying down exhausted. The German general immediately ordered for Ernst Jackh, the private doctor at the German Embassy in Istanbul, to be brought to them.

After his first examination of Mustafa Kemal, Doctor Jackh wrote in his diary: "Mustafa Kemal is gravely ill with malaria. He has grown so weak that I did not recognize him at first."

It took 20 days for him to recover. After that, he rested for a week at his mother's house in Istanbul.

In 1918, he was staying at the Pera Palas, room 101, with writhing kidney pain. He had been suffering from it since his return from Germany with Mehmed Vahdettin.

His left kidney was inflamed from E. coli.

He went to Vienna and checked into the Cottager Sanatorium upon suggestion from his friend Doctor Rasim Ferit, who was the provincial health director for Istanbul.

Europe's most famous urologist, Professor Otto Zuckerland, performed the examination. Mustafa Kemal underwent treatment for three weeks. His complaints lessened a bit, but they suggested he go to the hot springs in Carlsbad for a cure.

With a reference from Professor Zuckerland, he went under the control of Professor Vermer. He underwent treatment at the hot springs for 25 days. He took steam baths, mud baths, drank plenty of mineral water and dieted.

He caught the Spanish flu in February 1919, as he was making the final preparations to leave for Samsun, and he was burning up with a high fever.

This was no ordinary influenza. The flu epidemic was first seen in the United States, in New Mexico. Then it suddenly spread around the world, causing mass deaths. In the United States, 675,000 people died, 250,000 died in Britain, 400,000 in France and 17 million in India. It also swept through Ottoman lands. The true figures aren't known, but people were dropping like flies. News about the epidemic was censored in all of Europe due to World War I, except for in Spain. Since Spain wasn't participating in the war, news of this horrible epidemic was published, which is why it was called the Spanish flu.

He was treated by his friend, Doctor Refik Saydam, who was with him and his other compatriots going to Samsun. Since the illness could be fatal, his condition was followed extremely closely with blood tests. It continued for a month and Mustafa Kemal felt pressed. He groused that he had never had such restrictive examinations even when he was entering military school.

He had severe bouts of stomach pains before leaving for Samsun in April 1919. It was most likely the result of sleepless days and nights, stress, irregular eating, and excessive coffee and cigarettes. He was able to recover by the skin of his teeth in 17 days.

He left for Samsun in May of 1919, and caught malaria. It was the 11th time he'd had it.

It was a tertian fever that rose and fell every couple of days in paroxysm. He had no time to lie down and rest and was forced to be on his feet. When Doctor Arif İsmet Çetinoğlu conducted blood tests a year later at Ankara Cebeci Hospital, they showed that the malaria microbe was still in his bloodstream.

His kidney gave him writhing pain in the days the Grand National Assembly of Turkey opened in April 1920.

Of those days, Yakup Kadri Karaosmanoğlu wrote: "In all of the commotion, he also had kidney disease. He was suffering and holding his waist. He would sit until morning when he got to the state where he needed treatment. The doctors told him to sit in hot water, but there was no bath in which to do so. They bathed him in a tin wash basin, put him to bed there, and he got a little better. Then he'd have to come back to Parliament again and persuade the representatives."

A pustule appeared on his left cheek and quickly grew bigger during the Second Battle of İnönü in March 1921. Surgeon Ömer Vasfi Bey lanced and drained it. He was also suffering from ear pain at the same time.

On the eve of the Battle of Sakarya, his horse got spooked in Polatlı on August 16, 1921. He fell off on his back with his feet in the stirrups and broke three of his left ribs. They put pressure on his lung and making it difficult to breathe.

Aide-de-Camp Muzafer Kılıç placed wooden slats around his ribcage and tied it up with twine.

He went to Cebeci Hospital and got X-rayed. There was blood where the bones had been broken. He refused to stay at the hospital and instead had them bandage him up. He went to the front on the morning of August 17.

His kidney disease relapsed while he was in Akşehir in March 1922, and he took medication for 15 days. He wrote in his notebook: "My left kidney is causing me much pain and suffering and I was forced to rest immediately. Doctor Hulusi Bey came and found my heart to have an irregular beat. I suffered all night."

The pain didn't decrease despite those 15 days of medication in Akşehir. He went to the Ilgın hot springs, stayed there for two days and was relieved a little while under the supervision of urology specialist Major Arif Derman.

He was eating lunch with Latife at the Çankaya Mansion on November 11, 1923. All of a sudden, he put his hand to his chest and his face stiffened in discomfort. He had a shooting pain from his left arm to his chest. Doctor Refik Saydam just so happened to be at the table and he intervened with heart medication and morphine. After 20 minutes, he said it had passed and refused to be further examined.

He was walking through the yard two days later and experienced the same pain in his chest. Since he had refused treatment earlier, this time he was forcibly convinced to rest, if nothing else. He went to Izmir and convalesced at Latife's mansion there for two months.

The republic was declared on October 29, 1923. His speech of thanks in Parliament was surprisingly short. This is because his dentures were new and he had yet to get used to them. When he spoke, they hurt the roof of his mouth and there was a whistling sound.

He had lost his teeth at an early age due to problems with his gums, having been forced to neglect them in times of war. His top teeth were completely removable.

The size of his teeth was taken in a plaster cast, in accordance with the primitive conditions of the time. He had the dentures made in France. In addition to the dentures, he also had two teeth with gold crowns.

He had gone to Dentist Sami Günzberg's office on İstiklal Caddesi ever since he was a young man. During the final portion of his life, however, his teeth were so problematic and he needed to see a dentist so often that a dental chair was brought to Dolmabahçe Palace.

He had inflammation of the gums again three months before his death. Sami Günzberg came and performed surgery on his palate, but it started to bleed and the dentist couldn't stop it. This dentist with years of experience was overwhelmed and fainted. They immediately called for Doctor Mim Kemal, who came and stopped the bleeding.

Mustafa Kemal started experiencing nose bleeds in 1923. He would stuff cotton in his nostrils and lie on his back to manage it. The employees at the mansion had been warned about it. The bloody towels and pillows were washed secretly and ironed. The doctors didn't know about it because his aides had kept it a secret.

May 27, 1927... Upon suggestion from Refik Saydam, Professor Friedrich Kraus—the director of the Berlin School of Medicine—and Professor Ernst von Romberg, who was the director of the Munich School of Medicine, were brought to Ankara, where they conducted a consultation.

They said it was due to smoking and that even though he had a strong constitution, he should quit at once since his father had died young and his mother had died of heart failure. This diagnosis and advice, unfortunately, was to no use.

His legs began to itch in 1936. It was unbearable. It is a sign of liver failure, but that's not what it was attributed to. They reckoned it was from ants.

It's unknown who put forth this strange idea, but at the time, the Çankaya Mansion, being in the middle of open land, was rife with ants, so the idea seemed reasonable enough to everyone.

They put insecticide along the bottom of the walls.

That wasn't all, though. The pest control was performed as if it were a military operation. They got the opinion of the Ministry of National Defense's Department of Health Affairs' Poison Gas Office. It was decided to use hydrocyanic acid, which was used to kill rats on ships. Specialist officers were brought from the battleship Yavuz.

The ants at the Çankaya Mansion were bombed while Mustafa Kemal was in Yalova. All of the windows and doors were closed off with gummed cloth. They pumped intense gas inside and left it for 48 hours. Afterward, they ventilated the mansion and checked it over with sensors. It wasn't enough, though, so they washed the floors with a creosote solution. It took five days.

Of course, Mustafa Kemal's ailment had nothing to do with ants. His itching continued even worse. He had sores on his legs. Dermatologists were called to seek out an ointment to treat it.

And then, due to his liver failure, his nose bleeds became unstoppable. His nose was cauterized with electricity, but to no effect.

Two extremely important years were unfortunately wasted because of this.

He was in Trabzon on June 10, 1937. He stood up during dinner, put his hand in his pocket and turned it inside out. "They had me sign a salary contract, but there's no one who gives it or anyone to account for it," he said. "I have no need for money. I have no expenses in the first place. The love of the nation is enough for me, and if needed, the nation will look after me."

He sent an official letter from Trabzon to the Prime Ministry the next day and donated all his real estate holdings to the Treasury.

During the National Campaign, aid in the form of 500,000 liras came from Indian Muslims in what is now Pakistan. Mustafa Kemal entrusted the money to the command of the western front.

Three hundred eighty thousand liras were left after what was used for the War of Independence. It was transferred back to him with a government decision. He gave 250,000 liras for the capital to establish İş Bank of Turkey and he established farms with the remaining 130,000 liras.

The country had been burned to its foundation. Money was very valuable and land was cheaper than water.

He bought farms in Ankara that had been disused since 1924, and established the Forest Farm. He also set up the Yalova Farm, Silifke Farm, Tarsus Farm, and Dörtyol Farm.

There were 144 acres of fruit orchards, 173 acres of tree nurseries, 99 acres of vine nurseries, 5.5 acres of vineyards, 54 acres of olive groves, 93 acres of orange groves, nearly 4 acres of asparagus fields, 36.5 acres of agricultural land, 25 acres of parks, and 741 acres of forest.

He had 45 residential buildings built along with seven sheep pens, eight barns, six dairies, seven storehouses, four haylofts, six silos, four restaurants and two bakeries.

There was a malt house, ice factory, soda factory, soft drink factory, agricultural tools factory, two pasteurized milk factories, two yogurt factories, a creamery, brewery, winery, flour mills, and 19 irrigation facilities.

There were two chicken farms, five shops, 13,100 sheep, 443 heads of cattle, 69 riding and draught horses, 2,450 chickens, 16 tractors, 13 harvesters, a marine engine, five trucks, two cars, and a telephone switchboard.

All of the income from these farms was spent on the development of farms without touching a single *kuruş*. He took the profits and interest from deposits from his shares in İş Bank and used them to buy more land and transferred them to the farms.

He donated all of them to the state.

⁂

No one could figure out why he was doing this and why he had made such a sudden decision in Trabzon on that day. He didn't quite know what his health problem was, but he was sure that he wasn't well. On top of that, he started to get rid of his belongings.

⁂

December 31, 1937 was his last New Year's Eve.

A message of thanks was published: "On the occasion of the new year, telegrams are coming from citizens in all corners of the country telling of their feelings and sincere wishes. Moved by this, Atatürk has ordered that his thanks and well wishes be passed on."

He was at the Çankaya Mansion with his friends on New Year's Eve. He was weak and weary. He told them to come with him. He had difficulty climbing the stairs. They went to the top floor and into his bedroom. He opened his closet and gave away his shirts, ties, hats, handkerchiefs and everything else there was. It was as if he were bidding farewell and was distributing the final memories of him. "Let's see if I'm alive in the coming year," he said.

He arrived in Yalova on January 22, 1938, for the opening ceremony of the Merinos factory in Bursa. The director of the Yalova hot springs, Doctor Nihat Reşat Belger, examined him there.

He was the first to diagnose him correctly.

"I am convinced beyond a shadow of a doubt of my diagnosis," he told Mustafa Kemal. "Your liver is enlarged and hardened. It is the cause of your itching. It's liver disease."

As if liver diseases weren't enough, in February 1938, he ate outside at the Park Hotel in the dead of winter. He got cold and contracted pneumonia.

He had a consultation with a team of five doctors on February 28, 1938. They determined that he had an enlarged liver, the beginning of cirrhosis and an edema in his ankle.

Professor Erich Frank from the Istanbul School of Medicine was called to Ankara. He also diagnosed the onset of cirrhosis. There was no medicine to combat cirrhosis back then, and so he recommended Mustafa Kemal eat plenty of fruit, especially pineapple.

Professor Noel Fissinger, who was the most famous hepatologist in Europe, was invited and gave the same diagnosis.

It was much too late. The disease was progressing rapidly. Fluid began building up in his abdomen.

Medication was ordered from France. A telegraph was sent to the Turkish ambassador in Paris. They requested 25 boxes of Enterococcus. It was a special serum produced by a Doctor Cuny whose office was at 54 Rue du Faubourg Saint-Honoré. It was said to be good for itching. It cost 740 francs. The postage was 246 francs.

A second order was made 20 days later. This time it was for three boxes of Chophytol and three boxes of Hepascol—artichoke extract pills. There was also a list of mineral water, requesting a crate each of small bottles of Vichy Celestins and Vichy Grande Grille.

Ambassador Suat Davaz sent it off immediately.

The total bill was 483 francs. The postage was more expensive due to the large size of the crates, at 1,857 francs.

Mustafa Kemal had books in French on cirrhosis brought to him. He was learning what the disease was. He determined himself what stage he was in.

He knew he was going to die.

He was trying to set an approximate date of his death so as not to hobble state affairs and so that preparations would be made for after his passing.

In the meantime, he wrote a letter to his adopted daughter Afet İnan, who was in Switzerland. He was as realistic in it as he always was and spoke of the inevitability of the situation: "My condition has not been stopped and is progressing due to incorrect views and conclusions."

Professor Bergman was brought from Berlin. Professor Eppinger was brought from Vienna. These two professors gave a joint diagnosis. The cirrhosis couldn't have been caused by alcohol.

"It isn't possible to say whether or not malaria has an impact on the development of cirrhosis," they said.

In addition to their prescription of diuretic medication, they also recommended quinine for the treatment of malaria.

Professor Fissinger had made a similar determination. "The idea put forward that cirrhosis is caused only from alcohol is not correct," he said. "I have patients from Morocco, Tunisia and Algeria who have never had a spirit pass their lips in their lives. It is necessary to accept that there are other causes of cirrhosis."

❈

(They couldn't perform a liver biopsy at the time in Turkey. There also wasn't any post-mortem autopsy.

As such, it's impossible to say what was the cause of Mustafa Kemal's cirrhosis, whether alcohol, malaria or viral hepatitis.

This has become one of the most discussed topics in medicine. The overwhelming view of parasitologists and microbiologists is that Mustafa Kemal's cirrhosis was caused by Schistosoma parasites, which are a type of blood fluke. It's thought he most likely acquired the parasites in Alexandria or Tripoli, as these parasites were very wide spread in those primitive regions at the time.

In fact, the poet of the *National Anthem*, Mehmet Akif Ersoy, never drank a drop of alcohol in his life and developed cirrhosis in Cairo. He died from it two years before Mustafa Kemal.

The counterrevolutionaries who are quite fond of saying that Mustafa Kemal developed cirrhosis from drinking never mention that Mehmet Akif Ersoy died from the same disease. They never mention how common cirrhosis was in Turkey and North Africa in the 1930s. They also never mention that even as of 2018, children as young as 2 or 3 can develop cirrhosis.)

❈

Mustafa Kemal moved to the *MV Savarona* on June 1, 1938. It was adjacent to the palace and moored broadside to the pier. He placed his books in the library in his cabin. He was like a child who could not hide his joy.

Unfortunately, he was only able to stay on the ship for 56 days. His condition worsened and he couldn't walk. That summer was stiflingly hot and the breeze from the Bosphorus wasn't enough to cool down the cabins. Blocks of ice were placed in basins in the four corners of his bedroom in order to increase the airflow.

"My bowels are swimming in water like the ice in these basins," he commented. "How is a man to live like this?"

Kılıç Ali's mother prepared a refreshing concoction. She steeped linden, chamomile, marshmallow flowers and wall germander, added rose vinegar, cooled it in an ice bucket and brought it in a thermos.

He spread the concoction on his arms and legs. It was very refreshing and cooling.

He called Kılıç Ali's mother Luqman the Wise, who is a personality in the Quran. He held the thermos out to Doctor Refik Saydam, who was going around with a smile on his face, and said, "Don't laugh. Use a little bit yourself. I'm quite pleased with it. They had a laboratory 2,000 years ago!"

He still had a humorous look at life, but he was no longer able to stay on the *MV Savarona*. He refused to be put on a stretcher. On July 25, they waited for it to get dark so no one would see and sat him down on the sofa. "I've waited like a child waiting for a toy," he said. "Was this boat going to be a hospital for me?"

They lowered him off the *MV Savarona* on this sofa and carried him to his bed in Dolmabahçe Palace.

Fluid was going to be removed from his abdomen. There was the possibility it could result in his death.

Mustafa Kemal wrote out his last will in testament.

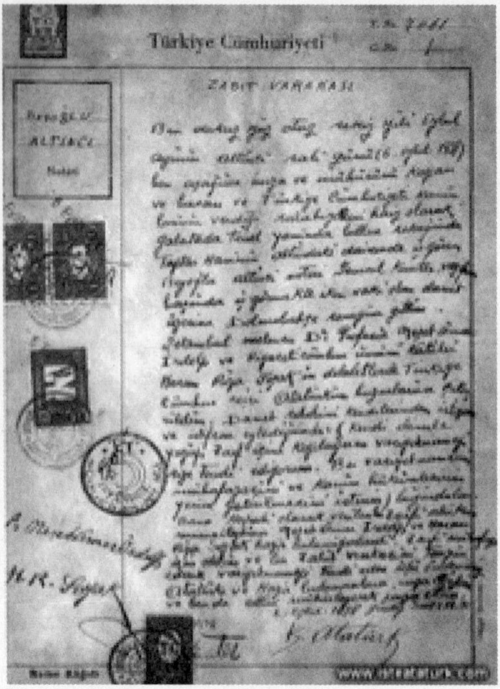
Türkiye Cumhuriyeti

ZABIT VARAKASI

He was in bed on September 4. They had placed large pillows under his head and he was lying on his back. Secretary General Hasan Rıza Soyak was called for. Mustafa Kemal held out his hand and sat up cross-legged with Hasan Rıza Soyak's help.

"It's difficult for both you and me to talk on this path, but we have no other option but to speak of it, my child" he said. "My bowels may be punctured or there could be some other trouble. Let's be cautious. Make a list of what I have and bring it at once."

A cloud of sadness passed over Hasan Rıza Soyak's eyes. He left the room with his shoulders slumped. He came back about an hour later.

Mustafa Kemal was sitting in the same position, gazing out the window. He examined the list and explained how everything should be distributed, and said, "Be careful this doesn't fall on deaf ears."

Member of Parliament and lawyer Salah Yargı drafted Mustafa Kemal's will on September 5. Hasan Rıza Soyak typed it up on a typewriter. Mustafa Kemal read the draft and changed some things by hand. He put it in a large envelope and then into the drawer of the nightstand.

İsmail Kunter from the 6th Notary of Istanbul in Beyoğlu was brought to Dolmabahçe Palace on Tuesday, September 6. He came with Doctor Neşet Ömer İrdelp and was introduced to the employees at the palace as a doctor friend who had come to do an examination so that they wouldn't know he was a notary.

Mustafa Kemal had bathed and was clean shaven. He was wearing silk pajamas and a dressing gown. He was sitting on a chaise lounge that had been put beside the window and he told them to come in.

Hasan Rıza Soyak, Doctor Neşet Ömer İrdelp and Notary İsmail Kunter all sat down on the chairs. They chatted a bit while they drank coffee.

Then Mustafa Kemal pushed the envelope on the coffee table toward the notary. "I consign this will that I wrote myself and put in this envelope to you," he said. "I would like my will protected and carried out according to the provisions of the law."

The notary kept the minutes.

Mustafa Kemal, Hasan Rıza and Neşet Ömer signed it. The notary signed it, as well, and sealed it with red wax.

The one-page will was opened at the 3rd Civil Court of Peace in Ankara, on November 28, 1938, 18 days after Mustafa Kemal Atatürk passed away. This is what was written:

I leave all the money and shares in my possession, as well as my belongings and property assets at the Çankaya Mansion to the Republican People's Party with the following conditions:

1) As it is now, İş Bank will be entrusted with my money and shares will accrue interest.

2) As long as the honor for them to be connected to me continues, for every year for as long as they live, every month 1,000 liras will be given to Makbule, 800 liras to Afet, 600 liras to Sabiha Gökçen and 200 liras each to Ülkü and Rukiye from the interest.

3) Sabiha Gökçen will also receive a house in addition to the money.

4) As long as Makbule is alive, the house where she lives in Çankaya will remain hers.

5) Aid will be given to İsmet İnönü's children so that they may complete their higher education.

6) Every year, what is left from the interest will be split half and half between the Turkish Historical Society and Turkish Language Association.

K. Atatürk

He had three deposit accounts at İş Bank. Nineteen thousand liras had accumulated in the account that received his pension. There were 53,000 liras in his personal savings account. There were 1.446 million liras in the expense account used for farm revenue and to further grow the farms, which hadn't had a single *kuruş* touched. There were also 119,215 shares in İş Bank.

∞

The fluid in his abdomen began to be removed with a syringe on September 7.

Three gallons had accumulated. It nearly filled the tin basin. He was relieved a little and sighed deeply for the first time in days.

He had grown very weak and had dropped to 101 pounds.

Fluid was removed for a second time on September 21. Again, 3 gallons of fluid had accumulated. He couldn't get out of bed. He was talking in his sleep.

Fluid was removed for a third time on October 14. Just less than 3 gallons had re-accumulated. He was severely nauseous. He was given small pieces of ice to swallow to ease his retching.

By October 29, 1938, he was exhausted. It was impossible for him to attend the Republic Day ceremonies. Sabiha Gökçen was at his bedside with tears streaming down her cheeks. She tried to cheer him up by telling him he would attend the ceremonies the next year, but he waved his hand for her to stop talking.

"Don't speak to me of future holidays, Gökçen," he said. "Don't mention the coming month, either. Even if I make it to October, I don't think I'll be able to make it to November."

He couldn't eat anymore.

On November 1, he was able to eat one slice of buttered bread from the corner. It was all he ate the entire day. He drank orange juice and sahlep.

On November 2, he had a few spoonfuls of mashed peas, orange juice and sahlep.

On November 3, he had buttered bread and two glasses of grape juice.

On November 4, he had coffee with milk and two glasses of grape juice.

On November 5, they tried mashed okra, but to no good. He was able to drink sahlep.

On November 6, he was only fed apple juice and milk. He could only take it by spoon.

On November 7, he was half asleep and half awake. He was losing consciousness from time to time. For the first time in his life, he wanted artichokes. They were impossible to find in Istanbul, so a telegraph was sent to Hatay.

He didn't make it. The food wasn't either.

On, November 8, he wasn't himself anymore. He would turn his head to the right and say *aleykümselam*—peace be with you.

It was his last word—*aleykümselam*.

On November 9, he had involuntary convulsions and was sweating profusely.

❉

On Thursday, November 10, at 9:05 a.m., the country lost Mustafa Kemal.

He was 57.

∞

Dolmabahçe Palace was in mourning and was startled by the sound of a single gunshot.

Salih Bozok.

The sound of a shot from the barrel of the Smith & Wesson with a mother of pearl handle screamed through the hall. They immediately ran downstairs. Salih Bozok was lying in blood on the floor. He had pulled the trigger.

He and Mustafa Kemal had been friends since their time in the neighborhood in Salonika, they'd been peers, and since the very beginning, since their time on the *SS Bandırma,* he had been Mustafa Kemal's aide and had volunteered for the ordeal.

They had been so close to each other that he had been Latife's witness when she married Mustafa Kemal and had been there to bury Zübeyde when Mustafa Kemal couldn't make it.

He had been at Mustafa Kemal's bedside at 9:05 a.m. He kissed his hand, left the room without saying a word and went to his room downstairs. He took the service pistol he always kept at his side, pointed the barrel at his breast and pulled the trigger.

Salih Bozok didn't die.

The bullet had just missed his heart and was lodged a hair's breadth to the side. He was hurried to the Şişli Medical Center and taken into surgery and his life was saved.

He continued his life as if it were a living funeral. He could not go without his beloved Mustafa Kemal and gave up everything in his life. He didn't leave his home or his room and was able to make another two years.

Not pierced by the bullet, his heart stopped by itself from grief.

A death certificate was written out for Mustafa Kemal. Nine medical professors signed it.

It said, "At 9:05, on the morning of Thursday, November 10, 1938, the honored and great patient lost his life."

Professor Mehmet Kamil Berk bound Mustafa Kemal's chin with one of his silk handkerchiefs monogramed with *M.K.A.*

On November 11, Mustafa Kemal's personal hafiz, Yaşar Okur, washed his body under the watch of Distinguished Professor Şerafettin Yaltkaya, who was the director of the Islamic Studies Institute at Istanbul University.

Professor of pathologic anatomy Lütfi Aksu conducted the embalming procedure under the watch of professor Mustafa Hayrullah Diker and professor Süreyya Hidayet Serter.

The solution used to ensure his body stayed intact consisted of 200 grams of formalin, 1 gram of mercuric chloride, 200 grams of salt, 10 grams of phenol and 1 liter of water.

After finishing the embalming process, professor Lütfi Aksu filled two small bottles with the solution, soldered the lids on, affixed labels listing the contents of the solution and placed them between Mustafa Kemal's arms.

A plaster cast was taken of his face and right hand.

He was placed in a lead coffin, and the lid was shut. That was then placed in a rosewood casket, and the lid was shut. Over it was laid a Turkish flag.

The casket was placed on a catafalque in the reception hall of Dolmabahçe Palace on November 16.

It opened for visitation at 10 o'clock in the morning. A flood of people flowed in.

Visitation was supposed to end at midnight, but it was impossible to so. More than 200,000 citizens passed by the flag-draped coffin in tears. There were hundreds of thousands of people in line, and it continued without interruption.

The sky grew dark on November 17, and the clock struck midnight. The end of the line extending toward Ortaköy couldn't be seen. Sadly, there was a stampede. There was no one to tell them to stop pushing and screams arose from around the Clock Tower in front of the entrance. Mounted police disbanded the crowd from behind, but the damage had been done. People had been squeezed and crushed—11 people lost their lives.

The next day, the newspapers ran the government's public notice.

Director of Sea Lines Raufi Mayasizade's 16-year-old daughter Bilun, Mrs. Anna who lived on İstiklal Caddesi, Rona Kişnir and her daughter Bella who lived on İstiklal Avenue, Hatice Hanım from Bakırköy, milk seller Diyamandi of Kurtuluş, Abdülhamid Bey from Topkapı, Mrs. Kecser Mehmed from Laleli in Aksaray, Satenik Ohannes of Tarlabaşı, 15-year-old student at Saint Benoit, Paul Kuto and Mr. Leon who had been staying at the Luxembourg Hotel in Beyoğlu had all died in the stampede.

Women and men; young and old; Muslims, Christians and Jews; local Greeks and Armenians—all citizens under the umbrella of the saying *How happy is the one who says I am a Turk*—wept for Mustafa Kemal—the commonality for the entire country.

The crowed continued to grow on November 18.

Reporter for the *Ulus* newspaper Cemil Kutay wrote, "How does an entire nation weep for being left an orphan from one compassionate father who bestowed dignity, liberty, independence and beautiful things? Here it is, that weeping.

"It is impossible to explain to those who did not witness the events of this century, this fidelity and flood of gratitude with writings, words, photographs, compositions and paintings. There is not one iota of protocol.

"There was no ephemeral sensation like that of a ceremony. There was a nation in solemn circumambulation. The majority was women."

The funeral prayer was performed at 8:10 a.m. on November 19.

Religious Affairs Minister Mehmet Rifat Börekçi had been consulted as to whether or not it was obligatory in Islam for Mustafa Kemal to be brought to a mosque.

Börekçi was a hero of the National Campaign and explained wonderfully: "The funeral prayer for Mustafa Kemal Atatürk can be done anywhere in the homeland that he himself made immaculate."

Distinguished Professor Şerafeddin Yaltkaya, the country's second religious affairs minister after Mehmet Rifat Börekçi, performed the funeral prayer at Dolmabahçe Palace.

(The main factor in this decision was the 11 people who were killed and more than 50 others who were seriously injured in the stampede. It would have never been possible to keep order with the hundreds of thousands of people who had come from everywhere in Turkey for the funeral prayer. It would have been impossible to keep the crowd orderly even if it were held in the Dolmabahçe Mosque, just next door to the palace. It was certain there would have been an even bigger tragedy. This was the main reason the funeral prayer was performed at the palace.

Beyond that, the governor and police chief of Istanbul were dismissed because of the tragedy that resulted from the stampede, and the Istanbul police chief and his deputy were charged with negligence as a result of the investigation by the prosecutor's office.)

Mustafa Kemal's casket was placed on two marble tables beneath the grand chandelier in the reception hall.

His friends, employees and religious officials lined up beside it.

Şerafeddin Yaltkaya took his place. Right behind him was Mustafa Kemal's personal hafiz Yaşar Okur and Hafiz İsmail.

Yaşar Okur called out, "O those present, perform the prayer for the sake of God, make the supplication for the deceased, and follow the imam."

The *Takbir* was said in Turkish.

Instead of saying the Arabic *Allahu Akbar*, it was *Tanrı Uludur* (in Turkish), both of which translate as God is Great.

The salutation at the end of the prayer, instead of the Arabic, *as-salamu alaikum wa rahmatullah*, was the Turkish, *esenlik üzerine olsun*—with the Turkish roughly corresponding to the Arabic meaning of *peace be upon you and God's mercy*.

At 8:30 in the morning, there were tens of thousands of colorful wreaths at the door of Dolmabahçe Palace and people as far as the eye could see. There wasn't even space for a needle to fall on the tree-lined street in front of the palace. Twelve generals carried Mustafa Kemal's coffin on their shoulders to a gun carriage with three teams of black artillery horses.

He was leaving Istanbul forever.

The funeral procession started precisely at 9:00 a.m. It followed the tram line through Tophane, Karaköy, over the Galata Bridge, through Eminönü, Bahçekapı, Sirkeci and Salkımsöğüt, and then from Gülhane Park to Sarayburnu.

The coffin was carried on a pontoon from the pier to the destroyer *Zafer*. From there it was transported to the battleship *Yavuz* moored off of Haydarpaşa and placed on deck.

A shot of mourning was fired every minute of its journey.

It was in a fleet with the *Hamidiye* cruiser, the *Zafer* and *Tınaztepe* destroyers, the *Dumlupınar* and *Gür* submarines, and the *Doğan* and *Martı* mosquito boats.

The Turkish Navy set out to perform the saddest duty in its history.

They docked at the Mayın Pier in İzmit. The coffin was put on the white train Mustafa Kemal had used to tour the country. It slowly pulled into the Ankara Train Station on the morning of November 20.

The Steering Building, which was used as the headquarters at the beginning of the National Campaign, now was hosting an eternal farewell.

President İsmet İnönü, Speaker of Parliament Abdülhalik Renda and Chief of General Staff Fevzi Çakmak were there to meet it. Prime Minister Celal Bayar had been on the white train and with the coffin since it left Istanbul.

Mustafa Kemal's coffin was placed on a catafalque in front of the Grand National Assembly building. From noon until midnight tens of thousands of citizens visited in tears. The line of people remained until the official ceremony was to begin on the morning of November 21.

Twelve members of Parliament shouldered the coffin to a gun carriage at 9:00 a.m. on November 21. A procession to the Ethnographic Museum began, accompanied by Chopin's *Funeral March*.

His coffin was placed on a marble catafalque at the entrance to the museum. President İnönü presided over a moment of silence.

The coffin stayed there for four months. A vigil was held with torches. During that time, people came to visit.

On March 31, 1939, the coffin was lowered into a chamber below the catafalque and stayed there for 15 years until Anıtkabir was completed.

(Mustafa Kemal hadn't chosen a resting place for himself. He didn't specify in his will where he was to be buried. He had said, "Let my nation bury me wherever they would like.")

Work began on Anıtkabir.

A commission was established with Professor Hermann Jansen, who had made the city plan for Ankara; Professor Clemens Holzmeister, who designed the Parliament building used today; and the architect of the Language, History and Geography Faculty Building, Professor Bruno Taut.

They proposed locations for it—Çankaya, the Ethnographic Museum, Ankara Castle, the Agricultural School, Gençlik Park, Altındağ and the Gazi Forest Farm.

A high commission of 15 members of Parliament was established. They had reached a consensus on Çankaya when the member from Trabzon, Mithat Aydın, who was a professional engineer, suggested Rasattepe.

Ankara was crescent shaped with one end in Dikmen and the other in Etilik. Rasattepe was like the star right in the middle. It would be a symbolic representation of the Turkish flag. They voted and decided on Rasattepe.

There was a meteorological station on the hilltop. It's where Rasattepe got its name, which means observation hill.

The people of Ankara wanted it to be in Beştepeler, as there were barrows there.

A committee headed by archaeologist Tahsin Özgüç was established. The barrows were excavated. It was determined that they were Phrygian. They found artifacts from kings, queens and princess, which were placed in the Museum of Anatolian Civilizations.

The owners of the land were paid and Rasattepe was expropriated.

The mausoleum would weigh 150,000 tons. But would Rasattepe be able to withstand that much pressure on top of it?

A committee was established, headed by Professor Salih Saya from Istanbul Technic University, and a geologic survey was conducted.

It was in the middle of World War II. They opened an international competition for the project.

German professor Paul Bonatz, Swedish professor Ivar Tengbom, Hungarian professor Karoly Wicker, professor Arif Hikmet Holtay, and master architects Muamer Çavuşoğlu and Muhlis Sertel were the impartial panel of judges.

A total of 49 projects were submitted from Turkey, Germany, Italy, Austria, Switzerland, France, and Czechoslovakia. Professor Emin Onat and Assistant professor Orhan Arda's project was selected.

The foundation was laid on October 9, 1944. It was completed on September 1, 1953.

The travertines were brought from Polatlı in Malıköy, and Pınarbaşı and Boğazköprü in Kayseri. The marble was brought from Çanakkale, Adana, Hatay, Bilecik and Afyon. The bar iron was produced at the Karabük Iron and Steel Factory. The cement came from the Sivas Cement Factory. The sand and gravel were taken from the bed of Çubuk Creek. The bronze torches were fabricated at the Boys Technical Teachers School in Ankara.

Hüseyin Özkan Anka fashioned the lion sculptures for the Aslan Yolu (Lion Way). Productions by İlhan Koman, Tankut Öktem, Zühtü Müridoğlu, Nusret Suman, Kenan Yontunç, Hakkı Atamulu, Emin Barın, Tarık Levendoğlu, Mehmet Özel, Erol Arda, Metin Yurdanur, Aydın Erkmen, Talih Salahov, Sergey Prisekin, Latif Rüstem, Sait Rüstem, Turan Erol and Ragıp Çiçen were also used.

Kâmile Şevki Mutlu.

Professor Kâmile Şevki was the chair of the Ankara University School of Medicine Histology. Her home telephone rang around 11 o'clock on the night of November 8, 1953. It was the governor of Ankara.

He informed the professor that the government had tasked her with opening Atatürk's casket and managing the embalming process.

(Kâmile Şevki Mutlu was a product of Atatürk's revolutions in all its meaning. She started the School of Medicine at Istanbul University in 1924, after the declaration of the republic, and graduated in 1930. Female physicians were not given public positions before. The Health Ministry first employed female physicians who graduated in 1930, and Kâmile Şevki Mutlu became a pathology assistant. She presented on her own at the Turkish Congress of National Medicine in 1931—which a first for a female doctor in Turkey. She was Turkey's first female professor of medicine and established the country's first electron microscope laboratory. She was the first female member of instruction in the Ankara University Senate. She also developed what is known in the medical community as the Şevki method concerning the adrenal glands.)

At 7:30 on the morning of November 9, 1953, Professor Kâmile Şevki Multu was shaking as she stood in front of the rosewood casket that had been removed from its temporary grave in the Ethnographic Museum and placed on a catafalque.

"I think I'm going to faint," she muttered.

They held a moment of silence.

"Let's get started, please," she said.

Ten teachers were brought from the Technical Teachers High School as assistants. They removed the screws from the rosewood casket and the soldered seam from the lead coffin and opened the lid. The odor of the embalming solution that had been used wafted around them.

His corpse was wrapped in a brown tarpaulin. The space between Mustafa Kemal's body and the walls of the coffin had been filled with sawdust so nothing would be damaged during its transportation. The sawdust was wet, which was a good sign, as it indicated that the embalming fluid had not evaporated away.

Professor Mutlu opened the tarpaulin down to the chest. Mustafa Kemal's body was wrapped in waxcloth and his face was covered with wet cotton.

It was as if time had stood still. No one made a sound. Everyone was holding their breath.

Professor Mutlu slowly lifted the layer of cotton and revealed Mustafa Kemal Atatürk's face.

There was no decomposition. His skin was the color of bronze. His blond hair hadn't lost its color. A few hairs from his thick eyebrows had fallen out and were on his left eyelid. His beard looked to have grown slightly. His thin lips were stuck together. He looked like he did when he was sleeping at Dolmabahçe Palace 15 years earlier.

In addition to there being no decomposition, there also wasn't any putrid odor. The embalming that Professor Lütfi Aksu, who had passed away two years earlier, had performed was completely successful.

Professor Kâmile Şevki Mutlu was face to face with Mustafa Kemal. She touched his cheek and caressed it.

This man who had liberated women was bade farewell to, 15 years after his death, by a woman stroking his cheek.

Like many of his features, this, too, was a world first and the only instance of such a thing in history.

What was Professor Kâmile Şevki Mutlu feeling in that moment? She later said, "For a moment, I felt as though we would talk."

There was a deep silence in the hall. Emotions were all over the place.

Mustafa Kemal's body was removed. A single photograph was taken. He was shrouded in prayers.

He was placed in a new, walnut casket and a Turkish flag was draped over it.

❉

The casket was placed on a gun carriage once again on November 10, 1953. Its route to Anıtkabir passed by the Opera House, Ulus, Parliament, the train station and Tandoğan.

The catafalque was placed in front of the Hall of Honor.

President Celal Bayar gave a speech:

"Atatürk, there were those who wanted to make you caliph and sultan. You paid them no attention. You chose the path of the national will. You dedicated your life and yourself to service to the nation. You possessed the qualities Turks admire: Be proud, work hard & be confident. You yourself were a Turk with all of these virtues. We now give you to the sacred land of the entire country you saved. Know that your true place is in the heart of the Turkish nation full of gratitude in which you believed and tied yourself to. Rest in peace."

His casket was lowered into an octagonal chamber just below the massive, 42-ton mausoleum.

It was 1:30 in the afternoon.

Mustafa Kemal was inturred in the homeland.

In order, President Celal Bayar, Parliament Speaker Refik Koraltan, second and former President İsmet İnönü, Prime Minister Adnan Menderes, Foreign Minister Fuat Köprülü, former Parliament Speaker Abdülhalik Renda and Mustafa Kemal's sister Makbule each shoveled a load of dirt over the casket.

After Anıtkabir commander Captain Halit Yener, 1st Lieutenant Cemal Tezgörücü, 1st Lieutenant Mustafa Eser, and the 12-man Guard Regiment finished the burial.

The funeral ceremony was broadcast by Ankara Radio. Twenty-eight presenters transmitted from 28 points along the route.

Suat Taşer reported live from the burial chamber.

Actors from the state theater and poets participated in the live broadcast with wise words about Mustafa Kemal Atatürk.

Behçet Kemal Çağlar was one of them.

"Does an idea die?" he said. "Does a work of art die? Does a man of the nation die? Does a man of the flag ever die? We who stand on this land, his heirs, regardless of date of birth, were all born on May 19, 1919. No matter what place of birth is shown on our birth certificates, we are all from Dumlupınar and Sakarya."

∞

Anıtkabir was opened to the public on November 17, 1953.

It was only allowed to be open for one hour on the first day. Seventy thousand people were able to enter.

On the 50th anniversary of his death, more than 500,000 people came in one day alone.

On the 75th anniversary of his death, more than 1.86 million people came in in a single day.

Every year, 5 million to 9 million people visit Anıtkabir.

About 455 million people had visited Anıtkabir when this book was first published in 2018. This is equal to the total current population of the 28 member states of the European Union.

There is no other example in the entire history of humanity of such love and respect forever growing over the years instead of cooling to ashes.

Turks have Mustafa Kemal's signature tattooed on their bodies. Those who don't have it tattooed stick it on their cars, motorcycle helmets, and baby strollers.

Nearing a century after his death, there is no other leader ever known or seen to have had people ink their signature on their bodies.

He is reborn every November 10.

1881-193∞

This isn't an epilogue—it is the preface forever more.
Mustafa Kemal is everlasting unto eternity.

∞

The world
as it was
with
Mustafa
Kemal.

1881...

The Ottoman Empire officially went bankrupt the year **Mustafa Kemal** was born. Abdülhamid II was sultan. The Public Debt Administration was established. Creditors seized government revenues in exchange for state debts.

A board of seven administrators was established—British, German, French, Austrian and Italian. It wasn't only established to track the payment of debts, but was set up to personally collect state revenues in order to manage the state's sources of income.

It was a foreclosure organization.

It became larger than the state, with 9,000 officials in the Public Debt Administration compared to the 5,000 civil servants in the state's Ministry of Finance. It was full of foreign earnings. Rather than the empire's educated young people availing their own state, they were competing for positions in the Public Debt Administration. There was a premium system. These officials who were strangling their own state were appreciated, and whoever strangled the state most was awarded. There were 26 regional offices and 720 collection offices in the cities and districts.

They imposed taxes and determined tax rates like a state. They didn't only appropriate revenue and pay foreign debt, they also kept the state budget book and paid domestic debt.

The Ottoman Empire became a toy for international loan sharks under the name of bankers. They didn't only milk the state coffers like a cow, they were addicted to credit like a junkie. They took new concessions by issuing new loans. They established railways, ports, banks, insurance companies, postal companies, telephone companies, tramway companies and power plants in Ottoman lands and managed the empire's underground resources as if they were their father's mines. They began to generate income on the debt hand over fist.

The people became slaves in their own country.

They came as the capitalism patrol.

They turned the Empire into a puppet of imperialism.

That is, until Mustafa Kemal came along.

The Public Debt Administration that had been set up in the year of Mustafa Kemal's birth was abolished with the Treaty of Lausanne.

Atatürk's Turkey paid off the Ottoman debt.

1881...

Mustafa Kemal was born the same year Pablo Picasso was and the year Dostoyevsky died. Thomas Edison and Alexander Graham Bell set up a joint telephone company. Kansas was the first U.S. state to ban alcohol. American outlaw Billy the Kid was killed. Andrew Watson took the title of being the first black soccer player in history, putting on the uniform for Scotland's Queen's Park squad. The world's first electric trolley was put into service in Berlin. Brahms premiered his *Piano Concerto No. 2* at a gala in Budapest. The Natural History Museum in London opened with dinosaur fossils, and 80 million specimens of plants, insects, minerals, animals and fossils. The majority of the collection were specimens Charles Darwin, the father of the theory of evolution, had collected.

1881 - 1886...

When **Mustafa Kemal** was 5 years old, Ömer Seyfettin was 2, Franz Kafka was 3, Karl Marx had died three years earlier and Victor Hugo had died one year before. The International Meridian Conference was held in Washington DC, and Greenwich was accepted as the mean meridian off of which international time zones were set. The Statue of Liberty was dedicated to New York. French microbiologist Louis Pasteur developed the rabies vaccine. German physician Robert Kock identified the cholera bacterium. Polish professors Karol Olszewski and Zygmunt Wróblewski successfully liquefied oxygen for the first time in history. German pathologist Edwin Klebs discovered that diphtheria was caused by bacteria. The world's first appendectomy was performed in the United States. German physicist Rudolf Hertz discovered radio waves. Carl Benz invented the first gasoline-powered automobile—a three-wheeler called the Motorwagen. American mathematician Henry Seely invented the electrical iron. Mark Twain published *Huckleberry Finn* in London. In the United States, workers led by the Federation of Organized Trades and Labor Unions went on strike against 12-hour shifts and May 1 became the milestone of Labor Day. American pharmacists John Pemberton began to sell glasses of his invention Coca-Cola at his pharmacy. Legendary Apache leader and medicine man Geronimo surrendered to prevent the massacre of his people. Venus passed in front of the sun, with its next transit not to occur for another 122 years in 2004.

1886 - 1891...

When **Mustafa Kemal** was 10, Namık Kemal had died two years earlier and Van Gogh one year earlier. The Eiffel Tower was constructed. Emile Berliner invented the gramophone, Nikola Tesla invented the transformer and Jesse Reno invented the escalator. *The Wall Street Journal* began publication. The Moulin Rouge, that symbol of French culture, opened its doors. The frigate *Ertuğrul* sank. Canadian-American physical education instructor James Naismith invented basketball. History's first fashion photography was published in *La Mode Pratique* periodical. Sir Arthur Conan Doyle wrote *A Study in Scarlet*—his first story with the fanciful detective Sherlock Holmes.

1891 - 1896...

When **Mustafa Kemal** was 15, the United States Supreme Court ruled tomatoes should be classified as a vegetable instead of a fruit—since United States tax law only envisaged taxation of vegetables, tomato producers argued tomatoes were a fruit to escape paying taxes, with the case eventually making it to the Supreme Court. The first modern Olympic Games were held in Athens, with the United States winning the most medals. Liverpool F.C. was founded. The Corinth Canal opened. The Lumière brothers invented the motion picture, German physicist Wilhelm Röntgen discovered X-rays, and American mechanical engineer Whitcomb Judson invented the zipper. Utah became a state. Âşık Veysel was born, and Tchaikovsky and Alexandre Dumas died.

1896 - 1901...

When **Mustafa Kemal** was 20, the first line of the Paris Metro opened. German chemist Felix Hoffman produced synthetic acetylsalicylic acid, which was released by Bayer as Aspirin. British mechanical engineer Hubert Booth invented the vacuum cleaner—its suction power was fine, but it was large enough to be towed by a horse-drawn carriage. American housewife Josephine Cochrane invented the electrically operated dishwasher. Count Zeppelin flew in his invention. Austrian neurologist Sigmund Freud published The Interpretation of Dreams in which he presented the basic principles of psychoanalysis. The Boston Marathon was run for the first time in history. The first ever World Figure Skating Championship was held in London. F.C. Barcelona and Juventus F.C. were founded. Hawaii became a United States territory. The world's first auto show was held in New York. Italian electrical engineer Guglielmo Marconi successfully established the first wireless connection and the radio was born. U.S. Steel became the first company ever to be valued at $1 billion. Walt Disney, Alfred Hitchcock, Humphrey Bogart, Ernest Hemingway and Louis Armstrong were born. Friedrich Nietzsche, Oscar Wilde and Giuseppe Verdi died. The global population was 1.65 billion.

1901 - 1906...

When **Mustafa Kemal** was 25, he was first arrested and then exiled to Damascus at the time Albert Einstein published the article on his theory of relativity with famous equation $E=mc^2$, changing the fundamental views on the concepts of space, time, energy and mass. Russian psychologist Ivan Pavlov put forth the definition of the conditional reflex with his experiment on dogs. Marie Curie was the first woman to receive a Nobel Prize. The Irish independence movement, Sinn Féin, was founded. Norway became an independent state. Cubism emerged. Mata Hari's exotic dances were written about in the press around the world. The Wright brother flew a motor-powered airplane for the first time. American mechanical engineer Alva Fisher invented the washing machine. The first Western film in cinematic history was shot by the Edison Manufacturing—the story of a train heist, and it ran for only 11 minutes. The world's first movie theater opened in Los Angeles. Puccini's opera *Madam Butterfly* was staged for the first time at La Scala in Milan. Italian tenor Enrico Caruso reached 1 million records sold. Creole American ragtime and jazz pianist Jelly Roll Morton composed *Jelly Roll Blues*, which was one of the earliest jazz recordings. American oil giant Texaco was founded. Harley Davidson began producing motorcycles. The Tour de France, the most prestigious cycling race, was held for the first time. William Kellogg produced Corn Flakes cereal. Pepsi Cola was established and its logo was trademarked. Italian-American ice cream maker Italo Marchioni patented the ice cream cone. Construction of the Panama Canal began. SOS was accepted as the international Morse code distress signal. Kemalettin Tuğcu, John Steinbeck, Salvador Dali, Christian Dior, and Ayn Rand were born. Jules Verne, Paul Gauguin, and Emile Zola died.

1906 - 1911...

When **Mustafa Kemal** was 30 years old and on his way to Trablusgarp, Norwegian explorer Roald Amundsen was the first man to reach the South Pole. The ancient Incan city of Machu Picchu, considered to be one of the new seven wonders of the world, was discovered by American archaeologist Hiram Bingham in the Peruvian Andes. American pioneer of radiochemistry Bertram Boltwood devised uranium–lead dating, with initial results that the world was 2.2 billion years old. IBM, the world's largest information technology company, was founded. Mother's Day was celebrated for the first time in the United States. Butch Cassidy and the Sundance

Kid were killed. Jack Johnson was the first black boxer to win the 'heavyweight champion of the world' title. Taxi meters were used for the first time in London cabs. General Electric produced the electric toaster. The Manhattan Bridge in New York, and Selfridges in London opened. Converse produced its first athletic shoe. The first Frankenstein movie was filmed in New York—it was only 14 minutes. Rıfat Ilgaz, Hulusi Kentmen, Nubar Terziyan, John Wayne and Frida Kahlo were born. Leo Tolstoy and Mark Twain died. Leonardo da Vinci's *Mona Lisa* was stolen from the Louvre—people lined up to see the empty wall where the painting was stolen and, two years later, the thief, Italian Vincenzo Perugia was caught when he tried to sell the painting to the Uffizi Gallery in Florence. Halley's Comet was seen with the naked eye, not to be seen again until 1984. The *RMS Titanic* was launched and was thought to be impervious to icebergs.

1911 - 1916...

When **Mustafa Kemal** was 35 years old, he first fought in Gallipoli, and then in Bitlis and Muş at the time the first ship passed through the Panama Canal. The recipe having been created by his wife, Richard Hellmann began selling Hellmann's Mayonnaise at his New York City deli. Italian fashion house Prada and German automotive giant BMW were founded. Istanbul's first fatal traffic accident occurred in which Italian Embassy driver Frederico Rasi hit an Albanian named Idris in front of the Şişli Mosque—Idris died and Rasi was arrested, but released after the Italian Embassy paid compensation to Idris' family. Russian mystic and self-proclaimed holy man Rasputin, who claimed to have supernatural powers, was killed. Pravda newspaper published its first issue. Charlie Chaplin made his first film. Arizona and New Mexico became U.S. states. The first home refrigerator was built in Chicago— its body was made of wood and the cooling apparatus was more than half its size. British metallurgical engineer Harry Brearley invented rustless steel, later called stainless steel, to protect the rifle barrels from corrosion. Albert Berry was the first man to parachute from a powered plane, which he did from 1,500 feet. Camel cigarettes hit the market. Josef Stalin was arrested as a young man and imprisoned in Siberia. Fifty thousand women demanded their rights in London's Hyde Park. Civil rights defender Rosa Park took a stand against discrimination of African-Americans and was arrested for not giving up her seat at the front of the bus to a white man, becoming a symbol of the African-American civil rights movement the United States. The racist Ku Klux Klan was re-established. Orhan Veli, Aziz Nesin, Albert Camus, Burt Lancaster, Anthony Quinn and Kirk Douglas were born. Tevfik Fikret and Jack London died. The most famous illusionist of all time, Harry Houdini, escaped from a trunk with his hands and feet chained for the first time, shocking the audience. German geologist Alfred Wegener introduced the theory of continental shift, claiming the continents had been one he called Pangaea 300 million years ago and that they dispersed over time to settle in their present positions. Pluto was viewed for the first time and was classified as a planet.

1916 - 1919...

When **Mustafa Kemal** was 38 years old and on his way to Samsun, the October Revolution erupted and the Soviet Union was established. Three small children in the Portuguese parish of Fátima claimed to have seen the apparition of the Virgin Mary who told them prophecies while they were herding sheep in what was called the Miracle of the Sun. Spanish influenza swept over the world and killed 30 million people—Mustafa Kemal also fell ill with it. Emiliano Zapata, a leading figure of the Mexican Revolution who campaigned to win land for poor villagers, was killed. Susan Hayward, Dean Martin, Robert Mitchum and Ray Charles were born. Emile Durkheim died. The first Pulitzer Prizes were given to American female writers Laura Richards and Maud Howe Elliott.

1919 - 1920...

When **Mustafa Kemal** was 39 and founding the Grand National Assembly of Turkey, the German Labor Party was renamed the National Socialist German Workers' Party, which was the foundation of Adolf Hitler's Nazi Party. A wagon loaded with dynamite exploded on Wall Street in New York, killing 38 people in the J.P. Morgan building in the 9/11 of the time. The League of Nations, the precursor to the United Nations, was established. Charles Bukowski was born and Omar Seyfettin died.

1920 - 1923...

When **Mustafa Kemal** was 42 years old, he proclaimed the republic at the time American astronomer Edwin Hubble discovered the Andromeda Galaxy—until then, the entire universe was thought to be made up of only the Milky Way. British archaeologist Howard Carter found King Tutankhamen's tomb. Canadian physician Frederick Banting discovered insulin and received the Nobel Prize in Medicine that same year. White Castle burgers opened in Kansas as the first ever fast food restaurant. A famine in Russia killed 7.5 million people. The Gucci fashion house was established. Wembley Stadium opened. American Garrett Morgan, a sewing machine repairman of African-American and Native American heritage with only an elementary school education whose parents had been slaves, invented the three-position traffic signal. The Hollywood sign was placed on Mount Lee in Los Angeles. Kemal Film, Turkey's first film studio, was founded by the brothers

Kemal and Şakir Seden, whose first film was Muhsin Ertuğrul's *Istanbul'da Bir Facia-ı Aşk* (A Tragedy of Love in Istanbul). Yaşar Kemal, Pierre Cardin and Charlton Heston were born. Alexander Graham Bell and Gustave Eiffel died. A 7.9-magnitude earthquake struck Japan, lasted four minutes, and killed 105,000 people. Benito Mussolini became the prime minister of Italy. Inflation in Germany exploded, with $1 equal to 4.2 trillion Deutsche Marks, making a wheelbarrow full of cash necessary to by a loaf of bread.

1923 - 1926...

When **Mustafa Kemal** was 45 years old, U.S. Congress granted citizenship to Native Americans. The first Winter Olympics was held in Chamonix, France, with the participation of 16 countries—Norway won the most medals. French bacteriologist Albert Calmette produced the tuberculosis vaccine. Turkey's first sugar factory began to operate in Alpullu. Norwegian chemical engineer Erik Rotheim invented the aerosol spray. Metro-Goldwyn-Mayer, one of the leaders of American cinema, was founded. Soviet silent film *Battleship Potemkin*, a classic of cinema the world over, was debuted. F. Scott Fitzgerald's masterpiece, *The Great Gatsby*, was first published. New York City took the title of the world's largest city from London. Queen Elizabeth II and Marilyn Monroe were born, as well as Rauf Denktaş, Sadri Alışık, Rock Hudson, Jack Lemmon, Tony Curtis, Jerry Lewis, Peter Sellers and Paul Newman. Vladimir Lenin and Franz Kafka died.

1926 - 1931...

When **Mustafa Kemal** was 50 years old, Turkey's first census was taken, showing a population of 13,648,270 people. German Jewish physicians Selmar Aschheim and Bernard Zondek produced a home pregnancy test. The first World Cup was played in Uruguay, with the participation of 13 countries—Uruguay defeated Argentina 4-2 in the final to win the trophy. American businessman Clarence Birdseye created a method of freezing food without destroying its flavor, and the first packaged frozen food on the market was fish. Scottish bacteriologist Alexander Fleming discovered penicillin. Adhesive tape, invented by American chemical engineer Richard Drew, entered into everyday life under the name Scotch tape. Belgian cartoonist Georges Remi, a.k.a. Hergé, published the first of his *The Adventures of Tintin*. The first Academy Awards were held. The Empire State Building opened. Wall Street crashed in what was the world's most devastating stock market tumble and was the beginning of the Great Depression, which lasted 12 years. Ernesto Che Guevara, Martin Luther King Jr., Yasser Arafat and Mikhail Gorbachev were born. Neil Armstrong, the first man to set foot on the moon, was born, followed by William Shatner—Captain Kirk and Mister Spock of *Star Trek*, respectively. Zeki Müren, Adile Naşit, Gazanfer Özcan, Eşref Kolçak, Nejat Uygur, Audrey Hepburn, Grace Kelly, James Dean, Steve McQueen, Clint Eastwood, Sean Connery and Larry Hagman—J.R. from Dallas—were also born. Thomas Edison died. An agreement was signed between Italy and the Catholic Church, and the independent Vatican state was officially established. The Republic of Turkey officially requested foreign countries use Turkish names for its cities, and afterward, letters addressed to Istanbul and Angora instead of Istanbul and Ankara were not delivered.

1931 - 1936...

When **Mustafa Kemal** was 55 years old, British physicist James Chadwick discovered neutrons, for which he received the Nobel Prize in Physics and which opened the way for the atomic bomb and nuclear energy. Nazi Hermann Göring created the Gestapo.

The military prison on Alcatraz Island was turned into a federal penitentiary. Reza Shah Pahlavi petitioned the League of Nations to refer to his country as Iran instead of Persia. The first Tarzan film was shot. The Venice Film Festival was held for the first time. Toyota produced its first car and Zippo produced its first lighter. The first beer can was introduced in Richmond, Virginia. *Monopoly* hit the market and has since become the world's most-played board game. It was a period for magnificent women, with the births of Türkan Saylan, Suna Kan, Elizabeth Taylor, Sophia Loren, Brigitte Bardot, and Ursula Andress. Yuri Gagarin, Oğuz Aral, Elvis Presley, Luciano Pavarotti, Umberto Eco, Omar Sharif, Jean-Paul Belmondo, Burt Reynolds, David Carradine, Karl Lagerfeld and Giorgio Armani were also born. British spy T. E. Lawrence, who had a large part in the Arab uprisings in the Ottoman Empire, died from a motorcycle accident in Dorset, England. African-American track-and-field athlete Jesse Owens won four gold medals at the Berlin Olympics, breaking both Olympic and world records and reportedly making Hitler fly into a rage and leave the stadium, unable to bear Germans falling behind.

1938...

When **Mustafa Kemal** died at the age of 57, oil was discovered in Saudi Arabia. The Spanish Civil War was a bloodbath. The world's first blood bank opened in Chicago. Volkswagen produced its first car. Hungarian journalist László Bíró patented the first successful ballpoint pen. American physicist Chester Carlson invented electrophotography for dry copying documents. The first modern nylon toothbrushes were produced in the United States. The first performance of the music of Sergei Prokofiev's ballet Romeo and Juliet was at the Mahen Theater in Czechoslovakia. Cüneyt Arkın, Yılmaz Güney, Tanju Okan, Neşet Ertaş, Jack Nicholson, and Dustin Hoffman were born. Created by author Jerry Siegel and illustrator Joe Shuster, the first Superman comic hit the shelves after having first been conceived in 1933 as a weak man transformed into a bald supervillain, but having not been able to sell the concept, he was transformed into the handsome, crime-fighting hero. Orson Welles presented the War of the Worlds on the radio with such wonderful storytelling that listeners believed it to be real, causing a panic throughout the country that the U.S. was being invaded by Martians. The Nazis perpetrated the Kristallnacht during which they attacked Jewish homes, shops businesses, cemeteries and Synagogues, leaving hundreds dead and the streets littered with shards of glass in what was another step toward the Holocaust.

❋

World War II was to start only 10 months after the death of **Mustafa Kemal**.